Globalization, Economic Development and Inequality

NEW HORIZONS IN INSTITUTIONAL AND EVOLUTIONARY
ECONOMICS

Series Editor: Geoffrey M. Hodgson
Research Professor, University of Hertfordshire Business School, UK

Economics today is at a crossroads. New ideas and approaches are challenging the
largely static and equilibrium-oriented models that used to dominate mainstream
economics. The study of economic institutions – long neglected in the economics
textbooks – has returned to the forefront of theoretical and empirical investigation.

This challenging and interdisciplinary series publishes leading works at the
forefront of institutional and evolutionary theory and focuses on cutting-edge analyses of modern socio-economic systems. The aim is to understand both the institutional structures of modern economies and the processes of economic evolution and
development. Contributions will be from all forms of evolutionary and institutional
economics, as well as from Post-Keynesian, Austrian and other schools. The overrid-
ing aim is to understand the processes of institutional transformation and economic
change.

Titles in the series include:

The Evolutionary Analysis of Economic Policy
Edited by Pavel Pelikan and Gerhard Wegner

The Evolution of Scientific Knowledge
Edited by Hans Siggaard Jensen, Lykke Margot Richter and Morten Thanning Vendelø

Evolutionary Economic Thought
European Contributions and Concepts
Edited by Jürgen G. Backhaus

Economic Institutions and Complexity
Structures, Interactions and Emergent Properties
Karl-Ernst Schenk

The Economics of Knowledge Sharing
A New Institutional Approach
Edited by Ernst Helmstädter

The Economics of Energy and the Production Process
An Evolutionary Approach
Guido Buenstorf

Institutional Economics and the Formation of Preferences
The Advent of Pop Music
Wilfred Dolfsma

Globalization, Economic Development and Inequality
An Alternative Perspective
Edited by Erik S. Reinert

Globalization, Economic Development and Inequality

An Alternative Perspective

Edited by

Erik S. Reinert

President, The Other Canon Foundation, formerly at SUM – The Centre for Development and the Environment, University of Oslo, Norway

NEW HORIZONS IN INSTITUTIONAL AND EVOLUTIONARY ECONOMICS

Edward Elgar

Cheltenham, UK • Northampton, MA, USA

Published by
Edward Elgar Publishing Limited
The Lypiatts
15 Lansdown Road
Cheltenham
Glos GL50 2JA
UK

Edward Elgar Publishing, Inc.
William Pratt House
9 Dewey Court
Northampton
Massachusetts 01060
USA

Paperback edition 2007
Paperback edition reprinted 2009, 2010, 2011, 2015

A catalogue record for this book
is available from the British Library

Library of Congress Cataloguing in Publication Data

Globalization, economic development, and inequality : an alternative perspective
/ edited by Erik S. Reinert.
    p. cm.—(New horizons in institutional and evolutionary economics series)
    Includes index.
    1. International trade—Social aspects. 2. Income distribution. 3. Technological innovations—Economic aspects. 4. Technological innovations—Social aspects. 5. Globalization—Economic aspects. 6. Globalization—Social aspects. 7. Economic development. 8. Evolutionary economics. I. Reinert, Erik S., 1949– II. New horizons in institutional and evolutionary economics.

HF1379.G593 2004
337—dc22

                                                                    2004045463

ISBN   978 1 85898 891 7 (cased)
       978 1 84720 472 1 (paperback)

Printed on FSC approved paper
Printed and bound in Great Britain by Marston Book Services Ltd, Oxfordshire

Contents

v

Contributors

David B. Audretsch holds the Ameritech Chair of Economic Development and is Director of the Institute for Development Strategies at Indiana University. He is also a Research Fellow of the Centre for Economic Policy Research, London.

Jürgen G. Backhaus holds the Krupp Foundation Chair in Public Finance and Fiscal Sociology, Faculty of Economics, Law and the Social Sciences, University of Erfurt, Germany.

Ådne Cappelen is Research Director of Statistics Norway, Oslo.

Arno M. Daastøl is a PhD candidate at the University of Erfurt, Germany.

Wolfgang Drechsler holds the Chair of Public Administration and Government, University of Tartu, Estonia.

Dieter Ernst is a Senior Fellow at the East–West Center, Honolulu, Hawaii, USA.

Chris Freeman is Emeritus Professor and Former Director of SPRU, Science and Technology Policy Research, University of Sussex.

Michael Hudson heads the Institute for the Study of Long-Term Economic Trends (ISLET) in New York. He is also a Research Fellow at the Levy Economics Institute of Bard College, New York.

Bengt-Åke Lundvall is Professor of Economics at the University of Aalborg, Denmark.

Carlota Perez is Honorary Research Fellow at SPRU, Science and Technology Policy Research, University of Sussex; Adjunct Senior Research Fellow, INTECH, Maastricht, The Netherlands; and Visiting Scholar 2002 and 2004 at Cambridge University. She is also an international consultant and lecturer based in Caracas, Venezuela.

Erik S. Reinert was formerly Senior Research Associate at SUM (Centre for Development and the Environment) at the University of Oslo, Norway, and Head of Research, Norsk Investorforum, Oslo. He is now President of The Other Canon Foundation, Hvasser, Norway, and Professor of Technology Governance at the Tallinn Technical University, Estonia.

Santiago Roca is Professor of Economics and Director of Research at ESAN, Escuela Superior de Administración de Negocios, Lima, Peru. He has also been Visiting Professor of Economics and Finance, College of Business, Department of Economics, Arizona State University, Tempe, AZ.

Luis Simabuko is Research Assistant at ESAN, Escuela Superior de Administración de Negocios, Lima, Peru.

Introduction

Erik S. Reinert

It is generally not recognized that two Nobel laureates in economics have provided two conflicting theories of what will happen to world income under globalization:

1. Based on the standard assumptions of neo-classical economic theory, US economist Paul Samuelson 'proved' mathematically that unhindered international trade will produce 'factor-price equalization', that is that the prices paid to the factors of production – capital and labour – will tend to be the same all over the world.
2. Based in an alternative dynamic tradition – which we here label The Other Canon – Swedish economist Gunnar Myrdal was of the opinion that world trade would tend to increase already existing differences in incomes between rich and poor nations.

We would argue that the second approach easily incorporates the main elements of evolutionary or neo-Schumpeterian economics, but with a broader theoretical and historical perspective and with a broader agenda. The aim of this book is to explore the contributions of today's evolutionary economics to the understanding of the increasing gap in global income inequality, that is to broaden the normal perspective of neo-Schumpeterian economics consciously into the realm of development economics.

The experiences since the early 1990s – since the fall of the Berlin Wall – have shown that in many cases globalization has followed the trend predicted by Myrdal. During the 1990s a large number of nations have experienced falling real wages and falling national income; in many cases real wages have declined both rapidly and considerably. In some of the former communist countries a humanitarian crisis of large proportions is evolving. In most Latin American countries real wages peaked sometime in the late 1970s or early 1980s, and have fallen since then. In several African countries it is no longer possible to talk about a 'state' as such; and this problem of 'failed states' is growing. Many institutions that used to be handled by the nation-state, like the educational systems, have broken down in these nations, and different areas of what used to be a nation are ruled over by different warlords. This is a type of political structure that a few years ago was thought of as belonging to a mediaeval past. If there is something called 'progress' and 'modernization', globalization has – particularly for many small and medium-sized nations – brought with it the opposite: many are experiencing 'retrogression' and 'primitivization'. Poverty and disease increase sharply in Sub-Saharan Africa, and we see a creeping 'Africanization' in parts of Latin America.

These developments profoundly challenge the present world economic order and the standard textbook economics on which this order rests. The increasingly globalized economy seems to produce opposite effects of what standard economic theory predicts, a Myrdal effect rather than a Samuelson effect. Instead of a convergence of world income (towards factor-price equalization), we find that a group of rich nations shows a tendency to converge, while another convergence group of poor countries seems to gather at the bottom of the scale. Mainstream logic would point to the opposite effect being the likely outcome: the more backward a nation, the more space will be available to catch up to some imaginary 'frontier'. In effect, what is actually happening may be something very different. From a Schumpeterian perspective, some nations may specialize in producing continuous flows of innovations that raise their real wages ('innovation rents'), whereas other nations specialize either in routine economic activities where there is very little or no technological change (*Maquila*-type activities) or, alternatively, where technological change takes the form of process innovations where technical change is taken out in the form of lower prices to the consumers rather than in higher wages to the workers. It is not well known today that this 'Schumpeterian' explanation of underdevelopment – that the fruits of innovation and technical change are taken out differently in the First World (higher wages) than in the Third World (lower prices) – was an integral part of the Prebisch–Singer theory of underdevelopment, recorded by Hans Singer, a student of Schumpeter in Bonn.

In response to the growing challenges, the focal points of the Washington Institutions have changed over time, reflecting a growing recognition of the complexities of economic development. The initial phase can be described as 'get the prices right', and development will more or less take care of itself. In this phase states and government policies were out, supposedly harmony-creating markets were in. A second phase can be described as 'get the property rights right'. It was understood that the market needed a legal setting. A third stage of understanding was reached in the latter part of the 1990s when the watchword became 'get the institutions right', followed by 'get the governance right'. Towards the end of the 1990s, evolutionary or neo-Schumpeterian elements were added to this moving target of prescriptions: 'get the competitiveness right' and 'get the innovation system right'.

There is a risk here, however, that these evolutionary elements are introduced on top of what is essentially a neoclassical theory: that a Schumpeterian icing is added to a solidly neoclassical cake.

It is not clear that these consecutive focal points of the Washington Institutions really have brought us any closer to understanding why economic development by its very nature seems to be so unevenly distributed. The risk is that we have not arrived at the root causes, synergies and conditions that make institutions, innovation and good governance viable and possible. We may be continuously pointing to new symptoms rather than to the actual causes of development, because we do not include in our analysis the preconditions that institutions, innovations and good governance need to take root. For example, institutions that took centuries to develop in an industrialized Europe are not likely to be successfully transferred to a feudal mode of production or to a hunting and gathering tribe. Likewise, as far back as in the late 1500s economists like Giovanni Botero were pointing to a diversified artisan and manufacturing base as a precondition both for 'good rule' and for the synergetic process that we call economic development to take place. If we accept Botero's analysis we can also explain why the very existence of both political freedom and generalized welfare was for so many centuries an urban phenomenon. Neither democracy, nor 'good governance' or effective 'national innovation systems' are likely to appear in a feudal production structure based on agricultural monoculture. This would also give us a hint as to why the process of deindustrialization in the 1990s (Chapters 5 and 6 of this book) – in effect removing the complex synergetic diversity and division of labour of a society – is a phenomenon that runs parallel to the growth of 'failing states'. In Chapter 1 of this book we attempt to resurrect a type of 'Renaissance economics' – The Other Canon – that takes these factors into account.

From this perspective democratic state formation, economic development and functioning innovation systems are probably all dependent on the very same conditions: a large diversity of economic activities subject to increasing returns, being synergetic phenomena built upon the mutual dependency created by finely knit and interlocking networks of divisions of labour. Antonio Serra's path-breaking theories (1613) in this regard are referred to in Chapter 1 and Chapter 6 of this book. This same perspective – including the city and its diverse activities as the nexus of innovations, growth and liberty – was raised again in the nineteenth century by Friedrich List (quoting Antonio Serra) and others, and formed the basis for the industrialization policies of all nations that followed England in the process of industrialization. As late as in 1945, it was obvious that Western Europe needed to rebuild its industry, even though – compared to the United States – its comparative advantage may not have been in that sector. In the view of this editor the failure to capture these common preconditions – for economic growth, innovation systems, good governance and democracy – make the sequential new insights of the Washington Institutions merely catchphrases that address symptoms rather than causes. We argue that by widening the evolutionary and neo-Schumpeterian perspectives, a case can be built connecting economic diversity and innovations with the growing problem of failing nation-states.

Two alternative theories based on two different metaphors compete for the attention of today's economists: mainstream economics based on an equilibrium metaphor from physics, and evolutionary economics based on biology, on Darwinian evolution. We argue that both suffer from an important common weakness: both metaphors fail to grasp the synergetic elements of economies and societies, both are in a sense based on methodological individualism. They both also emphasize the mechanics of development; in our view the Darwinian metaphor fails to carry economics sufficiently away from 'matter' towards 'mind'. Renaissance understanding of society was based on the thirteenth-century concept of *il bene commune* or 'the common weal'. This Renaissance understanding of the economy and society was – dating all the way back to Roman legal tradition – based on an entirely different biological metaphor; on the human body as the metaphor for studying society. In the tradition of English historiography this systemic thinking is referred to as the body politic. The idea is clearly visualized in the frontispiece of Thomas Hobbes's *Leviathan* (1651), where Leviathan himself is depicted as consisting, literally, of a huge number of human beings. Understanding society as a body of members and parts, each specialized in different tasks, very clearly brings across the idea of synergies, embeddedness, interdependencies and linkages in human societies and in their economies, and it also makes obvious the role of the human mind and human will as economic factors. These systemic dimensions – which we find largely absent in both mainstream and evolutionary paradigms today – are reflected in The Other Canon approach. We would argue that when the biological metaphor of economics shifted from the body politic to Darwinian (or Lamarckian) evolution, important elements were lost: the role of the human will – the head – and the synergetic elements of the evolution of economies and societies.

The Renaissance discovered the individual and opened up the way for great individual feats in art, science and entrepreneurship. However, the creative role of the individual in this tradition was superimposed on the earlier synergetic view of society and its common weal as expressed by the body metaphor. This created a dualistic view that also opened the way for tensions and required conscious political trade-offs between the interests of society and the interests of the individual. In this tradition of Renaissance civic humanism Italian economist Pietro Verri emphasizes, in the 1760s, that the private interest of each individual, when it coincides with the public interest, is always the safest guarantor of public happiness. With Adam Smith and his followers the direct connection between individual greed and the public interest tended to be taken for granted, and economics slowly opened up for Margaret Thatcher's famous dictum that 'there is no such thing as society'.

We would argue that the present weak understanding of the process of economic development also has its background in the development of economics since the Second World War. Stated in terms of the circular flow of the economy, focus over the past decades was increasingly put on the monetary side, not on the 'real economy' of goods and services, on what Schumpeter called the *Güterwelt*. The Fordist production system created a long economic boom following the Second World War. In this period a well-developed Keynesian toolbox succeeded in controlling the cyclical ripples in the economy, almost to the extent of creating an illusion of controlling the wave of economic growth itself. In the developed world, economic redistribution and Keynesian economic fine-tuning almost came to take for granted the huge productive and synergetic machinery that was once called industrialism. Only by looking at the Third World was it obvious that this was only an illusion, but 'development economics' as a field of academic research was declared dead by the mainstream sometime in the 1980s.

Already in 1954 – early in the development of the neoclassical synthesis – Swedish institutional economist Johan Åkerman had a perceptive comment on this development of economic science, how economic theory came to lose the very cause of twentieth-century wealth creation: industrialism. Åkerman explains these mechanisms well:

> Capitalism, property rights, income distribution came to be considered the essential features, whereas the core contents of industrialism – technological change, mechanisation, mass production and its economic and social consequences – partly were pushed aside. The reasons for this development are probably found in the following three elements: *Firstly*, Ricardian economic theory ... became a theory of 'natural' relations, established once and for all, between economic concepts (price, interest, capital, etc). *Secondly*, the periodic economic crises are important in this respect because the immediate causes of the crises could be found in the monetary sphere. Technological change, the primary source creating growth and transforming society, disappeared behind the theoretical connections which were made between monetary policy and economic fluctuation. *Thirdly*, and most importantly, Marx and his doctrine could capitalise on the discontent of the industrial proletariat. His teachings gave hope of a natural law which led towards the 'final struggle', when the pyramid of income distribution would be turned on its head, the lower classes should be the powerful and mighty. In this ongoing process the technological change came to be considered only as one of the preconditions for class struggle.

With the growth of evolutionary and neo-Schumpeterian economics in the 1990s, focus was again put on the production side of the economy. Evolutionary economics has been the branch of economics that has delved into the 'black box' of technology and production, into Schumpeter's *Güterwelt* – the world of goods and services. Although essentially equipped with the right focus on production and innovation, evolutionary economics has in our opinion delivered little research into the study of uneven economic growth from the point of view of the Third World. Also the crucial link between innovation and finance, which was so important to Schumpeter himself, has been largely ignored by his followers. The link between technology and wages – which was an important issue both for the German Historical School and the 'old' US institutionalists – has also been peripheral in evolutionary economics. The field has developed more towards the micro level, like the theory of the firm, than towards addressing the big issues that equally open up when one has grabbed the torch of technology and innovations as explaining not only economic growth in general, but also why this process is so uneven.

The Other Canon is an attempt to broaden the evolutionary and neo-Schumpeterian agendas by reintegrating important elements which distinguished the German Historical School – out of which Schumpeter's own theories originate – from English classical economics. Neo-Schumpeterian economics is the happy story of innovations and increasing returns. However, we tend to forget that when the synergies of increasing return activities are destroyed by the precipitous opening up of previously isolated economies – as was the case in so many countries in the 1990s – the gloomy Malthusian mechanisms of diminishing returns are still alive and well. These mechanisms explain why a large percentage of the world population still lives under the spell of David Ricardo's 'dismal science': wages tend to hover around subsistence level. These Myrdalian 'vicious circles' and 'perverse backwashes' are described in Chapter 6 of this book. The Other Canon opens the way for a Schumpeterian economic geography where creative destruction materializes as creation in one nation and utter destruction in another nation, and where the effects of changing techno-economic paradigms are widely different in paradigm-producing countries than in paradigm-using countries. It also opens the way for Schumpeterian development economics that – in the tradition of Hans Singer and the early development economists – recognizes that in some cases the fruits of innovations do not stick with the producing nations, but are given away to the consuming nations, and that some nations are locked into a specialization in activities where not even the innovation powerhouses of the world have managed to create innovations. In our view there is a risk today that the rich Schumpeterian vision boils down to a 'Schumpeterian variable' in mainstream equilibrium models, as a Schumpeterian icing on the thoroughly neoclassical cake.

The purpose of this book is to collect views and insights from contemporary evolutionary economists, many of them prominent, on the issues of technological change, globalization and uneven economic growth. The complementary perspectives of the book, focused around an evolutionary and Schumpeterian perspective, point to mechanisms that cause economic globalization to increase global economic inequality. This is of course the opposite conclusion of that reached by mainstream economics, but is consistent with the observed trend since the early 1990s. Several of the chapters point to a tendency that some nations may specialize in being innovative and wealthy, while others may specialize in routine activities with little potential for innovation, and stay poor. The book is an outcome of a sequence of conferences held during the last several years in Oslo, Norway and Venice, Italy, attempting to reconstruct and develop an alternative to the neoclassical paradigm. Financial contributions to The Other Canon from Norsk Investorforum and the Norwegian Shipowners' Association are thankfully acknowledged. The editor thanks Fernanda and Sophus Reinert for editorial assistance.

On the pages following this introduction, we have attempted to contrast the postulates and assumptions of a full-fledged alternative and evolutionary economic theory – The Other Canon – with today's standard theory. Whereas standard economics may relax one or two of its assumptions, later to put them back into the theoretical edifice, The Other Canon approach demands that all standard assumptions are relaxed simultaneously. As already mentioned, The Other Canon contains many elements both from the German Historical School of economics and from the kind of economics that dominated in the United States during most of the nineteenth century and in the early twentieth century.

In both cases – both in the mid-nineteenth century and in the early twenty-first century in the case of The Other Canon – these alternative *Weltanschauungen* were created as a reaction to liberalism, to a type of theory postulating markets as promoters of automatic economic harmony. In both cases the champions of liberalism were the leading world economies, England and the United States respectively. In both cases the proponents of the alternative theories were the laggard nations; in the case of nineteenth-century liberalism the main proponents of the alternative theory were found in Germany and the United States. Contrasting the economic postulates and economic policies promoted by the United States in the past – as a laggard country catching up with England – and the postulates and policies of the same United States today therefore becomes a particularly rewarding exercise in the connection between vested interests and economic theory. If we go further back in history we find that the same switch in theory – from an Other Canon type theory to liberalism – took place in England with Adam Smith. We would also argue that in both cases the economic harmony born out of liberal theory was already built into the core assumptions of the liberal theoretical edifice itself. A theory that contains no diversity between its actors or activities can hardly be expected to predict any diversity in outcome. Including and understanding diversity is therefore a core element in any theory of uneven development.

The eleven chapters of the book have been organized in four parts that approach the problem of uneven development from different angles. The logic of the sequence is the following. The first two chapters, grouped under the heading 'Foundations of an Alternative Theoretical Perspective', discuss the types of economic theory available and what type of theoretical framework is most appropriate in order to analyse why economic development by its very nature has proved to be so unevenly distributed among nations. The second part of the book, 'The Strategy of Success', is devoted to a discussion of the very successful economic strategies of two industrial latecomers, Germany and the United States. The third part of the book, 'The Strategy of Failure', contains case studies of two countries that have experienced a sharp reduction of real wages during recent decades, Peru and Mongolia. Part IV of the book contains five chapters on 'Technical Change and the Dynamics of Income Inequality'.

In Chapter 1 Erik Reinert and Arno Daastøl argue that the problem of world income inequality is best understood in a different tradition than that of today's mainstream economics. They describe the trajectory of an alternative type of economic theory – Renaissance Economics or The Other Canon – whose history is much longer than that of standard textbook economics. A canon of thought can be defined as a selection of authoritative authors who represent a theoretical tradition over time, a concept closely related to what Joseph Schumpeter calls a 'filiation of thought'. Reinert and Daastøl's chapter traces the history of this alternative Other Canon of economics, and documents six periods in the history of economic thought when the two canons have been in conflict, in other words six *Methodenstreite*. It is argued that no nation has ever made the difficult transition from poor to rich without a prolonged period of Other Canon economics, of what Werner Sombart called the 'activistic/idealistic' rather than the 'passivistic/materialistic' tradition of economics.

In Chapter 2 Wolfgang Drechsler discusses two alternative forms of human understanding in the German tradition, and argues for the reintroduction of a qualitative type of understanding in economics. Drechsler argues that this qualitative type of understanding, *verstehen*, is not a complex form of quantitative measuring, but something very different.

This form of qualitative understanding is a key feature of the alternative Other Canon of economics.

Opening Part II of the book, Jürgen Backhaus outlines the view of the German Historical School of Economics, the dominating economic theory in Germany for about a century, on international trade and world income distribution. Backhaus documents the scepticism about free trade before a nation had achieved a comparative advantage outside the primary sectors. In the next chapter, the fourth, Michael Hudson discusses an aspect of US economic history which today is almost completely ignored: the analysis of technology and of systemic competition that formed the foundation of US nineteenth-century trade and industrial policies. During the nineteenth century German and US economists formed a common front against the English tradition of Adam Smith and David Ricardo, in favour of the tradition that we call The Other Canon. Early in the century, the ideas of Americans Daniel Raymond and Mathew Carey were reflected in the work of German (and one-time American citizen) Friedrich List. Later in the nineteenth century, Henry Carey and Eugen Dühring formed another transatlantic economic front, frequently citing each other. This unification of the German–US tradition was much strengthened by the fact that for a very long time there were no graduate courses in economics in the United States. Virtually all US economists at the time received their PhD at German universities, as had all the founders of the American Economic Association.

Part III of the book opens with a case study of failed national policy, that of Peru since 1950. In this Chapter 5 Santiago Roca and Luis Simabuko analyse four cycles of industrialization and deindustrialization in Peru over the last 50 years. In these cycles, when the Peruvian manufacturing industry has gained one percentage point as a percentage of GDP per capita, real wages have risen by more than 10 per cent. The reverse, a relative increase in the primary sector at the expense of manufacturing, has had the opposite effect: one percentage point increase of the primary sector has reduced real wages by more than 5 per cent. We would argue that this reflects the view which was held by the German and US economists who were discussed in Part II of the book: it was a well-established truth that a nation with a relatively inefficient manufacturing sector would be much better off than a nation with no manufacturing sector at all. An inefficient manufacturing sector ought to be made more efficient, it should not be closed down – as it was in the 1990s from Argentina to Mongolia and Zimbabwe. We would argue that by not recognizing the crucial importance of a diversified manufacturing sector to the development of a nation, the Washington Consensus broke with a policy tradition dating back to the 1500s.

Chapter 6 is a second case study on failed economic policies, by Reinert on the Mongolian economy during the 1990s. This chapter argues that the mechanisms which were set in motion in Mongolia, deindustrialization accompanied by falling productivity in the agricultural sector, are the same type of mechanisms which were created in Germany by the Morgenthau-plan in the period immediately following the Second World War. In 1947 the US government recognized that in a deindustrialized Germany – which was the aim of the Morgenthau Plan – there were 25 million people too many. An immediate reversal of the Morgenthau Plan and the creation of a plan to reindustrialize Germany – the Marshall Plan – was the result. It is argued that a similar turnaround is needed today for a large part of the Third World.

Part IV opens with an overview of long-term technological development by Carlota Perez, in Chapter 7. Perez presents a qualitative understanding of technological change and business cycles that is very much in the production-based – rather than barter-based – Other Canon tradition of economics. Carlota Perez shows us that historically, technological revolutions pass through predictable phases, and that understanding these phases is crucial to the understanding of both business cycles and uneven development. New technological paradigms – quantum jumps in potential productivity – open the way for a great potential to increase general wealth. However, Perez emphasizes, the ability of the institutional and sociopolitical framework to take advantage of this potential will determine both the speed and the extent of its successful introduction.

In Chapter 8 Chris Freeman discusses the relationships between technical change, economic growth and income distribution. The impact of technical change is discussed as it affects both the level of unemployment and the level of earnings of those who are employed. It is argued that the Kuznets effect – a widening of income inequalities in the early stages of growth, later to be followed by a narrowing of inequalities – is in fact a phenomenon that is closely related to the stages of the techno-economic paradigms. The reaction towards a policy of narrowing inequalities has been a product of political revulsions against the hardships created under growing inequality. This counter-reaction against growing inequalities is exemplified in the United States by the Homestead Act of the 1830s, antitrust legislation and other reforms in the 1890s, and the New Deal in the 1930s and 1940s. Freeman points to the challenge of creating new ways of thinking and new policies in order to reverse the present trends towards increasing inequalities, a challenge which exists both within nations and between nations.

In Chapter 9 Dieter Ernst and Bengt-Åke Lundvall discuss the challenges facing developing countries during the present process of globalization, focusing on the dual face of knowledge in the learning economy. By comparing and contrasting tacit and codified types of learning, as exemplified by Japanese and American business practices respectively, Ernst and Lundvall discuss the different roles these symbiotic forms of knowledge have in the process of economic development. Challenging the standard view of globalization as the great equalizer, they show how the increased intensity of creative destruction in the production and implementation of new knowledge may give birth to a vicious circle where developing countries, lacking the necessary technological and institutional infrastructure, fall further and further behind. National policies must therefore intervene where the invisible hand fails to generate the desired result, as 'there is no way to reduce poverty other than to place learning and knowledge creation at the centre of development strategy'. National Innovation Systems – associated with Chris Freeman, Richard Nelson and Bengt-Åke Lundvall – is an important approach that opens the way for reintroducing the crucially important synergetic elements of economic development.

In Chapter 10 David Audretsch argues that differences in income distribution are likely to grow with increasing globalization. In a world where costs for transportation and diffusion are relatively low, while wage differentials between geographic areas are large, the author argues that routine economic activities will tend to be transferred out of high-cost locations to lower-cost locations. This will leave the presently wealthy nations specializing in search activities, in R&D. Audretsch revisits recent contributions to the rediscovered field of economic geography, and argues that economic diversity of a region is the driving force producing knowledge spillovers and innovation. Using Gunnar Myrdal's terminology, we could add that diversity is the starting point for cumulative causation of the positive kind, a precondition for innovations under increasing returns and Schumpeterian competition.

The editor would like to add here that Audretsch's chapter vindicates the view of the early Italian economists Giovanni Botero (Botero 1588) and Antonio Serra (Serra 1613) about the importance of diversity. In this tradition the diversity of economic activities – the degree of the division of labour – was the key to understanding why some cities, those with a strong artisan and manufacturing base, were wealthy, while purely administrative centres and farming areas tended to be poor. Antonio Serra developed this argument into a theory of uneven development that is discussed in Reinert's Chapters 1 and 6 of this book. Audretsch's chapter also indirectly revives the old debate in development economics about the problems of monoculture in development economics: the lack of a diversified economic base is a serious obstacle to innovations and consequently to economic development.

In Chapter 11 Ådne Cappelen presents thoughts on the continued relevance of the Kuznets curve for understanding convergence and divergence of income at local, national and global levels. Cappelen shows that European countries have alternated between diverging and converging trends of economic growth even in cases where structural symmetries seem to satisfy the assumptions of neoclassical growth models. Beyond the European theatre, it is clear that the long-term global picture is one of absolute divergence in GDP per capita. Convergence is thus clearly not a stable process, but erratic and heavily dependent on factors exogenous to neoclassical doctrine. The questions raised by Cappelen are important for policy-makers and economists alike, and he specifically calls for a comparative analysis of regional and individual income distribution for use in domestic policy.

Taken together, the chapters of this book also raise the issue of a 'minimum efficient size' of nations. Most of the many nations that have grown poorer during the last decade have been relatively small states. In the nineteenth century Friedrich List warned against small states – against what he called *Kleinstaaterei* – and argued for successive trade liberation in larger and larger units, until global free trade could be reached when all nations had achieved a solid manufacturing base. Not only have the apparent success stories of globalization, China and India, followed a conscious pro-manufacturing policy for more than 50 years, they are also the most populous countries of the planet. Seen through our perspective and that of List, many regions – Latin America among them – probably graduated too early into global free trade without having consolidated their regional trading system (under the Latin American Free Trade Association or the Andean Pact). Whereas small developed nations like Finland and Ireland have been spectacularly successful in industries that are 'born global', the smaller states in the periphery seemingly still retain the problems identified by List and require the regional integration among equals that List himself recommended.

Rapid technological change of the nineteenth century created what came to be called 'the social question' in Europe, growing economic inequality and increasing misery in the middle of a technological revolution. Among the most miserable were the 'home workers', specializing in the non-mechanized routine economic activities that had not become part of the industrial factory. Audretsch's chapter in this book points to a similar effect today: some nations may specialize in routine activities where the scope for innovation is minimal. This is a phenomenon we in previous publications have called 'Schumpeterian underdevelopment'.

'Creative destruction' is an important term in Schumpeterian economics, a term that entered economics via Friedrich Nietzsche and Werner Sombart. As Schumpeter, Nietzsche himself saw this process as a positive one. The eminent Renaissance historian Jacob Burckhardt – Nietzsche's friend and colleague at the University of Basel – was however of a different opinion. In his view absolutely destructive forces also existed, 'under whose hoofs no grass grows'. This is a perspective that presently seems most relevant in many poor countries that are cut off from any progress, increasingly falling behind into the category of 'failed states'. A theoretical vacuum surrounds their problems, but the situation really requires urgent policy measures. We find it is important that evolutionary economic geography highlights the fact that destruction and creativity may take place in entirely different parts of the globe, as when the textile mills of Manchester replaced the weavers of Bengal. The fact that the labour market is not globalized, in our increasingly globalized world economy, in our view seriously exasperates this problem, sometimes with very serious consequences, as in the case of Mongolia (Chapter 6).

As Chris Freeman and Carlota Perez both point out in their respective chapters in this volume, any improvement in the trend towards greater equality – a Kuznets effect where inequality diminishes – is a result of conscious economic policies and institutional change. The old 'social question' was only solved by creating institutions that, one by one, became building blocks of a system that produced generalized welfare: minimum wage, health and safety standards, health insurance, unemployment benefits and so on. These institutions were above all constructs of the German *Verein für Sozialpolitik* – the Association for Social Policy – working from 1872 to 1932, which received the political backing of Chancellor Bismarck at an important point. Their institutional innovations created the most important blueprints for solving 'the social question' across Europe. We are now faced with a new and global version of 'the social question', but this time the distributional problems are more between nations than inside nations. Not only are we faced with the challenge of developing economic theories that explain the increasing gap between rich nations and a large number of poor nations, we also need someone playing the role of Bismarck – picking up and acting on the new theories – on the international political level.

At the core of the increasing misery of many nations lies, in our view, the loss of what for centuries – until the mid-1980s – was accepted common sense: a poor nation would be much better off with an inefficient manufacturing sector than without any manufacturing sector at all. History has shown that the synergies and the division of labour arising out of the increasing return sectors – manufacturing and advanced services – are the core mechanisms behind economic growth, innovation systems, good governance and democracy. Inefficient manufacturing sectors are to be made efficient in a regional setting, not to be closed in a process that throws the nation back into a raw material monoculture devoid of any diversity, increasing returns or synergies, as it occurred in the 1990s. As happened at the end of the first wave of globalization, about 100 years ago, this means that we again shall have to revise our attitude towards instant free trade, although being the long-term goal, as always being the optimal solution also in the short run.

APPENDIX: TWO DIFFERENT WAYS OF UNDERSTANDING THE ECONOMIC WORLD AND THE WEALTH AND POVERTY OF NATIONS.*

Starting point for the standard canon	Starting point for 'The Other Canon'
Equilibrium under perfect information and perfect foresight	Learning and decision-making under uncertainty (Schumpeter, Keynes, Shackle)
Methodological individualism	Methodological holism *and* methodological individualism
High level of abstraction	Level of abstraction chosen according to problem to be resolved
Man's wit and will absent	Moving force: *Geist- und Willenskapital*: Man's wit and will, entrepreneurship
Not able to handle novelty as an endogenous phenomenon	Novelty as a central moving force
Moving force: 'capital *per se* propels the capitalist engine'	Moving force: new knowledge which creates a demand for capital to be provided from the financial sector
Metaphors from the realm of physics	Metaphors (carefully) from the realm of biology
Mode of understanding: mechanistic (*'begreifen'*)	Mode of understanding: qualitative (*'verstehen'*), a type of understanding irreducible only to numbers and symbols
Matter	*Geist* precedes matter
Focused on Man the Consumer. A. Smith: 'Men are animals which have learned to barter'	Focused on Man the Innovator and Producer. A. Lincoln: 'Men are animals which not only work, but innovate'
Focused on static/comparative static	Focused on change
Not cumulative/history absent	Cumulative causations/'history matters'/backwash effects (Myrdal, Kaldor, Schumpeter, German Historical School)

Increasing returns to scale and its absence a non-essential feature	Increasing returns and its absence essential to explaining differences in income between firms, regions and nations (Kaldor)
Very precise ('would rather be accurately wrong than approximately correct')	Aiming at relevance over precision, recognizes the trade-off between relevance and precision as a core issue in the profession
'Perfect competition' (commodity competition/price competition) as an ideal situation: a goal for society	Innovation- and knowledge-driven Schumpeterian competition as both engine of progress and ideal situation. With perfect competition, with equilibrium and no innovation, capital becomes worthless (Schumpeter, Hayek)
The market as a mechanism for setting prices	The market also as an arena for rivalry and as a mechanism selecting between different products and different solutions (Schumpeter, Nelson and Winter)
Equality assumption I: no diversity	Diversity as a key factor (Schumpeter, Shackle)
Equality assumption II: all economic activities are alike and of equal quality as carriers of economic growth and welfare	Growth and welfare are activity-specific – different economic activities present widely different potentials for absorbing new knowledge
Both theory and policy recommendations tend to be independent of context ('one medicine cures all')	Both theory and policy recommendations highly context dependent
The economy largely independent from society	The economy as firmly embedded in society
Technology as a free good, as 'manna from heaven'	Knowledge and technology are produced, have cost and are protected. This production is based on incentives of the system, including law, institutions and policies
Equilibrating forces at the core of the system and of the theory	Cumulative forces are more important than equilibrating ones, and should therefore be at the core of the system

Economics as *Harmonielehre*: the economy as a self-regulating system seeking equilibrium and harmony	Economics as an inherently unstable and conflict-rich discipline. Achieving stability is based on Man's policy measures (Carey, Polanyi, Weber, Keynes)
Postulates the representative firm	No 'representative firm'. All firms are unique (Penrose)
Static optimum. Perfect rationality	Dynamic optimization under uncertainty. Bounded rationality
No distinction made between real economy and financial economy	Conflicts between real economy and financial economy are normal and must be regulated (Minsky, Keynes)
Saving caused by refraining from consumption and a cause of growth	Saving largely results from profits (Schumpeter) and saving *per se* is not useful or desirable for growth (Keynes)

Note: *Authors: Leonardo Burlamaqui, Ha-Joon Chang, Michael Chu, Peter Evans, Jan Kregel and Erik Reinert.

PART I

Foundations of an alternative theoretical perspective

1. The Other Canon: the history of Renaissance economics

Erik S. Reinert and Arno M. Daastøl

1. TYPOLOGIES OF ECONOMIC THEORY AND THE FOUNDATION OF THE TWO CANONS

It has been said that economics as a science – or pseudoscience – is unique because parallel competing canons may exist together over long periods of time. In other sciences, periodic gestalt-switches terminate old theoretical trajectories and initiate new ones. In a paradigm shift, the scientific world moves from a situation in which everyone knows that the world is flat to a new understanding that the world is round (Kuhn 1970). This occurs in a relatively short time. In economics, the theory that the world is flat has been coexisting for centuries with the theory that the world is round. In this essay we shall argue for the existence of an alternative to today's mainstream theory: the continuation of the canon that dominated the worldview of the Renaissance – The Other Canon. Using a metaphor from Kenneth Arrow, 'this tradition acts like an underground river, springing to the surface every few decades'.[1]

We argue that during the Cold War the 'underground river' of Renaissance Other Canon economics all but disappeared from economic theory, and that it is time to reintroduce it. Traditionally, The Other Canon has been resurrected in times of crisis, such as national emergencies, which bring production – not barter – into focus. This occurs, for example, when an exclusive focus on barter has caused financial bubbles that subsequently burst, when nations are engaged in serious catching up with the prevailing world leader (as the United States, Germany and Japan were in the nineteenth century, or as Korea was until recently), or when a war economy forces a national political system to focus on production (of materials of war). Today the urgency of a change of focus toward the Renaissance conception of economics is particularly acute in the Third World and in formerly communist Eastern Europe. Unfortunately, this is not where economic theory is produced.

The two different canons are based on fundamentally different worldviews, which can be traced back to ancient Greece, where the term 'economics' was first used. Today's standard economics is based on a mechanistic, barter- and consumption-centred tradition – static in the tradition of Zeno – that explains human economic activity in terms of physics. Renaissance Other Canon economics is production-centred and dynamic in the tradition of Heraclitus, and tends to explain human economic activity in terms of biology rather than static physics (for a discussion of the traditions of Zeno and Heraclitus see Popper 1997, pp. 112–13). The mainstream tradition belongs to what Werner Sombart (1930) calls *ordnende Nationalökonomie*, which is concerned with organizing the economic sphere. The Renaissance tradition is what Sombart calls *verstehende Nationalökonomie* and what Nelson and Winter (1982) refer to as 'appreciative economics'. The first tradition is represented by Malthus's dismal science, the second by Christopher Freeman's *Economics of Hope*.

Present mainstream economic theory descends in a canonical sequence from the physiocrats via Adam Smith and David Ricardo to the neoclassical tradition beginning with William Stanley Jevons, Carl Menger and Alfred Marshall. The sequence has been made clear to generations of economists as the 'family tree of economics' featured in many editions of Paul Samuelson's *Economics*. The alternative canon in economic theory runs parallel in time with the tradition of Samuelson's 'family tree'. We have named this alternative canon The Other Canon, or alternatively 'Renaissance economics', because never before or since have the values that this canon represents dominated the world picture as they did during the Renaissance. The mainstream canon is a product of the Enlightenment, in opposition to Renaissance values and outlook. Rationality and individuality during the Renaissance were based on an image of man as a spiritual being: creative and productive. The Enlightenment had a more materialistic understanding of human rationality and individuality: mechanical and consuming. Today, the Renaissance canon disappears in the history of economic thought, as this branch of economics increasingly concentrates on the predecessors of neoclassical economics. We would claim that the absence of the history of economic policy as a branch of economics is responsible for pushing the alternative canon into virtual oblivion.

Renaissance economics is optimistic: the never-ending frontier of knowledge stands in sharp contrast with Malthus's dismal science and with the production theory of mainstream economics. Other main features of the Renaissance canon of economic theory are the following. The fundamental cause of economic welfare is human productive creativity and morality, the immaterial production factors. In order for these ideas to materialize, capital is needed. Capital *per se* is sterile. The Renaissance tradition can be contrasted with the mainstream using Schumpeter's description of the economics of John Rae, a nineteenth-century US economist of the Renaissance canon: 'The essential thing is the conception of the economic process, which soars above the pedestrian view that it is the accumulation of capital per se that propels the capitalist engine'.[2] Squarely put, whereas the Renaissance canon focuses on culture as the main source of production and welfare, the mainstream canon focuses on nature. Mainstream economics defines its origins in the French school of physiocracy (that is, 'the rule of nature'),[3] where value is created by nature and harvested by man. In Renaissance economics, value originates through man's wit and will (that is, 'ideocracy'). During the mechanization of the worldview that took place during the materialistically oriented Enlightenment, the defenders of the Renaissance tradition were the antiphysiocrats.[4] The Renaissance tradition is holistic and idealistic, not atomistic and materialistic. At the core of the system is the individual, set in a complex web of interrelations. The beneficial effects of these interrelations first became evident in Renaissance towns, giving birth to the Renaissance expression the common weal, *il bene comune* or *das Gemeinwohl* depending on the language (Latini et al. 1993, Henderson 1994) – a synergetic understanding of society as being more than the sum of its parts.[5]

Towns permitted communication, which unleashed individual freedom, creativity and diversification, which in turn engendered unprecedented wealth. Later nation-building in this tradition tried consciously to reproduce these synergetic benefits of towns on a national scale. In order to achieve this, law and administrative science had to be cultivated and promoted. Renaissance economics emphasizes the crucial role of nation-states and the duties of the ruler – that is, government – not only to regulate in order to provide incentives for the creation of welfare (in the ancient tradition of law and economics), but also to initiate projects creating a demand for knowledge-based production.

The strategy of the Renaissance Other Canon tradition included two tightly interrelated parts: (1) the promotion of new knowledge, and (2) the promotion of infrastructure in its broadest sense, thereby permitting the communication of knowledge and the exchange of goods at lower transportation and/or transaction costs. These two types of investments, typically being public goods – private investors would not be able to collect the benefits of such investments – need public entrepreneurship produced by a visible hand.

An integral part of this nation-building strategy was a notion that a national market had to be created, that it did not appear spontaneously. For this reason, communication and state-initiated investments in large-scale infrastructure projects hold a very strong position in the Renaissance Other Canon tradition, from the dams and irrigation canals of the Sumerian kingdoms to Colbert's canals to Eisenhower's interstate highways. We could say that the strategy of Renaissance economics was to create perfect competition within national borders and dynamic imperfect competition in the export trade. Contrary to the common preconceptions of economics before Adam Smith, 'Competition was often artificially fostered [nationally] . . . in order to organize markets with automatic regulation of supply and demand'.[6] It was commonly agreed that a national competitive advantage had to be created in knowledge-intensive activities before free trade with the most advanced nations could be established.

The two canons should be seen as 'ideal types' in the Weberian sense. Through time, several distinguishing features have clearly separated them. One of these is their different conceptions of the origin of wealth:

- In the mainstream canon, wealth originates from material sources: nature (land), physical labour and capital. The accumulation of these assets takes place through trade and war. This accumulation is static – more of the same.
- In The Other Canon, wealth originates from immaterial sources: human culture, creativity and morality. The accumulation of assets takes place through innovations cumulatively changing man's stock of knowledge and of his tools (technology). This accumulation is dynamic – something new and qualitatively different.

A second major distinguishing feature of the two canons is their analytical focus:

- In the mainstream canon, the focus of analysis is on barter, consumption and accumulation (man as trader and consumer).
- In The Other Canon, the focus of analysis is on production and innovation, productivity being the force that unites mind and matter (man as creative producer).

A third major difference between the canons is:

- In the mainstream canon economic development is spontaneous and independent of any collective will. (See Viner 1972 for a discussion of the invisible hand as it relates to beliefs in Fate and Providence.)
- Since the Renaissance, economic development in The Other Canon is the result of wilful and conscious creation and policy intervention in order to promote a synergetic common weal.

At a very fundamental level, the two canons of economics are founded on two different views of how Man differs from other animals. We shall let

Adam Smith represent the material and barter-based canon, and Abraham Lincoln represent Renaissance economics – the immaterial and production-based canon.

Adam Smith:

> The division of labour arises from a propensity in human nature to . . . truck, barter and exchange one thing for another . . . It is common to all men, and to be found in no other race of animals, which seem to know neither this nor any other species of contracts . . . Nobody ever saw a dog make a fair and deliberate exchange of one bone for another with another dog. (Smith 1976[1776], p. 17)

Abraham Lincoln:

> Beavers build houses; but they build them in nowise differently, or better, now than they did five thousand years ago . . . Man is not the only animal who labours; but he is the only one who *improves* his workmanship. These improvements he effects by *Discoveries* and *Inventions* . . .' (Speech of the 1860 Presidential Campaign)

There are, of course, inventions also in Adam Smith, but they are exogenous; they are created ouside his economic system. The term 'innovation', which was important in English economics from Francis Bacon's 'An Essay on Innovations' (ca 1605) until and including James Steuart (1767), disappears with Adam Smith (see Reinert & Daastøl 1997 for a discussion).

We argue the existence of an immaterial and production-based canon through time. (1) The continuity of this immaterial and production-based tradition in economic theory can be traced from the 1400s to the present, and this filiation of thought and its geographical movements from nation to nation can be documented, through citations and economic policy. (2) The roots of this economic theory, both in philosophy and in economic policy, can be traced back through the Byzantine and Carolingian empires to Platonic philosophy, to Ptolemy's Egypt and the Sumerian kingdoms. In other words, our approach is mainly diffusionist. However, we do not exclude 'independent discoveries' of the rational principles of Renaissance economics, particularly in times of national crisis and war. We also see a consistent pattern of application of The Other Canon in the framework of succesful economic catching up.

No nation-state has ever developed from poverty to affluence without taking the production-based canon as its fundamental guide for economic policy over long periods.[7] This was true in France (where a modern starting point for policy could be Louis XI, in 1461, and Barthélemy Laffemas (in 1597), Antoine de Montchrétien, Jean Bodin and the Duc de Sully for theory); in England (where a logical starting point for policy is the reign of Henry VII, in 1485); in Germany; in the United States (Benjamin Franklin,

Alexander Hamilton, Daniel Raymond (1820), Henry Clay, Matthew and Henry Carey, E. Peshine Smith); and in Japan (the Meiji Restoration). Today we see the production-based economic strategy at work in East Asia. The Third World has never fully experienced the production-based canon.

On the practical policy level, the two canons conflict because whereas in the Renaissance theory different economic activities offer different potentials for achieving national welfare, in the barter-centred theory (discounting the different circumstances under which the bartered goods are actually produced), all economic activities become qualitatively alike. If anything, in the standard canon superiority is awarded to agriculture, which is more 'natural' because (1) it delivers nature's produce, and (2) competition here is more 'natural', atomistic and 'perfect'.

Tracing the Renaissance canon of economic thought presents several problems. First, the history of economic thought has to a great extent developed into a genealogy of neoclassical economics. For this reason the 'unorthodox' economists who are not part of the canonical sequence are left out. Second, the overwhelming dominance of Anglo-Saxon economists – today generally with very limited skills in languages other than English and mathematics – and of Anglo-Saxon economic policy in the post-Bretton Woods period has added an ethnocentric dimension to this development. Third, in spite of their profound impact on economic policy, the people who represented the Renaissance canon are often not classified as economists. Even Schumpeter's *History of Economic Analysis*, which is unique in this tradition in its geographical and linguistic scope, leaves out people such as Gottfried Leibniz and Christian Wolff. As economists, Leibniz and Wolff were not only very important for the economic policy of their time, but they also laid the foundation for the whole German economic tradition, which largely coincided with the US and Japanese traditions during the nineteenth century up until the Second World War. Many of these German economists tend to be classified as sociologists, particularly Max Weber. Schumpeter (1954, p. 117) writes: '[T]he great names of Leibniz and that of his faithful henchman Christian Wolff, are left out advisedly: they were polyhistors, of course, and greatly interested, among other things, in the economic events and policies of their day; but they made no contribution to our subject.' It was only in the post-Bretton Woods era that Adam Smith and David Ricardo completely won the day in economic policy, so the economists of alternative traditions who were crucial to economic policy are therefore almost entirely left out of today's history of economic thought. The last history of economics to provide good coverage of the theories behind the nineteenth-century economic policy was Spann (1926). This was translated into several languages; interestingly, the British edition was published under the title *Types of Economic*

Theory, underscoring Spann's awareness that there are, indeed, different types of economics, not just one monolithic canon.

2. THE FAMILY TREE OF THE OTHER CANON

Traces of the Renaissance Other Canon can be found in pre-antiquity. Statecraft and the accumulation of knowledge – exemplified by the Library of Alexandria and the scientific academies of Sumeria under Hammurabi (2030–1995 BC) – were important features of the early Middle Eastern kingdoms of Sumeria and Egypt. These kingdoms also produced extensive literature and documents on economic and legal matters which survive today. As occurred later in Asia and in the Andes, irrigation seems to have been the first technology to create important increasing returns to scale, and consequently to require statecraft. Irrigation was therefore instrumental in the establishment of the first states. The cuneiform script of the Sumerians remained the standard for the Middle East region for the next 2000 years, and the Code of Hammurabi tells of an enlightened and humane system of law.

Later, during the Phoenician dominance of Mediterranean trade (from about 1500 to about 500 BC), there was clear practical recognition of the Other Canon principle that adding knowledge and labour to raw materials through the production of manufactured goods produces a superior standard of living to only extracting and selling the raw produce. We find this same theory clearly stated in Botero (1590), but only Serra (1613) would later explain the economic mechanisms behind this principle: why the Republic of Venice, with little or no raw materials, was so rich compared to the Kingdom of Naples, with its abundance of natural wealth. Later colonial and neocolonial projects would retain the pattern set by the Phoenicians and well expressed in the maxims of Charles King (1721): imports of raw material and export of manufactured goods are 'good trade', export of raw materials and import of manufactured goods are 'bad trade', while exchanging manufactured goods for other manufactured goods is 'good trade' for both trading partners. The 'New Trade Theory' of the 1990s again modelled Charles King's maxim, but alas with no practical consequences for the Third World.

The philosophical foundation of the Renaissance canon displays a clear continuity. Plato and other Greek philosophers were to some extent influenced by Egyptian civilization. Augustine's *De civitate dei* (413–426) was written in the Platonic spirit. Occasional rediscoveries of Plato such as this led to sporadic 'renaissances', among them the Carolingian Renaissance under Charlemagne (768–814). Charlemagne was counselled by Thomas of

York, a follower of Augustine. Under Charlemagne the fondness of Renaissance economics for education, industry and infrastructure was already evident. Charlemagne was actively promoting the textile industry; in Friesland, he built roads and worked on a canal linking Europe's greatest rivers, the Danube and the Rhine; and he promoted Latin as a standard administrative language in Western Europe.

No doubt inspired by the developments in Italian city states, France under Louis XI (1423–83) experienced an early mini-renaissance. Louis XI established a pattern that came to typify Renaissance economics: he allied himself with the middle class against the noblemen, establishing a tax system favouring the urban, middle-class value of industriousness against the landowning upper class's feudal valuing of agriculture and trade *per se*. Renaissance economics – creating centralized nation-states – was an important factor in bringing about the decline of feudalism. In Spain, with the 1521 civil war known as the Revolt of the Comuneros the feudal class won over the modernizing urban middle classes, thus contributing to the political foundations for Spain's deindustrialization following the inflow of precious metal from the Americas.

The Italian-born Renaissance was a rebirth of knowledge as the central engine of human change; it led to a reinterpretation of Man's place in the divine scheme. Innovations had previously been tantamount to heresy – all Man was supposed to know was already in the Holy Bible and in the writings of Aristotle. Knowledge production was confined to the interpretation of these scriptures. The influence of the Eastern church and the inflow of refugees from the crumbling Byzantine Empire to Italy completely reversed these perceptions: Man was created in the image of God, and God's most salient feature was his rational creativity. Consequently, innovations were no longer heretical; on the contrary, Man's essential and pleasurably duty was to innovate. Figure 1.1 shows the main contributions to the Renaissance and the philosophers who helped promulgate Renaissance economic thinking in Europe.

'To me the Renaissance will always mark the high point of this millennium', says Nietzsche (2000, p. 10288). The Renaissance worldview released enormous creativity; it gave us da Vinci, Michelangelo, Rafael, Kepler and Copernicus. In all arts and sciences, the people of the Renaissance still stand out in history, whereas the statesmen and economists of the Renaissance today are represented by the caricatures Adam Smith created. In the spirit of the Renaissance, Francis Bacon – Queen Elizabeth's Lord High Chancellor – wrote *An Essay of Innovations* (ca 1605). Bacon became the 'scientific leader of the new industrialists',[8] urging the use of science to produce manufactured goods and profits.

This conviction that a society based on manufacturing is fundamentally

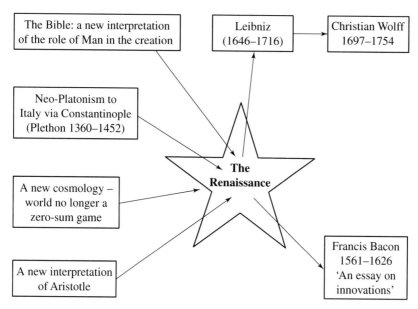

Figure 1.1   The Renaissance: influences and consequences for economics

superior to a society without a manufacturing base is an essential feature of what we label Renaissance economics. Emphasis on the 'intrinsic value of manufacturing' has been an integral part of the economic policy of all nations that have ever successfully embarked on a strategy of catching up with leading nations. Only when the catching up has been achieved have the industrialized nations (beginning with England) embraced the classical/neoclassical tradition. In other words, no nation has ever achieved general welfare without going through a period of Renaissance economics. In England this period lasted for more than 400 years, starting in the late fifteenth century; Korea achieved a great deal in only 40 years.

Bacon's emphasis on scientific knowledge was very similar to that of Friedrich List more than 200 years later: 'Industry is the mother and father of science, literature, the arts, enlightenment, useful institutions and national power . . . The greater the advance in scientific knowledge, the more numerous will be the new inventions which save labour and raw materials and lead to new products and processes.'[9] In this sense, there is a continuity of argument from the Renaissance through Bacon and List to today's evolutionary economics, which emphasizes the role of research and development and of innovations in improving economic welfare. As to natural resources, List (1904, p. 79) says that 'industrialisation will greatly increase the value of a country's natural resources'. This thinking was the basis for economic policy in the resource-rich nations that have achieved general welfare: Canada, Australia and New Zealand. A manufacturing sector (even though it was not competitive with England's) was needed to transform the natural resources of a nation into national wealth (Reinert 1998).

List (1904, p. 142) expressed the view of industry that prevailed among nations catching up with England during the nineteenth century:

> Let us compare Poland with England: both nations at one time were at the same stage of culture; and now what a difference. Manufactories and manufactures are the mothers and children of municipal liberty, of intelligence, of the arts and sciences, of internal and external commerce, of navigation and improvements in transport, of civilisation and of political power. They are the chief way of liberating agriculture from its chains. . . . The popular school [that is, Adam Smith and J.B. Say] has attributed this civilising effect to foreign trade, but in that it has confounded the mere exchanger with the originator.

Deindustrialization, on the other hand, has been a corollary to economic disasters and massive reductions in human welfare; examples include the deindustrialization of Holland after 1650, of Northern Italy following the French invasion, of France following the Napoleonic Wars, of Eastern Europe after the fall of the Berlin Wall, and of several Third World countries after the 'adjustment policies' of the Washington Consensus (see the case studies of Mongolia and Peru in this volume). List, who originally had been a free trader and continued to believe that free trade was the final goal of development, recognized the crucial role of manufacturing when he saw the devastating effects of the deindustrialization of France after the Napoleonic wars on the welfare of the nation.

In List we find again the synergy-based arguments of Renaissance economists such as Giovanni Botero and Antonio Serra. As stated earlier, the goal of the state's economic policy was to increase the common weal – the prosperity of the community. This is the starting point of virtually all economic writing of the period. To the Renaissance economists, systemic effects seem to have arisen first from the observation that widespread wealth appeared to accumulate in the cities, not in the countryside. This was the fundamental observation of one of the earliest best-selling books in economics, *Delle Cause della Grandezza delle Città*, by Giovanni Botero (1543–1617). The English translation, published in London in 1606, is titled *The Cause of the Greatnesse of Cities*. This argument was discussed in detail by Antonio Serra in 1613, whose work is cited nine times and with extensive comments by Friedrich List.

In the best theoretical works of the time, the difference between the wealth and poverty of cities and countryside, and between cities, is explained in terms of the following main factors: (1) size and density of population; (2) different 'qualities' of economic activities, manufacturing being 'good' and agriculture alone being 'bad'; (3) the presence or absence of diversity of economic occupations; (4) the different capacities of economic activities to initiate 'virtuous circles' or positive feedback mechanisms; and (5) a steady, orderly and liberal government providing economic policy based on the above principles. The systemic effects in the economy are described by Renaissance economists at three levels of sophistication:[10]

1. Observations that higher welfare is produced by some economic activities than by others, a static and nonsystemic observation of welfare being activity-specific. (To give a modern-day example: lawyers make more money than people picking lettuce; therefore, a nation of lettuce pickers will be poorer than a nation of lawyers.)
2. Observations that certain economic activities are at the core of systemic synergies which produce and spread welfare locally or nationwide. ('Where there are many people working with machines, the shopkeepers are wealthier than in other places where machines are not used.')
3. There are degrees of understanding how these systemic synergies develop into positive feedback systems, but the most sophisticated is that of Antonio Serra (1613), who describes Venice as a true autocatalytic system in which increasing returns and diversity – the latter expressed as the number of different professions in a nation (that is, degree of division of labour) – are identified as being at the core of virtuous circles that generate wealth. Naples represents the opposite effect in Serra's system, because the production of raw materials is not subject to increasing returns.

These synergy-based arguments are found today in the works on increasing return by authors such as Paul David, W. Brian Arthur and James Buchanan. In our opinion these authors are reinventing the role of knowledge, synergies and path-dependence, which are main characteristics of Renaissance economics throughout history. Take, for example, List's (1841/1904) view of manufacturing's role:

> The productive powers of agriculture are scattered over a wide area. But the productive powers of industry are brought together and are centralised in one place. This process eventually creates an expansion of productive powers which grow in geometric rather than in arithmetic proportion.
> This is why the population of an industrialised society is brought together in a few conurbations in which are concentrated a great variety of skills, productive powers, applied science, art and literature. Here are to be found great public

and private institutions and associations in which theoretical knowledge is applied to the practical affairs of industry and commerce. Only in such conurbations can a public opinion develop which is strong enough to vanquish the brute force, to maintain freedom for all, and to insist that the public authorities should adopt administrative policies that will promote and safeguard national prosperity . . .

In addition the manufacturers are the focus of a large, lucrative, and world wide trade with peoples of varied standards of culture who live in many distant countries. Industry turns cheap bulk raw materials, which cannot be sent long distances, into goods of low weight and high value which are in universal demand.

List was in many ways the main nineteenth-century propagandist of the Renaissance canon. He emphasized the immaterial foundations of wealth (knowledge and human 'wit and will'), the superiority of manufacturing over agriculture and raw materials, the crucial role of infrastructure, the systemic nature of economic growth (as a 'national innovation system') and free trade among nations at the same level of development. These are all typical traits in pre-First World War theories of economic policy in Germany, the United States and Japan. Later these ideas spread to Korea and Taiwan and are now the basis for China's economic strategy, where Sun Yat-Sen (Yat-Sen 1922) and Chang Kai Shek were followers of List's system.

However, List's analysis of why these policies were so efficient is somewhat lacking. No doubt his observations were accurate, but his theoretical concepts are vague and his explanations of the economic mechanisms at work are imprecise. Werner Sombart comments: 'His concepts levitate like undelivered souls on the banks of Hades'.[11] In spite of this, List's holistic vision of the fundamentals of economic development creating national wealth or poverty is almost unprecedented.

The Renaissance theory often works through abduction – the kind of intuitive knowledge that precedes induction and deduction. Lemons helped sailors in the Mediterranean prevent scurvy 800 years before the exact mechanisms through which these lemons work were established (that is, vitamin C). Similarly, economic growth was successfully promoted in the Renaissance tradition of economics using 'new knowledge' and 'use of machinery' as proxies for the underlying factors causing systemic economic growth. The German cameralist tradition in economics recognized the superior potential of manufacturing over any other activity as a basis for collecting taxes. This was one of several reasons why manufacturing was favoured in the German states, and increased economic wealth and technical change were by-products of this policy.

We argue that there is a strong continuity in this canon (see Figure 1.2). Serra (1613) provides a theoretical framework to the mercantilist view that

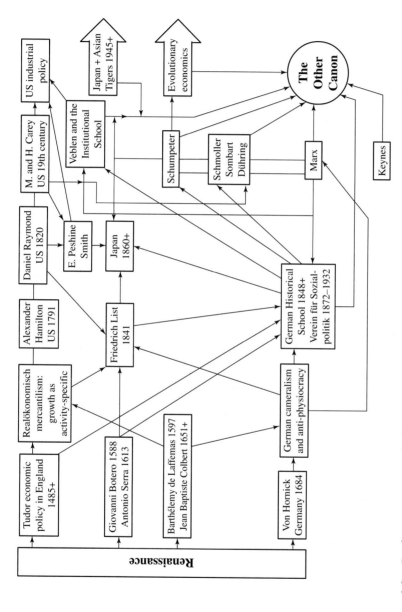

Figure 1.2   Reality economics: the knowledge- and production-based Other Canon of economics

some specific economic activities are carriers of economic growth. He also explains the mechanisms creating the synergies which the mercantilists called the common weal. At the core of these mechanisms Serra sees increasing returns in manufacturing but not in agriculture. The purpose of Serra's treatise is to explain the wealth of Venice and the poverty of Naples, despite the fact that Venice had virtually no natural resources and Naples abounded in natural resources. Serra provides a theory which can explain why the English strategy, starting with Henry VII, was so successful.[12]

In France, the seventeenth-century policies of Sully and Colbert are based on the same type of reasoning. Based on the theory provided by Laffemas (1597), the voluminous letters and instructions of Colbert make clear his role as a businessman in charge of a huge empire.[13] He was faced with what historians of technology call 'reverse salients'[14] – 'dynamic bottlenecks' – retarding the system and demanding managerial attention. In the German-speaking world an early spokesman for the same principles was Philipp Wilhelm von Hornick, whose 1684 work *Österreich über alles wann es nur will* appeared in 16 editions, the last one as late as 1784.

The bridge between English mercantilist policies and the industrial policy of the United States can be documented by two strong pillars: Benjamin Franklin's admiring and enthusiastic footnotes to the second edition of Whatley's (1774) late mercantilist tract, and Alexander Hamilton.

It has been shown that Hamilton knew his Adam Smith but rejected the free trade conclusion. Excerpts from Malachy Postlethwayt's *Universal Dictionary of Trade and Commerce* were scattered through Hamilton's *Army Pay Book*[15] and later provided much inspiration for his 1791 *Report on the Manufactures.*

When in the 1850s Wilhelm Roscher put increasing returns on the map again as a determinant of uneven economic development, he repeatedly quoted Antonio Serra just as List had done a decade or so earlier. Serra's work had been reprinted in Italian in 1803. The German Historical School of economics thoroughly understands and appreciates the wisdom of *realökonomisch* mercantilism, although Sombart jokingly admits to the risk of defending any economic theory older than Adam Smith's: 'I say this in spite of the risk of being branded as a neo-mercantilist, and as such to be transferred into the collection of the oddities of our profession.'[16]

A crucial feature of nineteenth-century economic thought is the theoretical cross-fertilization between the biggest nations that were attempting to catch up with England: Germany, the United States and Japan. They were united in their opposition to the theories of Smith and Ricardo, particularly as it applied to free trade. Michael Hudson (1969, p. 45) traces the 'institutionalist (historical) school of economists which flourished in

America during the final decades of the nineteenth century. The line appears to have run from the protectionist circle around Matthew Carey and Daniel Raymond, through Friedrich List to Germany and from there, via Roscher's circles, to American students such as Patten and Ely studying at German universities.' There were no graduate courses in economics in the United States at the time, and most US economists had their PhD from Germany. This includes all the founders of the American Economic Association. The transfer of Other Canon economic ideas to Japan after the Meiji Restoration was made by German economists – and by US economists who had studied in Germany – when 'a stream of German teachers of political economy and related disciplines continually flowed in'.[17]

The mercantilist inspiration for production-based economics can also be traced to the twentieth century. The main economist behind the Third Reich was Hjalmar Schacht, who was one of the two prisoners immediately freed after the Nürenberg trials. The subject of Schacht's PhD thesis at the University of Kiel in 1900 was 'Der theoretische Gehalt der englischen Merkantilismus' ('The theoretical content of English mercantilism').[18] Schacht's skilful use of mercantilist production-based war economics, combined with a Keynesian understanding of credit, for a long time worked wonders for Hitler's Germany. Schacht's work also proves, though, the fundamental point of the Other Canon Renaissance economics – that economics cannot and must not be separated from morality. The influential German economist J.F. von Pfeiffer (1715–87), an ardent antiphysiocrat, put it this way: 'You can make of human beings what you want. The way he is governed, commends man to good, or to evil.'[19]

3. THE TWO CANONS: SELECTIVE USE, METHODOLOGICAL SCHIZOPHRENIA AND OPPORTUNISTIC IGNORANCE

We do not imply that the world is a binary one, where all economists belong to one tradition or the other. On the contrary, a key characteristic of several important economists is their at times schizophrenic allegiance to both sets of theory. One example of this is the conflict between the Marshall whose 'Mecca of the economist' was based in economic biology (Marshall 1890, p. iv) and the Marshall of the appendices to his *Principles*, which were deeply steeped in 'physics envy'. In order to create the equilibrium that characterizes today's physics-based standard economic theory, Marshall paradoxically had to resort to a biological metaphor. Increasing returns had been an important argument for industrial policy beginning with Serra (1613) and continuing through the nineteenth century. To reconcile the existence of increasing returns with equilibrium, Marshall (1890, pp. 315–16) uses a lengthy metaphor of firms growing and dying like trees in the forests. This evolutionary growth process supposedly counteracts the tendency toward uneven accumulation caused by increasing returns to scale.[20] The argument that killed all future biological analogies in neoclassical economics was a biological analogy, which was important in making economics what it is today, a profession in which a physics-inspired equilibrium is the central gestalt.

Schumpeter emanated from the Renaissance tradition of the German historical school and spent his life on the hopeless task of formalizing the creative essence of Renaissance economics – entrepreneurship, novelty and creative destruction – into the framework of the dead equilibrium that is at the core of neoclassical economics. Schumpeter was indeed 'a living, breathing contradiction', as Mirowski (1994, p. 5) puts it. We would claim that this contradiction was a result of being steeped simultaneously in two irreconcilable paradigms (see Reinert 2002 for a discussion).

Marx was steeped in the same two irreconcilable paradigms. In his emphasis on technology and economic dynamics Marx, like Schumpeter, belongs to the Renaissance production-based canon. Marx's and Schumpeter's visions have a common basis in the German economic tradition. In Anglo-Saxon economics, these economists come across as extremely original; seen from the German side, they are both firmly rooted in that alternative canon. The one aspect of Marx's theory that belongs to the Anglo-Saxon canon is his use of Ricardo's labour theory of value. This theory is out of place in the German tradition, in which entrepreneurship, ideas, knowledge, leadership and management make vital contributions to the value added by physical labour.

Although he was – after John Locke and Bernard de Mandeville – the true founder of the mainstream canon, Adam Smith himself suffered from the same canonical mental split. In his discussion of the Navigation Act he was clearly in favour of the protectionist policy, blocking Dutch ships and imports. His argument was to a large extent based on considerations of national defence. To Smith (1976, vol. 2, p. 219), 'The art of war . . . is certainly the noblest of all arts'.

It is of great interest to note that to Smith, the father of free trade, the mercantilist and protectionist Navigation Act was 'the wisest of all commercial regulations in England' (1976, vol. 1, p. 487). This apparent double standard and selective use of the different canons in order to suit English interests was frequently denounced by German and US economists in the nineteenth century. Their slogan was, 'Do as the English did, not as they say'. Today an appropriate strategy for the Third World would be, 'Do as the Americans did, not as they say'. Part of this use of a double standard was, and is, an 'opportunistic ignorance' (to use Gunnar Myrdal's term) of the history of one's own nation's economic policy.

Before his meeting with the French physiocrats, Adam Smith clearly expressed the Renaissance view of the common weal as the motivating force for establishing manufactures. These were established neither to assist the producer nor to assist the consumer:

> The same principle, *the same love of system*, the same regard to the beauty of order . . . frequently serves to recommend those institutions which tend to promote the public welfare . . . When the legislature establishes premiums and other encouragements to advance the linen or woollen manufactures, its conduct seldom proceeds from pure sympathy with the wearer of cheap or fine cloth, and much less from that with the manufacturer or merchant. The perfection of police [that is, policy], the extension of trade and manufactures, are noble and magnificent objects. The contemplation of them pleases us, and we are interested in whatever can tend to advance them. They make part of *the great system of government*, and the wheels of the political machine seem to move with more harmony and ease by means of them. We take pleasure in beholding the perfection of so beautiful and grand a system, and we are uneasy till we remove any obstruction that can in the least disturb or encumber the regularity of its motions.[21]

As we have indicated, the two alternative canons have ebbed and flowed throughout history. However, quite often we find the same nation-state applying both canons at the same time, but for different end-users. For example it is clear that, starting in the 1830s, England used Ricardo's trade theory (the barter-based classical canon) for export and Charles Babbage's works on the importance of machinery and of science (the knowledge- and production-based Renaissance canon) for domestic purposes. The United States conveniently followed this same canonic dualism in the nineteenth century. At a time when the United States was busily protecting its own industries, US commodore Matthew Perry was sent to Japan to convince that nation of the benefits of free trade. This resulted in the 'unfair treaties' that hold such a dominant position in the Japanese perception of their own history.

The same contradictory policies continued into the twentieth century. A book from the Washington-based Institute for International Economics in 1986 introduces the description of US trade policy as follows: 'With bipartisan regularity, American presidents since Franklin Delano Roosevelt have proclaimed the virtues of free trade. They have inaugurated bold international programs to reduce tariff and non-tariff barriers. But almost in the same breath, most presidents have advocated or accepted special measures to protect problem industries. Together the two strands of policy have produced a contradictory profile.'[22] On these occasions, arguments from the

Renaissance-based canon – recognizing that both manufacturing and other knowledge-based activities matter – are invoked in order to protect both the national manufacturing base and the knowledge-based service sector. On the other hand the World Bank, following a strategy that 'manufacturing does not matter', carries out structural adjustment programmes which in many cases lead to the deindustrialization of whole nations, with a consequent collapse of national welfare (see the chapters on Mongolia and Peru in this volume). This is the paradigm of organized free trade, which in practice follows the Golden Rule: 'The one who has the gold makes the rules.'

An important feature of the opportunistic ignorance of today's leading industrialized nations is the fact that the history of their own economic policy – the policy that they used to catch up with the wealthy nations – to a surprising extent has been forgotten. This is very clear in the United States. The economists who laid the foundations for nineteenth-century US trade and industrial policy are hardly mentioned in today's history of economics, and if they are mentioned it is to point out their 'failures'. It is curious how today's American economists virtually unanimously declare that both the industrialization of their own country and the New Deal were carried out by 'bad economists'. Economists such as E. Peshine Smith,[23] who later played a key role in bringing the 'American System of Manufactures' to Japan, Matthew Carey, Daniel Raymond, Alexander Everett, Calvin Colton, Francis Bowen and Stephen Colwell are unknown today. Only Henry Carey is remembered by a few.

This is of course a parallel to the well-established 'fact' of economic science that the Renaissance economists who brought Europe out of the Middle Ages all belonged to the despised category of 'mercantilists'. We have collectively absorbed Adam Smith's caricature of all economists before himself: that they mistook gold for real wealth. German economist Eugen Dühring scorns *die Karikierer des Merkantilismus* – the caricature-makers of mercantilism – who 'only too often spoke as if the business people and the statesmen of the day almost believed that precious metal could be used as food for the human body'.[24] The important systemic and production-based aspects of the Renaissance theory – the creation of a national common weal – are left out of today's accounts. Recently however Cosimo Perrotta (1988) has published a book that resurrects Continental mercantilism as a theory focused on production and employment.

The strategy of 'theory juggling' is also present in the European Community. The Cecchini Report on the single European market identifies most of the benefits from the single market as coming from economies of scale. On the other hand, EU policy toward the Third World is based on a theory which denies that economies of scale and increasing returns exist. During the nineteenth century, the existence of increasing returns in industry was an important argument for the protection of industry in all the nations that followed the English path to industrialization. Today, this argument is used only internally in the European Union, not in its policy toward the Third World. The industrialized nations are today 'pulling up the ladder' of development from those who tried to industrialize later. Only in Asia, where the activity-specific Renaissance strategy is copied from Japan, do we see real catching up.

Friedrich List saw clearly that Adam Smith's theory contradicted the policy followed by England during its ascent to world power. List's succinct and accurate summary of the history of English economic policy states: 'The principle "sell manufactured products, buy raw materials" was for centuries the English substitute for an [economic] theory.'[25]

To List (1904, pp. 368–9), English classical economic theory

> conceal[s] the true policy of England under cosmopolitan expressions and arguments which Adam Smith had discovered, in order to induce foreign nations not to imitate that policy. It is a very common clever device that when someone has attained the summit of greatness, he kicks away the ladder by which he had climbed up, in order to deprive others of the means of climbing up after him. On this lies the secret of the cosmopolitical doctrine of Adam Smith, and of the cosmopolitical tendencies of his great contemporary William Pitt, and of all his successors in the British Government administrations. . . . William Pitt was the first English statesman who clearly saw in what way the cosmopolitical theory of Adam Smith could properly be made use of.

The actual historical record of free trade confirms that England carried out at home the very policies that its theoretical economists tried to prevent in the rest of the world. Conventional wisdom has it that in the nineteenth century, France was a fortress of protectionism while England was the bastion of free trade. Consulting actual trade data, however, yields the surprising conclusion that 'French average tariffs were . . . consistently below those of Britain throughout most of the Nineteenth Century, even after the abolition of the Corn Laws'.[26] The double standard is not new, but is still amazingly effective in maintaining and widening the gap between the leaders and the laggards of the world's nations.

4. COMMUNICATION, INFRASTRUCTURE AND FINANCE

In spite of its sparse treatment in economic theory, infrastructure is a key factor in any advanced economy. Infrastructure is the necessary policy response to the existence of geography and distance. Investments in transportation and communication are both productivity-enhancing and price-reducing (deflationary), and as such a prime engine of general invest-ment. Traditional infrastructure induces investment in engineering and in the production of heavy machinery, while advanced infrastructure, as for example in telecommunications, is highly science- and innovation-driven. In both cases, transaction costs are reduced, labour productivity and employment are increased and the tax base widened.

In the Renaissance tradition, the bases for increased economic welfare are knowledge and infrastructure, broadly defined. Knowledge concerns the human ability to think, to generate hypotheses and to communicate. This communication in turn depends on the phenomenon of *consensus gentium*, which we elaborated upon in our article on Leibniz and Wolff (Reinert and Daastøl 1997).

Initial public institutions and public works focused on the need for defending society and for establishing justice; later institutions facilitated the extension of commerce and the promotion of education. An early invention that brought wealth was the institution of the well-ordered city, with its tight communication, extended division of labour, markets, legal and political administration, and well-ordered communication with the outside world. This dates at least to the Indus civilization of 2300 BC, where Mohenjodaro was probably the first planned city in the world; it included a highly developed division of labour with many 'modern' inven-tions such as the wheel, the plough, intense irrigation, a sewer system, local markets and a vast international trading network.

As already mentioned, the concept of the common weal was synergetic, as had been observed already by Xenophon (Xenophon and Ambler, 2001). Serra (1613) specifically relates the wealth of a city to the number of differ-ent professions contained therein, that is to the extent and degree of the division of labour. Adam Smith's division of labour, known to the ancients and elaborated by numerous authors before him,[27] clearly implies increas-ing returns to scale. This is probably the reason why the division of labour has never been integrated into classical or neoclassical economic model-ling. The division of labour is in some very fundamental sense not compat-ible with constant returns to scale; rather, it is a result of fixed costs – either of knowledge or of other tools – which automatically cause increasing returns to some degree. In the Renaissance conception of economics, there-fore, returns increased with the size of population of a nation. Recreating and extending this observed urban advantage, the urban bias of develop-ment, to the whole nation-state was a central challenge to Renaissance rulers. Both List and Wallerstein point out that while England achieved this increased size through national unity, Italy, the Hansa and Holland did not develop beyond a collection of city-states, which they see as a main reason for their loss of leadership.[28]

Early municipal (city-state) mercantilists observed the beneficial effects of denser populations clustered in towns giving rise to productive synergetic effects through differentiation, personal and political freedom, and economies of scale. Having a large population was therefore regarded as a great benefit to any nation. Roscher (1882, p. 343 § 254) writes on the early policy of Henry IV that '[n]ot many had as much insight as Henry IV: la force et la richesse des rois consistent dans les nombre et dans l'opulence des sujets', and Petty 'would give up Scotland and Ireland entirely, and have the inhabitants settle in England'. For a discussion of early population theories, see Stangeland (1904). In this philosophy, building infrastructure became a key tool to later nation-building mercantilists and cameralists. State mercantilists tried to emulate on a national scale the agglomeration advantages found in urban areas through state-initiated construction of various means of infrastructure, communication and transportation. These economists and policy-makers tried to reconstruct artificially the observed benefits of the cities' high population densities in geographical areas with lower population densities. Law and order; industrial quality control; labour codes; labour discipline; standardization of language, measurements, coins and education; the construction of ports, roads, canals, postal routes and 'refuelling stations' along transportation routes were all parts of this strategy. These measures were intended to create widespread national welfare as opposed to the municipal mercantilist strategy which flourished, in the main, in coastal city-states. These city-states mostly functioned as enclave economies that were relatively isolated from the hinterland. State mercantilism or 'statism' changed this early merchant mercantilism. In its pursuit of public power and wealth, state mercantilism fused the monarchic and municipal mercantilist traditions. This alliance between the king and the middle class, which opposed the feudal aristocracy, created a powerful instrument: the nation-state, an instrument that unified formerly separate towns and regions.

In sparsely populated areas, a policy of corridor development was pursued, similar to the old Silk Road caravan tracks between the Roman and Chinese empires established by the first Han (206 BC–220 AD) or the Emperor's Grand Canal between Hangzhou and Beijing (1800 km). By creating dense populations in areas along transportation routes, construction of these arteries was made economically more worthwhile. This strategy also opened up marginal areas for development, the early railroad development of the United States being a prime example of such strategy. The purpose of the huge investments in infrastructure was in some ways similar to the purpose of the city-states itself: the realization of 'systemic increasing returns', an idea which is already very evident in Xenophon's *Cyropedia* (§ 8.2.5, in Xenophon 2001) and in his *Poroi* (Zincke 1753). This observed 'systemic increasing returns' to the size of a city was the basis for the pro-population stance of cameralists and mercantilists.

List (1985, p. 131) notes the importance of infrastructure for greater communication between citizens. Much like the Internet today, this increased direct communication made political control of the individual more difficult, and therefore created greater political freedom and by extension increased creativity and innovation. Only in densely populated areas could a critical mass of public opinion acquire enough strength to develop into democracy and generally promote political and human rights. At the same time, the expansion of markets through improved communication allowed for greater economies of scale, greater diversification and production for niche markets, and greater production for a monetary – as opposed to a barter – market. Economies of scale allowed for improved technology and made it possible for a higher percentage of the population to engage in new activities, again contributing to diversity, division of labour and economies of scale in a positive feedback circle. The mercantilists' promotion of manufacturing also intended to emulate these positive effects of the city modelled as a huge productive machine, the factory.

A major problem with promotion of infrastructure is how to initiate and finance it. The core factors of the Renaissance policy – knowledge, innovation and infrastructure – all have the character of public goods: concentrated costs for the investor and widely dispersed benefits for society. As is well known, this results in a systematic underinvestment if left to an unregulated market. This outcome is suboptimal from a public point of view, although perfectly rational from the individual investor's point of view. The public, including the individual investors, therefore needs a coordinator, such as a municipality, a regional authority (for example, German Länder or the states in the United States), the nation or an international body (for example, the EU or the UN), to initiate and direct credit to these sectors that produce public goods. The credit directing may be done more directly through a central planning agency, such as GOSPLAN in the former USSR, or more indirectly by ordering banks to offer favourable conditions to industrialists investing in these sectors, as in the French dirigisme system up to the reign of de Gaulle. Another solution is to have many of these public goods produced under the umbrella of national defence, as in the United States where defence spending was used to finance the interstate highways (the national system of interstate and defence highways was financed 90 per cent by the Federal Government) and where military basic research that has led to innovations as diverse as the ballpoint pen (by the US airforce during the Second World War), burglar alarms (the Vietnam War), advanced cellular telephone communication (the 'Star Wars' programme) and the Internet.

From the school of the state mercantilist Colbert, then Napoleon, St Simon and the Grandes Ecoles system came the dirigist system with 'qualitative bank control' in various softer and harder versions (Wiles 1977, p. 215). Wiles further writes (p. 322): 'We remark here again the flexibility, speed and secrecy of such arrangements, compared with the constitutional obstacles to continual changes in taxes by the government, let alone a command economy.' There is a strong tradition of using this kind of policy among nations when endeavouring to catch up, in France, the United States, Japan and Germany. There are several ways to solve this problem of credit directing in practice. They all call for cooperation among authorities, industrialists and bankers; among people, knowledge of the physical production process and of the credit system. Such collaboration and consequent public encroachment into what is otherwise today seen as the sphere of the private market is of course against mainstream economics, but the present national innovation system of the United States is replete with institutions of this sort. The website of the US Small Business Administration http://www.sba.gov reveals that this institution alone channels loans of more than $58 billion of federal funds to US businesses. This government institution assisted more than one million private US companies during 2002, a most visible US government hand. On the US state level a large number of tax incentives to manufacturing companies that are 'small' (by US standards) complements this policy. The problem, however, is that the conditionalities of the Washington Institution prevent these excellent US policies from being copied by poor nations.

Traditionally this way of thinking is accompanied by policy measures ensuring sufficient effective demand – or purchasing power – for the new production capacities thus created. The nineteenth-century US 'High Wage Strategy' was an efficient such strategy, as was the 'Fordist' wage regime, lasting until about 1970, whereby production wages were increased at the same pace as productivity increases in the manufacturing sector. This would prevent depressions due to 'overproduction', 'underconsumption' or 'oversaving'. This idea is also also expressed in the 'circular flow' of J.M. Keynes or the 'ecocirc' of Ragnar Frisch. In this system increasing the standards of living of the majority of the population is not only a moral imperative, it becomes an economic necessity in order to keep the economy growing. Once the virtuous circle of increased productivity/increased real wages starts operating, increasing the real wages of the common man becomes a necessary economic policy if the system is to be perpetuated.

The leading historian and theoretician of economics in Germany in the middle of the nineteenth century was Wilhelm Roscher, whose *Principles*, book IV, is devoted to consumption. As Roscher noted, financial investments are a kind of sterile storage until channelled into consumption. This may disturb the peaceful balance and equilibrium in the perfect model of the classical school. One of Roscher's chapters has the telling heading, 'Necessity of the Proper Simultaneous Development of Production and Consumption'. After a discussion of the two areas, he writes, 'Hence, one of the most essential conditions of a prosperous national economy is that the development of consumption should keep equal pace with that of production, and supply with demand.' In a footnote he declares:

> The necessity of an equilibrium between production and consumption was pretty clear to many of the older political economists. . . . *The moderns have frequently inequitably neglected the doctrine of consumption.* Thus it appears to be a very characteristic fact that in Adam Smith's great book . . . one might think that products were not made for the sake of man but for their own sake. But on the other hand there came a strong reaction . . . And so according to Carey, *Principles*, ch. 35, § 6, the *real difficulty does not lie in production but in finding a purchaser for the products.* But he overlooks the fact here that only the possessor of other products can appear as a purchaser. From another side, most socialists think almost exclusively of the wants of men, and scarcely consider it worth their while to pay any attention to the means of satisfying them. (Roscher 1882, book VI, Chapter 1, §CCXV; emphasis added)

The core motive of Friedrich List and the American protectionists was to promote production in order to elevate wages and consumption, thereby increasing the tax base and production of public goods, and then to promote more production and consumption in a virtuous circle.

Part of this development plan must therefore also have a strategy on how to increase consumption and avoid market crises. On such crises, Roscher (1882, §CCXV) writes:

> The growth of a nation's economy depends on this: that consumption should always be, so to speak, one step in advance of production. . . . Now, the politico-economic disease which is produced by the lagging behind of consumption, and by the supply being much in advance of the demand, is called a commercial [market] crisis.

He continues (§CCXVI), 'Most theorists deny the possibility of a general glut, although many practitioners stubbornly maintain it.' In the next paragraph (§CCXVII) Roscher continues:

> All these allegations are undoubtedly true, in so far as the whole world is considered one great economic system, and the aggregate of all goods, including the medium of circulation, is borne in mind. The consolation which might otherwise lie herein is made indeed to some extent unrealizable by these conditions. It must not be forgotten in practice that men are actuated by other motives than that of consuming as much as possible. . . .

There are, everywhere, certain consumption-customs corresponding with the distribution of the national income. Every great and sudden change in the latter is therefore wont to produce a great glut of the market. [Footnote: If all the rich were suddenly to become misers . . . a multitude of former consumers, having no employment, would be obliged to discontinue their demand. Over-production would be greater yet if a great and general improvement in the industrial arts or in the art of agriculture has gone before.] (Roscher 1882, §CCXVII)

The last point about general improvement in the industrial arts is reminiscent of the recent technological revolution and the consequent financial crisis (Perez in this volume). It should be noted that in this perspective the loss of purchasing power of national salaries and wages as documented in the case studies of Peru and Mongolia in this volume, to the order of around 50 per cent, constitute an enormous setback in the development process. Under the present economic policies there are no signs why this process should be reversed again.

The circulation problem therefore concerns not only directing credit to production but, according to Roscher, even more to channelling purchasing power to consumers in order to create a demand for this production. This brings our discussion into the age-old problem of the regulation of the financial sector as a servant of production and consumption. Such a regulation of the financial sector is found as far back as in Ancient Sumeria and in early Judaism, where sporadic debt forgiveness was an important institution. These were the Jubilee years, a financial institution that we find mentioned several times in the Bible. The famous Rosetta Stone, which made possible the deciphering of hieroglyphics, commemorates such a debt cancellation by Ptolemy V in 196 BC (Rostovtzeff 1941, II, p. 713). At one point the accumulated debt burden could cripple investment in productive activities, thereby undermining not only the ability to feed a population, but also the ability to pay interest. This in turn would cripple production. Not only would the financial community fail in directing credit to productive purposes, it would also gradually become the owner of empires and people. For this reason, authors such as Marx have seen the financial community as the great culprit of derailed development, quite opposite to the positive catalyst it might have been and actually has been in some instances, such as in early industrialist Germany and Japan.

This is clearly most relevant for the Third World debt problem today. If history is to be a guide, the vicious circles of debt and poverty can only be broken by creating a virtuous circle of production in the Third World, not by debt foregiveness alone.

5.   CANONICAL BATTLES: THE HEAD-ON CONFRONTATIONS

Occasionally the two canons meet head-on in what we have labelled canonical *Methodenstreite*. Next we describe six of these *Methodenstreite*.

5.1   Canonical *Methodenstreit* 1: De Santis versus Serra (1605 and 1613) and Misselden versus Malynes (1622–23).

Today's mainstream economics was born only in the eighteenth century with Bernhard Mandeville and Adam Smith. There were, however, important earlier skirmishes between the school of barter and the school of production. An early debate is the one in Naples in the early seventeenth century between Marc'Antonio de Santis and Antonio Serra (Schumpeter 1954, p. 344; Doléjal 1921). The battle-lines between exchange and production are clearer in the debate between de Santis and Serra, but the 'English' debate between Gerard de Malynes (1622, 1623) and Edward Misselden (1622, 1623) is better represented in the historiography of economics (Seligman 1920). The latter debate is also more personal and 'acrimonious, even abusive', where 'ink was shed like water'[29] (the authors swore to each other in ten languages, Misselden mocking Malynes for not knowing the eleventh one). Malynes represents a static theory rooted in barter and Misselden represents a theory centred around learning and production. Both Misselden and Malynes were Flemish, working in London.

In the history of economic thought, the debate between Misselden and Malynes is normally interpreted as being about exchange controls and the balance of trade.[30] However, by going back to the sources, one finds that Misselden's main line of attack is against Malynes's 'mechanical' view of man (see Mirowski 2002 for a parallel to neoclassical economics). According to Misselden, Malynes has left out man's 'art' and 'soul'. He (Misselden 1623, p. 8) quotes Malynes's reduction of trade to three elements, 'namely, Commodities, Money, and Exchange'. Objecting to this definition, Misselden writes: 'It is against Art to dispute with a man that denyeth the *Principles* of Art'. Misselden scorns Malynes for not seeing the difference between a heap of stones and logs and a house – because man's productive powers and his soul, which produce the house, have been left out. A similar criticism can be made of neoclassical economics.

Misselden represents the acute Renaissance awareness of the enormous territory to be covered between mankind's present poverty and ignorance on the one hand and its enormous potential on the other. This released enthusiasm and energy. The situation recalls Keynes's frustration with the suboptimal situation of the world during the Great Depression. We shall attempt to show that to the Renaissance philosophers and economists and to Keynes, the formula needed to 'free' society from its suboptimal position was what Keynes (1930, vol. 2, p. 102) called 'Salvation through Knowledge'. The parallel with the Third World today should be clear.

In the late eighteenth century a new type of economic theory came into being, focusing on the 'natural harmony' of nature. Malynes, and later Bernard de Mandeville (also a Dutchman), were the predecessors of this view. This theoretical development culminated with Adam Smith's *Wealth of Nations*, published in 1776 when the English had caught up with and forged ahead of the Dutch. Mandeville is best known for his work *Fable of the Bees* (1714, but an early version in 1705). An early parallel is that Malynes in 1655 published *The Commonwealth of Bees*. The use of bees in a harvesting economy as a metaphor for a human economy leaves out the role of creativity, novelty and intelligence. Even today, a fundamental and unresolved problem of standard economic theory is how to deal with knowledge and novelty.

This 'harvest economy' was central also to the French physiocrats: physiocracy, that is the rule of nature. As we shall see, the antiphysiocrats were defending the Renaissance tradition. In physiocracy all economic activities other than agriculture were seen as sterile. Within today's evolutionary economics we find the same schism: part of the evolutionary school tends to substitute 'biology envy' for 'physics envy', leaving out the creative dimension of man. Today Adam Smith's 'invisible hand' finds its equivalent in Paul Krugman's (1996, p. 99) view of the economy as a self-organizing system: 'Global weather is a self-organising system; so surely, is the global economy'. The implications are clear: Man is at the mercy of an irrational destiny we cannot influence, particularly not on a collective level.

In his *Theory of Moral Sentiments* Adam Smith makes it clear that tampering with destiny is not man's business:

> The care of the universal happiness of all rational and sensible beings, is the business of God and not of man. . . . Nature has directed us to the greater part of these [means to bring happiness about] by original and immediate instincts . . . [which] prompts us to apply those means for their own sake, and without any consideration of their tendency to those beneficent ends which the great Director of Nature intended to produce them.[31]

The parallel with Krugman's weather metaphor is obvious. Albert Hirschman's 1991 book *The Rhetoric of Reaction* traces the history of this theoretical school.

In our view, both Smith and Krugman fit the tradition of moral hedonism, exemplified in this quotation from Jeremy Bentham (1780, p. 11):

Nature has placed Man under two sovereign masters, pain and pleasure. It is for them alone to point out what we ought to do, as well as determine what we shall not do. . . . [E]very effort we make to throw off our subjugation, will serve but to demonstrate and confirm it. In words a man may pretend to abjure their empire: but in reality he will remain subject to it all the while. The principle of utility – the greatest happiness or greatest felicity principle – recognises this subjugation, and assumes it for the foundation. . . . Systems which attempt to question it deal . . . in caprice instead of reason, in darkness instead of light.

Typically, proponents of the barter-centred mechanical theories of wealth appear in well-consolidated and wealthy nations where the problems of creating the institutions of a civilizing state have long been forgotten. At the time of the Misselden–Malynes controversy, Holland was the leading nation and England and France were attempting to catch up. Many leading businessmen in England were at the time Dutch, and the same is true of many 'English' economists. We have already mentioned Misselden and Malynes. Jacob Vanderlint, an early 'English' free trader, was also a Dutchman working in London. Nicolas Barbon, another English free trader, was born in England but educated in Leiden (see Raffel 1905). In the tradition that local free traders were in reality citizens of the 'empire' of the day, the main German nineteenth century free trader in Germany was John Prince-Smith, an Englishman (Prince-Smith 1874).

The shift of emphasis in economics from human creativity (Botero, Serra, Misselden) to 'natural harmony' and barter (Malynes, Smith) was a true paradigm shift in Thomas Kuhn's sense. It must be admitted however that in Adam Smith's England the use of some of the incentives of Renaissance economics to produce knowledge had degenerated. Patents had been established starting in the late fifteenth century in order to promote what we have labelled dynamic and knowledge-producing rent-seeking or Schumpeterian Mercantilism (Reinert 1999). In Adam Smith's England this system in many cases had degenerated into static rent-seeking. Patents were no longer used to promote new knowledge; monopoly patents were sold by the King in order to raise money. As was previously argued by Pieter de la Court in the case of the Netherlands (de la Court 1662), free trade and the reduction of restrictions were necessary in Adam Smith's England to reduce production costs in order for the nation to remain internationally competitive.

Whereas the optimistic theory of the Renaissance focused on the limitless potential of 'man the producer', the new economic theory came to focus on 'man the trader and consumer'. The two theories were steeped in very different realities: the old one in man's ability to create and produce, and the new one in a world of barter, based on the mechanics of the 'natural order'. The old theory was dynamic and organic, centred around 'thought' and 'becoming'; the new theory was mechanical and static, centred around 'matter' and 'being'. In the old theory the market played the role of servant to active human beings who knew where they were going; in the new theory the market acquired many of the characteristics of 'providence', as the manifestation of the natural order (see Viner 1972). Sombart (1928, p. 919) fittingly calls the Renaissance economics activistic–idealistic, and the mainstream economics from Adam Smith onward passivistic–materialistic.

It is important to understand why such a paradigmatic shift at any historical moment may be in the interest of the leading nation, but detrimental to the laggard nations. Having created a strong nation-state and established itself in the most dynamic economic activities of the day, the hegemonic state can take the existence of such an efficient state and of its own technological capabilities for granted, and at that point – as did England and the United States in sequence – elevate the market to a goal in itself. A theory which assumes away the importance of technology and knowledge is not harmful to a nation which possesses the most knowledge and the most advanced technology, only to the laggard nations. Assuming away the existance of diminishing returns is not harmful to the nation that dominates the industries with the highest degrees of increasing returns, only to the nations specialized in activities dominated by the law of diminishing returns. Typically, the leading nations – England and the United States again in the same sequence – have produced economic theories that are void of any context.

Whereas Renaissance economics sees no limits to progress – it truly envisions 'a never-ending frontier of human knowledge' – in Adam Smith's system, which followed Malynes's, nations reach a stationary state where they can advance no further, when that 'full compliment of riches which the nature of its soil and climate . . . allowed it to require' had been reached (Smith 1976, p. 106). It is only here that we see the practical consequences of Smith's sharing the same assumptions as part of today's ecology movement: no new knowledge enters the system. The only logical consequence of a theory that does not allow for the production of new knowledge is either a stationary state (as with Smith and Ricardo) or an ecological disaster (as with Malthus). This disaster can be predicted by simple extrapolations; however, each level of knowledge carries its own level of 'sustainability'. Knowledge and institutions are the conspicuously and 'actively absent' factors in Adam Smith's system; that is, he not only ignores these factors but actively argues that they have no relevance.[32]

Whereas Renaissance economics focuses on production, neoclassical economics focuses on barter and exchange. Leibniz sees the origin of barter as being in production, and quotes Aristotle: 'Nam Maercaturs transfert tantum, Manufactura gignit' (Trade can carry only as much as the factories produce). To Leibniz, the poverty of the artisans was an important argument for the establishment of an active state: 'After all, is not the entire purpose of Society to release the artisan from his misery? The farmer is not in need, since he is sure of his bread, and the merchant has more than enough' (Leibniz 1992, p. 54).

5.2   Canonical *Methodenstreit* 2: Antiphysiocracy versus Physiocracy and Adam Smith (ca 1770–1830)

The second *Methodenstreit* between the knowledge-based Other Canon and the predecessor of today's standard economic theory starts in the 1770s with the rise of the physiocratic school in France. It may be said that the physiocratic school in some sense was a reaction to the excesses of Colbertism. But it can also be said that it was the reaction of the landowners against Colbert's policy of systematically diverting resources from agriculture to manufacturing: The physiocrates continued the animalistic view of Man '. . . sometimes they regard man as a browsing animal, concerned only with his nourishment, the maximum production of the fruit of the earth as his social ideal' (Higgs 1897, p. 107–8).

The antiphysiocratic movement has received little attention in the history of economic thought. These authors, however, represented the true continuation of Renaissance economics. Interestingly, two of the main opponents of physiocracy in France were clergymen: Abbé Mably and Abbé Galiani, the Neapolitan envoy to the Court of Paris.[33] Galiani was to take a position which in many ways foreshadowed the position of the historical school in late nineteenth-century *Methodenstreit*: 'Abstract principles are no good for commercial policy. Corn laws which are good in one time or place may be bad in another . . . The statesmen who admired Colbert should not imitate him, but ask himself, "What would Colbert do if he were here now?"' (Higgs 1897, p. 117). This criticism of a very abstract and context-free theory was similar to Richard Jones's reaction in 1820 against Ricardo's writings. Reverend Jones was the father of the English Historical School of economics, which became very influential during the latter half of the nineteenth century.

One of the main opponents of the physiocratic school in France was Forbonnais, who refused to admit that trade and industry are sterile.[34] Forbonnais believed that the main agent creating wealth is man, not nature: without human agency the land is doomed to absolute or relative stability. The anti-physiocracy movement was strong in France, Italy and Germany, but perhaps the most ardent antiphysiocrats were found in Germany. Under the heading 'Antiphysiokraten', Humpert's bibliography of the German cameralist school lists 25 works published between 1771 and 1832

(Humpert 1937, pp. 1031–2). The best-known of these is Johann Friedrich von Pfeiffer's *Der Antiphysiokrat* (1780).

5.3 Canonical *Methodenstreit* 3: The American System versus the British System (Nineteenth-Century United States)

The US opposition to English classical economic theory started with Benjamin Franklin and continued with US Secretary Alexander Hamilton's report on industrial policy to the House of Representatives in 1791. This *Methodenstreit* on the policy level lasted through the 1930s, although on the theoretical level English classical economics was to be increasingly taught at the Ivy League universities in the late nineteenth century. At one point Cornell University offered parallel courses in the two traditions. Important economists in this tradition included, as already mentioned, Daniel Raymond, Matthew and Henry Carey, John Rae and E. Peshine Smith. The last great economists of this tradition were Richard Ely and Simon Patten, who had both studied in Germany.

On the policy level, the nations industrializing in the nineteenth century were to take up the example that England had set – and later abandoned when it had achieved world hegemony. The great industrial nations in their pre-take-off period shared a core theme of the activity-specific nature of growth (see Reinert 1996b). Economic growth could only be achieved by including in the nation's portfolio of industrial activities activities with the following characteristics: (1) fast technological change, (2) a rapid growth in output ((1)+(2) representing what is normally called Verdoorn's Law), and (3) subject to increasing returns to scale. This theme can be followed in economic writings from the 1500s in Italy, England and France, and a little later in the German cameralists. It is introduced to the United States through Alexander Hamilton and his favourite economist, the English mercantilist Malachy Postlethwayt,[35] and from Friedrich List's involuntary exile in the United States it is reinforced again in the Germany of the Zollverein. In Meiji Japan, the *doitsugaku* school, which favoured the German model, became the most influential for the building of society, at least until 1945 (Yagi 1989, p. 29). The Japanese took over the autarkic views that dominated the German historical school. As we have already commented, in Japan after 1883 'a stream of German teachers of political economy and related disciplines continually flowed in' (Sugiyama and Mizuta 1988, p. 32).

Through the centuries, one common thread of successful long-distance catching up has been a shared distrust of free trade until the nation is firmly established in what was seen to be the 'right' economic activities – the specific activities which increased the nation's 'productive powers'. Through dynamic imperfect competition (Schumpeter's 'historical increasing returns', see Schumpeter 1954 and Reinert 1980) in these specific activities, real wages could be raised: first in the 'engine' industry and subsequently spreading through the whole national labour market. In the US tradition, adding skill to the labourer was the logical way of increasing his value (his wage). This tradition survived in the United States up to and including the economists who were taught by Ely's and Patten's generation. We would argue that in nineteenth-century US economic policy, the general view was that some economic activities were better than others. Differences in wage levels, both nationally and between nations, are to a large extent a result of varying degrees of imperfect competition, caused by both static and dynamic factors. The factors at work have long been identified both by businessmen and in industrial economics, and they are correlated. These factors were for many years discussed under the heading of 'industrialism'.

Figure 1.3 plots the 'quality' of economic activities at any given time on a scale from white (perfect competition) to black (monopoly). The whole system is constantly moving as new types of knowledge enter on top and, with varying speed, fall toward perfect information and perfect competition as they mature. We would claim that the gestalt expressed in Figure 1.3 corresponds to the nineteenth-century US view of why some nations were wealthier than others and why nations had to reach the top of the quality index before free trade would be beneficial to them. At the bottom of this hierarchy sit the world's most efficient producers of baseballs – in Haiti – making US$0.30 per hour. This type of production has not been mechanized anywhere. Higher up sit the world's most efficient producers of golf balls – in a mechanized production – making US$12 per hour. We maintain that no nation of any size has ever reached a high level of national welfare without going through a period of this kind of thinking, perhaps with the possible exclusion of tiny city-states. This was the vision of the *realökonomisch*-oriented mercantilist school. In the English literature Charles King's very influential 1721 volumes clearly express this thinking.

Figure 1.3 unites the economic factors that prevent factor-price equalization from ever taking place in the world economy. Within one nation – within the same labour market – the same forces are at work, but the dispersion in the wage level becomes much less pronounced. Within a nation several factors unite to create a tendency toward larger equality in wages: mobility of labour, similar education and knowledge levels, pressure from labour unions, and the like. The wage level of the traditional service sector seems to be determined by the existence or lack of 'high-quality' activities in each nation. If none are present, real wages in the service sector are low. In this sector (which includes barbers, bus drivers, chambermaids and so

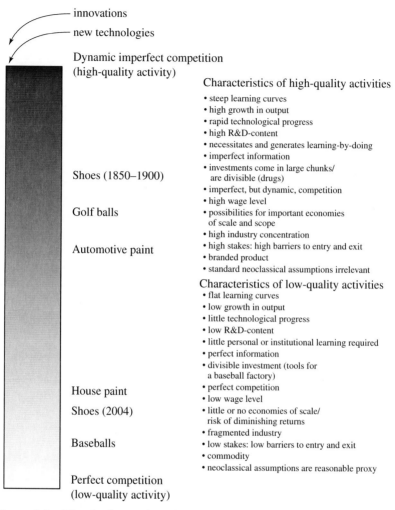

innovations

new technologies

Dynamic imperfect competition
(high-quality activity)

Characteristics of high-quality activities
- steep learning curves
- high growth in output
- rapid technological progress
- high R&D-content
- necessitates and generates learning-by-doing
- imperfect information
- investments come in large chunks/ are divisible (drugs)
- imperfect, but dynamic, competition
- high wage level
- possibilities for important economies of scale and scope
- high industry concentration
- high stakes: high barriers to entry and exit
- branded product
- standard neoclassical assumptions irrelevant

Shoes (1850–1900)

Golf balls

Automotive paint

Characteristics of low-quality activities
- flat learning curves
- low growth in output
- little technological progress
- low R&D-content
- little personal or institutional learning required
- perfect information
- divisible investment (tools for a baseball factory)
- perfect competition
- low wage level
- little or no economies of scale/ risk of diminishing returns
- fragmented industry
- low stakes: low barriers to entry and exit
- commodity
- neoclassical assumptions are reasonable proxy

House paint

Shoes (2004)

Baseballs

Perfect competition
(low-quality activity)

Figure 1.3   The Quality Index of economic activities

on), productivity levels all over the world tend to be very similar. Their real wages, however, are widely different. A barber or bus driver in Bolivia or Russia, although as efficient as those in the First World, earns real wages that are only a fraction of his Swiss or Norwegian counterparts.

The quality index of economic activities, in our opinion, answers the question of why the 'invisible hand' compensates workers of equal efficiency in the service sector so differently in different countries. We would claim that because of this mechanism, what to most people seems like a globally 'efficient' market does not maximize world welfare. By distributing production of knowledge-intensive, high-quality products to all labour markets – not by distributing capital – the average standard of living throughout the world may be raised considerably. Our argument is very close to those of the German philosopher Leibniz and of early US economists, starting with Benjamin Franklin,[36] Alexander Hamilton, Mathew Carey and Daniel Raymond in the late eighteenth and early nineteenth centuries.

The pre-Mandevillean and pre-Smithian attitude towards colonialism are also worth noting. Since they knew that a nation without a manufacturing sector could not develop to any extent, pre-Smithian economists tended to acknowledge that colonialism was not in the interests of the colonies themselves. Manufacturing being a key to wealth, this is an obvious part of the logic of the mercantilist system. Johann Heinrich Gottlob von Justi (1717–71), for example, recognized that colonial trading arrangements 'always will be in danger as soon as the foreign people starts getting wiser' (quoted in Roscher 1874, p. 91). Adam Smith and David Ricardo represent a real watershed in economics, in that it is only with their barter-based, rather than production-based, economic theories that colonialism becomes morally defensible. Colonialism is only defensible within an economic theory where national wealth grows independently of what the nation produces.

5.4   Canonical *Methodenstreit* 4: The Historical School versus the Classical and Neoclassical Schools and Marginalism (1848–1908)

The resounding success of Ricardian economics and its extreme *laissez-faire* policies during the 1840s provoked a theoretical counter-movement following the political events of 1848. The international depression in 1873 further increased opposition to the classical economic tradition all over Europe. The stronghold of the opposition was in Germany, where the older historical school founded by Bruno Hildebrand (1848), Karl Knies and Wilhelm Roscher increasingly challenged both the theoretical foundations and practical conclusions of Ricardian economics. Later a new generation of historical economists led by Gustav Schmoller – the younger historical school – dominated German academic and practical economics for a long time. Schmoller was instrumental in the founding of the *Verein für Sozialpolitik* – the Association for Social Policy – which was to build the theory and practice of the welfare state, piece by piece, between 1872 and 1932.

In 1883 Carl Menger, the founder of the Austrian marginalist school, published *Untersuchungen über die Methode der Sozialwissenschaften und der politischen Ökonomie insbesondere.* Menger dedicated his book to Wilhelm Roscher, the prominent German economist of the historical school. Menger closed the preface by praising recent German economics and hoping that his book would 'be regarded . . . as a friendly greeting from a collaborator in Austria'. Germany's reply was not friendly. Schmoller reviewed the *Untersuchungen* unfavourably in his *Jahrbuch*, and Menger responded in a small book titled *Errors of Historicism* in 1884.[37] Of all the *Methodenstreite* this, the most famous one, is paradoxically the least fundamental. Menger and Schmoller essentially shared the same critical attitude toward the mechanical and barter-based English theory. Their personalities and pride clashed, but compared to Ricardian economics the two are next of kin. This *Methodenstreit* created a debilitating civil war inside The Other Canon.

Schmoller wanted theory to be empirically founded, in opposition to the English classical tradition which founded theory on introspective assumptions and deduced far-reaching practical conclusions from these abstract structures. Schumpeter labelled this practice 'the Ricardian vice'. Today's standard explanation of this *Methodenstreit* generally fails to point out how similar the two men's criticism of Ricardian economics was. The New Palgrave describes the *Methodenstreit* as follows (Fusfeld 1987, p. 454):

> [Schmoller] rejected Menger's deductive method for three chief reasons: its assumptions were unrealistic, its high degree of abstraction made it largely irrelevant to the real-world economy, and it was devoid of empirical content. The theory was therefore useless in studying the chief questions of importance to economists: how have the economic institutions of the modern world developed to their present state, and what are the laws and regularities that govern them? The proper method was induction of general principles from historical–empirical studies.

However, reading through Menger's *Errors of Historicism* (1884) with the perspective of what economics has become, it becomes clear how 'Other Canon' both Schmoller and Menger were.

The historical school was steeped in the German tradition of embracing *die Ganzheit* – the whole. This search for *die Ganzheit* forced the historical school to cross the boundaries into what in the English tradition were considered unrelated academic disciplines. In the German historical tradition, it would make no sense to exclude any information relevant to the question asked – whether from the realm of climatology, pedagogy or any other branch of human knowledge. In the German tradition, economics was a science that integrated all the others and the criterion for including a factor or not was simply that of relevance. However, it is not at all clear that Menger disagreed with this. Menger formulated a model of the economic forces at work but, like Schumpeter later, he insisted that history was an 'indispensable' tool for the profession.

To Menger, the problem of the historical school was that it suffered from a kind of 'case-study syndrome': members of the school collected raw materials for a theory but failed to formalize their propositions on a higher level of abstraction. This is similar to Thorstein Veblen's view. However, this criticism is more appropriate to some members of the historical school than to others. It is crucial to define what is meant by 'theory'. The marginalist tradition came to seek 'pure theory', a formalist kind of theory that excluded from economics all the forces that in the Renaissance tradition were the driving forces of history and its auxiliary institutions: knowledge, creativity and morality. The criticism voiced by German economists at the time was similar to Misselden's accusations against Malynes: economics had become *entgeistet*, or void of human spirit. However, of all the marginalists, Menger was the closest to the historical school. As we shall discuss later, he both 'invented' marginalism and went far beyond it.

The criticism of the marginalists from the historical school was that the very source of wealth – human wit and will – had disappeared. The German ethical historical school, with its US followers such as Richard Ely and Simon Patten, followed the Renaissance tradition of seeing economics as a normative science, setting out to transform society for the benefit of the common weal. They considered morality to be rational and part of the *Ganzheit* of the economics profession. In contrast, in British empiricist philosophy and classical economics, morality was considered to be irrational and based on sympathy (feeling) in the tradition of David Hume and Adam Smith. Accordingly, to the English school morality was totally separated from science and therefore from economics.

5.5   Canonical *Methodenstreit* 5: The US Institutional School versus the Neoclassical School (Twentieth Century)

Institutional economics presents a continuation of the US and German nineteenth-century economics tradition. Institutionalism – a term originally coined to describe the work of the Norwegian-American economist Thorstein Veblen (1857–1929) – continued the radical trend of the 'American System' in opposing the abstract structures of English theory.

The institutionalists were very critical of the established economic doctrine, but most of them did not seek to throw it out completely. Since their theory was *praxisnah* – empirical and close to the reality of practical problems – the institutionalists attracted the attention of policy-makers. Academically and in terms of influence, US institutionalism peaked in the troubled 1930s, and it may be argued that institutional policy-makers in the early 1930s anticipated the Keynesian policy prescription without his elaborate theoretical framework.

Although institutionalism declined rapidly after the Second World War during McCarthyism, its influence on economic policy-making in Washington still lingers.[38] Today Paul Krugman complains, 'It is not just that economists have lost control of the discourse; the kinds of ideas that are offered in a standard economics textbook do not enter into that discourse at all' (quoted in Reder 1999, p. 6). To whom have the economists lost control? Krugman lists an alliance of 'policy makers, business leaders and influential intellectuals' (ibid.). These are the groups that today defend the common sense and pragmatism of institutional economics against the unmitigated rule of standard textbook economics. To the 'Ricardian vice' labelled by Schumpeter we may add the 'Krugmanian vice': the vice of possessing more relevant economic theories – such as new trade theory – but refusing to employ these principles in real-world economic policy.

5.6 The Coming Canonical *Methodenstreit* 6: The Other Canon versus Standard Textbook Economics and the Washington Consensus

Though neoclassicism won the day in academia and in our economic policy toward the Second and Third Worlds, the eclectic pragmatism of The Other Canon and of the old institutional school lives on in policy-making in both America and Western Europe. A clear focus on policies promoting innovations is just one indication of this. In academia today, the proponents of this school are mostly scattered in business schools and departments of government and international affairs. As a result of the virtual eradication of Other Canon economists from departments of economics, the poor countries of the world are still treated to a virtually undiluted version of neoclassical economics as administered by the Washington institutions. The centuries-old common sense – the core of the reconstruction of Europe after the Second World War – that a nation is better off with an inefficient manufacturing sector than with no manufacturing sector at all, was lost in the market euphoria following the fall of the Berlin Wall.

Over the last 50 years of the twentieth century, the mechanical model of neoclassical economics slowly gained a near monopoly position (Mirowski 2002). In a similar way Ricardian economics slowly gained prominence starting in the 1820s and culminating with the free trade movements of the 1840s. However, the 1848 revolutions that affected most Continental European nations provided an important backlash for this kind of policy, and marked the end of uncritical practical application of Ricardian theory. Between the summits in Rio in 1992 and the summit in Johannesburg in

2002, 66 developing nations had become poorer (http://www.johannes-burgsummit.org). In our view, today's increasing social problems and accompanying social protests are again caused by the uncritical application of the same Ricardian theory, now in the guise of immediate and absolute globalization of the poor world. Again a similar social reaction as that of 1848 is about to cause a similar backlash and standstill.

Enlightened economic policy, spearheaded by US and German economic theory and policy, and English social policy, slowly solved the 'social question', the most burning on the nineteenth-century European agenda. It is our conviction that the same kind of Other Canon economics without equilibrium is the only type of economics that can solve the social questions of today. In 1848, the United States and Germany had a healthy stock of Other Canon economists in their economics departments. This eased the search for policy solutions. Today's global village no longer holds such a diversity of approaches to economic policy, from which a search for solutions necessarily has to start. We are therefore more dependent than ever on using history, the only laboratory of economics, and the 'gene bank' provided by the writings of past Other Canon economists as our guides towards a world less dominated by poverty and misery.

6.   INTERNATIONAL TRADE POLICY AND THE TWO CANONS

A culmination of the barter-based canon – from the height of neoclassical economics – is Paul Samuelson's (1948, 1949) proof that international trade, under the usual assumptions of neoclassical economics, will produce factor-price equalization. If all nations would only convert to free trade, the price of the factors of production – capital and labour – would be the same all over the world. In response to the communist utopian idea that every man should give according to ability and receive according to need came the even more powerful neoclassical utopian idea that under capitalist free trade, all wage earners of the world would be equally rich. This theory is the foundation upon which the present world economic order rests.

The contraintuitive conclusion that all wage-earners of the planet will be equally rich under free trade in our view shows the affiliation of neoclassical economics with the pedantic and circuitous reasonings of scholasticism. This danger is inherent when the language of communication is mathematics; as Wittgenstein writes: 'All mathematics is self-referential.' In its extreme form scholasticism also 'proves' things that contradict common sense and intuition. Friedrich List accused the English classical canon of 'scholasticism'. In this same spirit the Danish economist L.V. Birck (1926) titled his article discussing the theories of Böhm-Bawerk 'Moderne Skolastik' (see Reinert 2000).

In the early nineteenth century, the immediate commonsense reply to Ricardian trade theory, such as the very influential writings of Daniel Raymond (1820) in the United States, was one intuitively appealing to the role played by knowledge, and the ability of each profession to absorb advanced knowledge. Pre-Ricardian common sense continued along this line of reasoning: if each lawyer in a nation has ten times the annual income of each person washing dishes, why should a nation of dishwashers be as rich as a nation of lawyers? Following Charles King (1721), it has been clear to The Other Canon that 'symmetrical' international trade – between nations at the same level of development – is beneficial to both nations, whereas 'asymmetrical trade' is beneficial only to the more advanced of the two trading partners. In our view – in the spirit of US and German nineteenth-century economics – symmetrical trade implies trade of goods at roughly the same level on the quality index in Figure 1.3, whereas asymmetrical trade implies trade of articles at very different positions on the quality index. Exceptions to this would be if a very large and dynamic nation or group of nations absorbed a smaller, poorer nation and upgraded its standard of living. Portugal in the EU might be a recent example of this, while Mexico's development under NAFTA may serve as an example of the opposite effect.

Samuelson, like Ricardo, failed to specify factors that were central in the Renaissance canon: (1) knowledge in and of itself, and (2) the differing capacities of economic activity to absorb knowledge. A key argument by Daniel Raymond (1820) was that because different professions have different capacities to absorb capital profitably (human or other), different professions have different 'windows of opportunity' for creating welfare. One cannot profitably add as much human capital to the job of washing dishes as to the job of being a lawyer. For this reason economists would recommend to their children professions which require a university education, although by doing this they express what – at the level of a nation – they would describe as a mercantilist preference for one profession over another. Adam Smith, however, is very consistent on this point: all risks considered, it is safer to let your son become a shoemaker's apprentice than to become a lawyer (see Reinert 1999 for a discussion).

A succinct version of the Renaissance view of the role of international trade in the creation of the common weal is found in James Steuart (1767, vol. 1, p. 336): 'If the greater value of labour be imported, than exported, the country loses.' This argument became the crusading slogan for US protectionists. The more advanced Renaissance economists also focused on this aspect, which Reinert (1980) calls the 'labour-hour terms of trade'.

This was the important variable to watch if one was interested in increasing the welfare of the common man. As noted earlier, the world's most efficient producers of baseballs (which are hand-sewn) work in Haiti earning US$0.30 per hour today, whereas the world's most efficient producers of golf balls (a mechanized production) in an industrialized country make at least $12.00 per hour. In the mercantilist/Renaissance view, by exporting baseballs and importing golf balls, Haiti exchanges 40 hours of labour (in baseballs) for one hour of labour (in golf balls). Haiti and Honduras together have a very large share of the world market in baseballs. The key point to remember here is that both baseball producers and golf ball producers are in this example producing with state-of-the-art technology: whereas golf ball production is mechanized, all the capital of the United States has yet to mechanize the production of baseballs. This uneven advance of technical change makes it possible for a nation to be locked into a comparative advantage of being poor and ignorant. This possibility is ignored in today's economic theory, but was clearly perceived by the more sophisticated Renaissance mercantilists, who held the variables of skill and knowledge up front in their theoretical edifice.

Since the time of the *Methodenstreit* between Misselden and Malynes, free trade has consistently been a logical strategy of the leading technological and economic power. Protecting and building knowledge has been the pattern of nations that have caught up, and later overtaken, the leader. Only the Netherlands, having had a first-mover advantage, introduced protection at a later stage (around 1725) as a defensive measure against its neighbours who were catching up.

In our opinion it is evident that the core assumptions of standard economic theory may play a political role in protecting the vested interest of the leader against the laggards. To a nation that possesses unique technical knowledge, the assumption of 'perfect information' and 'perfect competition' is beneficial. Likewise, an assumption of constant returns to scale will benefit a nation that engages in mass production of manufactured goods, but will be very damaging to nations specializing in agriculture and extractive activities subject to diminishing returns. Therefore, in our opinion it is legitimate to talk about 'assumption-based' rents in economic theory. The rents accruing to the nation exchanging one hour of labour exporting golf balls for 40 hours of labour importing baseballs is such an 'assumption-based' rent. One may divide today's world into two groups of nations: those that at some point have been through a stage of Renaissance economics – the industrialized nations – and the others, the poor South, which continues to produce assumption-based rents for the industrialized North.

7. THE TWO CANONS IN PRESENT ECONOMICS: THEORY AND PRACTICAL POLICY

In the preliminary remarks to his *Principles of Economics*, John Stuart Mill (1987 [1848], p. 3) states:

> It often happens that the universal belief of one age of mankind – a belief from which no one *was*, nor without any extraordinary effort of genius or courage, *could*, at that time be free – becomes to a subsequent age so palpable an absurdity, that the only difficulty is to imagine how such a thing can ever have appeared credible . . . It looks like one of the crude fancies of childhood, instantly corrected by a word from any grown person.

Today the strongest conclusion of standard economic theory is that of world factor-price equalization: if worldwide free trade is adopted, all wage earners of the world will be equally rich. In our view, this 'law' of factor-price equalization – on which our policy toward the Third World is based – qualifies as one of the beliefs which to a subsequent age will become a palpable absurdity. No doubt free trade is a cornerstone in world welfare among the rich nations. But the enormous gains from symmetrical free trade are not the static gains of Smith and Ricardo; they are the synergetic, dynamic and scale-based gains from trade to which *realökonomisch* mercantilists in the Renaissance tradition have long pointed, and which modern economists such as Paul David, W. Brian Arthur and, at times, Paul Krugman are rediscovering.

Occasionally other intuitive flashbacks from Renaissance economics appear in today's formal theory. One important example is Robert E. Lucas's (1988) article in which he argues, as in US nineteenth-century economics, that the potential to learn differs between economic activities. In his model, the nations that acquire most human capital also attract more physical capital, which will be applied more productively there. Because of this, increasing the world mobility of capital under a free trade regime will increase, not diminish, both international inequalities and international migratory pressure. We would argue that Lucas (who later won a Nobel Prize in economics) in this article has recreated a classical mercantilist argument for why vicious and virtuous circles dominate the world economy: because economic activities are qualitatively different, unrestricted free trade between nations of different stages of knowledge development will lead to significant loss of welfare for nations below a certain threshold of knowledge.

Lucas (1988, p. 8) writes, 'The consequences for human welfare involved in questions like these are simply staggering: Once one starts to think about them, it is hard to think about anything else.' One important problem in today's standard economics is that any graduate student in the profession is able to produce a model that 'proves' any pet idea he might have. As long as the profession continues to confuse theory with science – as long as models are produced with only very limited, if any, testing in the real world – the science of economics will continue to produce models that can 'prove' anything. This gives politicians a virtual smörgåsbord of alternative theories, often contradictory, to choose from and to apply according to national preferences and vested interests. Lucas's 1988 model – which is really relevant for the problems of world poverty – disappears in a sea of other elegant but alas irrelevant models.

Three factors have, in our opinion, led to a near-disappearance of the Renaissance tradition in the post-Second World War era. Firstly, the Cold War created an enormous demand for economic and political arguments against the totalitarian threat to the West. The perfect markets of neoclassical theory provided an ideological defence line. Communism promised that everyone would receive according to his needs. Neoclassical economics returned with an even more powerful argument: under its system all wage earners of the world would become equally rich. Although the basis for the theory was there earlier, in our view it is not merely coincidence that the influence of neoclassical formality reached its height in the Cold War. Samuelson's 'proof' of factor-price equalization came during the Berlin blockade, and Milton Friedman's 1953 defence of the use of any assumptions so long as they worked came at the height of the McCarthy era. The Cold War needed Ricardo and Smith, and they did their duty (see Mirowski 2002 for the development of post-Second World War economics).

Secondly, the mechanization of the world picture which started with the Enlightenment will probably, with the benefit of hindsight, prove to have peaked during the same post-Second World War period. The choice of mathematics as the lingua franca of economics – and the way in which the profession was mathematized – contributed to the demise of Renaissance economics. Key variables in Renaissance economics are irreducible to mathematics (see Drechsler in this volume). Renaissance economics depends on a different form of understanding, the qualitative understanding that German philosophers call *verstehen*, as opposed to the quantitative *begreifen* which characterizes the hard sciences. Trying to bridge these two worlds was the impossible task that Schumpeter assigned himself (Reinert 2002). The creative processes underlying economic change proved impossible to reduce to linear mathematics based on nineteenth-century physics. Modern complexity theory, however, seems to be able to achieve what Schumpeter desired.

Thirdly, research and production for the Second World War produced a formidable knowledge base which fed the post-war innovation and production boom. Once the Fordist technological paradigm had been set in motion, there was no demand for the Renaissance economics idea of human creativity as the primary engine of growth. Post-Second World War society was living off the stock of human creativity which, as so often before, had been set free in a war economy. Having learned from Keynes how to even out the ruffles of the business cycle, the economics profession was confident. Paraphrasing Krugman (1990, p. 4) economic research proceeded – undisturbed by the real world – down the path of least mathematical resistance. Unfortunately, the discovery of how to iron out the business cycle was mistaken for the philosopher's stone for creating welfare. Keynesianism's emphasis on financial and monetary aspects, though justified in the crisis of the 1930s, helped financial capitalism take the upper hand over production capitalism in the late 1990s, leading to a predictable collapse (Perez 2002).

In our opinion, these three factors reinforced each other in a most unfortunate spiral to virtually eliminate The Other Canon of economics. Economics was elevated to a level of abstraction where it became unscientific to be relevant.

Today, evolutionary economics is growing as an alternative to the standard, neoclassical-based economic theory. With the TEP Programme (Technology and Economy) of the Organisation for Economic Cooperation and Development (OECD) of the early 1990s, evolutionary economics gained prominence as a policy guide in the industrialized world. At its best, this evolutionary theory captures the essence of Renaissance economics. At its worst, it merely substitutes a mechanical economic understanding based on biology ('biology envy') for the standard canon's mechanical economic understanding based on physics ('physics envy'). Evolutionary economics needs to be moved along the axis from matter to mind, not only from physics to biology. Since the early 1990s Schumpeterian economics flourishes at the micro level, but very few attempts are made to evaluate the consequences of this kind of microeconomics at the macro level. Schumpeterian economics remains a thin icing on a thoroughly neoclassical cake, allowing the juggling of assumptions that we have criticized above.

Although the potential benefits from applying evolutionary and institutional theorizing would be much larger in the Third World than in the First World, this theory has not yet had any influence on the Third World policy of international institutions such as the International Monetary Fund and the World Bank. This is probably because the vast majority of World Bank economists, regardless of their nationality, are educated in economics departments of American and English universities, where evolutionary theory is not taught. In the same way that Renaissance knowledge was created outside the old university structure – in the scientific academies – in most countries, Schumpeterian evolutionary economics is practised mostly outside university economics departments.

Economics as it is practiced in the economics departments is essentially no longer in demand in the OECD countries. These theories are too general and too abstract, and are perceived as being irrelevant to any practical purpose in the real world. Today, standard textbook theories in their pure form are applied in practical policy only in the Third World by IMF and World Bank economists who have virtually no experience in the economic policies of the wealthy nations. This is, in our view, an ethically disturbing case of selective use of economic theory, which has enormous implications for the welfare of poor countries. Although standard economics preaches the same medicine for all nations regardless of context, presently the world community is administering different medicines to the poor nations than to the wealthy nations. Perversely, however, Other Canon economics is practised in the developed nations but not contained in the prescriptions from the Washington instututions to the poor countries which need it the most. The need to resurrect Renaissance non-equilibrium economics – the Other Canon – for application in Eastern Europe and in the Third World is an urgent one.

NOTES

1. Quotation from Arrow's foreword to Arthur 1994. Arrow uses this metaphor to describe the place of increasing returns in economic theory. Increasing returns has, explicitly or implicitly, been at the core of the economic analysis of the Renaissance canon ever since Antonio Serra described this phenomenon in 1613. Serra explicitly associated increasing returns with manufacturing industry.
2. Schumpeter 1954, p. 468.
3. Of which Schumpeter (1954, p. 175) writes: 'Its analytical merit is negligible, but all the greater was its success.'
4. In Germany, the main antiphysiocrat was Johann Friedrich von Pfeiffer; in France, Gabriel Bonnot, Abbé de Mably, Accarias de Serrionne, Jacques Necker, François Veron de Forbonnais, Jean Graslin, Ferdinando Abbé Galiani – a Neapolitan envoy at the Court of Paris – and, most critical of them all, Simon-Nicolas-Henry Linguet. For a list of works by German antiphysiocrats, see Humpert 1937, pp. 1031–32.
5. These synergetic effects are clearly described in Botero 1590 and even more so in Serra 1613. To Serra these 'virtuous circles' have their origins in the increasing returns found in the manufacturing sector, which are absent in agriculture. Machiavelli is also clear on this point: 'Il bene comune è quello che fa grandi le città.'
6. Eli Hecksher, quoted in Polanyi 1944, p. 278.
7. With the possible exception of small city-states, such as Hong Kong and San Marino.
8. Crowther 1960, p. 97.
9. List 1904, pp. 66–7.
10. These arguments are thoroughly discussed in Reinert 1999.
11. '[S]eine Begriffe "schweben" umher wie die unerlösten Seelen an den Ufern des Hades', Sombart 1928, p. 929.
12. For a discussion of this strategy, see Reinert 1994.

13. See Clément 1861–1872.
14. For a discussion of this concept, see Bijker et al. 1989.
15. See Morris 1957, p. 285.
16. 'Ich sage das auf die Gefahr hin, als Neo-Merkantilist abgestempelt und in das Raritätenkabinett unseres Faches übergeführt zu werden', Sombart 1928, p. 925.
17. Sugiyama and Mizuta 1988, p. 32.
18. The author's full name appears on the dissertation as Horace Greeley Hjalmar Schacht. Horace Greeley (1811–1872) was – like the important US protectionist E. Peshine Smith – a protégé of the US statesman William Seward, a secretary of state and one of the founders of the Republican Party. This party was the main proponent of 'Renaissance economics' in the United States at the time. Greeley founded the New York *Tribune* and was its editor for 31 years. One of the *Tribune*'s European correspondents was Karl Marx, whose dispatches became classics of Marxian socialism.
19. 'Man kann aus den Menschen machen, wass man will; die Art, mit der er regiert wird, entschliesst ihn zum Guten, oder zum Bösen', Pfeiffer 1777, p. 2.
20. This problem is discussed in Hart 1990.
21. Smith 1812, vol. 1, p. 320 (emphasis added).
22. Hufbauer et al. 1986, p. 1.
23. On E. Peshine Smith, see Hudson 1969. In the 1970s Hudson edited a series of reprints of the writings of nineteenth-century US economists.
24. Dühring, *Kritische Geschichte der Nationalökonomie* (1879), quoted in Sombart (1928), p. 913.
25. List 1959, p. 12. Our translation. This is part of List's foreword, which has been drastically reduced in the English edition.
26. Nye 1991, p. 23.
27. Roscher (1882, vol. 1, p. 189 § 58) refers to the works of Xenophon, Plato, Aristotle, Aquinas, Luther, Petty, Mandeville, Berkeley, Harris, Rousseau, Turgot, Diderot, Tucker and Beccaria.
28. List 1904, Chapters 1, 2 and 3; Wallerstein 1978, vol. 2, pp. 90–93.
29. Schumpeter (1954, pp. 344–5) discusses the controversy between the two men. See also their respective entries in the *New Palgrave*. In all cases these references are purely to the mechanics of money and exchange.
30. Buck 1942, p. 23.
31. Smith 1976a, p. 237. Interestingly, this appears in a book that is said to represent the diametric opposite of *Wealth of Nations*, the first based on altruism, the latter on self-love.
32. This point is discussed in Reinert 1996a.
33. A good description of Galiani and his unique standing in French society at the time is found in Pecchio 1849, pp. 80–86.
34. The antiphysiocrats are discussed in Weulersse 1910, vol. 2, pp. 256–682, and in Higgs 1897, pp. 102–22.
35. Excerpts from Postlethwayt's *Universal Dictionary of Trade and Commerce* were scattered through Hamilton's *Army Pay Book*; see Morris 1957, p. 285. Hamilton's views on the English classical economists was echoed in that of the Japanese 80 years later; see Tessa Morris-Suzuki 1989.
36. See particularly Franklin's comments printed as footnotes in Whatley 1774.
37. Menger 1884; see also Ritzel 1950.
38. Two informative books (Yonay 1998; Morgan and Rutherford 1998) trace the demise of institutional economics in the United States.

REFERENCES

Arthur, W. Brian (1994), *Increasing Returns and Path Dependency in the Economy*, Ann Arbor, MI: University of Michigan Press.

Bentham, Jeremy (1780), *An Introduction to the Principles of Morals and Legislation*, London: University Paperback.

Bijker, Wiebe, Thomas P. Hughes and Trevor Pinch (eds) (1989), *The Social Construction of Technological Systems*, Cambridge, MA: MIT Press.

Birck, L.V. (1926), 'Moderne Scholastik: Eine kritische Darstellung der Böhm-Bawerkschen Theorie', *Weltwirtschaftliches Archiv*, **24** (2), 198–227.

Botero, Giovanni (1590), *Delle Cause della Grandezza delle Città*, Rome: Vicenzio Pellagalo.

Buchanan, James, and Yong J. Yoon (eds) (1994), *The Return to Increasing Returns*, Ann Arbor, MI: University of Michigan Press.

Buck, Philip (1942), *The Politics of Mercantilism*, New York: Henry Holt.

Carey, Henry Charles (1864), *Financial Crises: Their Causes and Effects*, Philadelphia, PA: Henry Carey Baird.

Carey, Henry Charles (1967 [1851]), *Harmony of Interests: Agricultural, Manufacturing and Commercial*, New York: Augustus M. Kelley.

Clément, Pierre (ed.) (1861–72), *Lettres, Instructiones et Mémoires de Colbert*, Paris: Imprimerie Impériale/Imprimerie Nationale.

Commons, John (1963 [1893]), *The Distribution of Wealth*, Fairfield, NJ: Kelley.

Crowther, J.G. (1960), *Francis Bacon: The First Statesman of Science*, London: Cresset Press.

Court, Pieter de la (1662), *Interest van Holland*, Amsterdam, German translations 1665 and 1668, English translations, London 1743 and 1746.

Doléjal, Oscar (1921), *Le milieu politique et économique du Royaume de Naples au XVI et au début du XVII siècle. Les doctrines économiques de Marc'Anonio de Santis, d'un Anonyme Génois et d'Antonio Serra*, PhD Thesis, Université de Poitiers, Ligugé: E. Aubin.

Freeman, Christopher (1992), *The Economics of Hope*, London: Pinter.

Fusfeld, Daniel R. (1987), 'Methodenstreit', in *The New Palgrave Dictionary*, Macmillan: London.

Hart, Neil (1990), 'Increasing returns and economic theory: Marshall's reconciliation problem', University of Western Sydney, Discussion Paper Series, no. E9004.

Henderson, John (1994), *Piety and Charity in Late Medieval Florence*, Oxford: Clarendon.

Higgs, Henry (1897), *The Physiocrats*, London: Macmillan.

Hildebrand, Bruno (1848), *Die Nationalökonomie der Gegenwart und Zukunft*, Frankfurt: Literarische Anstalt.

Hirschman, Albert O. (1991), *The Rhetoric of Reaction: Perversity, Futility, Jeopardy*, Cambridge, MA: Harvard University Press.

Hornick, Philipp Wilhelm von (1684), *Österreich über alles wann es nur will*, no place (but Nürnberg), no publisher.

Hudson, Michael (1969), 'E. Peshine Smith: A study in protectionist growth theory and American sectionalism', PhD diss., New York University; Ann Arbor, MI: University Microfilm.

Hufbauer, Gary C., Diane T. Berliner and Kimberly A. Elliot (1986), *Trade Protection in the United States: 31 Case Studies*, Washington DC: Institute for International Economics.

Humpert, Magdalene (1937), *Bibliographie der Kameralwissenschaften*, Cologne: Kurt Schroeder.

Keynes, J.M. (1930), *A Treatise on Money*, 2 vols, London: Macmillan.

King, Charles (1721), *The British Merchant: Or Commerce preserv'd*, 3 vols, London: John Darby.

Krugman, Paul (1990), *Rethinking International Trade*, Cambridge, MA: MIT Press.

Krugman, Paul (1996), *The Self-Organizing Economy*, Cambridge, MA: Blackwell.

Kuhn, Thomas (1970), *The Structure of Scientific Revolutions*, Chicago, IL: University of Chicago Press.

Laffemas, Barthélemy (1597), *Reiglement [sic] general pour dresser les manufactures en ce rayaume, et couper le cours des draps de soye, & autres merchandises qui perdent & ruynent l'Estat: qui est le vray moyen de remettre la France en sa splendeur, & de faire gaigner les pauvres . . .*, Paris: Claude de Monstr'oil and Jean Richter.

Latini, Brunetto, Paul Barrette and Spurgeon W. Balwin (1993), *The Book of the Treasure = Li livres dou Tresor*, New York: Garland.

Leibniz, Gottfried Wilhelm (1992 [1671]), 'Society and Economy', reprinted in *Fidelio*, **2** (1), 63–9.

List, Friedrich (1904 [1841]), *The National System of Political Economy*, London: Longman.

List, Friedrich (1959 [1841]), *Das Nationale System der politischen Oekonomie*, Basel: Kyklos.

List, Friedrich (1985 [1937]), *Die Welt bewegt sich: Uber die Auswirkungen der Dampkraft und der neuen Transportmittel*, ed. Eugen Wendler, Göttingen: Vandenhoek & Ruprecht.

Lucas, Robert E. (1988), 'On the mechanics of economic development', *Journal of Monetary Economics*.

Malynes, Gerard de (1622), *The Maintenance of Free Trade, according to the Three Essentiall Parts . . . Commodities, Moneys and Exchange of Moneys*, London: William Sheffard.

Malynes, Gerard de (1623), *The Center of the Circle of Commerce, or, A Refutation of a Treatise . . . Lately Published by E. M.*, London: Nicholas Bourne.

Marshall, Alfred (1890), *Principles of Economics*, London: Macmillan.

Menger, Carl (1883/1963), *Problems of Economics and Sociology (Untersuchungen über die Methode der Socialwissenschaften und der Politischen Ökonomie insbesondere)*, Urbana, IL: University of Illinois Press.

Menger, Carl (1884), *Die Irrtümer des Historismus in der deutschen Nationalökonomie*, (Errors of Historicism), Vienna: Alfred Hölder.

Mill, John Stuart (1987 [1848]), *Principles of Political Economy*, New York: Kelley.

Mirowski, Philip (1994), 'Doing what comes naturally: Four metanarratives on what metaphors are for', in Philip Mirowski (ed.), *Natural Images in Economic Thought*, Cambridge: Cambridge University Press.

Mirowski, Philip (2002), *Machine Dreams. Economics Becomes a Cyborg Science,* Cambridge: Cambridge University Press.

Misselden, Edward (1622), *Free Trade and the Meanes to Make Trade Flourish*, London: Simon Waterson.

Misselden, Edward (1623), *The Circle of Commerce or the Ballance of Trade*, London: Nicholas Bourne.

Morgan, Mary S. and Malcolm Rutherford (eds) (1998), *From Interwar Pluralism to Postwar Neoclassicism*, annual supplement to *History of Political Economy*, **30**.

Morris, R.B. (1957), *Alexander Hamilton and the Founding of the Nation*, New York: Dial Press.

Morris-Suzuki, Tessa (1989), *The History of Japanese Economic Thought*, London: Routledge.

Nelson, Richard and Sidney Winter (1982), *An Evolutionary Theory of Economic Change*, Cambridge, MA: Harvard University Press.

Nietzsche, Friedrich (2000), *Digitale Bibliothek Band 31: Nietzsche*, Berlin: Directmedia (CD-ROM)

Nye, John Vincent (1991), 'The myth of free-trade Britain and fortress France: Tariffs and trade in the nineteenth century', *Journal of Economic History*, **51** (1), 23–46.

Pecchio, Giuseppe (1849), *Storia della Economia Pubblica in Italia*, Lugano: Tipografia della Svizzera Italiana.

Perez, Carlota (2002), *Technological Revolutions and the Mechanisms of Bubbles and Golden Ages*, Cheltenham: Edward Elgar.

Perrotta, Cosimo (1988), *Produzione e Lavoro Produttivo nel Mercantilismo e nell' Illuminismo*, Galatina: Congedo Editore.

Pfeiffer, J.F. von (1777), *Lehrbegrif sämtlicher oeconomischer und Cameralwissenschaften*, vol. 3, part 1, Mannheim: Schwan.

Pfeiffer, J.F. von (1780), *Der Antiphysiokrat, oder umständliche Untersuchung des sogenannten physiokratischen Systems für eine allgemeine Freyheit und einzige Auflage auf den reinen Ertrag der Grundstücke*, Frankfurt am Main: Schäfer.

Polanyi, Karl (1944), *The Great Transformation*, Boston, MA: Beacon Press.

Popper, Karl (1997), *The Poverty of Historicism*, London: Routledge.

Prince-Smith, John (1874), *Der Staat und der Volkshaushalt*, Berlin: Springer.

Raffel, Friedrich (1905), *Englische Freihändler vor Adam Smith*, Tübingen: Laupp.

Raymond, Daniel (1820), *Principles of Political Economy*, Baltimore, MD: Fielding Lucas.

Reder, Melvin W. (1999), *Economics: The Culture of a Controversial Science*, Chicago, IL: University of Chicago Press.

Reinert, Erik S. (1980), 'International trade and the economic mechanisms of underdevelopment', PhD diss., Cornell University; Ann Arbor, MI: University Microfilm.

Reinert, Erik S. (1994), 'Catching-up from way behind: A third world perspective on first world history', in Jan Fagerberg, Bart Verspagen and Nick van Tunzelmann, *The Dynamics of Technology, Trade and Growth*, Aldershot, UK and Brookfield, US: Edward Elgar, pp. 168–97.

Reinert, Erik S. (1996a), 'Diminishing Returns and Economic Sustainability: The dilemma of resource-based economies under a free trade regime', in Stein Hansen, Jan Hesselberg and Helge Hveem (eds), *International Trade Regulation, National Development Strategies and the Environment: Towards Sustainable Development?*, Oslo, Centre for Development and the Environment, University of Oslo, pp. 119–50.

Reinert, Erik S. (1996b), 'The role of technology in the creation of rich and poor nations: Underdevelopment in a Schumpeterian system', in Derek H. Aldcroft and Ross Catterall (eds), *Rich Nations – Poor Nations. The Long Run Perspective*, Aldershot: Edward Elgar, 1996, pp. 161–88. Spanish translation (2002) 'El rol de la tecnología en la creación de países ricos y pobres: El subdesarrollo en un sistema Schumpeteriano', *Cuadernos*, **7** (12).

Reinert, Erik S. (1998), 'Raw materials in the history of economic policy; or, Why

List (the Protectionist) and Cobden (the Free Trader) both agreed on free trade in corn', in G. Cook (ed.), *The Economics and Politics of International Trade. Freedom and Trade: Volume II*, London: Routledge, pp. 275-300.

Reinert, Erik S. (1999), 'The role of the state in economic growth', *Journal of Economic Studies*, **26** (4/5), 268–326. A shorter version published in Pier Angelo Toninelli (ed.) (2000), *The Rise and Fall of State-Owned Enterprises in the Western World*, Cambridge: Cambridge University Press.

Reinert, Erik S. (2000), 'Full Circle: economics from scholasticism through innovation and back into mathematical scholasticism. Reflections around a 1769 price essay: "Why is it that economics so far has gained so few advantages from physics and mathematics?"', *Journal of Economic Studies*, **27** (4/5), 364–76.

Reinert, Erik S. (2002) 'Schumpeter in the context of two canons of economic thought', *Industry and Innovation*, **6** (1), 23–39.

Reinert, Erik S. and Arno M. Daastøl (1997), 'Exploring the genesis of economic innovations: the religious gestalt-switch and the duty to invent as preconditions for economic growth', *European Journal of Law and Economics*, **4** (2/3), 233–83 reprinted (1998) in *Christian Wolff. Gesammelte Werke, Materialien und Dokumente*, Hildesheim: Georg Olms Verlag, 1998.

Ritzel, Gerhard (1950), *Schmoller versus Menger*, Frankfurt am Main: n.p.

Roscher, Wilhelm (1874), *Geschichte der National-Oekonomik in Deutschland*, Munich: Oldenbourg.

Roscher, Wilhelm (1882), *Principles of Political Economy*, Chicago, IL: Callaghan.

Rostovtzeff, Mikhail (1941), *Social and Economic History of the Hellenistic World*, 3 vols, Oxford: Oxford University Presss.

Samuelson, Paul (1948), 'International trade and the equalisation of factor prices', *Economic Journal*, **58**, 163–84.

Samuelson, Paul (1949), 'International factor-price equalisation once again', *Economic Journal*, **59**, 181–97.

Schumpeter, Joseph A. (1954), *History of Economic Analysis*, New York: Oxford University Press.

Seligman, Edwin A. (1920), *Curiosities of Early Economic Literature*, San Francisco, CA: John Henry Nash.

Serra, Antonio (1613), *Breve trattato delle cause che possono far abbondare li regni d'oro e argento dove non sono miniere*, Naples: Lazzaro Scoriggio.

Smith, Adam (1812 [1759]), 'The Theory of Moral Sentiments', in *Collected Works*, London: Cadell & Davies.

Smith, Adam (1976 [1776]), *Wealth of Nations*, Chicago, IL: University of Chicago Press.

Sombart, Werner (1928), *Der Moderne Kapitalismus*, vol. 2, *Das Europäische Wirtschaftsleben im Zeitalter des Frühkapitalismus*, Munich: Duncker & Humblot.

Sombart, Werner (1930), *Die Drei Nationalökonomien*, Munich: Duncker & Humblot.

Spann, Ottmar (1926), *Die Haupttheorien der Volkswirtschaftslehre*, Leipzig; Quelle & Meyer. US edition (1930): *The History of Economics*, New York: Norton.

Stangeland, Charles Emil (1904), *Pre-Malthusian Doctrines of Population: A Study in the History of Economic Theory*, New York: Columbia University Press.

Steuart, James (1767), *Principles of Political Economy*, London: Millar & Cadell.

Sugiyama, C. and H. Mizuta (1988), *Enlightenment and Beyond: Political Economy Comes to Japan*, Tokyo: University of Tokyo Press.

Viner, Jacob (1972), *The Role of Providence in the Social Order: An Essay in Intellectual History*, Philadelphia, PA: American Philosophical Society.

Wallerstein, Immanuel (1978 [1974]), *Det moderne verdenssystem*, 2 vols, Oslo: Gyldendal.

Weulersse, Georges (1910), *Le mouvement physiocratique en France*, Paris: Alcan.

Whatley, G. (1774), *Principles of Trade. Freedom and Protection Are Its Best Suport* [sic]: *Industry, the Only Means to Render Manufactures Cheap*, London: Brotherton and Sewell.

Wiles, P.J.D. (1977), *Economic Institutions Compared*, Oxford: Basil Blackwell.

Xenophon and Wayne Ambler (2001), *The Education of Cyrus*, Agora Editions. Ithaca, NY: Cornell University Press.

Yagi, Kiichiro (1989), 'German model in the modernisation of Japan', *Kyoto University Economic Review*, **59** (1–2).

Yat-Sen, Sun (1922), *The International Development of China*, New York: Putnam.

Yonay, Yuval (1998), *The Struggle over the Soul of Economics*, Princeton, NJ: Princeton University Press.

Zincke, Georg Heinrich (1753), *Xenophon's Buch von den Einkünften, oder, dessen Vorschläge, wie das bereiteste Vermögen grosser Herren und Staaten nach ächten Grund-sätzen des Finanz-Wesens zu vermehren*, Wolfenbüttel: Meissner.

2. Natural versus social sciences: on understanding in economics*

Wolfgang Drechsler

Verstehen ist der ursprüngliche Seinscharakter des menschlichen Lebens selber.

(Gadamer 1990, p. 264, 1989, p. 259)

Half a century ago, Ludwig von Mises concluded an essay with a title very similar to the present one by addressing the proponents of mathematical economics thus: 'If it may some day be necessary to reform economic theory radically this change will not take its direction along the lines suggested by the present critics. The objections of these are thoroughly refuted forever' (1942, p. 253).[1] Mises's first statement was factually wrong; this does not mean, however, that the second one was incorrect as well.

Indeed, it seems to me that the problem of the current mainstream, mathematical, usually neoclassical approach to economics[2] is two-fold. It is flawed both practically and theoretically: practically because it does not deliver, theoretically because it rests on premises that are problematic at best, and extrapolates from them by equally questionable means. The argument by its protagonists has been to excuse practical problems by pointing to theoretical truth-value, and theoretical ones by pointing to practical success.

This chapter concentrates on the theoretical problems. It rests on the assumption, rather than tries to demonstrate, that mathematical economics does not deliver; if one feels that it does, then one need not read on. But of course the theoretical problems have a practical connection (see Kant 1992, pp. 23–5), because the purpose of pursuing economic scholarship is not to create an aesthetically pleasing theoretical system, but rather to say something meaningful and consequential, directly or indirectly, about reality.

Therefore I should first state that the premise of this chapter is that this is possible. (This is by no means a given; were the topic focused on the humanities side of economics, where one would have, for example, to deal with the linguistic turn and occasionally even yet with postmodernism, one could not dismiss this point so quickly.) Thus, truth is defined here as congruence with reality, and reality as all that is the case rather than all that exists, including options and myths *as* options and myths. This means that 'the world is significantly stratified independently of our interpretations of it' (Eagleton 1996, p. 35), but that our perceptions enter into it and become part of the world.

This truth may be hidden and difficult if not impossible to ascertain, but if one has a concept or an idea one can, as Xenophanes says, 'indeed accept this assumingly, as alike the real' (fragm. B 35). We can act as if we had the truth, as if we were right, so long as we remember that we might be wrong; as Aristotle put it, 'not only he who is in luck but also he who offers a proof should remember that he is but a man' (*On the Good*, fragm. 27 in 1886, p. 40; fragm. 1 in 1952, pp. 116–117). In that sense only working hypotheses are possible, but they *are* possible.[3]

The demand put to a theory is therefore that it mirror reality, and the claim is that it can do so. It is recognized that this is exceedingly difficult to do or to prove, but once the truth-connection, the search for the truth, is lost, the connection with reality is too. If a theory does not mirror reality, it is untrue or wrong; if it cannot, it is self-referential. The question in consequence is then whether mathematical economics can and does mirror reality or is at least on the way thither. It is argued here that it neither does nor can mirror reality, nor is it on the way to doing so, at least not sufficiently.

As a caveat, it should be added that in such an essay one must be careful not to knock down a straw man. Indeed, I have the impression that the leading economists of our time would hardly claim, nor did many of their predecessors, any more or less absolute theoretical validity of mathematical economics (which I am very aware is neither defined nor dealt with in any detail here). But general academic discourse leads to, or embodies, exactly this view. And once such a discourse is established it is, for soft-knowledge reasons, very difficult to break – until, if so much Kuhnianism is permitted, the system seems all too wrong.

Finally, the classic purpose of any, and certainly of this, essay is to remind rather than to explain, and it does so not by treating its subject comprehensively but rather by reminding its reader by means of exemplary or indicative thoughts. This chapter uses quotations heavily; that seemed to be necessary because on such a potentially contentious question there appeared to be some safety in borrowed authority. This is especially comforting because the author himself is grappling with the problems at hand and is less decided about them than the following paragraphs, which presumably have a tendency to err on the side of oversharpening their points, might indicate.

1. NATURAL VERSUS SOCIAL SCIENCES

If one conceives of the social sciences as of something somehow 'between' the natural sciences and the humanities, then economics generally, and certainly the mathematical kind, has a very strong tendency towards the natural sciences side, even a tendency to make economics a natural science. This chapter addresses that orientation.

The difference between natural and social sciences may at first appear trivial: natural sciences deal with objects, social sciences with subjects, that is with human beings. This basic difference would have a decisive impact on the transferability of concepts from one to the other; we will return to this point. But if we look at the two 'kinds' of sciences from another perspective, the opposite view may stand out. It is this view which in 1874 the economist, statistician, physics PhD and member of the Historical School Wilhelm Lexis, when assuming his first Chair at the University of Dorpat (now Tartu), in his inaugural address 'Natural and Social Sciences' (1903) spelled out as follows:

> Right away, a certain analogy is noticeable which exists between the social and the natural sciences . . . The means of realisation for the one as well as for the other class of sciences is supposed to be experience. As the natural sciences are taken to be the specific empirical sciences, the temptation is close at hand to put the social sciences under the guidance of her older sister by presenting to her the tried method of the latter. (p. 235)

Lexis goes on to argue that in the (ideal) end of all natural-scientific explanation there are the differential equations of dynamics, having as variables the coordinates of moved points in time and space: 'If one envisions these equations in an integrated format, one receives a system of equations through which in any point in time the spatial situation of all moving points is determined' (p. 239). This 'world formula' approach, the 'inductive concluding towards the future' (p. 239), is still at the basis of much natural-scientific thinking:

> The method of the natural sciences in its ideal execution thus consists of the objective assessment of the phenomena in space and time, its division into basic facts, and the erection of a purely quantitative mathematical scheme for the relations of the phenomena. Is this method applicable to the matter of the social sciences and, if so, is the purely quantitative scheme, which only expresses outside relations, sufficient to embody the totality of our possible experiences in this area? (p. 240)

Lexis says, 'The answer to the first question is yes; to the second one, no' (p. 240). In this chapter, it is argued that the answer to both is no. (Cf. Sombart 1967, p. 292.)

2. MATHEMATICS

Complaints about the use of mathematics in economics are not rare, although not as frequent as they perhaps should be. Heinrich v. Stackelberg, in the preface to his book that played a key role in the re-mainstreaming and thus mathematizing of German economics during and after the Second World War, says:

> It is also stated that mathematics would fake an exactness and rigidity of economic relations which in reality would be flowing and inexact; it would fake necessities of natural-scientific laws where in reality the human will would be able to decide and shape freely . . . This view completely mistakes the role of mathematics in economic theory. How often have experts said that 'more never jumps out of the mathematical pot than has been put in'! Mathematical symbolics change neither the preconditions nor the results of the theoretician, as long as they are concludent. (Stackelberg 1951, pp. x–xi; 1952, p. xiii)[4]

This is wrong, or at least flawed, in three central points. First, in everyday academic discourse mathematization *is* taken to somehow 'guarantee truth' – it becomes more than a tool, it becomes a safety-foundation of an almost mythical nature (see Kenessey 1995, pp. 304–5). Note that this is usually not claimed explicitly, but very frequently indeed it is tacitly implied.

But this is misleading, as Einstein pointed out: 'As far as the statements of mathematics refer to reality, they are not certain, and as far as they are certain, they do not refer to reality' (Einstein 1970, pp. 119–20).[5] Wittgenstein put it even more clearly: 'All mathematical propositions mean the same thing, namely nothing'.[6] Or, again Einstein: 'mathematics as such is incapable of saying anything about . . . things of reality' (1970, p. 120).[7]

Once just one variable (that is, one symbol for anything) is introduced, the floodgates are opened for definition, representation, conception and language problems, that is, problems of language and philosophy. And this is inevitable, for 'one cannot want to look into the world of language . . . from above. Because there is no position outside of the linguistic world-experience from which the latter itself could possibly become an object' (Gadamer 1990, p. 456; 1989, p. 452). 'The objectivising science thus experiences the linguistic being-formed of the natural world-experience as a source of prejudices' (1990, p. 457; 1989, p. 453).[8] And this means that even the current highly sophisticated and complex ventures into new 'forms' of mathematics that try to encapsulate uncertainties and variabilities fall prey to this point, because they still try to 'count in' the larger paradigm which, however, sets the framework.

Second, and this is even more frequently overlooked, the mathematical connection is not, as Stackelberg says, simply a logical one. Although the mathematics of economics Stackelberg refers to is quite different from that of Lexis's day, let alone that of today, Lexis makes a point which is still valid when he explains:

> Scientific thinking . . . consists in the connecting of terms according to certain general basic relations. These connections at first only have [a] logical signifi-cance. However, as every empirical science wants to recognise the real connec-tion of the phenomena which are in front of it, at a certain point it has to give to the merely logical connections also a real significance for the relations of the things themselves. (1903, p. 236)

Therefore, mathematics as a connection of the objects under investigation does not add certainty to the statement, but it might easily be mistaken for a real connection between the objects. (See also v. Mises 1942, pp. 243–5.)

The third point, linked to the question of objects and how one sees them, is that the mathematical connection invariably tempts its disciples into the abstraction and definition of the objects under review in the form of a clear-cut determinedness:

> The scientific concepts are idealisations; they are derived from experience obtained by refined experimental tools, and are precisely defined through axioms and definitions. Only through these precise definitions is it possible to connect the concepts with a mathematical scheme and to derive mathematically the infi-nite variety of possible phenomena in this field. But through this process of idealisation and precise definition the immediate connection with reality is lost. (Heisenberg 1958, p. 171)

3. PHYSICS

The second major cause of this problem is the scientifically illegitimate use in another sphere of natural science concepts, which have worked well in the fields in which they were developed, by people who have 'excessive faith in laws and methods derived from alien fields, mostly from the natural sciences, and apply them with great confidence and somewhat mechani-cally' (Berlin 1996, p. 51; see also p. 50 and Knight 1935, p. 147). But are these natural science fields really alien to the social science ones? They are not if one can treat human beings as objects to begin with – in other words, if one is a positivist:

> The characteristic theses of positivism are that science is the only valid knowl-edge and facts the only possible objects of knowledge; that philosophy does not possess a method different from science; and that the task of philosophy is to

find the general principles common to all the sciences and to use these principles as guides to human conduct and as the basis of social organisation. Positivism, consequently, denies the existence or intelligibility of forces or substances that go beyond facts and the laws ascertained by science. (Abbagnano 1967, p. 414)

This handy view is still to be found in social science faculty lounges and in social science journals, but it is recognized as wrong even on its own principles and by its own protagonists in the natural sciences. Because it seems that this fact has not yet been fully grasped in the social sciences, three decisive fallacies of this approach will briefly be outlined.

First, to physicists, this kind of physics is dead. One of physics' insights during the last 75 years was 'that even such fundamental concepts as space and time could be changed and in fact must be changed on the account of new experience' (Heisenberg 1958, p. 170):

> Coming back now to the contributions of modern physics, one may say that the most important change brought about by its results consists in the dissolution of this rigid frame of concepts of the nineteenth century. Of course many attempts had been made before to get away from this rigid frame which seemed obviously too narrow for an understanding of the essential parts of reality. But it had not been possible to see what could be wrong with the fundamental concepts like matter, space, time and causality that had been so extremely successful in the history of science. Only experimental research itself . . . and its mathematical interpretation, provided the basis for a critical analysis – or, one may say, enforced the critical analysis – of these concepts, and finally resulted in the dissolution of the rigid frame. (Heisenberg 1958, p. 170)

Second, philosophically positivism rests on an exceedingly naive view of determinacy. This is best summed up by Timothy Kautz in his important study of Ernst Cassirer, in the chapter on Cassirer's 1939 argument against the 'first emotivist', Axel Hägerström, who claimed that 'reality means the same as determinedness', and that 'determinedness only exists in those sciences which determine events or things in space and time' (Kautz 1990, p. 209). But 'determinedness is a result of an interaction, or a sum of interactions, which come into existence, or are kept, in a matrix of judgement. "Determinedness" in the sciences is thus precisely not a simple situation or a simple, given intuition but rather the result of (symbolic) negotiations [*Vermittlungen*]' (p. 213). 'And determinedness never derives solely from the "things" in space and time, just *because* they are in space and time: an apparent objectivity in the imagined placement of every thing in a space–time system of coordinates is not a *sufficient* description of the world because it is precisely the kind of relation that remains undetermined' (p. 214).[9]

Third, there is the profound hermeneutic critique, pointing to the circu-

lar reasoning of positivism and to the subsidiarity of science to understanding:

> But is it really so that [the world of physics] is a world of the being-as-such,
> which leaves all *Daseinsrelativität* behind and whose realisation might be called
> an absolute science? Is not already the concept of an 'absolute thing' a wooden
> iron? Neither the biological nor the physical universe can in truth deny the
> *Daseinsrelativität* which belongs to it. Physics and biology have insofar the same
> ontological horizon which, as sciences, they cannot cross at all. They recognise
> what is, and, as Kant has demonstrated, this means how it is given in space and
> time and how it is the subject of experience. This defines outright the progress
> of realisation which is achieved in the sciences. The world of physics, too, cannot
> at all want to be the whole of what is. Even a world equation which would display
> all that is, so that even the observer of the system would appear in the equations
> of the system, would still require the physicist, who as the calculating one is not
> the calculated. A physics which would calculate itself and would be its own cal-
> culation would remain a contradiction in itself . . . The being-as-such upon
> which its research is focused, be this physics or biology, is relative towards the
> *Seinssetzung* situated in its research program [*Fragestellung*]. Beyond that, there
> is not the slightest reason to give credit to the claim of physics that it could realise
> the being-as-such. As science, the one as well as the other has its object-area pre-
> designed, the realisation of which signifies its mastery. (Gadamer 1990,
> pp. 455–6; 1989, pp. 451–2)

4. QUANTITATIVE VERSUS QUALITATIVE

To sum up, the problem with quantitative modelling is not its abuse and
possible mistakes (so Spengler 1961, p. 274), but the 'thing in itself'. This is
not to argue for a romanticist thrust against measuring and calculation generally, which it would be silly to propose for economics. As Isaiah Berlin
has stated:

> whatever can be isolated, looked at, inspected, should be. We need not be obscu-
> rantist . . . Whatever can be illuminated, made articulate, incorporated in a
> proper science, should of course be so . . . [The] argument is only that not every-
> thing, in practice, can be – indeed that a great deal cannot be – grasped by the
> [natural] sciences. (Berlin 1996, p. 48)[10]

The basis of natural science however, its ideal, as Lexis puts it and as has
been mentioned previously, is in the end 'the purely mathematical concept
of its subject in space and time, through which the *quality* of the phenomena is dissolved in *quantitative* determinations' (Lexis 1903, p. 238). This is
legitimate if one follows positivism as explained, based on outdated
physics, and in this context most strongly stated by Ernst Mach: '*quantitative* investigation is only a *particularly simple case of the qualitative one*'

(1926, p. 322). But, as we have seen, this is not true. Try as we might, 'the experience of the social-historical world cannot be lifted up to science by the inductive process of the natural sciences' (Gadamer 1990, p. 10; 1989, p. 4):[11]

> Socrates the Younger: 'This is correct; only what does now follow?'
> The Stranger: 'Obviously, we will now divide the art of measuring into two parts, according to what has been explained: one part in which we put all arts which measure numbers, lengths, widths, depths and speed against their contrary; as the other one all those who do it against the appropriate and decent and convenient and proper and all which has its place in the middle between two extreme ends.'
> Socrates the Younger: 'Very great is each of these segments, and very different one from the other.' (Plato, *Politikos*, 284e; see 283e–285c)

5.   THE QUANTITATIVE PROPENSITY

One might at this point ask what led to the use of quantitative methods in economics. According to Spengler, it was 'the state of mathematics and statistics, the degree of acquaintance of economic writers with quantitative methods, the cultural *Weltanschauung*, the example of other sciences, the availability of data, and the role of the state in economic affairs' (1961, p. 261). But that is only part of the answer.

The rise of numerical thinking and quantification is perhaps put best by Ernst Mach, who traces it to something like a need and natural, biological necessity of the human species and the development of society (Mach 1926). For economists, this is a particularly tempting approach because their field is quantitative by nature. Indeed, the economic world caused mathematics to develop, rather than the other way round: 'Traffic and trade, buying and selling *demand* the development of arithmetic' (p. 327). Mindsets are important, and those who choose economics as their field usually have a quantitative inclination to begin with. And there is a tendency for those who do not to be institutionally screened out.

Further, although well into the twentieth century natural science was usually, depending on the country, less prestigious than the humanities, today there is a celebrated inferiority complex towards 'lab coats': in an age dominated by the truth-claim of science, it is nice to be on the winning side. This also has something to do with the (at least apparent) decline of the humanities into '*Laber- und Orchideenfächer*', with the obvious *Mumpitz* of many contemporary theories, with the 'Czech cartoon' effect (that is, gifted people fleeing from politically charged and thus dangerous fields towards neutral areas), and with raging unemployment and thus the declining prestige of the entire humanities side (and, admittedly, the social sciences except economics as well).

In other words, if we believe at all in human inclinations towards different ways and approaches, then it is easy to see why those who end up with a degree in economics prefer the quantitative path. If 'science is what recognised scientists recognise as science' (Marquard 1989, p. 199), this is not a problem. But if we want to avoid self-referentiality and instead look for the truth, then we need to follow Plato's division of the two kinds of measuring, and we need to accept that qualitative is not a complex form of quantitative, but rather something else.

6.   NORMATIVITY

There are two interrelated possibilities for proceeding from here. One, which will be discussed later, is to search for a method for economics that takes this problem into account. The second possibility is normative reasoning, and it will be very briefly addressed here, less because of its own vitally important ramifications, which I hope soon to address elsewhere, but because of its epistemological ones.

In the case of economics, dealing as it does with the human sphere (see v. Mises 1942, p. 245), there is always at the basis, 'explicit or implicit, a concept of the human being' (Baumgardt 1990, p. 112). And neoclassical economics' concept, the *homo oeconomicus*, is problematic at best; Baumgardt flatly states that 'from today's perspective, it must be seen as an aberration of the human' (p. 113).

This is significant for the truth-value of neoclassical economics, for if human beings simply do not behave according to the specifications of the model, then the model does not have predictive capability.[12] The 'egotism of the masses' is not calculable; 'there is a strong irrational remainder, caused by indolence, custom, prejudice, which as a decisive factor contributes to the shaping of the economic general circumstances; but also more ideal motives intervene in fact in the clockwork of economic personal profit, in order to disturb the Ricardian circle' (Lexis 1903, p. 245).

This is, to repeat, precisely the case not only with individuals but also with larger groups. Dealing with human beings means that statistical likelihood is ephemeral because humans can decide quite in contrast to the statistical propensity of a group in which they are numbered (cf. Oettingen 1868), any true decision-making situations forming 'neutral threshold-situations, zero-points of indifference, so to say' (Jonas 1987b, p. 63), in which, regardless of all previous experience, things can go either way.

7.   *VERSTEHEN*

'To demand or preach mechanical precision, even in principle, in a field incapable of it is to be blind and to mislead others' (Berlin 1996, p. 53). But do we, normativity aside, have another chance to do economic scholarship? Fortunately, we do: it is the concept of understanding, *Verstehen*.

To say it right away: to understand is not less or less scientific than to assess from the outside, as in the natural science world; but it is more or more so. The great economist of the Younger Historical School, Werner Sombart, whom we will follow as an example of an understanding approach to economics, has put this extremely well, in terms quite similar to the thesis of Gadamer's *Wahrheit und Methode* (1990, trans. 1989): the natural sciences' successful attempt to monopolize the truth is a reversal of the real situation. '"True" realisation reaches as far as we "understand", that is, it is limited to the area of culture and fails towards nature' (Sombart 1923, p. 9). As Nicolai Hartmann put it, '"Understood" can only be "meaning", as well as all that which is related to it: value, goal, significance' (Hartmann 1951, p. 33; see also pp. 64–76). And Sombart: 'Realisation that wants to arrive at the being of nature, is metaphysics' (1929, p. 75; see 1967, pp. 204–5). This does not mean, of course, that *Verstehen* inevitably leads to the truth, but it means that there is a chance that it does, or might.

This means that although we cannot talk very meaningfully about things in biology and physics, the situation in the social sciences 'is completely different: here, our realisation is capable of immediate penetration of the inner causal connection of the outer phenomena, and we would sacrifice a central part of our possible knowledge if we gave up the question for this causal connection' (Lexis 1903, pp. 242–3; see also v. Mises 1942, p. 246).[13]

Today we would call this the hermeneutic approach. We might be more cautious about the penetration being immediately possible, perhaps. In addition hermeneutics has become so fashionable that it has a weasel connotation;[14] it is used here in the very classical sense of the Schleiermacher–Dilthey–Gadamer triad (which of course denotes fundamentally different ways of *Verstehen*). And especially in economics, forays into economic hermeneutics have not been too successful either.

This is one of the reasons why Werner Sombart's approach is used here, although this presents several problems as well, such as Sombart's unpopularity in post-Second World War economic theory, his political reputation and the peculiarly Platonism-based and somewhat simplistic format of his concept of understanding. (See Drechsler 1996, pp. 287–9.)

Why, then, Sombart? Because he makes the case for *verstehende National-ökonomie* particularly lucid and he is explicitly hermeneutic. (See Sombart 1929, p. 76; 1967, pp. 157–9; cf. Koslowski 1996, p. 300.) Sombart developed this approach at length in his book *Die drei Nationalökonomien* (1967, esp. pp. 140–276) and concerning sociology and the social sciences generally in three short and very accessible essays (1923, 1929 and 1936). Whether one traces Sombart's understanding back to Heinrich Rickert, Wilhelm Windelband, Wilhelm Dilthey or even Max Weber, or whether Gustav von Schmoller would have been the more obvious example (all of which, incidentally, could have been employed very profitably indeed for this chapter), is not really important – in our context one must instead ask, 'Is it true or isn't it?'[15]

There are, according to Sombart, two 'truths': '*All society is spirit*, and *all spirit is society*' (1936, p. 115). Thus, '*all humanities* are *social sciences*' (1936, p. 117; 1967, p. 175).[16] Understanding is immanent realization, while the realization of nature is transcendent (1929, p. 75; 1967, p. 197). Based on these ideas, Sombart realizes that one can only understand what one already has: 'Schleiermacher expressed the same when he says: "Where there is no community, there cannot be a connecting point for understanding, either"' (1929, p. 80; see 1967, p. 200).

Sombart sees the difference between the two ways of looking at society in 'their different positions towards the two central concepts of our science: the one of Understanding and the one of Law' (1923, pp. 8–9). The cultural sciences – that is, the humanities – try to realize from the inside to the outside (that is, to understand), whereas the sciences can only '*begreifen*',[17] that is, only the other way round (1923, p. 9; 1967, p. 193).

'But what does it mean to understand? It means first, that we gain insight into the meaning. What is now meaning? As much as connection. But this is not enough . . . "Meaning" means connection within a spiritual whole, within an idea' (1929, p. 78; see 1967, p. 197). This is important because 'in the spirit-world surely there are *only* wholes . . . which then . . . will take on very different forms' (1929, pp. 78–9).

The superiority of this kind of realization stems from its immanence, because the subject and object of realization are identical, as they are both spirit (1929, p. 79; see 1967, p. 197).[18] 'Culture is objectivised spirit . . . subjective or human spirit is the specific capability of the human being to behold ideas, to set goals, to give norms, the specific capability of the spiritual person which, as far as we know, is only existent in the human person' (1929, p. 79).

This anticipates Gadamer's famous dictum, 'To recognise one's own in the strange, to become at home in it, is the basic movement of the spirit, whose being is only the return to itself from the being different' (Gadamer 1990, pp. 19–20 [1989, p. 14]).[19] Hans Jonas expressed it thus:

> As far as the so-called 'understanding' is concerned, the mode of realisation of the humanities, it is evident that a 'personal experiencing', as a feeling-into the matter which in itself is a result of experience, belongs in the realisation insepa-rably from the beginning to the end, that is, until its result, and that it permeates the entire exegesis. (Jonas 1987a, p. 9)

'Because subject here meets with subject, which even in the most extreme strangeness of historical distance remains a human one and thus one accessible to us, if infinitely interpretable' (p. 9).[20]

How to employ this for economics? Frank Knight's recommendation seems to me well taken:

> The first step to getting out of this slough, we suggest, is to recognise that man's relations with his fellow man are on a totally different footing from his relations with the objects of physical nature and to give up, except within recognised and rather narrow limits, the naïve project of carrying over a technique which has been successful in the one set of problems and using it to solve another set of a categorically different kind. (Knight 1935, p. 147)

I cannot say how to go on in concrete economic research terms, especially in light of the practical tasks economics has to fulfil. But this is no reason not to point 'to the deficits [of the "*status praesens*"] and to initiate the respective strategies' (Kolb 1994, p. 195), especially as it seems possible to take the way of *Verstehen*, be it Sombart's variant or not, while the other way does not appear to be a valid option.

CONCLUSION

This, finally, leads us to a look at normativity again. Its reinclusion into eco-nomics would be a return to the Greeks, at least in perspective, a basic focus on 'that which is lucrative and that which is conducive' ('*Einträgliches und Zuträgliches*'; Baumgardt 1990, p. 113). And here understanding and nor-mativity are linked in such a way as to produce a possible, meaningful, truth-focused approach: 'The Aristotelian program of a practical science seems . . . to be the only science-theoretical model according to which the "understanding" sciences can be thought' (Gadamer 1977, p. 87 [1993, p. 499; 1985, p. 183]).[21] Therefore the problem of the two kinds of measur-ing which is at the heart of this essay – the reminder that the qualitative is not a complex form of the quantitative, but *etwas ganz anderes* – might for the social sciences, where human beings are concerned, be solved by Aristotle himself, who says that 'the good is the most accurate measure of all things' (*Politikos*, fragm. 79 in 1886, p. 81; fragm. 2 in 1952, p. 68).

NOTES

* This chapter was originally presented to the 'Evolutionary Economics and Spatial Income Distribution: International, National and Regional Dimensions' conference in Oslo, Norway, 15 May 1997. First of all, my thanks go to Erik S. Reinert for his invitation, indeed his persuasion, to write and to present it as a paper at Oslo. My graduate assistant, Rainer Kattel, was as always extremely helpful in providing both critical comments and research support. For the shaping and development of my argument, discussions with two 'hard-nosed' social scientists par excellence, who represent the very best of this tradition and who both disagree with me on the issues of this essay, were more than crucial: my thanks go to my Dean, Academician Jüri Allik, and especially to Peter R. Senn, with whom I have discussed these topics intensively, personally and in writing, for almost a decade. For discussions at Oslo I thank the participants of the conference; for additional research support, Maarja Soo.

I should point out, however, that the present chapter only presents my first thoughts on the subject, now (2002) half a decade old. During these five years, I have dealt with the matter more thoroughly, and several points and contentions I would now rephrase or argue quite differently, or even retract. For the most recent development of my argument in writing – which is still not complete itself, either – see Dreschler 2000b.

This present chapter includes some ideas and phrases from Drechsler 2000a.

Some support for this project came from the 'State Sciences and Politics' *teadussummad* project area for 1997 at the University of Tartu Faculty of Social Sciences, ref. no. SOAH 005 SO; parts also derived indirectly from the 'Karl Bücher in Dorpat' project of the Estonian Science Foundation, grant no. 3094.

1. I have correlated the following words: *Ansichsein* as 'being-as-such', *Geistes-* and *Kulturwissenschaften* as 'humanities', *Naturwissenschaften* (and *Wissenschaften*, when it clearly refers only to *Naturwissenschaften*) as 'natural sciences', *Sozial-* and *Gesellschaftswissenschaften* as 'social sciences', *Wissenschaft* as 'science' and *Forschung* as 'research'. Also, *anschaulich* as 'visible', *Beziehung* as 'relation', *Erkenntnis* as 'realization', *schlüssig* as 'concludent', *Sinn* as 'meaning', *sprachlich* as 'linguistic', *Zusammenhang* as 'connection' and *Zweck* as 'purpose' (always with derivatives). If the reference is to non-English sources, all translations are mine, but in the cases of Gadamer and v. Stackelberg, I have given the reference to the standard English translation as well (without using it). Particularly short and difficult German quotations have been given in the original language either in the notes or in the main text; so were the Greek ones originally, but – perhaps not insignificantly – the press could not deal with that, in spite of all attempts by the editor. Non-English passages quoted only in the notes have generally not been translated.

2. Mathematical and neoclassical economics are not the same, but in the present context the latter stands and falls with the former to such a degree that the distinction has not been made. Of course, neoclassical economics can be very profitably critiqued from other angles as well.

3. Peter Senn would say that this 'is true for every case that is *not* confirmed by experience. "All human beings grow old and die." This is one of the thousands (millions?) of bits of knowledge accepted as scientific knowledge and without the need of further verification. It is not a working hypothesis in the usual meaning of the words. It is what is commonly called a "fact"' (personal correspondence, 12 May 1995).

4. In German and in full, the quotation reads: 'Ferner wird [gegen die Anwendung der Mathematik in der Nationalökonomie] eingewendet, die Mathematik täusche eine Exaktheit und Starrheit der volkswirtschaftlichen Beziehungen vor, die in Wirklichkeit fließend und unexakt seien; sie täusche naturgesetzliche Notwendigkeiten vor, wo in Wirklichkeit der menschliche Wille frei entscheiden und gestalten könne. Deshalb sei die Anwendung der Mathematik in der Volkswirtschaftslehre abzulehnen. Diese Auffassung verkennt völlig die Rolle der Mathematik in der Wirtschaftstheorie. Wie oft ist schon von sachkundiger Seite hervorgehoben worden, daß "aus dem mathematischen Topf nie

mehr herausspringt, als in ihn vorher hineingelegt worden ist"! Die mathematische Symbolik verändert weder die Voraussetzungen noch die Folgerungen des Theoretikers, sofern sie schlüssig sind' (Stackelberg 1951, pp. x–xi; 1952, p. xiii).

5. In German: 'Insofern sich die Sätze der Mathematik auf die Wirklichkeit beziehen, sind sie nicht sicher, und insofern sie sicher sind, beziehen sie sich nicht auf die Wirklichkeit' (Einstein 1970, pp. 119–20). Also quoted (and translated almost identically) in v. Mises 1942, p. 252.

6. Quoted in Heath 1974, p. 25n.5 (as 'the remark attributed to Wittgenstein').

7. In German and fuller: 'die Mathematik als solche [vermag] weder über Gegenstände der anschaulichen Vorstellung noch über Gegenstände der Wirklichkeit etwas auszusagen' (Einstein 1970, p. 120).

8. In German: 'Man kann nicht die sprachliche Welt . . . von oben einsehen wollen. Denn es gibt keinen Standort außerhalb der sprachlichen Welterfahrung, von dem her sie selber zum Gegenstand zu werden vermöchte' (Gadamer 1990, p. 456 [1989, p. 452]). 'Die objektivierende Wissenschaft erfährt infolgedessen die sprachliche Geformtheit der natürlichen Welterfahrung als eine Quelle von Vorurteilen' (1990, p. 457 [1989, p. 453]). Of course, prejudices are nothing bad in the Gadamerian universe.

9. In addition, specifically for the social sciences, Norman Bradburn has emphasized the salient fact that 'whether or not things are viewed as "data" and worthy of being measured, lies in the question being asked, not in the thing itself' (1997, p. 8).

10. Paracelsus' dictum 'he who heals is right', coined for medicine, is applicable to economic modelling also. The Machian point that the reality of a given hypothesis is of no importance whatsoever, as long as the object under consideration is performing *as if* it were so (see P. Zühlke in Mach 1926a, p. 4), is a strong one. Along these lines, Senn argues that 'there are two ways to judge the "usefulness" of a system, logically and empirically . . . The empirical judgement of "usefulness" is quite separate. It depends, along with other things, mainly on how the system performs and the goals of the evaluator' (personal communication, 12 May 1995). But the assumption of this essay, remember, is that mathematical (and neoclassical) theory does *not* 'deliver'.

11. In German: 'Die Erfahrung der gesellschaftlich-geschichtlichen Welt läßt sich nicht mit dem induktiven Verfahren der Naturwissenschaften zur Wissenschaft erheben' (Gadamer 1990, p. 10 [1989, p. 4]).

12. Baumgardt 1990, p. 107: 'Die Realitätsferne der Annahmen beim homo-oeconomicus-Modell und die daher sehr bedingte und auf Extreme beschränkte Aussagekraft des Modells, wird für immer mehr Wirtschaftstheoretiker unbefriedigend. Auch innerhalb der Wirtschaftswissenschaften selbst gibt es deshalb gewichtige Ansätze, die problematisch gewordene Vorstellung vom homo oeconomicus zu korrigieren. Diese Ansätze sind freilich (noch) nicht wirtschaftswissenschaftliches Allgemeingut.'

13. Lexis (1903, p. 243) continues: 'Das Element der sozialwissenschaftlichen Erscheinungen ist das nach Motiven handelnde menschliche Individuum. Für die Kausalität des menschlichen Individuums aber, für die menschlichen Motive und deren Wirkungen, haben wir vermöge unseres eigenen Bewusstseins ein unmittelbares Verständnis . . . So sind wir also imstande, die menschlichen Dinge mit Rücksicht auf die *Kausalität* und *Wechselwirkung* der sich nach ihrem eigenen Wesen bestimmenden Individuen wissenschaftlich zu betrachten.'

14. Already in 1977, Gadamer put it this way: 'Many others – especially since hermeneutics has become a fashionable term and every "interpretation" wants to call itself hermeneutics – abuse the word and the thing for which I had taken the floor contrarily in such a way that they see in it a new *Methodenlehre* with which in truth they legitimise methodical unclarity or ideological cloaking' (1977, pp. 80–81; 1993, pp. 494–5 [1985, p. 177]). An excellent sketch of the sophisticated yet realist use of hermeneutics is Kaiser 1997, pp. 58–9.

15. 'Stimmt es oder stimmt es nicht?' So Julius Ebbinghaus regarding the work of Hermann Cohen, quoted in Orlik 1993, p. 143.

16. In German: '*alle Gesellschaft ist Geist* und *aller Geist ist Gesellschaft*' (Sombart 1936, p. 115). Thus, '*alle Geisteswissenschaft* [ist] *Gesellschaftswissenschaft*' (Sombart 1936,

p. 117). It is important to realize that this is Nicolai Hartmann's, rather than Hegel's, *Geist* (not in the sense that it derives from there, but that it is the same concept). See Hartmann 1949, p. 460, as well as Drechsler 1997, pp. 67–8.

17. Mises (1942) translates *begreifen* as 'conceive', but then the wordplay (the German implies 'to touch with your hands, from the outside') is lost, and I also think 'conceive' means something else even on the abstract level.

18. Sombart (1967, pp. 197–198n.76, 198) sees a parallel to his own idea of the mode of *Verstehen* as being determined by the concept of immanence in Martin Heidegger's approach in *Sein und Zeit*.

19. In German: 'Im Fremden das Eigene zu erkennen, in ihm heimisch zu werden, ist die Grundbewegung des Geistes, dessen Sein nur Rückkehr zu sich selbst aus dem Anderssein ist' (Gadamer 1990, pp. 19–20).

20. In German: 'Was aber speziell das sogenannte "Verstehen" betrifft, die Erkenntnisweise der Geisteswissenschaften, so ist evident, daß dabei das "persönliche Erleben", als Einfühlung in den Gegenstand, der selber ja Niederschlag von Erlebnis ist, in das Erkennen von Anfang bis zu Ende, d.h. bis in sein Ergebnis unzertrennlich hineingehört und die ganze Auslegung durchdringt' (Jonas 1987a, p. 9). 'Denn Subjekt begegnet sich hier mit Subjeckt, das auch in der äußersten Fremdheit geschichtlicher Ferne ein menschliches und daher uns zugängliches, jedoch unendlich deutbares bleibt' (p. 9).

21. In German: 'Das aristotelische Programm einer praktischen Wissenschaft scheint mir das einzige wissenschaftstheoretische Vorbild darzustellen, nach dem die "verstehenden" Wissenschaften gedacht werden können' (Gadamer 1977, p. 87; 1993, p. 499; 1985, p. 183).

REFERENCES

Abbagnano, Nicola (1967), 'Positivism', in Paul Edwards (ed.), *The Encyclopedia of Philosophy*, New York and London: Macmillan and Collier Macmillan, vol. 6, pp. 414–19.

Aristotle (1886), *Aristotelis qui ferebantur librorum fragmenta*, ed. Valentin Rose, Leipzig: Teubner.

Aristotle (1952), *The Works of Aristotle*, vol. 12, *Select Fragments*, trans. and ed. Sir David Ross, Oxford: Oxford University Press, reprint 1967.

Baumgardt, Johannes (1990), 'Der Mensch als Homo Oeconomicus – gilt das noch heute? Der Beitrag der Wirtschaftswissenschaften zum Menschenbild der Gegenwart und Zukunft', in Gert Hummel (ed.), *Der Beitrag der Wissenschaften zum gegenwärtigen und zukünftigen Menschenbild*, Bonn: Deutscher Hochschulverband, pp. 97–120.

Berlin, Isaiah (1996), *The Sense of Reality: Studies in Ideas and Their History*, London: Chatto & Windus.

Bradburn, Norman (1997), 'Social information, social policy and social science', *ZUMA-Nachrichten*, **40** (May), 7–20.

Drechsler, Wolfgang (1996), 'The revisiting of Werner Sombart: implications for German sociological thinking and for the German debate about the past', in Jürgen G. Backhaus (ed.), *Werner Sombart (1863–1941): Social Scientist*, Marburg: Metropolis, vol. 3, pp. 287–96.

Drechsler, Wolfgang (1997), 'On German *Geist*', *Trames*, **1** (51/46) (1), 67–77.

Drechsler, Wolfgang (2000a), 'Zu Werner Sombarts Theorie der Soziologie und zu seiner Biographie', in Jürgen Backhaus (ed.), *Werner Sombart: Eine kritische Bestandsaufnahme*, Marburg: Metropolis.

Drechsler, Wolfgang (2000b), 'On the possibility of quantitative-mathematical social science, chiefly economics: some preliminary considerations', *Journal of Economic Studies*, **27** (4/5), 246–59.

Eagleton, Terry (1996), *The Illusions of Postmodernism*, Oxford: Blackwell.

Einstein, Albert (1970 [1921]), 'Geometrie und Erfahrung', in *Mein Weltbild*, Frankfurt/Main: Ullstein, pp. 119–27.

Gadamer, Hans-Georg (1977), 'Hans-Georg Gadamer', in Ludwig J. Pongratz (ed.), *Philosophie in Selbstdarstellungen*, Hamburg: Meiner, vol. 3, pp. 60–101. Now also in (1993), *Hermeneutik*, vol. 2, *Wahrheit und Methode. Ergänzungen, Register = Gesammelte Werke*, 2nd edn, Tübingen: Mohr/Siebeck, vol. 2, pp. 479–508. Standard English translation [partial]: (1985), 'On the origins of philosophical hermeneutics', in *Philosophical Apprenticeships*, trans. Robert R. Sullivan, Cambridge, MA: MIT Press, pp. 177–93.

Gadamer, Hans-Georg (1990), *Hermeneutik*, vol. 1, *Wahrheit und Methode: Grundzüge einer philosophischen Hermeneutik*; vol. 1 of *Gesammelte Werke*, 6th edn, Tübingen: Mohr/Siebeck. Standard English translation: (1989), *Truth and Method*, trans. Joel Weinsheimer and Donald G. Marshall, 2nd rev. edn, London: Sheed & Ward.

Hartmann, Nicolai (1949), 'Nicolai Hartmann', in Werner Ziegenfuß with Gertrud Jung (eds), *Philosophen-Lexikon: Handwörterbuch der Philosophie nach Personen*, Berlin: de Gruyter, vol. 1, pp. 454–71.

Hartmann, Nicolai (1951), *Teleologisches Denken*, 2nd repr. edn, Berlin: de Gruyter, 1966.

Heath, Peter (1974), *The Philosopher's Alice*, New York: St. Martin's Press.

Heisenberg, Werner (1958), *Physics and Philosophy: The Revolution in Modern Science*, London: Allen & Unwin.

Jonas, Hans (1987a), 'Wissenschaft als persönliches Erlebnis', in *Wissenschaft als persönliches Erlebnis*, Göttingen: Vandenhoeck & Ruprecht, pp. 7–31.

Jonas, Hans (1987b), 'Im Kampf um die Möglichkeit des Glaubens: Erinnerungen an Rudolf Bultmann und Betrachtungen zum philosophischen Aspekt seines Werkes', in *Wissenschaft als persönliches Erlebnis*, Göttingen: Vandenhoeck & Ruprecht, pp. 47–75.

Kaiser, Otto (1997), 'Zwischen Interpretation und Überinterpretation: Vom Ethos des Auslegers', *Variations herméneutiques*, **6** (May), 53–70.

Kant, Immanuel (1992 [1793]), *Über den Gemeinspruch: Das mag in der Theorie richtig sein, taugt aber nicht für die Praxis*, 5th edn, Frankfurt/Main: Klostermann.

Kautz, Timothy (1990), 'Ernst Cassirer und die Ethik: Eine Studie zur Philosophie der symbolischen Formen', diss. phil., University of Düsseldorf; Darmstadt: Dissertations Druck Darmstadt.

Kenessey, Zoltan E. (1995), 'The emergence of quantitative thinking about mortality and life expectancy', *International Review of Comparative Public Policy*, **6**, 291–311.

Knight, Frank H. (1935), 'The limitations of scientific method in economics', in *The Ethics of Competition and Other Essays*, 2nd printing, 1951, London: Allen & Unwin, pp. 105–47.

Kolb, Gerhard (1994), 'Volkswirtschaft als Kulturtheorie – Georg Weippert zum Gedenken', in *Jahrbuch für Philosophie des Forschungsinstituts für Philosophie Hannover*, Vienna: Passagen, vol. 5, pp. 181–97.

Koslowski, Peter (1996), 'Economic ontology – Cultural philosophy of the economy – Business ethics: Sombart as a proponent of a philosophical econom-ics', in Jürgen G. Backhaus (ed.), *Werner Sombart (1863–1941): Social Scientist*, Marburg: Metropolis, vol. 1, pp. 297–301.

Lexis, Wilhelm (1903 [1874]), 'Naturwissenschaft und Sozialwissenschaft', in *Abhandlungen zur Theorie der Bevölkerungs- und Moralstatistik*, Jena: Gustav Fischer. Reprinted with a preface by Wolfgang Drechsler and with the original 1874 newspaper article from the *Neue Dörpt'sche Zeitung* as University of Tartu Working Paper in Public Administration and Government 97-04.

Mach, Ernst (1926), 'Zahl und Maß', in *Erkenntnis und Irrtum: Skizzen zur Psychologie der Forschung*, 5th (≈ 4th) edition, reprinted 1980, Darmstadt: Wissenschaftliche Buchgesellschaft, pp. 320–36.

Marquard, Odo (1989 [1985]), 'Über die Unvermeidlichkeit der Geisteswissen-schaften', reprinted in Westdeutsche Rektorenkonferenz (ed.), *Hochschulaut-onomie, Privileg und Verpflichtung*, Hildesheim: Lax, pp. 193–203.

Mises, Ludwig [v.] (1942), 'Social science and natural science', *Journal of Social Philosophy and Jurisprudence*, **7** (3), 240–53.

Oettingen, Alexander v. (1868), *Die Moralstatistik: Inductiver Nachweis der Gesetzmäßigkeit sittlicher Lebensbewegung im Organismus der Menschheit*, vol. 1 of *Die Moralstatistik und die christliche Sittenlehre: Versuch einer Socialethik auf empirischer Grundlage*, Erlangen: Deichert.

Orlik, Franz (1993), 'Einige Probleme des Cohenschen Idealismus und die Versuche zu ihrer Bewältigung bei Nicolai Hartmann und Ernst Cassirer', in *Philosophisches Denken – Politisches Wirken: Hermann-Cohen-Kolloquium Marburg 1992*, Hildesheim: Olms, pp. 144–62.

Sombart, Werner (1923), 'Soziologie: Ein Vorwort', in *Noo-Soziologie*, Berlin: Duncker & Humblot, 1956, pp. 1–12.

Sombart, Werner (1929), 'Das Verstehen', in *Noo-Soziologie*, Berlin: Duncker & Humblot, 1956, pp. 75–93.

Sombart, Werner (1936), 'Soziologie: Was sie ist und was sie sein sollte', in *Noo-Soziologie*, Berlin: Duncker & Humblot, 1956, pp. 95–123.

Sombart, Werner (1967 [1930]), *Die drei Nationalökonomien: Geschichte und System der Lehre von der Wirtschaft*, 2nd (≈ 1st) edition, Berlin: Duncker & Humblot.

Spengler, Joseph S. (1961), 'On the progress of quantification in economics', *Isis*, **52**, pt 2 (168), 258–76.

Stackelberg, Heinrich v. (1951 [1943]), 'Vorwort zur ersten Auflage', in *Grundlagen der theoretischen Volkswirtschaftslehre*, 2nd edn, Tübingen and Zürich: Mohr/Siebeck and Polygraphischer Verlag, pp. vii–xi. Standard English transla-tion: (1952), 'Preface to the first German edition', in *The Theory of the Market Economy*, trans. Alan T. Peacock, New York: Oxford University Press, pp. ix–xiii.

PART II

The strategy of success: nineteenth-century United States and Germany

3. The views of the German historical school on the issue of international income distribution

Jürgen G. Backhaus

The title of this chapter needs a few words of explanation. First, the views discussed here are theory-based and tested against specific policies within well-defined institutions. Second, the reference to the German Historical School is purely a convenience; these views are likewise held in different language areas, such as the French, the Dutch and the Italian traditions, but when the institutions through which economic policies are to be carried out differ, then specific policies informed by the same basic outlook will differ as well. Third, the term 'Historical School' refers to a body of literature before the advent of econometrics, which used historical evidence systematically in order to test theories against empirical evidence. Historical economics also tended to be defined more broadly than economics is today; institutions, legal issues, rules of law and customs as well as issues of geography and technology tended to be part of the explanatory apparatus. We can refer to Friedrich List (1789–1846), Wilhelm Roscher (1817–1894), Gustav von Schmoller (1838–1917) and Werner Sombart (1863–1941), in chronological order.[1] The list could easily be augmented with authors from other language areas.

In a nutshell, the views of the Historical School on the international distribution of income resulting from international trade were inspired neither by nationalism (the issue of state building) nor by anti-market sentiment (the choice of state command rather than market forces as the preferred allocation mechanism). Nor were the Historical School's views based on unbridgeable methodological differences from free-market advocates. Rather, the questions asked by members of the Historical School were different from those asked, for example, by David Ricardo or Adam Smith and therefore demanded different answers. Typically, members of the Historical School emphasized the dynamic process through which an economy grows, and their basic question was not what causes the wealth of nations, but what causes productive forces to spring up so as to produce the wealth of nations.

The argument in this chapter develops in five steps. First I contrast Ricardo's (1772–1823) basic argument in *Principles of Political Economy and Taxation* (first published 1817), repeated in a simpler form in so many textbooks, with the standard body of theory then taught on the European continent. Second, I briefly explain the leading economic doctrines of cameralism and mercantilism as they were taught on the Continent when Adam Smith's *Wealth of Nations* appeared in 1776. Third, I examine the emphasis on money and the importance of gold within this body of doctrines. Fourth, I offer a summary assessment of the British free-trade argument as it was commonly held on the European continent. Finally, using the concept of protective tariffs as developed by Friedrich List, I explain the purpose of this economic policy instrument and why it continues to be frequently misunderstood.

The standard wisdom about the views of members of the Historical School on international trade is that they were critical of the distribution of income resulting from international trade and therefore subscribed to protectionist arguments. It is then generally implied that these authors were anti-market to begin with and tended to ignore or at least discount classical economic theories. A few examples may illustrate these points. One of the leading textbooks on the history of economic thought sketches the views of the Historical School thus:

> *The older historical school.* The important writers of *the older historical school* are Friedrich List (1789–1846), Wilhelm Roscher (1817–1894), Bruno Hildebrand (1812–1878), and Carl Knies (1821–1898). They contended that classical economic theory did not apply to all times and cultures and that the conclusions of Smith, Ricardo, and J.S. Mill, though valid for an industrializing economy such as England, did not apply to agricultural Germany. There was a great deal of nationalistic feeling in the economic analysis of these writers. Furthermore, they asserted that economics and the social sciences must use a historically based methodology and that classical theory was mistaken in attempting to ape the methodology of the physical sciences, particularly in the hands of Ricardo and his followers. Some of the more moderate members of the school acknowledged that theoretical/deductive methods and historical/inductive methods were compatible. But others, particularly Knies, objected to any use of abstract theory.
>
> List expressed particularly strong nationalist views and refused to admit that the laissez-faire conclusions of classical theory were applicable to countries less developed than England. Where classical theory held that national well-being will result from the pursuit of individual self-interest in an environment of laissez faire, List argued that state guidance was necessary, particularly for Germany and the United States. He contended that whereas free trade would be beneficial to England, given the advanced state of its industry, tariffs and protection were necessary for Germany and the United States. (Landreth and Colander 1994, p. 325)

In fact, Harry Landreth and David Colander's argument echoes a similar argument made by Wesley Mitchell (1967, Chapter 19). There, to our amazement, we read:

> List wrote his great *Das nationale System der politischen Ökonomie* (The National System of Political Economy) in 1842 on national economics as a man who was interested in the unification of Germany, who believed in building up a strong nation, and who thought that the application of protection with the principles was desirable in the view of that larger political aim. Whether or not for the time being the country was better off under free trade or under protection from a stricter material point of view made comparatively little differences in his eyes. To him, the major controlling consideration was the ultimate construction of a powerful Germany . . . So when economics seemed more and more to be running out to the practical conclusion of free trade in England, it was running more and more counter to the disposition of the Germans under the influence of such ideas as List represented. (p. 535)

It is difficult to see where Mitchell got this. As the editor, Joseph Dorfman, points out in an appended footnote, Mitchell wrote this passage in 1918 (when the United States was at war with Germany). In fact, List recommended to other countries – including the United States – the same economic development policies in order to achieve industrialization, and argued that Germany should form a customs union with England.

The climate in which this intellectual debate took place was more complex than these assessments reveal. Mitchell makes this point explicitly, and it is well worth quoting:

> That is to say, they [the German political economists] found that classical economics with its insistence upon a thorough-going individualism, with a doctrine that it is best for the group to interfere very little in the affairs of the individual, that on the whole, society will be best off in the material sense if every man is left free to follow his economic interest as he sees it, they saw that these ideas were not compatible with the kind of social life which had produced as a home-grown product *Cameralwissenschaft*. The same class of men were engaged in teaching the two subjects. (p. 533)

But where did this difference in outlook come from?

When *The Principles of Political Economy and Taxation* appeared, political economy had not yet taken hold as an academic discipline in Britain or the United States. In Britain, William Nassau was appointed to the first chair in political economy at Oxford in 1826. On the Continent, however, the first chairs in political economy had been established a century earlier (1727) in Halle and Frankfurt on the Oder. The purpose of these chairs was to instruct future civil servants in those principles of political economy that they needed in order to help design and implement enlightened economic policies that would bring prosperity and welfare (*Glückseeligkeit*) to their respective countries, when it was understood that a country's prosperity meant that the state could also financially prosper and participate in this wealth. The major way the state participated in the wealth of its subjects was to tax transactions by means of either the excise tax or the older forms of regalia, concessions and fees. Another important source of revenue was customs duties.

Ricardo's well-known example of England trading with Portugal, where England produced the cloth and Portugal the wine, depicted a static situation which did not reflect what would happen if the agriculture-based trading partner adopted policies to broaden its industrial base. Also, the example clearly referred to a situation in which the industrial producer's raw materials came from a different country and therefore the example assumed the industrial country's reliance on the supply of raw materials, in all likelihood from its colonies. Hence, members of the German Historical School saw Ricardo's example as an apt description of England's position *vis-à-vis* its less developed trading partners but not an effective argument for free international trade. The issue at hand is not the comparative advantage at the moment but the development of commerce and industry in the agriculture-based country.

Political economy was thus taught on the European continent as the science that enabled public administrators to develop the economies of their respective countries. At the centre of such an approach, naturally, was the state with its policy instruments bent on creating markets. We can distinguish two variants of the Historical School doctrine, fitting the respective geopolitical conditions of the countries in which they were taught. Large contiguous territories with access to the sea, such as France or Spain, strongly relied on closing their markets through customs duties to both imports of manufactured goods and exports of raw materials, and on selling concessions – sometimes even public offices – as bonds.[2] In contrast, central Europe consisted largely of smaller states, some of which had far-flung and not always contiguous territories. Nevertheless, these territories required a common economic and commercial policy which could not rely on high tariffs to the same extent as countries with contiguous territories and sea access; rather, the princes of these more than 300 smaller central European states had to rely on policies to encourage the immigration of skilled workers; other state revenues would stem from public enterprises in agriculture and manufacturing, excise taxes, concessions and regalia as well as the circulation of currency. Only if the currency was considered more stable than those of competing currency issuers could the circulation of currency be a sustainable revenue source. Herein lies a basic difference between mercantilist and cameralist policies: the cameralist policy-maker always competed with other similarly motivated princes for commerce, crafts and means to industrialize the country. Many countries, such as Prussia, resorted to policies of selective immigration, thereby relieving pressure on religious minorities. Almost every prince engaged in furthering the production of knowledge, itself an export industry, by founding or expanding existing universities. Thus the chequered political landscape of central Europe gave rise to very competitive economic policies and a large university landscape, in which political economy likewise grew as a state-centred economic doctrine designed to help future administrators. [3]

Another difference between mercantilist and cameralist doctrine is the strong emphasis that cameralists placed on technology. The typical cameralist textbook emphasized not only economic principles but also a wide range of issues concerning their implementation, down to even very practical suggestions. In particular, there was a strong emphasis on introducing new technologies (for example, in mining), new types of machinery and work organization (for example, in manufacturing), and new techniques (for example, more efficient practices in agriculture and forestry). Sometimes the state directly sponsored such projects, often at great expense and not always with sufficient success. However, the state of Prussia, which went far in implementing cameralist doctrine, developed a policy that relied on market forces to support the state effort. New initiatives would be launched, and if they proved commercially viable they would be privatized in order to generate new funds for development.

The Prussian Trading Corporation (Preussische Seehandlung), founded in 1772, may be a good example to make the point. The trading corporation started to borrow from private lenders and without any state guarantee. In 1804 it offered 4 per cent interest (later 3 per cent) and borrowed a total of 25 million taler. Its assets were Prussian bonds which could not be redeemed in 1806. Instead of liquidating, the bank received a state guarantee in 1810 and henceforth started to combine the activities of a state bank with those of an industrial development corporation with activities in road and rail construction, shipping, wool and salt trade, mills, mechanical weaving, paper factories, engineering and shipbuilding. Because not all of these enterprises could be operated successfully, it was the practice of the trading corporation to sell unprofitable undertakings and retain those that were profitable. In this way the company not only managed the very considerable public debt – the extent of which was among the best-kept secrets of the Prussian state – but it even made net contributions to the state's budget to the tune of about 0.2 per cent of net state revenues. In addition, the company made an important contribution to the process of industrializing Prussia. It should be noted in this context that the company enjoyed no legal monopoly.

Since these development strategies involved the transformation of almost exclusively agricultural economies into commerce- and crafts-based economies with the advent of industrial production in manufacturing, market penetration of the self-sufficient agricultural economies in order to further the division of labour clearly required money. Hence, both the mercantilists and the cameralists were bent on increasing the use of money and keeping enough money in circulation. Where these countries did not own gold or silver mines, an ancillary concern was the need to keep enough precious metal within the home economy. Precious metals are not an end in themselves in these doctrines, however; they are the means to monetize self-sufficient economies in order to introduce markets and deepen the division of labour.

When free-trade arguments appeared in larger numbers, originally inspired by the British literature but rapidly spread into France, Germany and Italy, the consensus among the established writers nevertheless remained that each country adopted a trade policy in order to further its own advantage. While the policies internally were designed to foster the development of markets, this meant externally that these same emerging markets had to be protected against international competition which would erode the local base from which the developmental take-off could be launched. In summarizing the mercantilist and cameralist consensus in the literature, Schmoller (1919–23, vol. 1, p. 87) says:

> The literature in the various European nations which took part in this intellectual movement are mainly different in that according to the specific geographical position and the general national interests different state administrative measures are being suggested. In Holland one praises the admiralties, large monopolistic trade companies and all those regulatory measures which make Amsterdam the centre of international trade. Outside the Netherlands one generally suggests the imitation of this small but active people of merchants, but in England one insists above all on national navigation acts mainly aimed at the Netherlands, on supporting ocean fishing, on the East Indian trade, on depressing the rate of interest and on supporting domestic industry. In Germany above all measures against the import of foreign products of manufacture are suggested in order not to endanger local commercial lives through overwhelming foreign imports. The different measures are different indeed, but the goals are the same everywhere: The egotistical support of one's own economy with all the measures the state has available.[4]

In many ways Friedrich List presents the best example of how this developmental strategy had been designed.

Friedrich List was the first professor of administrative practice at the University of Tübingen, the state university of the newly created kingdom of Württemberg. The kingdom had been created as a consequence of the

Napoleonic occupation of Germany and comprised a large number of formerly independent territories and free cities. List had risen through the state tax service and had been employed by the prime minister's office for various special tasks. For instance, he was charged with an inquiry into the causes of mass emigration from Württemberg to North America; in his report, based on interviews with emigrants in the port of Heilbronn on the Neckar river, he emphasized the harsh tax system – which did not take into account individuals' ability to pay – as a major cause of emigration. The country had had to contribute an army to Napoleon's Russian expedition, and many farms and businesses had lost their major breadwinners, who had either died or returned as disabled veterans. These war-related burdens were simply put onto the taxpayers without regard for their sustainability. At the time of List's appointment to the University of Tübingen, which trained the kingdom's future civil servants, political economy was taught by Friedrich von Fulda (1774–1847) in the physiocratic tradition, a doctrine rightly considered impracticable. List's appointment against the express wish of the faculty was unusual in that he had not passed the usual university qualifying exams.[5] The prime minister's wish in appointing List was not only that he turn out more practice-oriented graduates but also that he design a tax reform for the kingdom of Württemberg. In this tax reform, the protective tariff was of pivotal importance.

List's oft-repeated ideal scenario of economic development is as follows. The country's public administration carries on its traditional tasks of establishing law and order, thereby creating a favourable business climate; of meeting the needs of public transportation, such as for improved roads and waterways as well as railways, which were of particular importance in List's analysis; of establishing a simple tax administration and of carrying out a programme of regulatory reform in order to simplify the procedures faced by business; and of supporting publications, improving public health services and increasing awareness of new technologies by organizing fairs and industrial and technological exhibitions and by setting up prototype sites of production. There is no bureaucratic expansion, since the central instrument – the protective tariff – is handled by an existing administrative body and requires no additional resources whatsoever (List 1983; see also 1930, p. 330). As a consequence of all these complementary and secondary administrative measures, of the protective tariff and of occasional direct measures such as the attraction of particular entrepreneurs, competition in home markets eventually intensifies, prices decline and quality improves at the same time (p. 389). This also affects agriculture, which is never subject to protective tariffs, by stimulating a general increase (shift) in the demand for agricultural goods and by leading to an increase in the value of land due to increased demand for land for industrial purposes (pp. 330, 389) and for housing, with the additional consequence (not mentioned by List) that yields from traditional property taxes also increase. The revenues from customs decline, since local price levels decline as well. Eventually this leads to a drying up of revenues from customs, in the case of both high and low tariff rates. True to traditional administrative practice, the (by now) insignificant custom duty (*bagatelle* duty)[6] is discontinued; and thereby the desired goal of free trade is reached.

In conclusion we can note that the views of the Historical School with respect to international trade have often been misunderstood. The scholars of the Historical School were not protectionists as such, although they advocated temporary protective tariffs for well-specified conditions, provided they carried the seeds of their own destruction. Nor were the Historical School economists anti-market. On the contrary, the trade and development policy they set out to teach and test practically was designed to further the development of markets in order to develop their respective countries economically.

NOTES

1.   List's most prominent work was *Das nationale System der politischen Ökonomie (The National System of Political Economy)*. Various editions have been published in German, English and French. Roscher's most important publication for the issue at hand was *Geschichte der Nationalökonomie in Deutschland (History of Political Economy in Germany)*. Schmoller's magnum opus was *Grundriß der allgemeinen Volkswirtschaftslehre (Blueprint of Political Economy)*. Sombart's magnum opus was *Der moderne Kapitalismus (Modern Capitalism)*.
2.   The bond would be redeemed through the income from the office (for example, income to a judge or a bridgemaster).
3.   In 1798 in Germany alone there were already 23 chairs of political economy at universities.
4.   'Die Schriften der verschiedenen europäischen Nationen, welche an dieser geistigen Bewegung teilgenommen haben, unterscheiden sich hauptsächlich dadurch, daß sie je nach der Lage und den nationalen Gesamtinteressen verschiedene staatliche Verwaltungsmaßregeln empfehlen. In Holland rühmt man staatliche Admiralitäten, große monopolisierte Handelsgesellschaften und alle die Maßregeln, die Amsterdam zum Mittelpunkte des Welthandels machen. Ausserhalb Hollands empfielt man allgemein die Nachahmung dieses kleinen rührigen Handelsvolkes, aber man dringt in England in erster Linie auf nationale Schiffahrtsgesetze, die gegen Holland gerichtet sind, auf Pflege der Seefischerei, des ostindischen Handels, auf eine staatliche Herabdrückung des Zinsfußes und eine Förderung der heimischen Industrie: In Deutschland empfiehlt man vor allem Erschwerung und Verbot der fremden Manufaktureneinfuhr, um das gewerbliche Leben der Heimat nicht ganz durch die fremde Konkurrenz erdrücken zu lassen. Die einzelnen Mittel sind verschieden, die Ziele sind überall dieselben: Die egoistische Förderung der eigenen Volkswirtschaft mit allen Mitteln des Staates.'
5.   List was forced – as was the custom – to give his inaugural lecture in Latin, a language he did not understand.
6.   As part of traditional administrative procedures in continental European tax administration, there are regularly evaluations of tax yields and administrative costs. Bagatelle duties

are duties resulting in insignificantly small net revenues, with sometimes very substantial gross revenues being consumed entirely by the costs of collection. Duties found to have fallen into this category are routinely discontinued.

REFERENCES

Landreth, Harry and David C. Colander (1994), *History of Economic Thought*, 3rd edn, Boston, MA: Houghton Mifflin.

List, Friedrich (1983), *National System of Political Economy*, London: Frank Cass. German edition: (1930), *Das nationale System der politischen Ökonomie*, Berlin: Hobbing.

Mitchell, Wesley C. (1967), *Types of Economic Theory from Mercantilism to Institutionalism*, ed. Joseph Dorfman, New York: Augustus Kelley.

Ricardo, David (1821 [1817]), *The Principles of Political Economy and Taxation*, 3rd edn, reprinted (1917) London and New York: Everyman's Library.

Roscher, Wilhelm (1874), *Geschichte der Nationalökonomie in Deutschland*, Munich: Oldenburg.

Schmoller, Gustav (1919–1923), *Grundriß der allgemeinen Volkswirtschaftslehre*, 2 vols, Leipzig: Duncker & Humblot.

Smith, Adam (1776), *An Inquiry into the Nature and Causes of the Wealth of Nations*, ed. Edwin Cannan from the text of the 5th edn, New York: Modern Library.

Sombart, Werner (1916–1927), *Der moderne Kapitalismus*, 3 vols, Leipzig: Duncker & Humblot.

4. Technical progress and obsolescence of capital and skills: theoretical foundations of nineteenth-century US industrial and trade policy

Michael Hudson

This chapter reviews some early technological theories of competitiveness and (what often is left out of account) economic obsolescence. The implications of technological change and industrial head starts for the problem of economic backwardness in societies where progress was not occurring were analysed by mid-nineteenth-century American economists who are largely forgotten today: Calvin Colton, Henry Carey and E. Peshine Smith. These American School writers were associated with Whig (and after 1853, Republican) politicians in shaping the industrial policies that transformed the United States from a raw-materials-producing ('Southern') economy into the world's major industrial power (a 'Northern' economy).

Members of the American School, if they are discussed at all, typically are dismissed as protectionists. A more accurate name for them would be technology theorists, futurists or prototypical systems analysts. Their theory of productive powers focused on industrial and agricultural technology, especially the substitution of capital for labour and land. A quarter century ago (Hudson 1972a and 1975) I collected examples of their theorizing. More recently (Hudson 1992, especially Chapters 7 to 9) I placed them in the context of the evolution of international trade theory. But inasmuch as mainstream theory continues to ignore their remarkable contributions, it is not out of place to present a summary of their work. This chapter therefore contrasts their technological assumptions with the narrower assumptions adopted by subsequent *laissez-faire* orthodoxy. I conclude by suggesting some features needed to formulate a modern theory of the financial and social preconditions for international competitiveness versus backwardness.

Twentieth-century trade theory has diverted economists down the path of hypothetical 'what if' reasoning unabashedly at odds with economic reality. Year after year, Nobel economics prizes have been given for mathematical demonstrations that under certain highly restrictive assumptions economies tend to settle at stable and equitable equilibria. Under these assumptions, international wage and profit rates tend to converge.

There is reason to suspect that the selection of unrealistic assumptions underlying this economic orthodoxy is not innocent. It is axiomatic to historians of economic thought that when a speculative theory is chosen in preference to a more realistic one, some industry's or nation's self-interest is acting as an invisible hand, turning economic doctrine into a public relations ploy to promote specific desired policies. The effect is to divert analysis from economic reality.

Today's economics discipline has become a science of assumptions whose badge of scientific reasoning is simply the internal consistency of these (arbitrary) assumptions. If trade theory bears much of the blame for economics' circular reasoning and practical irrelevance, it is largely because of the role played by the tariff debate during the formative period of classical economics and the mobilization of economic theory to promote status quo dependency patterns today.

The factor-price equalization theorem, for instance, diverts attention from the reasons why, in practice, wages and profits do not converge (much less equalize) in the international economy. What is remarkable to the historian of economic thought is that more than a century ago international trade theory recognized an everyday fact of life that proves fatal to the factor-price equalization theorem: capital competes with other inputs (labour and land) as well as with other capital. This means that the market for goods is not shaped mainly by low-wage labour competing against high-wage labour, as unsophisticated protectionists argue. (More sophisticated protectionists progressed beyond this assumption a century and a half ago.) High-productivity, power-driven capital competes with manual labour and also, to a lesser degree, with skilled high-wage labour.

When Japanese auto makers captured a large part of the American automotive market from the 1960s onward, for instance, it was Japanese capital that undersold American labour as Japan's scientific mechanization of production – and the yen's rising international value – raised the remuneration of Japanese auto workers above that of their US counterparts. Likewise, when American grain undersells that of Argentina and other countries, it is not simply because of the higher natural fertility of US soil. Rather, American agriculture has become more highly mechanized and capital-intensive than that of any other nation. Agricultural capital has been substituted for land and farm labour. Meanwhile, US foreign aid lending provides easy grain credits to food-deficit countries and World Bank lending (reinforced by chronic currency depreciation) diverts their agricultural investment toward the production of plantation export crops. These two

pressures combine to enforce the status quo, keeping these 'Southern' economies in debt to 'Northern' economies, preventing them from developing
more profitable industries and destabilizing their governments if they
attempt to chart an independent course. Thus Guatemala, Cuba, Chile,
Nicaragua, Brazil and other countries undertaking serious land reform have
found themselves the objects of political and economic destabilization.

What do the factor-price equalization theorem and other free-trade
orthodoxies have to say about these phenomena actively shaping trade patterns? Very little.

The world's major nations – England throughout the Industrial
Revolution, and the United States, Germany and Japan prior to the 1940s
– developed dynamic industrial policies not based on free-trade orthodoxy
and its 'equilibrium economics'. However, as these nations have achieved
industrial leads they have adopted international economic orthodoxy, at
least as an ideology to export to increasingly dependent customer countries.
International dependency and unequal gains from trade thus find their
counterpart in asymmetrical economic policies and early theorizing.

The American School of political economists reflected their nation's
position as a less-developed country. They did not want their nation to
develop in the 'normal' way, as a 'hewer of wood and drawer of water' providing raw materials to help England remain the workshop of the world;
they viewed this as *mal*development. Instead they wanted to create something more than economic growth: a new kind of economic civilization
based on the productive powers of capital – above all energy-driven, mechanized production. They recognized that this high-productivity capital
required skilled high-wage labourers as operators and managers.

1.   THE ECONOMICS OF INTERFACTORAL COMPETITION: HOW CAPITAL UNDERSELLS LABOUR

An economic novice might imagine that only since the Second World War
has the role of capital productivity in displacing labour become a subject
on the economic horizon. Was it more natural a few centuries ago to reason
that an economy's labour competed with the labour of other countries, not
with capital?

Actually the theory of how capital produces labour power (and horsepower) equivalents has a long history. James Steuart (1767, p. 159) noted
that machines provide work effort without needing food. To be sure, he
added, new labour is needed to make this machinery, so the result does not
tend to be unemployment. Josiah Tucker (1931, pp. 241–2) had made the

same point in 1757, and William Petty had said much the same thing in 1691 (in a passage probably written in 1665, in *Verbum sapienti*; Petty 1899, p. 118). Adam Smith (*Wealth of Nations*, book I, Chapter i) believed that capital and labour would simply grow together in a natural proportion rather than capital displacing labour. (For a critique of his neglect of machinery in this respect see Hollander 1973, pp. 215, 217, 209.) But Lauderdale (1804, pp. 298–9), in his critique of *The Wealth of Nations*, noted that the nation need not fear that rising wages would stifle business upswings, for employers could substitute capital equipment. (The literature is reviewed in Hudson 1992, pp. 170ff.)

Writers in both Great Britain and the United States tracked machine power in terms of its labour equivalents, but it was the Americans who emphasized that capital was being substituted for labour at different rates internationally. British power looms supplanted labour not only domestically, but in India and the United States as well. If one country possessed machinery that doubled the output of its workers, Alexander Hamilton (1893, pp. 17, 35) wrote in his 1790 'Report on the subject of manufactures', its labour cost to produce a given article would be halved, giving it a corresponding international advantage. Henry Clay picked up this idea in 1824, multiplying Hamilton's example a hundredfold: 'One man at home did the work of two hundred, less or more' (cited in Colton 1846, pp. 159–60).

American economists also perceived another fact that British economists overlooked: the machinery that displaced the most poorly paid manual labour needed skilled high-wage labour to operate it as well as to design and build it. 'It is not by reducing wages that America is making her conquests,' US labour secretary Jacob Schoenhof (1884, p. 19) concluded, 'but by her superior organization, greater efficiency of labor consequent upon the higher standard of living ruling in the country . . . High-priced labor countries are everywhere beating "pauper-labor" countries.'

Steam-powered production not only increased labour productivity, it also threatened to render unskilled and low-wage labour redundant, not only at home but in less industrialized countries as well. These poorer countries, which were 'rich' in low-wage labour, did not develop a comparative advantage in 'labour-intensive' manufactures because there was no such thing as inherently labour-intensive manufactures – or land-intensive agriculture, for that matter. In every sector, labour was being replaced by capital. This was the universal dynamic of industrial progress. Countries that failed to mechanize their production thus were in danger of finding their labour forces becoming industrially obsolete. Low wages were a curse, not an advantage.

The diplomat-lawyer-journalist Erasmus Peshine Smith viewed economic development in terms of energy per worker. Smith was a close

associate of William Henry Seward and, in his economic theorizing, a follower of Henry Carey. His *Manual of Political Economy* (1853) became one
of the most famous American economic books of the period and was translated into French, Italian and German. Smith himself went to Japan as
advisor to the Mikado following the Meiji restoration.

Smith's basic premise was that mechanization lowered the cost of work-
effort applied in the production process (as measured in joules or, by logical
extension, horsepower or kilowatt-hours). The economic imperative of
technological progress was to raise labour from the role of providing merely
brute force to that of applying skills. Smith proceeded to develop a refined
theory of what subsequently would be called human capital.

Following David Ricardo, the English economists had viewed capital
merely as an adjunct to their value theory: the value of capital in production reflected the labour embodied in its manufacture. But as Carey had
pointed out, the value of commodities reflected their reproduction costs.
These costs tended to fall steadily with the progress of technology. It followed that comparative advantage among nations was to be gauged mainly
by the productive powers of the capital with which labour operated.

Smith accordingly formulated what might be called an energy-productiv-
ity theory of value in which capital played a more important role than in
English economics. Rejecting the 'pauper labour' argument that industrial
tariffs were needed to keep out the products of low-wage countries, he
described the American System of political economy as resting 'upon the
belief, that in order to make labor cheap, the laborer must be well-fed, well-
clothed, well-lodged, well instructed, not only in the details of his handi-
craft, but in all general knowledge that can in any way be made subsidiary
to it. All these cost money to the employer and repay it with interest' (Smith
1852, p. 42). What appeared to be highly paid labour on a per diem basis
thus turned out to be inexpensive on a unit-cost basis.

Employment of labour required a complementary investment in capital,
noted Smith (1853, p. 107): 'As we rise to labor in connection with more
complicated machinery, the value of general intelligence becomes distinctly
apparent.' As Schoenhof observed a generation later (1892, p. 27): 'In
almost every employment of an industrial nature a very great amount of
training is requisite to make it effective or to make it serviceable at all. Only
in times of a very great demand and scarcity of labour would any one
employ crude labor in factories where skill is required.' The minimum necessary educational level rose over time, as labour required increasingly
intensive training and education as a precondition for employment – not
only within the national economy, but internationally as well. It followed
that nations that promoted education would be in the best position to ride
the wave of technological progress and undersell other nations. This inci-

dentally seemed to favour democracies over autocracies (a principle long noted by British writers as well).

If there is no such thing as inherently labour-intensive commodities (given the tendency of machinery to displace labour), then factor endowment theories miss the point in viewing countries as having a natural advantage in either labour- or capital-intensive products. Trade does not necessarily provide a demand for each nation's particular mix of labour and capital. Countries may be left behind if their unskilled labour becomes too poor and technologically obsolete to work with high-productivity capital.

In focusing on steam-powered production as the mainspring in economic development, Peshine Smith exemplified the dictum of Friedrich List (1885, p. 170) that political economy should not aim simply at increasing 'the values of exchange in the nation, but of increasing the amount of its productive powers'. But he went further. List had remained in the German Romantic tradition in not explaining just how to quantify productive powers economically. It is a reflection of how far Smith's generation of American protectionists progressed beyond List that in reviewing the first American translation of List's *National System*, Smith complained (in Horace Greeley's *New York Tribune*, 12 April 1856) that the book was too historical and empirical. In terms of actual economic theory, 'all he has done is to substitute the "Theory of Productive Force" for that of Values'. To be sure, Smith granted:

> He shows that the European Economists overlook the truth that 'the power of creating wealth is vastly more important than wealth itself.' . . . Their system ignores what may be called virtual or latent wealth, and treats nations as if they were actually exerting the whole productive power of which they are capable; and the only question was how their forces should be directed. The moment this idea is introduced, their theory explodes.

The obsolescence function – the degree to which existing capital equipment and labour find their revenue reduced because of rising productivity from newly produced capital and more recently educated labour – applies in agriculture as well as industry. It reflects the tendency of technological innovation to render existing technologies – and the labour required to operate them – obsolete. The upshot has been that the industrial nations have become supreme not only in manufactured products but also in food-stuffs. While North American and European agriculture has enhanced soil fertility by the application of fertilizers, pesticides and herbicides, and freed labour by mechanizing production, the socially backward 'Southern' economies have been unable to compete. Over the past century the world has seen raw materials monocultures from Latin America to Africa deteriorate into food-deficit economies.

Most European economists rejected the technological analysis of economic development. Reviewing the *Manual* in France, Jean Gustave Courcelle-Seneuil (1853), just before leaving for a decade-long professorship in Santiago, Chile, complained that Smith's approach was too 'specifically American' for him to understand: 'In order to found his theory on purely physical laws, Peshine Smith has simply left the realm of economic science.' The *Manual*'s emphasis on the effect of international trade on soil productivity (in viewing ecological depletion as a by-product of single-crop monocultures) entailed propositions 'in truth, more agricultural than economic'.

This did not say much for the relevance of economic science to the dynamics set in motion by industrial and agricultural technology. Ricardo's theory that each nation gained from specializing in 'what it was good at producing' turns out, upon examination, to be static and obsolete when applied to real-world development. Today's trade theory remains in the Ricardian tradition by not recognizing the technological imperatives analysed a century and half ago by the American School.

2. FITTING TECHNOLOGY AND OBSOLESCENCE INTO TRADE THEORY (AND ECONOMICS PROPER)

By failing to trace the effect of trade on national productive powers, free-trade theorizing (and neoclassical economics in general) remains merely a theory of market-clearing price equilibrium achieved through the forces of supply and demand, not a dynamic analysis of how economies evolve in terms of their long-term trends and social structures. It would be more than a century before modern economists would rediscover the principle that production costs fall as capital is substituted for labour, and the corollary that economies (or specific companies within given industries) may achieve such great progress as to render existing technologies commercially obsolete, along with outdated machinery and relatively untrained labour. The obsolescence function applies to labour because 'low-paid laborers cannot afford to acquire the training or education necessary to raise their status in production at the rate required by twentieth-century technology' (Hudson 1972a, pp. 125–6). These phenomena are fatal both to the factor-price equalization theorem and to its twin factor endowments theory of comparative advantage.

Instead of asking what conditions might lead wages and profits to equalize in the world economy, economics could gain greater respectability as a discipline by asking why the world's economies are polarizing rather than converging. But a methodological trap lurks for economists who imagine that the badge of scientific method is the ability to mathematize problems. A single determinate mathematical solution emerges only in a world of diminishing returns. Increasing returns would not produce an equilibrium tendency, and certainly would not lead to factor-price equalization but rather to a polarizing world in which lead nations extend their advantage over economically obsolete countries. Such countries are not so much 'less developed' as maldeveloped. Latin American and African agriculture, for instance, is blocked by inequitable land tenure patterns, rendering these continents dependent on the industrial economies for their basic food needs and hence subject to potentially coercive diplomacy (Hudson 1972b and 1977). Diplomatic coercion, especially in reinforcing agricultural back-wardness, shows up, for example, in the financial pressures that the IMF and the World Bank applied in Russia, Indonesia and elsewhere in the late 1990s. These loan programmes promote capital-intensive export sectors, whose proceeds accrue to the large multinationals, side by side with capital-starved low-wage domestic subsistence sectors.

3.   THE FINANCIAL CONTEXT FOR CAPITAL-INTENSIVE TECHNOLOGY

In addition to failing to analyse competitive advantage in terms of capital productivity, today's economic theory neglects to analyse how capital is 'costed'. By this term financial analysts refer not merely to the purchase price of a machine amortized over its productive lifetime on a unit-cost basis, but also to its financial costs, reflecting the interest rate charged, the debt maturity and the mix of debt and equity financing. The important point is that in today's world, technology is not only a product of engineer-ing; it exists in a financial context. As technological paths become more capital-intensive, the decision to employ a given technology turns largely on how it is financially costed. Direct investment in machinery and factories must be financed either internally (with retained earnings) or externally by some combination of bonds, equity stock issues and bank debt. Interest rates on such debt vary from country to country, as do price–earnings ratios for stocks (and hence the cost of equity capital).

Modern economies accordingly must be analysed not just in terms of their factors of production, but also in terms of their growth (often over-growth) of financial and other rentier claims on income and wealth. Yet today's 'value-free' economics mistakes the FIRE-sector (finance, insu-rance and real estate) overhead for wealth itself. It counts all labour and other remunerated economic activity as productive, regardless of its eco-nomic consequences.

Yet when we examine the competitiveness of specific industries (for example, electronics, autos and other manufacturing), the key variable often turns out to be the cost of capital. Countries are financially uncompetitive when their banking systems provide credit at so high a price that producers must factor in higher interest rates, higher debt–equity ratios, lower price–earnings ratios and shorter debt maturities than their foreign competitors. Austerity programmes which tighten domestic credit block new capital-intensive investment.

Such financial considerations are central to any corporate planner but have not found their way into academic economics. Economists have no perception of countries falling so deeply into debt that most of their income must go to service their debt, which, in turn, prevents them from competing with low-debt and low-rent economies. Although the same physical technology is available to all countries, financial considerations may render any given technology less remunerative in one economy than in others. Unfortunately, economists avoid having to cope with such problems by dismissing them as 'external economies', that is, considerations lying outside the narrow scope of factors recognized by most policy-making theory.

The fact that new technology requires lead time for research and development means that profits cannot simply be paid out to investors as dividends. They must be reinvested in research to develop more new products or to cut costs on existing output. But the spread of corporate raiding in the 1980s led companies to make quick pay-outs rather than invest in long-term development. Such pay-outs were needed either to support stock prices against potential raiders or (in the case of companies that were already raided) to pay off the high-interest ('junk') bond-holders.

Postclassical economics has dropped the study of land as a distinct factor of production, telescoping it into capital in general. This obviates the study of land tenure as a cause of backwardness and agricultural obsolescence. To be sure, the mechanization of farming is largely responsible for America's remarkable growth in agricultural productivity. But land also has a pure site value. Fortunes are made by reclassifying rural land as developable suburban land. And to the extent that savings are recycled to create a real estate bubble (as distinct from a stock market bubble), rents may be raised.

Fiscal, financial and related rentier charges do not reflect factor prices as such. They are claims on income or wealth that do not reflect actual inputs. If they have been neglected by most economic theorists, the reason seems largely to reflect the FIRE sector's interest in not allowing its behaviour to become a subject of economic analysis, part of the screen of invisibility which has been erected around the FIRE sector and its rentier income overhead.

4. THE ROLE OF CAPITAL TRANSFERS IN FACTOR-PRICE POLARIZATION AND THE CHOICE OF TECHNOLOGIES

An implicit corollary of the factor-price equalization theorem is the purchasing parity theory of exchange rates. This theory (perhaps 'rule of thumb' might be a more accurate label) states that currency values tend to reflect the cost of a similar market basket of commodities in different countries. The logic is that if such prices vary (at least under free-trade conditions), trade will occur to equalize prices in a unified world economy. But as any traveller knows, international prices tend to vary widely, especially in Third World debtor economies. And any balance of payments analyst knows why: most foreign transactions (like most transactions within domestic economies) are not for goods and services but for capital investments and their reciprocal debt service or earnings remittances. These capital account items (and I include debt service as being functionally a part of the capital account of assets and liabilities) overshadow commodity trade. Stated another way, currency values have become primarily a function of capital transfers. In balance of payments terms, the capital account drives the current account.

To be sure, international prices are plugged into certain common denominators. Raw materials have a common world price, as do physical capital goods. Capital and management also have more or less common world prices. These prices typically are set in US dollars, and hence are not influenced by currency depreciation.

When currencies are devalued, the major price influenced is that of domestic labour. In addition, foreign debt service becomes more expensive as calculated in the local currency. Devaluation therefore diverts purchasing power from the domestic sector to the foreign sector. The case of Latin America is instructive in this regard. Debt service, along with domestic capital flight, exerts chronic downward pressure on the entire region's currency values as governments devalue their currencies in a desperate (and vain) attempt to stimulate trade in order to service their debt and replace lost domestic capital.

Austerity programmes deny the credit needed to apply capital-intensive technologies. The policy of 'stabilizing public budgets' by taxing domestic income while depreciating the currency favours crude labour-intensive technologies rather than more capital-intensive ones

CONCLUSION

If the purpose of economic theory is to explain existing (and future) production and trade patterns, it is necessary to take into account not only the physical engineering aspects of technology but also the broad array of financial, fiscal and institutional factors that determine the economy-wide costs of such technologies. All these factors contribute to making Third World countries and the formerly socialist economies 'hewers of wood and drawers of water', as the American technology theorists put it in the nineteenth century.

A total economic theory is needed – not merely a theory of market-clearing prices, but an overall development theory. As long as such theories are marginalized into special subdisciplines of academia, economics will remain sidetracked by a non-developmental, asocial and apolitical theory based on tenets it takes as God-given, not to be questioned. Neoclassical economic theory does not accurately describe or adequately explain what actually happens in the real world. As Groucho Marx put it in one of his movies, 'Who are you going to believe – me, or your eyes?'

REFERENCES

Colton, Calvin (1846), *Life and Times of Henry Clay*, 2 vols, New York: Barnes and Co.

Colton, Calvin (1848), *Public Economy for the United States*, New York: Barnes & Co.

Courcelle-Seneuil, Jean Gustave (1853), 'Comte rendu du "Manuel d'economie politique" de M. Peshine Smith', *Journal des Economists*, **38**, 239–42.

Hamilton, Alexander (1893 [1790]), 'Report on the subject of manufactures', reprinted in Frank Taussig (ed.), *State Papers and Speeches on the Tariff*, Cambridge, MA: Harvard University.

Hollander, Samuel (1973), *The Economics of Adam Smith*, Toronto: University of Toronto Press.

Hudson, Michael (1972a), 'Obsolescent factors in the international economy', *Review of Social Economics*, **30**, 112–40.

Hudson, Michael (1972b), *Super Imperialism: The Economic Strategy of American Empire*, New York: Holt, Rinehart & Winston.

Hudson, Michael (1975), *Economics and Technology in Nineteenth-Century American Thought: The Neglected American Economists*, New York: Garland Press.

Hudson, Michael (1977), *Global Fracture: The New International Economic Order*, New York: Harper and Row.

Hudson, Michael (1992), *Trade, Development and Foreign Debt: A History of Theories of Polarization versus Convergence in the World Economy*, 2 vols, London: Pluto Press.

Lauderdale, James Maitland, Eighth Earl of (1804), *Observations by the Earl of*

Lauderdale, on the Review of His Inquiry into the Nature and Origin of Public Wealth, Edinburgh: Constable & Co.

List, Friedrich (1885), *National System of Political Economy*, London: Longmans, Green & Co.

Petty, William (1899), *The Economic Writings of Sir William Petty*, ed. C.H. Hull, vol. 1, Cambridge: Cambridge University Press.

Schoenhof, Jacob (1884), *Wages and Trade in Manufacturing Industries in America and in Europe*, New York: New York Free-Trade Club.

Schoenhof, Jacob (1892), *The Economy of High Wages*, New York: Putnam's Sons.

Smith, E. Peshine (1852), 'The law of progress in the relations of capital and labor', *Hunt's Merchants' Magazine*, **26**.

Smith, E. Peshine (1853), *Manual of Political Economy*, New York: Putnam.

Steuart, James (1767), *An Inquiry into the Principles of Political Œconomy*, vol. 1, London: Millar & Cadell.

Tucker, Josiah (1931), *Josiah Tucker: A Selection from His Economic and Political Writings*, ed. R.L. Schuyler, New York: Columbia University Press.

PART III

The strategy of failure: late twentieth-century deindustrialization and the economics of retrogression

5. Natural resources, industrialization and fluctuating standards of living in Peru, 1950–97: a case study of activity-specific economic growth*

Santiago Roca and Luis Simabuko

Peru's recent economic policy, like that of most Latin American countries,[1] has followed the so-called Washington Consensus. This set of policies precludes the implementation of strategic industrial policies or any active, deliberate construction of competitive advantages by promoting particular sectors or economic activities. In the Washington Consensus, all economic activities are seen as qualitatively alike. Indiscriminately opening any nation to the 'magic of the market' will allow that nation to acquire the necessary long-term external competitiveness, promote economic growth and enhance its standard of living, regardless of the country's productive specialization.

This chapter evaluates whether the type of productive specialization and trade in specific products has affected economic growth and standards of living in Peru. It seeks to determine if the prevalence of producing or trading goods from specific sectors – whether natural resources, industrial or service – has an impact, positive or negative, on the people's standard of living and well-being. To this end, we analyse Peruvian data for the last 50 years of the twentieth century, paying special attention to expansion and recession cycles and to industrialization policies implemented in Peru's economy since the end of the 1950s.

Our two core hypotheses, which are strongly related, are as follows. (1) In Peru during the last 50 years of the twentieth century, the standard of living was inversely related to the weight of the primary sector in the total economy. In other words, the standard of living of the population declines as raw materials and extractive activities grow at the expense of the manufacturing sector. We have named the combination of a shrinking manufacturing sector and a growing primary sector 'deindustrialization'. (2) The economy becomes increasingly fragile if, as a result of international specialization, the nation sells increasing amounts of simple raw materials in exchange for foreign goods which require greater manufacturing skill and more advanced technology.

The first section provides a brief overview of the theoretical framework that explains how economic activities are differentiated and why countries that specialize in producing and trading goods of 'lower quality' eventually erode their standards of living. The second section presents quantitative data on standards of living and the major types of activities that dominated in the Peruvian economy over the last half of the twentieth century. The third section presents our main findings concerning the relationship between deindustrialization, industrialization and real wages, and the fourth section provides an evaluation of the increasing gap of quality and value between Peruvian exports and imports. And finally, we offer some recommendations on how Peru can benefit from the era of globalization.

1.   THEORETICAL CONSIDERATIONS

Most classical literature about economic growth holds that a nation's choice of economic activities is not the critical element; rather, theory holds that economic growth depends on the abundance and best use of capital, labour or natural resources. In more complicated models factors such as technology, infrastructure, free trade, government's efficiency, savings and investment, education, individual effort and the driving force of the people are included as well. However, little or no attention has been paid to economists who underscore the type of products a country turns out as a major factor in economic growth. Reinert (1995, 1996, 1998) has explored more than 500 years of economic history to show that economic growth and real wages to a large extent have been determined by the type of activities nations pursue. Graham (1923) presents the essence of the extremely important nineteenth-century argument for a nation to specialize in economic activities subject to increasing rather than diminishing returns to scale. Graham shows that the standard of living and income level of two countries that specialize in production and engage in trade on the basis of their comparative advantages will improve if, and only if, both countries can produce similar returns.

If one country specializes in producing goods with increasing returns while the other specializes in producing goods with diminishing returns, the income of the world at large will increase, but revenues in the country that produces goods at diminishing returns will decrease while revenues in the country with increasing returns will rise. This means that one country will be wealthier and the other poorer although the world as a whole will become wealthier.[2] We have further elaborated on Graham's initial exercise to show that trade between countries with similar returns favours both countries, but if one country has growing or constant returns and the other has diminishing returns, the former will prosper to the disadvantage of the latter (Appendix).

Another argument underscoring the influence of the type of productive activity on economic growth was advanced in the 1950s and 1960s by authors such as Hirschman (1961), Prebisch (1970), Singer (1981), Seers and Leonard (1975) and Myrdal (1963). Prebisch holds that countries specializing in raw materials and natural resources are harmed because the prices of raw materials grow relatively less rapidly than prices of manufactured products. Hirschman believes that agriculture lacks the upstream and downstream linkages and the complex division of labour that characterize manufacturing. Myrdal mentions the 'cumulative causation' present in manufacturing but not found in natural resources development. Others point to higher income elasticity and increased growth of demand for manufacturing goods compared to primary products.

In the 1990s, Matsuyama (1992) and others pointed to the fact that manufacturing shows positive growth effects that are absent in agriculture and stem from higher induced learning. This means there are a number of learning externalities that neither agriculture nor the service sector – in the absence of a healthy manufacturing base – can provide.

Sachs and Warner (1995) present an empirical, comparative world survey showing that countries richly endowed with natural resources grow less than countries specializing in tradable manufactured products. Yet they fail to explain the reasons underlying those differences and then argue that free trade is beneficial for all parties involved.

Within the theory of trade, Krugman (1991) and Krugman and Obstfeld (1995) maintain that one economic activity may be better than another only if there are market imperfections that include positive externalities originating in technological innovation or the existence of rents in highly concentrated oligopolistic industries.[3]

Graham's 1923 paper shows how the choice of economic activity will determine wealth or poverty in a world with important scale effects but without technical change. Reinert (1980) discusses the intrinsic difficulty of separating increasing returns and technical change during nineteenth- and twentieth-century industrialization. Although clearly separable in theory, increasing returns and technical change are often inseparable in reality. Previous technologies are most often not available in the new scale of operations. For this reason Schumpeter coined the term 'historical increasing returns', which includes the combined effect of increasing returns and technical change over time.

Reinert (1996, 1998) takes a more dynamic, encompassing and integrating viewpoint of economic history that addresses and complements theories about competitiveness and corporate strategy by authors including Porter (1990), Marrus (1984) and David (1986). Reinert argues that economic activities are different from a qualitative vantage point and that they determine economic growth and income disparities among nations. He proposes a 'quality index' for economic activities, in which countries that grow are those that focus on producing 'high-quality' goods while nations that engage in 'low-quality' activities grow less or retrogress.

High-quality goods typically feature increasing returns and are produced under conditions of imperfect competition with steeply sloping learning curves, rapid technological changes, large-scale R&D and investment, high growth and income demand elasticity rates, economies of scale, numerous linkages, a high and complex division of labour, a significant need to 'learn by doing', high industrial concentration, imperfect yet extremely dynamic information flows, high barriers to market entry and exit, and high salaries. All of these industries closely follow the assumptions of Schumpeter's theory of imperfect though dynamic and changing competition.

Low-quality goods are characterized by precisely the opposite conditions – that is, all of those activities that closely reflect the traditional assumptions of the neoclassical theory of production, trade and growth.

According to Reinert (1996), trade among industrial and non-industrial nations is characterized by asymmetrical exchanges between industries that on the one hand feature rapid technological change and large economies of scale, competing under conditions of imperfect competition, and on the other hand industries characterized by diminishing returns and perfect competition. Moreover, he holds that present-day industrial economies historically chose to follow an active and deliberate path to 'high-quality' goods production by enforcing highly successful industrial and commercial strategies. Having established themselves firmly in high-quality activities, wealthy nations subsequently do not permit developing nations to copy the strategy they used to make the transition from poor to wealthy nations. This was the accusation that the young United States levelled against England.

2. STANDARD OF LIVING AND TYPE OF ECONOMIC ACTIVITY: PERU 1950–97

Based on the hypothesis that growth and standards of living depend on the type of activity in which a country specializes, this section analyses the evolution of standards of living and the major economic activities that characterized Peru in the last half of the twentieth century.

2.1   Legal and Institutional Aspects: Industrial and Labour Policies

Both the type of economic activity and the standard of living of any economy are influenced not just by economic and market cycles, but also by industrial, labour and income policies and by institutional factors and diverse cultural elements. Although we do not attempt to identify every one of these factors, it is necessary to take into account the wider trade, industrial and income policy periods that Peru experienced in the last 50 years of the twentieth century.

Since 1959, Peru's productive activities were to varying extents influenced by the Industrial Promotion Law, which introduced substantial incentives for industrial investment. Some of the schemes included in this law underscored tax incentives for reinvestment and effective protection of the manufacturing industry by reducing tariffs on capital goods imports, parts and raw materials while increasing them on consumer goods imports (Ferrari 1992, Portocarrero and Nunura 1984).

The 1959 law was followed by the 1970 Industrial Promotion Act and 1981 and 1986 bills that slightly modified the initial regulations. However, the crucial role afforded to incentive policies, and to the state's role as regulator, planner and even producer, was maintained. These were the characteristics of the industrial policy introduced in 1970 when state-owned companies started to expand.

The concept of priority industries was introduced in 1970 to promote the development of basic industries including cement, paper, basic chemicals, steel, fertilizers and oil refining, all of which were reserved exclusively for the state. Manufacturing was promoted through the tax structure, tariffs, credits and administrative schemes. In 1981 and 1986, although the existing industrial policy was largely preserved, the state's monopoly and the definition of priority industries were cancelled, as were tax exemptions for reinvested profits.

From the 1960s to the 1980s industrialization policies generally favoured permanent protection for all types of industries devoted to producing finished products for a local market where there was little internal competition. There existed no learning processes or linkages with foreign countries, technology was imported, and the policy as a whole was enforced with a static planning vision of the world and of business. This policy sought to create an industry to assemble imported parts and components without paying much attention to education, creativity and training. It thus had little chance of linking up with a broader market. Income and job allocation in industry were ruled by a static rent- and profit-seeking attitude, and by a culture based on nepotism rather than merit. Government assumed an oversized entrepreneurial role that lacked synergy and eventually excluded and displaced domestic and foreign private investment.

The first half of the 1970s saw the emergence of revenue measures and reforms that initially fostered wage and salary growth and that were related to the land and company reforms. Likewise, a number of labour regulations enacted during that period made lay-offs more difficult while giving workers job tenure and strengthening unions.

In the 1990s all the previous industrial, labour and income policy schemes were cancelled. The new government policy suspended the main tax exemptions, reduced tariff structure and lifted price controls while financial, exchange and trade regulations were liberalized. Job tenure was eliminated and labour legislation was made more flexible, thus dramatically reducing the power of unions. A radical government downsizing programme through privatization and the sale of state-owned assets was introduced and restrictions on the flow of foreign private capital were lifted.

As we shall see, the relative importance of the manufacturing sector grew through the enforcement of industrial policies only until the mid-1970s and was later reduced in the wake of earlier stabilization programmes. To the extent that industrial development was based on developing the domestic market through industrialization that focused on import substitution, the enforcement of adjustment programmes inevitably led to receding national industrialization. Concurrently, standards of living and income levels fell as a result of booming population growth and lower factor productivity.

2.2 Evolution of GDP and Major Economic Activities

Peru's economy grew at an annual 3.3 per cent average rate[4] from 1950 to 1997 but its annual performance was very irregular and less than satisfactory (see Figure 5.1). In the 20 years from 1950 to 1970, the annual average growth rate reached 5 per cent with only two years of recession and stagnation in 1958 (−0.6 per cent) and 1968 (0.4 per cent).

Between 1970 and 1990, annual growth was 1.7 per cent including several periods of strong economic contraction caused by weather difficulties such as the 1983 El Niño anomaly (−12.6 per cent) and drought in 1992 (−1.4 per cent) as well as by adjustment and stabilization programmes in 1976–78, 1988–89 and 1990. Finally, during the 1990–97 period, the economy grew at an annual 5.7 per cent rate despite the fact that production in 1997 was only 13 per cent greater than in 1987.

A breakdown of GDP by period and economic sector in the 1950s and 1960s reveals that fisheries activities led growth at an annual average rate of 19 per cent and 9.3 per cent respectively, while energy (electricity, gas and water) grew 8.8 per cent and 7.4 per cent, and manufacturing expanded 7.1

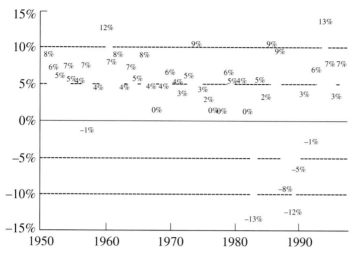

Figure 5.1 Gross domestic product, 1950–2000 (% change annually)

Table 5.1 GDP annual average growth by activities (%)

	1950–60	1960–70	1970–80	1980–90	1990–97	1950–97
Global	5.0	5.0	3.6	−0.3	5.7	3.3
Agriculture	1.5	3.1	0.5	2.4	5.7	2.0
Fisheries	19.0	9.3	−4.6	9.3	5.1	5.5
Mining	7.2	3.8	7.8	−3.3	2.8	3.8
Manufacturing	7.1	5.5	2.9	−0.4	5.4	3.4
Electricity, gas and water	8.8	7.4	9.4	3.0	6.6	7.1
Construction	4.9	3.5	3.1	−0.5	12.1	3.1
Housing	3.4	2.9	2.9	1.6	1.4	2.6
Government	4.7	5.4	4.7	0.7	0.7	3.5
Other	5.2	6.0	3.8	−0.9	6.3	3.5

Source: Perú National Statistics Institute (INEI).

per cent and 5.5 per cent for the respective years. Such levels of growth gave these productive sectors a significantly larger share in global GDP in the first two decades of the periods under consideration (see Table 5.1).

In the mid-1970s, macroeconomic imbalances and stabilization policies reduced the pace of economic growth to 3.6 per cent per annum. The most dynamic industries in that period were energy, mining and government services. However, fisheries fell, agriculture stagnated and manufacturing grew barely above population growth. Evolution in the 1980s was even more dramatic, given the higher vulnerability of the external sector. To this we may add populist policies enforced during 1985–89 that eventually led to a 0.3 per cent yearly drop in GDP. Excepting fisheries and energy, all other economic activities performed poorly, in particular mining, construction and manufacturing.

By 1997 annual average growth had reached 5.7 per cent for that decade, with construction leading growth, followed by electricity, gas and water and commerce and services. The most obvious laggard sectors were government services, rental housing and mining. Product mix during 1990–97 underwent substantial restructuring to the benefit of agriculture and construction, with less importance attributed to mining and government services.

Generally, the industrial policy enforced since the end of the 1950s led to the development of the manufacturing industry, which increased its share from 19 per cent in 1950 to a maximum 25.5 per cent in 1976. However, together with poor management of the agricultural companies created by the state, this industrial policy led to the relative fall of agriculture, which dropped from 23.7 per cent in 1950 to 9.9 per cent of GDP in 1980 (Table 5.2).

In the 1980s and 1990s, manufacturing took a step backwards compared to the 1970s, with a clear trend towards deindustrialization. The reasons can be found in the effects of the recession provoked by stabilization programmes and by the suspension since 1990 of various industrial promotion and protection schemes and incentives that had been in place since 1959. Evolution in most other sectors was basically influenced by exogenous factors, be they foreign (as in mining), weather (fisheries), population

Table 5.2   GDP structure by activity (%)

	1950	1960	1970	1980	1990	1997
Agriculture	23.7	17.1	14.2	9.9	13.4	13.2
Fisheries	0.2	1.0	1.9	0.5	1.3	1.1
Mining	7.6	10.3	9.1	12.9	10.1	8.3
Manufacturing	19.0	23.6	24.9	23.8	22.1	22.0
Electricity, gas and water	0.3	0.5	0.6	1.1	1.6	1.8
Construction	5.9	5.4	5.3	5.5	5.9	8.8
Housing	4.1	3.3	2.6	2.4	3.2	2.5
Government	5.9	5.5	5.7	6.4	6.7	4.6
Other	33.2	33.4	35.7	37.5	35.7	37.8

Source: INEI. Prepared by the authors.

(electricity, gas and water) or relating to the expansion of government expenditure (as in construction and government services).

An easier way to classify productive specialization in Peru over the past half century is by dividing GDP into four large economic groups or sectors: (1) extractive or primary activities (agriculture, fisheries and mining); (2) basic transformation or infrastructure (construction); (3) intermediate or industrial transformation (manufacturing); and (4) services (home rentals, government, electricity, gas and water, commerce, services and others).

Although this standardized classification is rather broad and does not accurately reflect the 'quality index for economic activities' proposed in the theoretical framework, we still do not have a methodology that will allow us to classify economic activities by use-intensity and technological upgrading capabilities, nor from the viewpoint of their relationship to increasing, constant or diminishing returns.[5]

Despite these constraints, we can assume that on average, natural resources activities are extractive and create goods with diminishing returns in perfectly competitive markets with low salaries. Infrastructure and manufacturing activities are processes with increasing returns, operating in imperfect markets, with larger technology investments, higher salaries. The service sector falls somewhere between the two.[6]

Table 5.3 shows GDP structure according to the four suggested sectors. Clearly, in the third quarter century, from 1950 to 1975, the primary sector's participation decreased by a significant 12 points. In the 1980s and 1990s, this sector's importance increased again, from 19.2 to 22.5 per cent.

Manufacturing activities (including processing of primary resources

Table 5.3   GDP structure by activity (%)

	Primary	Industrial	Construction	Services
1950	31.6	19.0	5.9	43.5
1955	27.5	21.7	7.9	42.9
1960	28.4	23.6	5.4	42.6
1965	24.9	24.6	5.8	44.6
1970	25.2	24.9	5.3	44.6
1975	19.2	25.1	6.7	49.0
1980	23.3	23.8	5.5	47.4
1985	25.1	21.8	4.6	48.5
1990	24.7	22.1	5.9	47.2
1995	22.7	22.2	8.5	46.5
1997	22.5	22.0	8.8	46.7

Source: INEI. Prepared by the authors.

such as fishmeal, frozen fish, sugar, non-ferrous metals and refined oil) also increased their share as a result of industrialization policies and reached a maximum 25 per cent of GDP in 1975 then to fall again in 1980, 1990 and 1997.

Throughout the period under consideration, construction never increased its share of GDP above 7 per cent, except in 1955 when it reached 7.9 per cent and in more recent years when, propelled by government expenditures and expanded home building in the private sector, it reached almost 9 per cent of GDP.

And finally, services increased their relative share from 43 per cent in the 1950s to 47 per cent in the 1990s.

2.3   Standard of Living: Per Capita Product, Per Capita Consumption and Remuneration

A simple way to classify levels of income and standards of living is through indicators like per capita product and consumption, and salaries (white-collar income) and wages (blue-collar income). Although it is true that these indicators may hide inequality and income distribution disparities, they do constitute reasonable criteria for this essay.

Taking into consideration that population grew at an annual average rate of 2.6 per cent, GDP per capita from 1950 to 1997 grew annually at a 0.7 per cent rate, and private per capita consumption grew by 0.6 per cent. It would take at least 100 years for income per capita and the population's purchasing power to double at these rates. Despite such overall poor performance, we can observe rapid growth in the first 25 years of the period under study, which led GDP and consumption per capita in the mid-1970s to rise 80 per cent above the corresponding 1950 figures. However, in subsequent years there was a notorious falling trend so that per capita income in 1997, although 69 per cent higher than in the 1950s, was 11 per cent lower than the historical record reached in 1981. Moreover, current per capita private consumption is 52 per cent higher than that of the 1950s but 17 per cent below the historical record achieved in 1975 (see Figure 5.2).

Table 5.4 shows that GDP and per capita consumption growth have not evolved in parallel. Quite the contrary, there have been alternating periods where income growth exceeded consumption growth and, conversely, in other periods consumption exceeded the growth of income. Thus, in the 1950s, 1970s and 1990s per capita GDP growth exceeded the growth of private consumption while it was lower in the 1960s and 1980s.

Between 1960 and 1997, real salaries (white-collar) and wages (blue-collar) fell at an average annual 4.2 per cent and 3.7 per cent rates, respectively, thus diminishing more steeply than per capita revenues and

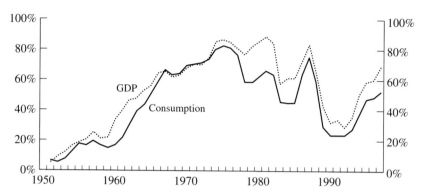

*Figure 5.2   GDP and private consumption per capita (cumulative %
change)*

consumption. Workers' earnings were most severely hit during the 1980s
when they fell between 9 per cent and 10 per cent annually, so that earnings
in 1990 were scarcely between 21 per cent and 29 per cent of those prevailing in 1960 (Figure 5.3).

Economic growth in the 1990s was basically reflected in higher compensation for white-collar employees (salaries), and to a lesser degree in blue-
collar labourers (wages). Real salaries in 1997 were 50 per cent higher than
in 1990, while wages were only 10 per cent higher. Despite growth in recent
years, real earnings in 1997 fell by 68 per cent compared to 1960.

Generally, living standards over the last half century measured either by
per capita private consumption or by real wages and salaries were characterized by an upward trend until the mid-1970s, and then by a strong
contraction with the introduction of economic stabilization programmes.
However, wages and salaries suffered a stronger decline (−75 per cent since
1973) than per capita consumption (−17 per cent since 1975), showing that
those white- and blue-collar salary and wage earners bore the brunt of economic adjustment.

3.   THE RELATIONSHIP BETWEEN PRIMARY
ACTIVITIES, INDUSTRIALIZATION AND
STANDARD OF LIVING

This section analyses the relationship between Peru's productive specialization categorized by product as proposed in Section 2.2, and the population's standard of living and income estimated in Section 2.3. More
specifically, it determines whether higher relative development of primary

Table 5.4   Annual Average Growth: GDP, Private Consumption and Remuneration (%)

	1950–60	1960–70	1970–80	1980–90	1990–97	1950–97	1960–97
GDP per capita	2.4	2.2	0.9	−2.5	3.9	0.7	−0.06
Consumption per capita	1.5	3.8	−0.7	−1.8	3.5	0.6	−0.2
Real salaries (white-collar)	NA	−1.0	−5.8	−9.0	6.6	NA	−4.2
Real wages (blue-collar)	NA	0.6	−2.2	−10.5	0.9	NA	−3.7

Source: INEI. Prepared by the authors.

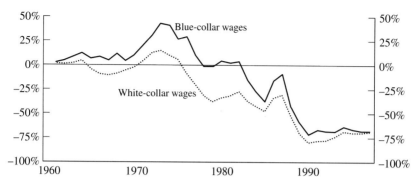

Figure 5.3   Real remuneration, 1960–2000 (cumulative % change)

goods, infrastructure, manufacturing or services is linked to higher living standards measured through wages and salaries or per capita private consumption.

A relationship between productive specialization and standard of living is proposed for both the long- and short-term periods. In the long run, the most relevant economic growth factors are increased productivity, economies of scale, technological innovation, labour specialization and capital stock increases. In the short term, macroeconomic fundamentals and imbalances are the key factors.

3.1   The Long-Term Factor: Specialization in Sectors with Diminishing Returns and Poor Technological Development

By plotting the percentage variation in living standards to the vertical axis and the changes in primary activities as a percentage of GDP to the horizontal axis we observe an inverse (or negative) relationship between the relative importance of primary or extractive activities (such as agriculture, fisheries and mining) and private per capita consumption or real earnings (Figure 5.4). Simply put, higher participation of primary activities leads to lower private per capita consumption, salaries and wages.

Figure 5.5 shows a similar but opposite relationship for manufacturing. As industrialization increases, higher per capita consumption and earnings (salaries and wages) are observed, meaning that increases in the industrialization index would imply higher standards of living.

A simple regression analysis by least squares for the period 1950–97 shows that for every incremental percentage point of extractive activities, private consumption falls by approximately 2.6 per cent while white-collar salaries fall by –5.4 per cent and blue-collar wages by –7.4 per cent (Table

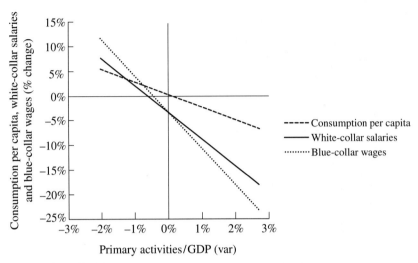

Source: See Table 5.5.

Figure 5.4 *Consumption per capita, white-collar salaries, blue-collar wages and deindustrialization*

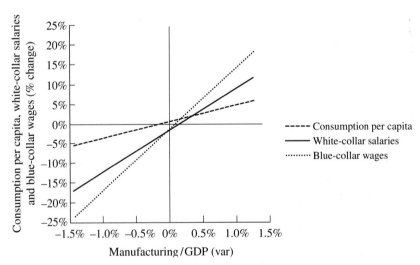

Source: See Table 5.5.

Figure 5.5 *Consumption per capita, white-collar salaries, blue-collar wages and industrialization*

Table 5.5   Impact of productive specialization on standards of living, 1950–1997

Independent variable:	Primary	Manufacturing	Construction	Services
Dependent variable:				
Consumption per capita, 1952–1997				
Coefficient (c_0)	0.46	0.66	0.68	0.86
Impact (c_1)	−2.58[1]	4.22[1]	3.12[1]	0.05[2]
R-squared	0.41	0.43	0.28	0.18
Durbin Watson Stat.	1.85	1.83	1.65	1.64
White-collar salaries, 1962–1997				
Coefficient (c_0)	−3.16	−1.66	−2.71	−2.33
Impact (c_1)	−5.41[1]	10.60[1]	5.79[2]	0.28[2]
R-squared	0.39	0.47	0.26	0.21
Durbin Watson Stat.	1.89	1.78	1.78	1.71
Blue-collar wages, 1962–1997				
Coefficient (c_0)	−3.22	−1.43	−2.73	−2.31
Impact (c_1)	−7.36[1]	15.52[1]	6.97[2]	0.54[2]
R-squared	0.35	0.50	0.11	0.05
Durbin Watson Stat.	2.13	1.97	1.92	1.90

Notes:
[1] Statistically significant at 5%
[2] Statistically not significant at 5%
Model estimated by least squares: $Y_t = c_0 + c_1 (X_t - X_{t-1})$
When Y_t ... Standards of living (real percentage change):
• Consumption per capita
• White-collar salaries
• Blue-collar wages
X_t ... Productive specialization (as percentage of GDP):
• Primary
• Manufacturing
• Construction
• Services

5.5). In other words, the adverse impact is greater on earnings as a whole than on consumption.

On the other hand, an extra percentage point in the share of manufacturing activities would increase per capita consumption by 4.2 per cent, white-collar real salaries by 10.6 per cent and blue-collar real wages by 15.5 per cent. This means that manufacturing specialization not only increases standards of living but has a proportionally larger impact on blue-collar wages, thus leading to a positive effect on income distribution.

In the construction industry, the impact on the various standard-of-living indicators would also be positive although the respective parameters are substantially smaller than those for manufacturing and are of little statistical significance.[7] Finally, impact in the service sector would be close to zero with little statistical significance in either private consumption or earnings.

If economic deindustrialization has the long-term effect of reducing the population's standard of living, why has there been such a long-term insistence on producing primary goods? Two fundamental explanations are in order. The first, presented below, deals with the way the country participates in the world economy. The second relates to macroeconomic imbalances and will be analysed later when we deal with the short-term factors affecting industrialization.

Peru's conventional exports and a large portion of its nonconventional exports are resource-based. Approximately 80 per cent of total exports are related to agricultural, mining and fisheries industries while only 20 per cent are related to manufacturing. This type of participation in international trade based on the use of natural resources has led to the growth of exports in the last 50 years. It has also led to increasing economic deindustrialization, a fact confirmed by a positive correlation ($r^2 = 0.36$) between deindustrialization and exports as a percentage of GDP (Figure 5.6). Likewise, a positive correlation exists between real exchange rate and deindustrialization, where $r^2 = 0.29$ (Figure 5.7), which proves that devaluation in real terms would increase the relative importance of primary activities.

Why would a higher real exchange rate lead to the increased relative participation of primary activities, that is, to deindustrialization? (1) The physical quantity of raw material exports would increase as a higher real

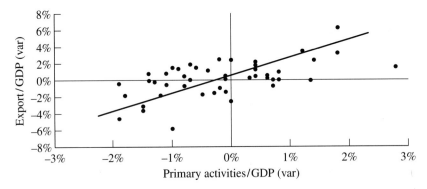

Figure 5.6   Export/GDP and deindustrialization

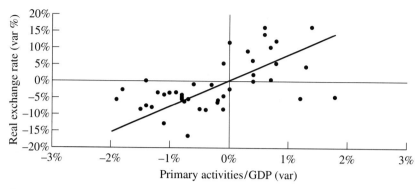

Figure 5.7 Real exchange rate and deindustrialization

exchange rate increases their profitability. (2) The increase of raw materials exports is higher than the expansion of manufacturing products (for either the domestic or external market) which would also grow as the real exchange rate increases. (3) Indirectly, deindustrialization grows as manufacturing output is reduced given the eventual negative impacts of higher real exchange rates on domestic demand. In these three instances real-term devaluation would reduce the manufacturing to GDP ratio, which would translate into higher participation of primary activities.

This occurs because the country's industrialization process revolved around the domestic market and not the external market, that is, it was not supported by the active and efficient promotion of manufacturing exports. If industrialization and the implicit trade policy were export oriented, the slope of the curve in Figure 5.7 would be steeper and may even become negative because devaluation would eventually reduce economic deindustrialization. For this to happen, however, the whole national industrial and trade strategy would have to be redefined, compared to recent decades.

3.2 Short-Term Factors: Macroeconomic Imbalances

A second reason why it has not been possible to reverse economic deindustrialization relates to short-term macroeconomic imbalances.

Although we showed that, in the long term, industrial development would lead to increased standards of living and revenues, there is a fundamental difficulty in maintaining basic macroeconomic balances. This difficulty determines swings between industrialization and deindustrialization (see Figure 5.8).[8]

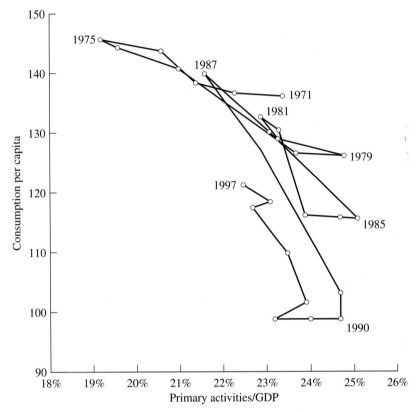

Figure 5.8   Consumption per capita and deindustrialization, 1971–97

If we separate into three periods the relationship between per capita consumption and primary activities to GDP, 1971–78, 1979–84 and 1985–90, we may see that within each period there are years when primary activities contract and therefore industrialization and standards of living increase. These might then be followed by other years where the reverse occurs, that is, the relative importance of extractive activities grows again with the consequent reduction in living standards.

For example, from 1971 to 1975 (Figure 5.9), the rate of primary activities to GDP fell from 23.4 per cent to 19.2 per cent while per capita consumption increased by 6.9 per cent (from 136 to 146, in 1979 soles). However, in the three years that followed, primary activities grew again while consumption declined, for a standard of living that was 7 per cent lower than at the beginning of this stage in 1971 – despite quite similar deindustrialization levels.

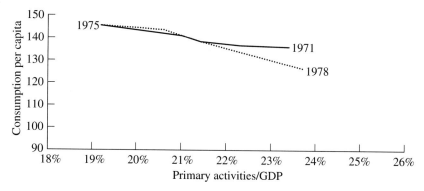

Figure 5.9   Consumption per capita and deindustrialization, 1971–78

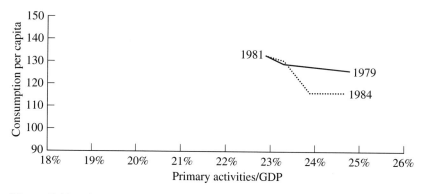

Figure 5.10   Consumption per capita and deindustrialization, 1979–84

In the second case (Figure 5.10) we observe that from 1979 to 1981, participation of the primary sector dropped, pushing consumption up by 5 per cent. In the subsequent three years, primary activities grew again to 24.7 per cent while consumption fell by 12.7 per cent, even below 1979 consumption levels. However, the effects of the 1983 El Niño weather phenomenon could largely account for this fact.

In Figure 5.11, our third example shows that primary activities as a percentage of GDP fell by 3.5 percentage points while per capita consumption increased strongly by 20 per cent. However, in the four years that followed, the importance of extractive activities rose again to 24.7 per cent of total GDP while per capita consumption plummeted by 29.4 per cent or below its 1985 level when the process started.

In these three instances, such pendulum movement led the level of deindustrialization almost to its point of departure; however, per capita

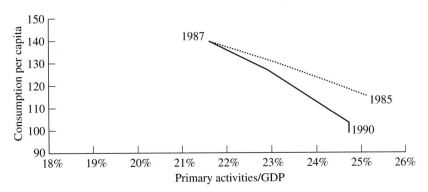

Figure 5.11   Consumption per capita and deindustrialization, 1985–90

consumption ultimately fell to a significantly lower level than its initial point. Consequently, these processes are extremely damaging to the standards of living of the population at large, because besides the pendulum swing from right to left, we can also see a downward trend. By comparing the coordinates for 1979, 1985 and 1990, we note that the level of primary activities to GDP is roughly similar. Still, per capita consumption was significantly lower in 1990 than in 1985 and 1979. In other words, from the viewpoint of standards of living, the progress made in the 1980s was totally wasted.

The trend toward deindustrialization began in 1976, 1982 and 1988, when the trade gap became unbearable and the country's foreign currency reserves did not suffice to sustain the imports of goods and services (see Table 5.6).[9]

In the 1990s (up to 1997), the liberalization policy translated into a slight decrease in the level of primary activities from 24 per cent in 1991 to 22.5 per cent in 1997, parallel to an increase in per capita consumption of 22.7 per cent propelled by higher earnings and expanded consumer loans (see Figure 5.12).

An important factor in the 1990s leading to falling primary activities to GDP ratio was the strong growth of the construction industry to reconstruct the basic social infrastructure damaged by external factors such as weather and terrorism. Also influential was the opening of the economy and privatization that led to substantial investment growth, in particular foreign investment, in non-tradable activities such as commerce, transportation, communications and energy which for purposes of this chapter have been grouped as services.

However, declining primary activities has not led to the growth of the manufacturing industry, implying that the economy is deindustrializing

Table 5.6 Main economic indicators 1974–97

	Primary activities to GDP (%)	Inflation (%)	GDP (Δ%)	Domestic demand (Δ%)	Trade balance (US$ millions)	Foreign reserve (US$ millions)	Foreign reserves (as % of imports)	Terms of trade (Δ%)	Prime rate (%)
1974	20.6	19.2	9.2	14.1	(405)	693	28.2	4.6	10.80
1975	19.2	24.0	3.4	2.0	(1097)	116	3.8	-31.0	7.86
1976	19.6	44.7	2.0	-1.8	(675)	(752)	-30.1	12.7	6.84
1977	21.0	32.4	0.4	-1.9	(422)	(1101)	-43.2	2.3	6.82
1978	23.7	73.7	0.3	-7.9	304	(1025)	-49.9	-18.8	9.06
1979	24.8	66.7	5.8	4.3	1722	554	22.5	31.9	12.67
1980	23.3	60.8	4.5	14.0	826	1276	32.1	10.2	15.27
1981	22.9	72.7	4.4	8.9	(553)	771	15.8	-18.1	18.87
1982	23.3	72.9	0.2	-0.6	(429)	896	18.6	-17.5	14.86
1983	23.9	125.1	-12.6	-17.6	293	856	23.2	7.4	10.79
1984	24.7	111.5	4.8	-1.4	1007	1103	36.4	-8.8	12.04
1985	25.1	158.3	2.3	-0.3	1172	1383	49.6	-10.2	9.93
1986	23.1	62.9	9.2	16.8	(65)	866	24.0	-26.7	8.35
1987	21.6	144.5	8.5	13.1	(577)	81	1.9	0.8	8.21
1988	22.9	1722.3	-8.3	-8.7	(99)	(317)	-8.0	8.2	9.32
1989	24.7	2775.3	-11.7	-19.7	1197	546	15.9	-3.5	10.92
1990	24.7	7649.7	-5.4	0.1	346	682	16.8	-9.7	10.01
1991	24.0	139.2	2.8	3.9	(166)	1933	40.8	-4.9	8.46
1992	23.2	56.7	-1.4	1.2	(566)	2425	44.4	-1.8	6.25
1993	23.9	39.5	6.4	5.9	(599)	2910	52.6	-8.1	6.00
1994	23.5	15.4	13.1	14.2	(1022)	6025	84.1	10.4	7.14
1995	22.7	10.2	7.2	11.5	(2185)	6693	69.2	6.5	8.83
1996	23.1	11.8	2.6	-0.0	(1967)	8862	88.9	-5.2	8.27
1997	22.5	6.5	7.2	6.7	(1738)	7982	73.6	5.2	8.44

Note: *GDP fell, strongly influenced by El Niño weather anomaly.
Source: INEI, Central Reserve Bank (Banco Central de Reserva del Perú), IMF. Prepared by the authors.

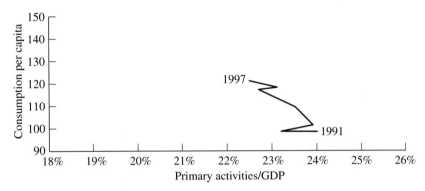

Figure 5.12   Consumption per capita and deindustrialization, 1991–97

because construction and services are expanding their respective shares. The standard of living improves and incomes grow because construction and services are activities of 'higher quality' than primary ones.

If we determine the speed at which the economy reduces its primary level of activities during the various periods when the phenomenon effectively occurred, we may observe that in the recent economic liberalization period from 1991 to 1997, primary activities fell by 0.25 points per year. In those periods where import-substitution industrialization policies were enforced, the drop was 1.0 point per year from 1971 to 1975 and 1979 to 1981, and 1.7 points per year from 1985 to 1987. This means that in the 1990s market liberalization policies led to lower deindustrialization ratios but at a significantly slower speed than when the process was induced or strategically driven by industrialization policies in the 1970s and 1980s.

Such 'slow' reduction of deindustrialization during the period when the economy opened up was not exempt from macro-economic imbalances which were also present during the industrialization processes analysed above. It is worth noting, for instance, that in 1993 and 1996, the deindustrialization index rose rather than fell (see Figure 5.12) because of the 1992 drought, in the first case, and due to excess domestic demand in 1994 and 1995 in the second case. This led to macroeconomic adjustment to prevent a further widening of the trade gap. In other words, deindustrialization grows precisely when there is imminent danger of macroeconomic instability and because of prudent short-term management of macroeconomic fundamentals. If macroeconomic imbalances were not immediately prevented, it is possible that primary activities would have diminished further on, thus making possible a strong swing back toward greater deindustrialization at the time the economy finally gets adjusted.

Sustained growth of foreign currency reserves in recent years largely contributed to revert deindustrialization in 1992, 1994, 1995 and 1997. An extremely favourable international environment accounted for larger foreign reserves. Terms of exchange have remained relatively stable, interest rates dropped and capital flows became increasingly global and international. These factors allowed for financing of a large trade gap. These wider options between 1991 and 1997 permitted progress, albeit slowly, toward diminishing the ratio of primary activities to GDP.

It is therefore particularly important to underscore that macroeconomic stability and good management of macroeconomic fundamentals (whether through industrialization-promoting policies or in an openly neoliberal framework) are necessary conditions to achieve the long-term objective of reaching a lower economic deindustrialization index on a sustained basis, thus improving standards of living.

Peru's case shows, though, that reducing the level of primary activities may occur more quickly if carried out through the active and deliberate design of industrialization policies, as was the case in 1971–75, 1979–81 and 1985–87, than if guided by the hand of free markets and liberalization, as occurred in 1991–97. The problem in the last 50 years stemmed from the lack of consistency and coherence between short-term macroeconomic management and industrialization policies, meaning that the type of industrialization policies implemented in Peru failed to prevent trade balance deficits.

4.   UNCOUPLING DEMAND AND SUPPLY STRUCTURES, THE QUALITY OF ECONOMIC ACTIVITIES AND VIABLE ECONOMIC GROWTH

If a country increasingly produces goods with a lower level of processing, quality and value, and on the other hand consumes foreign goods that include a larger amount of knowledge, undoubtedly it will exchange growing amounts of simple goods for the same (or a smaller) amount of elaborate goods.

If domestic supply, including exports, shifts toward primary products with diminishing returns, simple processing or minimum know-how, while demand moves toward increased consumption of sophisticated, complex and always newer products, there will be a gradual uncoupling of quality and value between what the country produces and what it consumes. This uncoupling occurs because not all economic products and/or activities are alike. It is precisely the more elaborate goods or services that eventually translate into higher standards of living. Elaborate goods incorporate a higher degree of technology and knowledge, show positive externalities, and generate a higher value and have a larger systemic and synergistic effect over the rest of the economy.

Conditions will deteriorate even further if the terms of trade fall because of market effects. Declining terms of trade implies prices of exported goods growing more slowly than the prices of imported goods. Although it is true that the terms of trade reflect a difference in the quality and value of economic activities, it is also true that these prices are subject to short-term fluctuations that are not related to these factors.

Short-term macroeconomic stability and the viability of long-term sustained growth become ever more complex if the uncoupling described above is reproduced in supply and demand patterns. This is true to the extent that in this kind of trade increasingly larger exports of simple products will be required to finance similar purchases of more elaborate goods, given the diminishing returns of the first type of products. If under those circumstances exports fail to grow, the emerging external account deficits will eventually hamper all attempts at sustained economic growth, as mentioned in section 3.2.

Depending on available resources and the country's capacity to produce an increasing amount of simple or primary goods, from a long-term perspective the nation will quite likely end up producing and working more but living under worsening conditions.

What evidence is there for Peru? Is the uncoupling of quality and value between supply and demand taking place already? How will this uncoupling hamper economic growth?

A review of the composition of Peru's domestic demand leads to the following remarks:

1. Figure 5.13 shows that imports as a percentage of domestic demand, after having plummeted to 16 per cent at the end of the 1980s, climbed back to 28 per cent in 1997, thus implying that in general, in the 1990s Peruvians consumed more imported goods as a percentage of their demand than in the late 1980s.
2. Table 5.7 shows that imports of durable and nondurable consumer goods followed by purchases of capital goods for industry recorded the largest relative share increase. These three items together accounted for 46.1 per cent of imports in 1997 while they were only 26.8 per cent in 1988, a difference of 19 percentage points.
3. On the contrary, the share of inputs and raw materials for industry fell from 43.4 per cent in 1988 to 28.7 per cent in 1997, about 15 percentage points less.
4. A flat review of the list of durable and non-durable inputs and of capital goods for industry shows that these goods incorporate relatively

Table 5.7   FOB imports by economic use

	US$ millions			Structure (%)		
	1988	1993	1997	1988	1993	1997
Consumer goods	273	934	1910	9.5	22.7	22.3
Nondurable	244	555	1107	8.5	13.5	12.9
Durable	29	379	803	1.0	9.2	9.4
Inputs	1593	1859	3437	55.6	45.1	40.2
Fuels, lubricants and related	253	322	780	8.8	7.8	9.1
Raw materials for agriculture	98	116	202	3.4	2.8	2.4
Raw materials for industry	1243	1422	2455	43.4	34.5	28.7
Capital goods	728	1143	2816	25.4	27.7	32.9
Construction materials	24	68	244	0.8	1.6	2.9
Goods for agriculture	40	37	28	1.4	0.9	0.3
Goods for industry	496	704	2037	17.3	17.1	23.8
Transportation equipment	168	334	507	5.9	8.1	5.9
Other goods	272	187	390	9.5	4.5	4.6
Total	2866	4123	8552	100.0	100.0	100.0

Source: Central Bank (Banco Central de Reserva del Perú). Prepared by the authors.

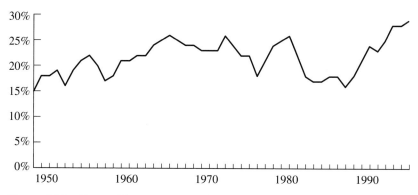

Figure 5.13   Import/domestic expenditure (%)

more knowledge and require a more complex technical manufacturing process, therefore pointing to a greater capacity to create value. On the other hand, raw materials for industry are less sophisticated and therefore create less value.

Some preliminary conclusions may be drawn from the above observations. First, Peru is increasing its demand for imported products. Second, if we analyse the mix of imports, it becomes obvious that Peru is importing increasingly sophisticated products with a higher technology or knowledge component (durable consumer goods and capital goods for the industry) while imports of less sophisticated products continue to fall (imports of raw materials for industry). This means that the country increasingly buys abroad products of higher quality and value content that cost more.

Such a demand bias is a consequence not only of Peru's commercial and financial expansion but also of increased globalization and communications, which are promoting consumption of 'cutting edge' or 'innovative' products.

At the microeconomic level, this demand trend has been confirmed through household surveys that measure increasing ownership of electric appliances in recent years. For instance, colour TVs equipped with remote controls have progressively substituted for black and white television sets and those without remote controls. This is evidence of demand propensities for innovative and improved-quality products that are not produced internally but imported.

This type of phenomenon is not necessarily negative because progress always comes with increased demand for products that provide a higher level of comfort and quality. The problem emerges when the country lacks sufficient capacity to import. At the heart of the matter seems to be the capacity to produce and export goods that are 'similar in value and quality' to the imports. For this the quality structure of imports should match the value of exports. If this occurs, there is a circle of growth through international trade that in Graham's model leads to exchange among countries that specialize in activities with constant returns.

But if the structure of production and/or exports shows that production of primary goods with little or no incorporated knowledge continues to grow, that is of goods with little value added, it is obvious that Peru will have to work harder to meet the observed trend in demand patterns.

A review of the structure of domestic supply (section 3 in this essay) shows that liberalization in the 1990s led to a slower fall in economic deindustrialization when compared to the period of active industrial policy. On the other hand, industrial policies or free-market schemes that ignore basic macroeconomic principles will unfailingly abort if there is lack of coherence with fiscal, external and/or monetary balances.

Empirical evidence shows that when the market is left on its own, the economy will move toward producing slightly more elaborate non-tradable services due to growing demand by consumers, but will never manage to produce the industrial-type tradable goods that consumers demand. Thus, because the demand for manufactured goods cannot be met by domestic supply, those goods are imported. And because domestic production of primary goods exceeds local consumption, they are exported. However, the process originates a growing 'uncoupling of quality and value' given that the world's demand for the goods Peru exports grows at a slower pace than its imports.

Figure 5.14 shows that Peru's terms of trade from the beginning of the 1950s to date fell toward the end of 1996 and in 1997 to a fifth of their value at the beginning of the 1970s and currently stand where they were in the mid-1950s.

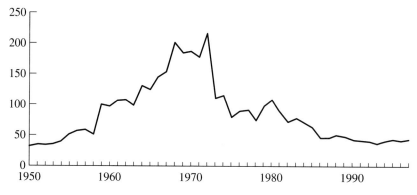

Figure 5.14   Terms of trade (1979 = 100)

This means that prices of exports since 1972 have grown considerably less (or have decreased) compared to the price of imports, leading to the most substantial fall in standards of living and income ever, excepting the periods from 1975 to 1977, and from 1979 to 1980. In other words the price of Peru's export products fall more or rise less than that of its imports, with the subsequent negative effect on domestic revenues and standards of living of Peruvians, who have to work more but are worse off.

The question then is, what caused terms of trade to improve in the 1960s and at the beginning of the 1970s and then decline since 1972.

An explanation may be that at the beginning of the 1960s given productivity levels and demand for materials, inputs and technology, there was an increase in demand and prices of minerals. In the 1970s, the world oil crisis led to radical technological changes in energy conservation and more efficient use of raw materials, which diminished demand and prices of raw materials. In the 1980s and 1990s, the communications, electronics and information revolutions introduced massive use of knowledge to produce goods in industrial countries that put Peruvian production and exports at a disadvantage because local industries were unable to incorporate new knowledge at the required speed.

Another hypothesis refers to the extremely poor management of fundamental economic balances since 1970 and the lack of a truly coherent industrial policy that would diversify the supply of exports and promote new activities for which world demand and prices would not fall steadily.

These are, however, hypotheses that must be explored further. The concrete fact is that Peru is not producing or exporting the types of good that would ensure and allow it to finance its new consumption structure, a structure that is constantly evolving as the world's demand fluctuates and changes.[10]

5. WORK MORE AND LIVE BETTER: SOMETHING PERUVIANS HAVE YET TO ACHIEVE

5.1 Major Conclusions

This chapter has demonstrated that deindustrialization of economic activities is intimately linked to declining standards of living. For the period 1950–97, for each additional percentage point of deindustrialization, per capita consumption fell by 2.6 per cent while white-collar real salaries dropped by 5.4 per cent and blue-collar wages by 7.4 per cent. The impact on the manufacturing industry is just the opposite, since for each point of increased industrialization, per capita consumption grew by 4.2 per cent and white-collar and blue-collar earnings rose 10.6 and 15.5 per cent respectively (see section 3).

If wages, salaries and standards of living increased with growing industrialization, why has Peru not gradually moved toward the production of manufactured goods? The answer is three-pronged.

In the first place, Peru wrongly participates in the world economy basically as an exporter of raw materials and natural resources with diminishing returns.

Second, an erroneous industrial policy has favoured permanent protection for all types of industries aimed at producing final goods for the domestic market without link-ups to other processes and no learning curve. Technology was imported as a package revealing a static business view of the world. There was an insufficient emphasis on education, creation of value and training, few possibilities of tuning up to a broader market, a static rent-seeking attitude, and total disdain for 'merit-based' promotion. In addition, the government sector lacked synergies with private investment and failed to understand the critical role played by market forces. In summary, an industrial policy is illustrated by the slope of the PR_0 curve in Figure 5.15.

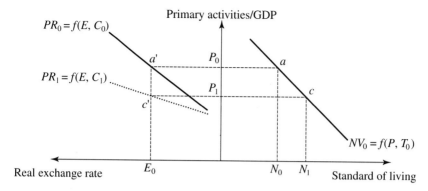

Figure 5.15   Exchange rate, deindustrialization and standard of living

Third, managing macroeconomic stability and fundamentals is extremely important. Section 3.2 proved that as the current account, government accounts and/or private deficits became unbearably large, a crisis emerged leading to the corresponding reversal of the industrialisation process.

If to these three characteristics we add events on the demand side, a rapidly deteriorating situation emerges. Section 4 showed how the structure of demand shifted toward consumption of foreign goods of higher quality, value, knowledge and technology. Moreover, if these changes in demand are accompanied by supply that continues to favour the production and export of primary goods, the country will inevitably end up with a 'value or quality mismatch'. It will end up working harder to earn the same units of imports. The country therefore specializes in producing and exporting goods with diminishing returns that are exchanged for products with increasing returns. As average productivity falls, so do standards of living (see sections 1, 3 and 4).

Our most important conclusion is that contrary to most neoclassical theory, we hold that growth and standards of living depend on the types of goods and services produced by a country. A country may master all the exogenous and endogenous factors that are responsible for economic growth as highlighted by neoclassical theory, that is, labour, capital, natural resources, savings, investment, technology, efficient use of resources, financial markets, infrastructure, sound macroeconomic indicators, efficient government and so on. However, if all these elements are directed toward producing the wrong types of products, the nation may end up working harder and living worse off.

5.2   A Framework to Design a Strategy for Growth and Increasing Standards of Living

Peru needs to devote time and energy to 'rethink' or review the goods it produces. Figure 5.15 provides a good initial framework for this analysis. The right-hand quadrant shows the reverse postulated relationship between deindustrialization[11] (primary activities/GDP) and standard of living. The left-hand quadrant shows the positive relationship between the real exchange rate and the deindustrialization ratio, as explained in Figure 5.7 in section 3.1.

Line NV graphs the negative impact of primary activities on standard of living. It has as implicit parameters a given level of technology, productivity, returns to scale, externalities and other elements that may be grouped as factor T. Likewise, line PR describes the positive impact of the real exchange rate on deindustrialization. It involves parameters related to the type of participation in the world economy and the country's industrial development policy, which depend on the varying focus on the domestic or external markets. These parameters are summarized by factor C. Thus, for instance, if the country's participation in global trade is based on using natural resources or if the national industrial strategy is basically directed toward its domestic market, PR's slope increases. On the contrary, if industrialization shifts toward promoting manufacturing exports, the slope drops (PR_1 in Figure 5.15).

A close look at these relationships reveals that standards of living would increase, *ceteris paribus*, by developing an outward industrialization process, which would imply a change in the type of participation in the international economy. In terms of Figure 5.15, line PR_0 would shift downward to PR_1 when the strategy to participate in the world economy moves away from the advantages derived from natural resources to the dynamic competitive advantages provided by manufacturing (from C_0 to C_1). Under these circumstances, given a certain real exchange rate (E_0), deindustrialization will fall from PR_0 to PR_1, from a' to c', and standards of living would increase from N_0 to N_1 sliding along the NV_0 curve, from a to c.

Alternatively, we could introduce a qualitative transformation in primary activities to gradually include technological development in them. Line NV_0 would move to the right, to NV_1 (see Figure 5.16). For the same level of deindustrialization (P_0), the population's standard of living would rise from N_0 to N_1.[12] Technological upgrading (from T_0 to T_1) in agriculture and mining, for instance, would improve standards of living, given a certain level of primary activities. For this process to be sustainable, technological progress in these primary activities would have to occur on an ongoing basis in order to set off the eventual negative weight of diminish-

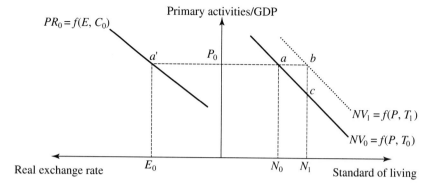

Figure 5.16 Exchange rate, deindustrialization and standard of living

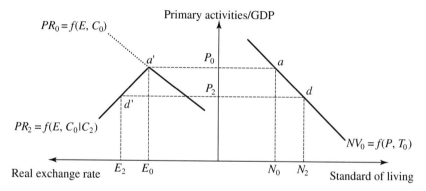

Figure 5.17 Exchange rate, deindustrialization and standard of living

ing returns in extractive activities, if this variable is effectively the key factor separating industrial from extractive processes.[13]

A third option, much in the style of countries with large endowments of natural resources such as Australia, New Zealand and Canada, is to resort to primary comparative advantages at relatively low real exchange rate levels while promoting manufacturing exports at higher real exchange rates.[14] In terms of Figure 5.17, this would mean that PR would be a kinked, upside down V, so that at low exchange rates, below E_0, deindustrialization would increase. Conversely, with higher rates of exchange, above E_0, deindustrialization would fall. The fundamental precept is to curtail total specialization on primary resources and thus prevent the spreading of this sector's diminishing returns throughout the economy.[15]

In this case, by shifting parameter C from C_0 to C_2, starting at point a', an increase of the exchange rate above E_0 would lead to a declining deindustrialization quotient and to increased industrialization. For this reason, given an E_2 exchange rate, if manufacturing output has been efficiently directed toward either the external or domestic market, manufactured products would be competitive and primary products would be significantly profitable. However, the higher profitability of the primary sector would have to be offset to prevent new entrants or expansion of incumbents in areas of diminishing returns. Countries with abundant natural resources that have successfully increased their population's living standards generally have regulated and restricted the use of their resources for both strategic and environmental reasons. In this case, developing a complementary manufacturing sector with either an inward or outward orientation depending on the size and volume of the market is crucial for any such economy to improve its standards of living.[16]

Obviously, it is possible to combine the three approaches mentioned above or try other paths that will modify the implicit parameters on both the left and right quadrants.

One initial proposal for Peru is to devote itself to primary activities at low real exchange rate levels, preventing the country from entering into areas with diminishing returns when the real exchange rate increases. As the real exchange rate rises, it should speed up promotion of a strong export-oriented manufacturing sector very much in the style of the inverted V curve shown in Figure 5.17. Rents should be extracted from primary activities when real exchange rate increases like in Canada, Australia and New Zealand, as a way to limit their expansion and address environmental concerns. The other two approaches, shown in Figures 5.15 and 5.16, could also be followed but with much more limited results.

5.3   Free Markets and Strategic Supply Policies in a Global World

How should Peru then face the new era of globalization and free trade that is promoted by multilateral organizations and the industrial economies?

Assuming that open markets by themselves will automatically lead Peru to the kind of specialized productive structure implicit in point d' of Figure 5.17 is a fallacy that was tested in the liberalization of the 1950s and 1990s. On the other hand, assuming that any kind of industrial policy will ensure that this path will be followed is another fallacy tested in the 1960s, 1970s and 1980s. Peru needs to design productive strategies that will consciously and deliberately allow it to 'create' and 'ensure' permanent increasing returns and dynamic competitive advantages over time, by producing higher value goods and services and maintaining well-balanced macroeconomic fundamentals.

Peru must therefore enter the new global and trade era not necessarily following the dictum of multilateral organizations and developed economies but ensuring the production of those goods and services that will generate faster growth and increased standards of living.

Neither free trade and free markets *per se* nor industrial and commercial policies that are inconsistent with market forces will prove successful in this venture. To improve Peru's standards of living it is essential to combine strategic policies and market orientation in order to create dynamic competitive advantages in the production of high value, high quality goods.

NOTES

*   A draft of this chapter was presented at the International Conference on 'Globalisation and Marginalisation in the 1990s: An Evolutionary and Activity-Specific Perspective', organized by SUM (Centre for Development and the Environment), University of Oslo, and Norsk Investorforum, Oslo, 5–6 September 1998.
1.   Rosenthal (1996) provides a historical overview of how development ideas and policies have evolved in Latin America in the last half century.
2.   Almost all classical and neoclassical international trade theory – from Adam Smith and David Ricardo to the present – is based on the assumption that constant returns and perfect competition will prevail. From this we can infer that under these conditions international commerce will benefit all nations. In the 1980s Krugman focused on part of Graham's work to redesign the whole theory of trade under the assumption of increasing returns and verified that in this case trade would also benefit all countries. However, as pointed out by Reinert (1996), Krugman failed to consider the possibility that one country would show increasing returns and the other decreasing ones, in which case the former becomes richer and the latter poorer, as demonstrated by Graham in 1923.
3.   If undertaking an economic activity results in knowledge used by other sectors without payment, Grossman argues, the industry will produce a marginal social benefit or will generate positive externalities that spread to the rest of the economy. In such cases there should be in theory some subsidy mechanism to allow the high-technology industries (for example, biotechnology, electronics, the space industry) to capture some of those social benefits and thus further foster its own development (Grossman 1991). In the case of oligopolistic industries, given the small number of companies that trade on a world scale, windfall profits are a logical consequence. Under such circumstances a country may subsidize its own company to push other countries' companies out of the market, a practice commonly called 'strategic commercial policy'. However, such a policy may unleash a trade war if all the other countries react likewise (Brander 1991). Despite these arguments, the fundamental implications for economic policy derived from such proposals are still valid. Thus, for instance, it is held that no conclusive empirical evidence allows that markets will necessarily fail. And even if this were true, the criteria selected to foster new activities are not clear, nor is there sufficient information to evaluate and determine what industries should be promoted. Finally, it is also held that this policy is not free from various pressures that would, in the best of cases, hamper final decisions (Grossman 1991).
4.   The annual average growth rate was computed from the $ln(Y) = a_0 + a_1*$ time regression where the a_1 coefficient is the annual average rate for the period under consideration. Prepared by the authors.
5.   More recently, the Organization for Economic Cooperation and Development (OECD 1992) suggested a difference between supplier-driven activities, economy-of-scale

intensive activities and those based on science. However, so far national statistics bureaus continue to use the International Industrial Uniform Classification presented in Tables 5.1 and 5.2 and proposed by the UN.

6. Obviously, this classification implies some oversimplification that must be corrected in later work. For instance, the garment and electronic industries are not comparable from a qualitative viewpoint for their effect on technological development, use of R&D, level of salaries, economies of scale, externalities and so on. Likewise, there is a substantial difference between extensive agriculture, and capital- and technology-intensive mining or fisheries. Despite these constraints, this type of classification makes it possible to establish the differences between and quantify those activities that generally allow a nation to reach increasing returns compared to those where only diminishing returns are possible if we follow Ricardo's terminology.

7. Impact is statistically significant only at 5 per cent per capita consumption but not for earnings, where statistical significance starts at 15 per cent.

8. A broader view integrating political and social factors other than purely economic considerations can be found in Gonzáles de Olarte and Samamé 1991.

9. Insufficiency of foreign currency reserves can be partly accounted for by excess domestic demand, which in the periods before the adjustment grew more than GDP. An important factor generating this growth of demand is obviously the increased private consumption, meaning that such swings are also explained by increased standards of living that create bottlenecks in the external sector. Of similar importance is the adverse impact of external shocks, such as falling terms of trade or higher international interest rates during the 1980s. Thus, for instance, a drop in terms of trade in 1975 (-31 per cent), in 1981 and 1982 (-32 per cent) and again in 1986 (-27 per cent) also had a substantial impact on the trade balance and the amount of net foreign reserves which eventually sparked the stabilization programmes.

   The gap model used for Peru (Canales and Fairlie 1996) covering a period of 20 years shows that external constraints were the basic factor limiting growth. This occurred even in the 1990s despite capital inflows, which did not necessarily lift the restriction but may have offset it temporarily, an effect similar to that of increased foreign flows during the 1970s.

10. A review of Japanese experience from 1950 to 1970 shows that the key to higher exports is found not only in Japan's ability to produce better-quality exports but principally in its capacity to adjust its export mix by introducing goods for which world demand was growing. In other words, Japan stopped producing and exporting those goods for which the world's demand was falling and which therefore had lower value, and shifted towards production of goods in greater demand.

11. The relative importance of manufacturing can be measured by moving in the opposite direction (downward) along the axis.

12. Technological change probably will turn PR_0 around point a, slightly increasing the impact of the real exchange rate on the degree of deindustrialization.

13. We must bear in mind that a key element separating primary from manufacturing activities is the former's diminishing returns and the latter's increasing returns.

14. It is also possible to develop a manufacturing sector on the bases of the internal market if this is sufficiently large to benefit from economies of scale as Friedrich List proposed in the nineteenth century.

15. Total deindustrialization, as depicted in Figure 5.17, would appear if we continue along the PR_0 dotted line, given parameter C_0.

16. Developing the internal market might be a second option but its success will depend upon its openness, size and competitive arrangements.

REFERENCES

Banco Central de Reserva del Perú (various years), *Memorias*, Lima: Banco Central de Reserva del Perú.

Brander, J. (1991), 'Justificaciones de política comercial e industrial estratégica', in P. Krugman (ed.), *Una política comercial estratégica para la nueva economía internacional*, Mexico City: Fondo de Cultura Económica, pp. 31–53.

Canales, G. and A. Fairlie (1996), 'Apertura, cuenta corriente y transferencia externa en el Perú', Documento de trabajo #131, CISEPA, PUC.

David, F.R. (1986), *Fundamentals of Strategic Management*. Columbus, OH: Merrill.

Ferrari, C. (1992), *Industrialización y desarrollo. Políticas públicas y efectos económicos en el Perú*, Lima: Fundación Friedrich Ebert.

Gonzáles de Olarte, E. and L. Samamé (1991), *El péndulo Peruano: Políticas económicas, gobernabilidad y subdesarrollo, 1963–1990*, Consorcio de Investigación económica. Instituto de Estudios Peruanos.

Graham, F. (1923), 'Some aspects of protection further considered', *Quarterly Journal of Economics*, **37**, 199–227.

Grossman, G. (1991), 'Promoción estratégica de la exportación: una crítica', in P. Krugman (ed.), *Política comercial estratégica para la nueva economía internacional*, Mexico City: Fondo de Cultura Económica, pp. 51–74.

Hirschman, A. (1961), *La estrategia del desarrollo económico*, Mexico City: Fondo de Cultura Económica.

Krugman, P. (ed.) (1991), *Política comercial estratégica para la nueva economía internacional*, Mexico City: Fondo de Cultura Económica.

Krugman, P. and M. Obstfeld (1995), *Economía internacional: Teoría y política*, New York: McGraw-Hill.

Marrus, S.K. (1984), *Building the Strategic Plan: Find, Analyze and Present the Right Information*, New York: John Wiley & Sons.

Matsuyama, K. (1992), 'Agricultural productivity, comparative advantage, and economic growth', *Journal of Economic Theory*, **58**.

Myrdal, G. (1963), *Economic Theory and Underdeveloped Regions*, London: Duckworth.

OECD (1992), *Industrial Policy in OECD Countries: Annual Review*, Paris: OECD.

Perú: Compendio Estadístico (various years), Lima: Instituto Nacional de Estadística.

Porter, M. (1990), *The Competitive Advantage of Nations*, New York: Macmillan.

Portocarrero, J. and J. Nunura (1984), *Industria y crisis: La década de los 70's*, Lima: Desco.

Prebisch, R. (1970), *Transformación y desarrollo: La gran tarea de América Latina*, Mexico City: Fondo de Cultura Económica.

Reinert, E. (1980), 'International trade and the economic mechanisms of underdevelopment', PhD diss., Cornell University; Ann Arbor, MI: University Microfilm.

Reinert, E. (1995), 'Competitiveness and its predecessor: a 500-year cross natural perspective', *Economic Dynamics and Structural Change*, March.

Reinert, E. (1996), 'Diminishing returns and economic sustainability: The dilemma of resource-based economies under a free trade regime', in S. Hansen, J. Hesselberg and H. Hveem (eds), *International Trade Regulation, National Development Strategies and the Environment: Towards Sustainable Development?* Oslo: University of Oslo.

Reinert, E. (1998), 'Raw materials in the history of economic policy, or why List (the protectionist) and Cobden (the free trader) both agreed on free trade in corn', in G. Cook (ed.), *The Economics and Politics of International Trade*, London: Routledge.

Rosenthal, G. (1996), *La evolución de las ideas y las políticas para el desarrollo*, Revista de la Cepal 60, Santiago, Chile: CEPAL.

Sachs, J. and A. Warner (1995), 'Natural resource abundance and economic growth', National Bureau of Economic Research, Working Paper 5398.

Seers, D. and J. Leonard (eds) (1975), *Desarrollo en un Mundo Dividido*, Mexico City: Fondo de Cultura Económica.

Singer, H. (1981), *Estrategia del desarrollo internacional: Ensayos sobre el atraso económico*, Mexico City: Fondo de Cultura Económica.

APPENDIX: GRAHAM'S MODEL

In an initial situation of autarky (case 1), Country A produces and consumes 800 units of wheat and 800 units of watches. Average productivity of both activities is 4 units per worker-day and the labour used in each activity is 200 worker-days.

Country B produces and consumes 800 units of wheat and 600 units of watches. Wheat productivity is 4 units per worker-day and that of watches is 3 units per worker-day. Each activity employs 200 worker-days.

Based on these assumptions, the world's wheat production would be 1600 units and 1400 watches, or a total production of 3200 units in wheat terms, given the relative price of the two products. Country A's product is 54 per cent of the world's production (or 1714 wheat units) while Country B accounts for 46 per cent of the total (or 1486 wheat units).

Case 1: Without Trade

	Country A			Country B			World
	Man-days	Output-man	Product	Man-days	Output-man	Product	Product
Wheat	200	4	800	200	4	800	1600
Watches	200	4	800	200	3	600	1400
Total	400			400			

Price: 1 wheat = 0.875 watches.

Product**		(%)
Country A	1714	54
Country B	1486	46
World	3200	100

Note: ** In wheat terms.

When opening trade (case 2), and given their respective comparative advantages, Country A specializes partially in watch making while Country B turns to wheat production. Presumably, Country A will transfer 100 worker-days from wheat cropping to watch making, while country B transfers labour in the opposite direction, that is, from watches to wheat.

Since both activities show constant returns, the world's watch output should increase by 100 units while wheat production remains stable.

Consequently, global world production in wheat terms grows by 114 units, or 3.6 per cent.

Increased world production (equivalent to the added balance of commerce between the two countries) is distributed equally, thus demonstrating that the specialization through trade, given each nation's comparative advantages, is beneficial for both countries, to the extent both activities show constant returns.

Case 2: With Trade and Constant Returns to Scale

+ Specialization by comparative advantage
  Country A transfers workers from wheat to watches
  Country B transfers workers from watches to wheat
+ Constant returns in both activities

	Country A			Country B			World
	Man-days	Output-man	Product	Man-days	Output-man	Product	Product
Wheat	100	4	400	300	4	1200	1600
Watches	300	4	1200	100	3	300	1500
Total	400			400			

Price: 1 wheat = 0.875 watches

Product**		(%)	(+/−)	(+/−)%var
Country A	1771	53	57	3.3
Country B	1543	47	57	3.8
World	3314	100	114	3.6

	Country A			Country B			World
	Domestic demand*	Product	Trade balance	Domestic demand*	Product	Trade balance	Trade balance
Wheat	800	400	(400)	800	1200	400	0
Watches	800	1200	400	600	300	(300)	100
Total**	1714	1771	57	1486	1543	57	114

Notes:
* Production before trade.
** In wheat terms.

However, if wheat has diminishing returns, and watches increasing returns (case 3), international trade, based on comparative advantages, will be beneficial only for Country A, that is, product will grow by 16.3 per cent when compared to the autarchic situation, while B will suffer from a 13.9 per cent decline in production.

In this example, the world's wheat production drops by 100 units, and that of watches grows by 150 units. Consequently, product and world trade, in wheat terms, will grow in 2.2 per cent (or 71 units).

Graham's model predicts that the country specializing in production of goods with diminishing returns will experience both a drop in its GDP and a trade gap. Just the opposite will happen to the country specializing in goods with increasing returns.

Case 3: With Trade: Wheat Diminishing Returns and Watches Increasing Returns

+ Specialization by comparative advantage
  Country A transfers workers from wheat to watches
  Country B transfers workers from watches to wheat
+ Increasing returns in watches and diminishing returns in wheat

	Country A			Country B			World
	Man-days	Output-man	Product	Man-days	Output-man	Product	Product
Wheat	100	4.5	450	300	3.5	1050	1500
Watches	300	4.5	1350	100	2	200	1550
Total	400			400			

Price: 1 wheat = 0.875 watches

Product**		(%)	(+/−)	(+/−) %var
Country A	1993	61	279	16.3
Country B	1279	39	(207)	−13.9
World	3271	100	71	− 2.2

	Country A			Country B			World
	Domestic demand*	Product	Trade balance	Domestic demand*	Product	Trade balance	Trade balance
Wheat	800	450	(350)	800	1050	250	(100)
Watches	800	1350	550	600	200	(400)	150
Total**	1714	1993	279	1486	1279	(207)	71

Notes:
* Production before trade.
** In wheat terms.

If one of the activities shows either increasing or diminishing returns, trade will hurt one of the two countries. In other words, trade will not be equal if there are differences in returns.

Should wheat have diminishing returns and watches constant returns (case 4), trade specialization reduces Country B's GDP, leading to a trade gap. That is, trade will adversely affect the nation with the comparative advantage in the good with diminishing returns.

The world's production would grow very slightly, and so would commercial exchanges, and, in general, the gain in Country A almost equals Country B's loss.

Case 4: With Trade: Wheat Diminishing Returns and Watches Constant Returns

+ Specialization by comparative advantage
  Country A transfers workers from wheat to watches
  Country B transfers workers from watches to wheat
+ Constant returns in watches and diminishing returns in wheat

	Country A			Country B			World
	Man-days	Output-man	Product	Man-days	Output-man	Product	Product
Wheat	100	4.5	450	300	3.5	1050	1500
Watches	300	4	1200	100	3	300	1500
Total	400			400			

Price: 1 wheat = 0.875 watches.

Product**		(%)	(+/−)	(+/−) %var
Country A	1821	57	107	6.3
Country B	1393	43	(93)	−6.2
World	3214	100	14	0.4

	Country A			Country B			World
	Domestic demand*	Product	Trade balance	Domestic demand*	Product	Trade balance	Trade balance
Wheat	800	450	(350)	800	1050	250	(100)
Watches	800	1200	400	600	300	(300)	100
Total**	1714	1821	107	1486	1393	(93)	14

Notes:
* Production before trade.
** In wheat terms.

If watch production shows increasing returns and wheat production constant returns (case 5), the final result will be quite similar to the previous example, since the production in Country B will fall and in Country A it will grow. A's trade balance will show a surplus while B's will be negative.

In spite of this similarity, the world's product and commercial trade will grow more than in the previous case.

Case 5: With Trade: Wheat Constant Returns and Watches Increasing Returns

+ Specialization by comparative advantage
  Country A transfers workers from wheat to watches
  Country B transfers workers from watches to wheat
+ Increasing returns in watches and constant returns in wheat

	Country A			Country B			World
	Man-days	Output-man	Product	Man-days	Output-man	Product	Product
Wheat	100	4	400	300	4	1200	1600
Watches	300	4.5	1350	100	2	200	1550
Total	400			400			

Price: 1 wheat = 0.875 watches.

Product**		(%)	(+/−)	(+/−) % var
Country A	1943	58	229	13.3
Country B	1429	42	(57)	−3.8
World	3371	100	171	5.4

	Country A			Country B			World
	Domestic demand*	Product	Trade balance	Domestic demand*	Product	Trade balance	Trade balance
Wheat	800	400	(400)	800	1200	400	0
Watches	800	1350	550	600	200	(400)	150
Total**	1714	1943	229	1486	1429	(57)	171

Notes:
* Production before trade.
** In wheat terms.

6. Globalization in the periphery as a Morgenthau Plan: the underdevelopment of Mongolia in the 1990s

Erik S. Reinert

I apprehend [the elimination of diminishing returns] to be not only an error, but the most serious one, to be found in the whole field of political economy. The question is more important and fundamental than any other; it involves the whole subject of the causes of poverty . . . and unless this matter be thoroughly understood, it is to no purpose proceeding any further in our inquiry.

(Mill 1848)

'Woe to the vanquished' – a saying of the ancient Romans – came to mind when I attended a conference in the Mongolian Parliament building in March 2000.[1] As the only non-Asian I participated in a forum addressing the severe economic problems of the country. The local newspapers vividly reported that not far away from the snug heat of Parliament, an estimated 2 million animals pasturing on the plains were starving to death in the bitter cold. Permanent desertification threatened the country, and it was clear that this disaster was manmade. What was not reported was the important fact that the 2 million animals dying during the winter of 1999–2000 were only the increase in the animal population over the previous two or three years. The fundamental cause of the disaster was the same type of diminishing returns that has afflicted mankind since biblical times: too much economic pressure on one factor of production, land, the supply of which was fixed. Rooted in this phenomenon, vicious circles of poverty were already well established.

In terms of economic theory, the Mongolian situation takes us back to economics as the 'dismal science', to Thomas Malthus (1820), John Stuart Mill (1848) and even Alfred Marshall (1890). In spite of the recurrence and description of these phenomena since the biblical Genesis, the mechanisms at work in Mongolia during the 1990s apparently were not recognized, even when the disaster was a consummated fact. The underlying cause was clearly not global warming, as the Western press reported.

The more I studied Mongolia in the months that followed, the clearer it became that this nation, vanquished in the Cold War, for all practical purposes was being subjected to a Morgenthau Plan (Morgenthau 1945). The subjugated Germany of the Second World War was, according to this plan, to be deindustrialized and made into an agricultural and pastoral nation. Early in 1947, in an astonishing mental and political turnaround, the United States ditched the Morgenthau Plan when former President of the United States Herbert Hoover reported back from Germany: 'There is the illusion that the New Germany left after the annexations can be reduced to a "pastoral state". It cannot be done unless we exterminate or move 25 000 000 out of it' (Hoover's report no. 3, 18 March 1947, quoted in Baade 1955). Secretary of State George Catlett Marshall announced the Marshall Plan, which had precisely the opposite objective of that of the Morgenthau Plan, during a speech at Harvard on 5 June 1947. According to the Marshall Plan – officially the Economic Recovery Program – the industrial production of Germany should, as soon as possible and at all costs, be brought back to its 1936 level, the last year that was considered 'normal' (Economic Cooperation Administration 1949, Balabkins 1964).

During the 50 years preceding the reforms of 1991, Mongolia slowly but successfully built a diversified industrial sector. The share of agriculture in the national product had declined steadily from 60 per cent in 1940 to about 16 per cent in the mid-1980s (International Monetary Fund 1991, p. 13). However, the de facto Morgenthau Plan proved exceedingly successful in deindustrializing Mongolia. In Mongolia 50 years of industry building was virtually annihilated over a period of only four years, from 1991 to 1995, not to recover again. In a majority of industrial sectors, production is down by more than 90 per cent in physical volume since the country opened up to the rest of the world, almost overnight, in 1991 (see Tables 6.2–6.4 in Appendix 2).

An unexpected effect of the Morgenthau Plan in Germany was that a reduction in agricultural productivity paralleled the decline in industrial production (Balabkins 1964, p. 87). This phenomenon – which would not have surprised nineteenth-century economists – was extremely strongly felt in Mongolia, as well. The jobless industrial workers were forced to take up the pastoral way of living of their ancestors, adding 8 million pasturing animals during the 1990s. This depressed productivity and strongly increased the ecological pressure on the pastures of the sub-Arctic steppe (Tables 6.7–6.8). The productivity decline in agriculture is even more notable. Since 1991, average yields for all crops are down by more than 50 per cent, and in the case of the most important fodder crop the reduction in yield per hectare is an impressive 71 per cent (Tables 6.5–6.6). Real wages are difficult to estimate meaningfully, since a shrinking number of people have 'real' jobs. It has been estimated, however, that the purchasing power of the average Mongolian has been roughly halved since 1991 (Malhotra 1998). Already in 1996, before the last decline started, 36 per cent of the Mongolian population lived below the weighted national poverty line of US$17 per month (World Bank 2000b).

The Mongolian balance of payment deficit equals 50 per cent of annual exports. Still the normal market mechanisms which, in the textbooks, are supposed to correct this situation have not been allowed to do their job. An artificially overvalued currency coupled with a real interest rate of 35 per cent make it impossible for the productive structure to regain international competitiveness. Priority is given to short-term financial stability, a choice which, at the next turn of the screw, will hit the financial sector again as the real economy deteriorates even more.

The causal roots of Mongolia's unrestrained economic decline can, however, no longer be traced through the normal sources in the West, since the industrial statistics provided by the Washington institutions – the International Monetary Fund (IMF) and the World Bank – only start in 1994 or 1995 (International Monetary Fund 2000). By then most of the economic damage had already been done. The picture of deindustrialization *à la* Morgenthau becomes clear only when we study the official Mongolian statistics (National Statistical Office of Mongolia 1999). IMF data after 1994 appear consistent with the data provided by the National Statistical Office of Mongolia, which is the source used by the IMF. There is therefore no reason to distrust these important data that the IMF chooses not to publish.

Mongolia only has 2.5 million people, so the disaster is not of the magnitude of the spectre of 25 million human beings exterminated or forced into migration. The matter-of-fact and pragmatic way in which Herbert Hoover presented this drama to the United States had a remarkable impact on Allied economic policy towards the loser of the Second World War. But the fundamental forces behind the drama of Germany in 1945 and the drama of Mongolia in 2001 were the same: the carrying capacity – in terms of both number of human beings and ecological sustainability – is infinitely higher in an industrialized nation than in an agricultural nation. Even a relatively inefficient manufacturing sector provides much greater welfare to a nation than having no manufacturing sector at all. The important synergies between manufacturing and agriculture, as made visible by the collapse of Mongolian agriculture, are but one reason for this. The solution is the same as it was in post-war Germany: the only way to save both the people and the ecology of Mongolia is reindustrialization with a prolonged transition period before free trade is introduced.

The big difference is that today there is no Herbert Hoover, no person or institution with the common sense and authority to overcome what Hoover managed to overcome in 1947: 'all the fallacies of logic, the evasion of issues, and the deliberate disregard of essential economic relationships' (Balabkins 1964, p. 13). The same type of zealots who today fight for instant free trade at any cost also propelled Morgenthau's strategy. Balabkins describes the fanatics then, who 'freely substituted normative views for positive propositions, and out of this mixture arose [a] "scientific" mixture for the treatment of post-war Germany' (ibid.). The economic theory behind the deindustrialization of Mongolia and large parts of the Second and Third Worlds is mostly concerned with the manipulation of monetary phenomena, with a very limited regard for the whole productive apparatus of which these monetary phenomena are but superficial ripples.

Imagine national economies as vehicles moving ahead at different growth rates. A parable for the management of the Second and Third Worlds since the early 1990s would be that of someone who has learned a theory on how to steer the US economy like a vehicle. Then this person attempts to apply the same steering principles to the economies of Mongolia, but without having given any thought whatsoever to what forces actually propel the vehicle. It is taken for granted that a production system like that of the United States and Europe – which has needed centuries of conscious and deliberate cultivation – with all its knowledge and all its technologies will appear spontaneously with 'the market'.

This is the type of problem that the Stanford economist Moses Abramowitz called to the attention of the profession in 1956: standard economic theory explains only a fraction of the economic growth actually observed (Abramowitz 1956). Only about 10 to 15 per cent of economic growth can be explained by the traditional factors of production; the balance became the unexplained 'residual' that Abramowitz called 'a measure of our ignorance about the causes of growth'. Many years later, Abramowitz returned to the same argument. His comment on the progress of economic science since 1956 was not positive:

> [T]he old primitive Residual is really an understatement, a lower-bound measure of our ignorance about the sources of growth . . . Perhaps some of you are thinking, 'If we are already ignorant of 90 percent of the sources of per capita growth, how much worse can it be? Can it be worse than 100 percent?' In a sense, it can . . . 'It ain't what we don't know that bothers me so much; it's all the things we do know that ain't so.' That is really the nub of the matter. (Abramowitz 1993)

Abramowitz points to the shaky theoretical foundations on which the uncompromising policies imposed on Mongolia rest. 'Laying the policy foundations for sustained growth' in Mongolia (World Bank 2000a, p. 2) has, in practice, meant eliminating many institutions without putting anything in their place. Economically, a belief in 'spontaneous order' has produced something closer to spontaneous chaos.

The structure of the rest of this chapter is as follows: section 1 outlines the basic mechanisms that created the vortex of economic contraction in Mongolia starting in the early 1990s. Section 2 discusses how economic theory lost the categories needed in order to explain both economic growth and economic contraction. Section 3 explains the synergies between increasing- and diminishing-return activities. These synergies were reversed in Mongolia in the 1990s. The collapse of the industrial sector starting in 1990 led to a partial and parallel collapse of the agricultural sector as well. I describe in theory the causal mechanisms leading into this vicious circle. Section 4 gives a description of the Mongolian setting, history and economy. Section 5 discusses in detail how the vicious circles described in theory in section 4 developed, interacted and reinforced each other in Mongolia during the 1990s. Section 6 argues that the Washington institutions have failed to meet the challenges that the Mongolian economy presents, using policies that effectively block the market mechanisms that, in theory, are supposed to bring relief. Section 7 discusses the mismanagement of the Mongolian economy by the Washington institutions. Finally, section 8 discusses the implications for the global periphery as a whole and outlines a way out.

Appendix 1 gives an account of the theory of economic thought as it applies to the understanding of uneven economic development, a theory that is highly relevant to this case. Appendix 2 gives statistical data for the Mongolian economy from 1989 to 1998. These data, taken from the records produced by the National Statistical Office of Mongolia, are of great importance, since the official IMF data have eliminated all documentation on the collapse of the manufacturing sector that took place from 1990 to 1995 (International Monetary Fund 2000). Appendix 3 gives a numerical example of one of the main mechanisms at work in Mongolia during the 1990s from an article published in 1923 by Frank Graham, and Appendix 4 gives a stylized version of the vicious circles at work.

1. THE BASIC MECHANISMS AT WORK

The mechanisms at work in Mongolia are the same that have reduced the standard of living during the 1990s in a number of countries, particularly in the former communist countries and in Latin America. According to the United Nations Conference on Trade and Development, 90 nations were poorer in 1997 than they had been in 1990. Thirty-seven of them were poorer in 1997 than they had been in 1970. Mongolia is a typical, but in many ways extreme case. Mongolia's economy is not very complex, which makes it a good case for illustration purposes. Comparing the post-Cold War economic policies with the policies implemented after the Second World War, I argue that Mongolia and large parts of the Second and Third Worlds have, in effect, been subjected to a Morgenthau Plan rather than to a Marshall Plan. The core of the Marshall Plan was not the transfer of funds; it was the reconstruction of manufacturing industry and a strategy focused on increasing the productivity of this industry.

Successful economic policy since the Renaissance had recognized the fundamental difference between diminishing-return industries, in which specialization increases unit costs, and increasing-return industries, in which specialization decreases unit costs. A policy basing a national strategy on the distinction between these two categories of goods has been successfully practised at least since 1485 in England (Reinert 1994). A remarkably clear statement of the theory and the vicious and virtuous mechanisms that emanate from the two types of economic activities was published in 1613 (Serra 1613). This type of consideration dominated the nineteenth-century discourse on economic policy (Schumpeter 1954, p. 259). The importance of these mechanisms was reiterated by Alfred Marshall (Marshall 1890, p. 452) and shown in a numerical example by Frank Graham, a president of the American Economic Association (Graham 1923; see also Appendix 3 in this chapter).

In the history of economic thought over the last 500 years, the dichotomy of increasing versus diminishing returns as a proxy for good versus bad exports was absent in economic theory for only a brief period, from the mid-1930s until the late 1970s. In the 1930s the Harvard economist Jacob Viner eliminated the concept of increasing returns from international trade theory because it was not compatible with equilibrium (Viner 1937, pp. 475–82). Thus a real-world phenomenon that economists for centuries had seen as a key to explaining wealth was sacrificed in order to maintain the 'purity' of the model. A key aspect of the economic terrain was airbrushed out of all maps in order to accommodate the weaknesses of the technical tools that the mapmakers insisted on using. The logical alternative would have been to change tools, but this would have meant sacrificing the assumption of equilibrium and opening up economic theory to a type of market that not only no longer created harmony, but also potentially created disharmony. The abstract principles of the profession created an analytical framework in which the factor left out, increasing returns, was crucial in explaining the growth of welfare. It was indeed a paradox that this happened in the middle of the ascendancy of the 'Fordist' paradigm, which placed increasing returns at the core of the wealth-creating economy.

The attitude of Viner and his followers – that is, virtually all neoclassical economists – was very different from the attitude of the founder of neoclassical economics, Alfred Marshall. In his celebrated *Principles of Economics*, Marshall clearly recognizes that a nation could improve its position by subsidizing economic activities subject to increasing returns and taxing those subject to diminishing returns, such as agriculture (Marshall 1890, p. 452). During the twentieth century, neoclassical economics slid away from its founder into Ricardian and Walrasian models. When the concept of increasing returns was brought back into the theory, it formed a new fashion in economics modelling (Krugman 1980, 1988, 1996). This economic fashion had no influence whatsoever on the policy recommendations of the Washington Consensus, however, which had a devastating effect on Mongolia's economy.

The loss of increasing-return activities has often been observed in nations that have lost wars. After wars, 'Morgenthau Plans' may occur spontaneously. The devastating effects of deindustrialization in France after the Napoleonic Wars convinced the young Friedrich List – previously a free trader – of the need to build a national industry before the final goal of global free trade could be achieved. In 1947, Herbert Hoover was rephrasing what economists had known since the sixteenth century: a pastoral nation could not come close to supporting as dense a population as an industrial/agricultural/pastoral state. If industry is killed off, a nation's ability to support its population is seriously curtailed.

The economic mechanisms set in motion by the free trade shock in Mongolia were the same as those normally observed when free trade is suddenly opened between a relatively advanced nation and a relatively backward one. Experience shows that the first casualty of free trade, the first industry to close, tends to be the most advanced industry in the least advanced country. This was the case, for example, in the nineteenth-century unification of Italy and in the Czech computer industry after the fall of the Berlin Wall. Reinert has described this as the 'winner-killing effect' and Jaroslav Vanek has called it 'the herbicide effect of international trade' and 'destructive trade' (Reinert 1980). This 'Vanek–Reinert' effect is fully compatible with standard international trade theory: under free trade each nation reinforces its comparative advantage – the wealthy First World reinforces its comparative advantage in higher skills in increasing-return industries, while poor nations fall back on their comparative advantage in diminishing-return industries. A comparative advantage in a diminishing-return activity is a 'natural advantage' based on nature's bounty, whereas a comparative advantage in an increasing-return activity is a 'created advantage', based on human innovation and skill.

The problems facing a nation specializing in diminishing-return industries with a relatively weak industrial sector, such as Mongolia, can be observed in Appendix 3 of this chapter. This primary or 'first-round' effect is followed by secondary effects which tend to reinforce each other, creating a downward spiral of underdevelopment. We shall return to these secondary effects and the vicious circles in the case of Mongolia.

2.   KNOWLEDGE LOST: NEOCLASSICAL ECONOMICS AND EARLY MEDICINE

> Just as we may avoid widespread physical desolation by rightly turning a stream near its source, so a timely dialectic in the fundamental ideas of social philosophy may spare us untold social wreckage and suffering.
>
> (Foxwell 1899)

A striking feature of the economic theory followed by the Washington institutions in the 1990s, is that, implicitly and explicitly, all economic activities are considered to be qualitatively alike in terms of creating economic development. This is the outgrowth of an economic theory that increasingly came to focus on monetary and trade phenomena at the expense of the real economy producing goods and services. Periodic crises in the economy had apparently been brought under control through the fine-tuning of monetary factors, and the fundamental engine of economic wealth – the growth of new knowledge and technology – became marginalized in theory. Controlling the ripples of the economic cycles of the industrial world gave the economics profession the illusion of having understood and controlled the extremely complex and varied underlying productive machinery.

The productive machinery underlying industrial economies is, however, propelled by factors that are all external to standard economic theory: new knowledge, technical change under enormous scale effects, and human initiative. All these 'true' factors of production were excluded from the neoclassical production function. Economic theory thus came to externalize the real factors that create economic wealth and to focus on superficial monetary factors. The 'real economy' of production of goods and services was tucked away in a black box, the content of which was assumed to be completely homogeneous, devoid of scale effects and fully accessible to all individuals inhabiting the planet (under the assumption of 'perfect information'). The illusion after the Cold War was that 'perfect' markets – 'getting the prices right' – and 'sound fiscal and monetary policy' would automatically fill the black box of production of goods and services in poor nations. Paradoxically, the enormous productive powers of capitalism were taken for granted by capitalist theory; the focus was on superficial movements of trade and of monetary quantities. Mainstream economics and the Washington Consensus suffered from 'the pedestrian view that it is the accumulation of capital per se that propels the capitalist engine' (Schumpeter 1954, p. 468). A naive view of the economy as automatically creating harmony led to a disregard for the productive apparatus in the second and third worlds.

This reduction of economics to monetary and trade phenomena was not harmful in the industrialized world, where the 'true' factors of production were in abundant supply. But for nations with weak or non-existent industrial sectors it created a dangerous and enduring illusion that economic development could be produced by adding capital to labour in a process analogous to adding water to instant coffee. The activity-specific element of economic welfare, the fact that all rich nations were riding on an industrial wave in which rapid innovation and increasing returns were the key factors, was forgotten. The mature economic activities pursued in poor countries did not present attractive investment opportunities. In other words, these nations could not absorb capital in a profitable way and therefore ceased to attract capital. Having lost touch with the real economy of production, many mistook the symptom of capital shortage as the root cause of their lack of development. The causal arrows of economic change had been inverted; the agent was considered the cause.

In this chapter I apply to the Mongolian case a set of principles different from those of standard economic theory – the principles of the 'Other Canon' of economics (see Chapter 1). I shall attempt to show how development policies based on the principles of the Other Canon would have prevented the poverty, social suffering and environmental degradation that haunt Mongolia. The principles of the Other Canon were applied by the United States during its period of spectacular catching up from 1820 until the First World War. I am, in a sense, holding up the economic policy theories of Abraham Lincoln as the example to follow for the poor world, rather than those of the IMF, the World Bank and the present US Treasury.

A key stumbling block in mainstream economics is the loss of categories. The fact that all economic activities are seen as being qualitatively alike represents a curious break with long-standing scientific tradition. Early scientists saw it as their main task to order observable objects and phenomena into categories and components. Classification put an end to an impression of chaos, creating perceived order in the world. Starting in the Renaissance, scientists embarked on a huge but slow project of mapping and classifying the natural world. Linnaeus's classification of the world of plants is a well-known example. The completion of mapping the human genome in 2000 can be seen as a milestone in this project of classification of nature.

Medicine and economics are the two sciences that most acutely affect human welfare. Medical science and, thus, human welfare benefited enormously from the early classification project. Symptoms were described and classified into different illnesses or syndromes. This classification was a prerequisite for the later development of medicines directed specifically at specific clusters of symptoms. Our great advances in medicine would not have been possible without a prior project of classification of medical symptoms. Here mainstream economics of the 1990s again differed: the same medicine was prescribed for all nations, regardless of their different symptoms and degrees of poverty.

Traditional medicine depended on centuries of experience, as when, starting in the twelfth century, lemons and oranges were used against scurvy in the Mediterranean. The scientific explanation for why lemons prevented scurvy was found only with the discovery of vitamin C in the late 1920s. In economic policy as in medicine, remedies were used without knowing why they worked. As the English economist Edward Misselden put it in 1622, 'Before we knew it by sense; now we know it by science.'

By dividing all economic activities into two categories – those subject to increasing versus those subject to diminishing returns – Antonio Serra in 1613 did for economics what Linnaeus did for botany. It was crucial for a nation to understand whether costs would increase if it specialized in a certain activity (diminishing returns) or whether costs would decrease and create formidable 'barriers to entry' in its favour (increasing returns). In practice, however, the targeting of increasing-return activities had already been going on for centuries before Serra.

In the eighteenth century when Captain Cook sailed around the world, scurvy was again the biggest threat to long voyages. Knowledge of traditional medicine had been lost. Generic 'cure-all' medical treatment such as bleeding had come to dominate medicine. This was, in a sense, a 'Dark Age', when useful traditional knowledge had been lost and before 'scientific' medicine had developed.

Today's debate on the benefits of 'open economies' is similar to the long European debate about bleeding sick patients. In his treatise on bleeding, economist and physician François Quesnay (1750) praises the great curative effects of bleeding on most diseases, including inflammatory diseases and fevers. The discussion then was not whether to bleed sick patients but how to bleed them – how much, where, when. The principle of bleeding was not questioned. In much the same way, the principle of 'openness' of all national economies is not questioned today.

In the other canon tradition from Serra all the way up to the Second World War, it was accepted that no nation could ever grow out of poverty without an increasing-return sector. Only when the increasing-return sector was firmly established should the nation 'graduate' to free trade. As the twentieth century advanced, the habit of dividing economic activities into two categories disappeared from economic theory, essentially because the dichotomy between increasing and decreasing returns was incompatible with equilibrium. The true engine of development – technological change under increasing returns (Schumpeter's historical increasing returns) – was thrown out because it did not fit the tools of textbook economics.

Today we observe the clustering of the world's nations in two convergence groups, one rich and one poor. This process can never be understood as long as the Washington institutions insist on using an economic theory that is devoid of categories of economic activity, a theory in which all economic activities are qualitatively alike as carriers of economic development. Everyone intuitively understands that a nation of stockbrokers will be richer than a nation of people specialized in washing dishes. Pre-Serra economic policy was based on this intuition, that of Henry VII of England (from 1485) being a prime example. However, this insight is not compatible with the theory on which the world economic order rests. The increasing poverty of the 'middle-income nations', which got poorer during the 1990s, is directly related to the enforcement of neoclassical economics in these nations. The middle-income nations had some manufacturing activities, but these were too inefficient to survive the sudden shock of open markets. In many former planned economies, managers in charge of these increasing-return industries probably did not even have time to figure out what their real costs were before their firms were wiped out.

With the loss of categories in economics, depth and quality of understanding are also lost. Antonio Serra's simple model gave him the extremely important insight that the very same economic policy can have very different effects in different industries: 'like the sun which makes clay hard but makes wax soft, like a low whistle which irritates the dog but quiets the horse' (Serra 1613). In Mongolia this insight that specializing in pastoral activities would have a very different outcome than specializing in manufacturing would have spared the country much damage. Standard economics works under what the Nobel laureate James M. Buchanan calls the 'equality assumption' and its models operate in a straitjacket: The theory can only operate at a level of abstraction where all economic activities are assumed to be identical.

The foundations of the present world economic order's theories are fundamentally ahistorical, devoid of any categories that would help in understanding economic phenomena. The underlying theory is, in Kuznets's term, not a 'tested theory'. Too often the main variable discussed is the relative openness of the economy, in a setting where the beginning of time is around 1973. In its simplest form, the argument is that rich countries are open economies; therefore openness is the key to riches. This kind of reasoning is typical of scientific scholasticism (see Reinert 2000b for a discussion). What the Washington institutions fail to recognize is that this combination of wealth and openness is, without exception, the result of a prolonged period of conscious building of increasing-return activities, under whatever name. In the next section we shall see how a simple system of dividing economic activities into two categories provided important policy guidance in Europe for centuries.

3.   DEVELOPMENT SYNERGIES: HOW THE PRESENCE OF INCREASING-RETURN ACTIVITIES BENEFITS DIMINISHING-RETURN ACTIVITIES

'Promoting husbandry . . . is never more effectually encouraged than by the increase of manufactures' wrote David Hume, Adam Smith's close friend, in his *History of England* (Hume 1768, vol. 3, p. 65). The economic changes which have taken place in the Republic of Mongolia in the 1990s show us that the reverse is also true: the destruction of animal husbandry and agriculture is never more effectually ensured than by the destruction of manufacturing. The application of the standard economic theory of the Washington consensus in Mongolia in the 1990s has given us a chance to observe – as in a laboratory experiment – how the classic vicious circles of poverty and environmental degradation set in and reinforce each other in a downward spiral of underdevelopment. The Mongolian experience is almost a textbook case for the theoretical framework in Reinert (1980).

During the early industrialization of Europe, agriculture and industry were often seen as being in competition. The first economist who expressed Hume's view of the complementarity of national investments in agriculture and manufacturing was Gottfried Wilhelm von Leibniz (Roscher 1874, p. 337). This view, later spread by authors as different as Johan Peter Süssmilch, James Steuart and Hume, was to influence profoundly both economic policy and economic development all over Europe. Later, Mathew Carey, starting in 1820, propagated the same basic view in the United States: the synergistic effect of manufacturing and agriculture in a nation. This idea made US industrial policy acceptable to US farmers throughout the rest of the nineteenth century. Leibniz's insight had an enormous impact on nineteenth-century economic policy. For centuries, undoing these synergies – as in Mongolia in the 1990s – would have been seen as a recipe for economic disaster. Just as knowledge of the simple cure for scurvy of eating lemons disappeared, so did this long-tested economic knowledge. The Mongolians are in the same situation as Captain Cook's sailors were: they must suffer because age-old knowledge has been forgotten.

Building the complementarity of agriculture and manufacturing from a purely agricultural nation required a period of protecting and nurturing manufacturing. The principle 'import raw materials, export manufactured goods' for centuries took the place of economic theory in England, as Friedrich List correctly observed (List 1841, Reinert 1998). This principle had been applied in economic policy since Henry VII came to power in England in 1485. In England one important theoretical foundation was Charles King's (1721) three-volume work, *The British Merchant, or Commerce Preserved*. To King and his contemporaries, exporting raw materials was 'bad trade' whereas exporting manufactured products was 'good trade'. Interestingly, trading manufactured goods for other manufactured goods was also considered 'good trade'.

In fact, King's recommendations make excellent sense if we assume that raw materials are produced subject to diminishing returns, whereas manufactured goods are produced under increasing returns. In Germany a stream of authors consistently presented the same conclusions on this issue. Johan Friedrich von Pfeiffer's (1764–78) monumental five-volume *Lehrbegriff sämmtlicher Ökonomischer und Cameralwissenschaften* is one example. All European nations, large and small, attempted to follow these same principles for centuries. As Alfred Marshall (1890) points out, the forces of diminishing returns, presently at work producing increasing poverty in Mongolia, are clearly set forth in the Bible: 'The land was not able to bear them that they might dwell together; for their substance was great so they could not dwell together' (Genesis 13:6).

I suggest that the decline in living standards experienced in many nations since the 1990s is a result of fundamental flaws in the economic models that support the Washington Consensus and consequently the management of the economies of the Third World. As indicated, the core ideas of this essay are that economic activities are qualitatively different and that economic development therefore is highly activity-specific. Some economic activities create development, others do not. And to complicate the matter, some types of economic activities create wealth only if other activities are present, as the quotation from David Hume at the beginning of this section suggests.

The role of increasing and diminishing returns in creating self-reinforcing cycles of, respectively, wealth and poverty also gives us a clue to one of the major puzzles confronting the economics profession: how was it possible for the notoriously inefficient centrally planned economies to produce standards of living that were considerably higher – in the case of Russia and Mongolia two times higher – than the living standards produced under capitalism today? The theoretical framework used here was first published in Reinert (1980) and later discussed and elaborated in Reinert (1994, 1996a, 1996b, 1998).

I also claim that evolution of the institutions enabling development is activity-specific. It is the presence of certain economic activities that gives birth to institutions (a view that represents the mid-eighteenth-century consensus in European economic policy). Insurance was created around 2000 BC because camel caravans and sea trading created demand for such a financial tool and the institutions that provided it, not the other way around. Getting the causal mechanisms of this apparent chicken-and-egg problem right is highly significant. Today there is a tendency to try to create in poor countries, based on traditional agriculture, institutions that are the product of centuries of advanced manufacturing and commercial activities. As it was put in a German price essay written for the King of Prussia in 1749: 'It is not that a primitive people civilise, later to introduce manufacturing. It is the other way around' (see Reinert 2000b). Understanding this causality is indispensable to understanding economic development. In this chapter, using Mongolia in the 1990s as an example, I try to explain why.

Continuing a long economic tradition starting with Antonio Serra in 1613, I claim that economic wealth and poverty can be understood only if 'Malthusian activities' (subject to diminishing returns with international specialization) are separated from 'Schumpeterian activities' (subject to increasing returns with international specialization). 'New trade theory' in the early 1980s (Krugman 1980) essentially resurrected the existence of increasing and diminishing returns, an argument that had been important, if not crucial, to economic policy through the nineteenth century. However, in new trade theory the dichotomy between increasing versus diminishing returns was, for all practical purposes, lost: the 'equality assumption' in neoclassical theory – the fact that all economic activities are seen as qualitatively alike – overruled any other tendency in economic theory.

The elements in each of the two columns reinforce each other and create the virtuous and vicious circles of development and underdevelopment, respectively. In Mongolia, the de facto Morgenthau Plan started in 1991 virtually wiped out the Schumpeterian activities that had slowly been built up over 50 years, and the Malthusian mechanisms took over.

Antonio Serra pointed out these mechanisms when he explained the relative poverty of Naples compared to the wealth of Venice, which he saw as a result of increasing returns. To German authors the principle of diminishing returns was equally important. In the 1850s, Wilhelm Roscher highlighted diminishing returns and related them to the 'bearing capacity' or 'carrying capacity' of lands and nations – terms strikingly close to today's 'sustainability' (Roscher 1882, Reinert 1996a). Not only do different eco-

Table 6.1 'Good' and 'bad'; economic activities from the point of view of a nation-state

Characteristics of Schumpeterian activities ('good' export activities)	Characteristics of Malthusian activities ('bad' export activities unless a Schumpeterian sector is present)
Increasing returns	Diminishing returns
Dynamic imperfect competition	Perfect competition ('commodity competition')
Stable prices	Extreme price fluctuations
Irreversible wages ('stickiness' of wages)	Reversible wages
Technical change leads to higher wages for the producer ('Fordist wage regime')	Technical change tends to lower price to consumer
Create large synergies (linkages, (linkages, clusters)	Create few synergies

nomic activities at any point in time present widely different potentials for economic growth, the presence of some types of activities is also crucial to the development of others, as David Hume claimed. The principles of increasing returns and cumulative causations now underlie the theories of W. Brian Arthur (1994).

Indirectly we also revisit the 'golden age' of development economics of the 1950s and 1960s, with its 'vicious circles' and 'perverse backwashes', of which Gunnar Myrdal (1956) gives perhaps the most concise expression. I claim that at the core of the mechanisms causing Myrdalian virtuous circles are increasing returns, and at the core of vicious circles are diminishing returns. Curiously, like Friedrich List (1841), Myrdal describes the effects of diminishing returns without pinpointing the core mechanisms themselves.

4.   MONGOLIA: A BRIEF DESCRIPTION

4.1   The Mongolian Setting

Ulaanbaatar, the capital of Mongolia, is nestled in a spacious valley at 1300 metres above sea level. Its 650 000 inhabitants do not come close to filling the valley. The country's average altitude is 1600 metres. At this altitude and latitude (about 48 degrees north) the landscape is bleak and nature seems fragile as in the sub-Arctic, where the tracks of a car remain visible for centuries. Mongolia's highest mountain, Khuiten, rises to 4374 metres above sea level.

When one arrives in Ulaanbaatar, the association that comes to mind is an Andean mining town at 4000 metres altitude. The German geographer Karl Troll once described the climate in the high Andes as 'winter every night and summer every day'. This description fits the extreme continental climate of the Mongolian *altiplano*. When I visited during late March, night temperatures still fell below minus 20 degrees Centigrade, rising to a few degrees above zero during the daytime. Because the country is shielded from the oceans by high mountain chains, its climate is very dry, so the cold, though bitter, is less unpleasant than a clammy cold would be.

Mongolia is blessed with an enormous variety of natural landscapes, ecosystems and fauna. The climate ranges from the Gobi desert, through steppe and *taiga* (cedar and larch forests), to the sub-Arctic mountain world of glaciers and frozen rivers. The country is inhabited by 665 species of vertebrates.

On the steppe, only July is frost-free, but the dry climate still offers unique possibilities for herding and raising animals. The animals graze outside all year on grass that appears to have been naturally freeze-dried on the root. The little snow that falls in flurries is extremely light and tends to blow away from the plains. The total population of 2.5 million Mongolians shares an enormous territory of 1.5 million square kilometres, more than the combined territories of Italy, France, Germany, Austria and Great Britain. In 1998 the 2 420 500 Mongolians shared their land with 32 897 500 domesticated animals: 356 500 camels, 3 059 100 horses, 3 725 800 cattle, 14 694 200 sheep and 11 061 900 goats.[2] In 1998 animals outnumbered people by a ratio of 14 to 1. The precipitous deindustrialization of the 1990s was accompanied by a human population growth of 16 per cent and an animal population growth of 33 per cent.

The Mongolian sky is an intense blue and the sun shines about 250 days a year. The dark blue sky in this dry climate is almost like a second national symbol. However, on the outskirts of Ulaanbaatar this image is tarnished by symbols of industrialization: four gigantic smokestacks spew smoke. The smokestacks belong to four power plants that provide electricity and heat to the city. Heating is by hot water, distributed through a citywide system of water pipes. The different plants produce smoke in varying shades of brown, testifying to different generations of technology and thus to the age of each plant. The World Bank recommendation is to privatize the most modern plant, the one which produces the least brown smoke.

This is a truly 'Fordist' and centralized heating system. For the newly poor of the 1990s the heating conduits that run underground through the city provide shelter from the bitter cold at night. Here is where the growing number of homeless children finds refuge. The Japanese social workers call them 'manhole children', from their dwellings.

4.2 Brief History

After having spent ten years uniting the tribes of Mongolia, Genghis Kahn proclaimed the Mongolian Empire in 1206. Under his grandson Kublai Khan (1215–94) the Mongolian Empire reached its largest territorial extension, including a large part of the former Soviet Union, China, Korea, Turkey and Persia. In Europe the Mongols penetrated far into Poland. The Venetian Marco Polo stayed in the old capital of Kharakhorum from 1236 to 1240 and wrote a good description of life in old Mongolia.

Like the Vikings, the Mongolians ended their period of colonizing hundreds of years before Europe's colonial period started. The Mongolian Empire deteriorated after the Chinese invasions starting in 1380, and in 1691 Mongolia became itself a colony of the Manchu Empire. Eastern and Western Mongolia split up, and the Western Mongolian state later joined the Chinese Empire. This part, Inner Mongolia, today forms the Autonomous Republic of Inner Mongolia in China. When the Russian tsars invaded Siberia, Outer Mongolia remained relatively independent. What I refer to here as Mongolia is in fact Outer Mongolia.

In December 1911, Manchu domination ended and Mongolia was declared an independent kingdom. Ten years later, in 1921, a communist revolution led to the establishment of a socialist republic that lasted until 1990. During the Second World War, Soviet-Mongolian troops fought against the Japanese. Prisoners taken in this war built the huge building which today houses both Parliament (the Great Hural) and the government offices in the present-day capital, Ulaanbaatar. This is the building where the economics conference took place in March 2000.

Communism was the first foreign-induced shock to twentieth-century Mongolia. The communist purges in Mongolia in the 1930s were brutal. Buddhist temples and statues were destroyed and monks massacred. The communists outlawed the traditional Mongolian script and substituted the Cyrillic alphabet that is still used today to write the Mongolian language. Mongolians also lost their family names and thereby their traditional clan identity because the communist rulers believed that clan identification could constitute a threat to the system. Only in 1999 were new last names officially put back into use.

4.3   The Economy

The traditional Mongolian lifestyle is that of a nomadic herder who gets all of his essentials from his animals. Nomadic life in Mongolia is organized around five species of animals: sheep, goats, cattle, horses and camels, the largest number being sheep, the smallest number being camels. The traditional household follows the livestock along the vast steppes in search of new pastures and water. Even today only 4 per cent of rural Mongolian households have access to electricity.

The traditional Mongolian house is the *ger*, a round tent with a wooden frame covered with animal felt. Though it appears smallish from the outside, the *ger* is surprisingly spacious inside. The growing shantytowns of Ulaanbaatar consist of a mixture of traditional shantytown buildings and *gers*.

Traditional Mongolian food is the food of the herdsmen. Meat – predominantly mutton – is the staple diet. Tea with milk and salt is a traditional drink, while the favourite drink is *airag*, fermented mare's milk, which is generously served at weddings, parties, and ceremonies. Horse milk is very rich in vitamin C, which compensates for the lack of vegetables in the diet. Vegetables such as cucumbers are grown in small greenhouses surrounding Ulaanbaatar. The true Mongolian barbecue – as opposed to the mock Mongolian barbecue that has spread in the Western world during recent years – consists of whole animals roasted over the fire. The special local feature is that boiling hot stones are added inside the animal in order to cook the meat from both sides. The hot stones from this process are given to the arriving guests so they can warm up.

The Soviets carried through an ambitious industrialization programme in Mongolia. The country was to convert its raw materials into finished products: canned and other processed meat, leather products (jackets, boots and so on), and wool products such as carpets, mostly machine-made but also some handmade. Luxury products processed from mohair goat wool and camel hair are also traditional export items. In addition typical import substitution industries – from soap to clothing and matches –were set up. The non-luxury items were largely traded within the former communist countries which made up the Council for Mutual Economic Cooperation (COMECON), which had an advanced division of labour. The machinery used in Mongolian industry came mainly from Czechoslovakia and East Germany. This policy considerably reduced Mongolia's dependence on husbandry and agriculture. The share of agriculture in the gross domestic product (GDP) was reduced from more than 60 per cent in 1940 to about 16 per cent in the mid-1980s.

5. MEETING THE 'FLEXIBLE WALL': MONGOLIA AND THE VICIOUS CIRCLES OF THE 1990s

In 1990, Mongolia embarked on two simultaneous transitions, one economic and one political. In this sense, Mongolia is more similar to most Eastern European countries than to the former planned economies in Asia. While the People's Republic of China and Vietnam essentially started with an economic transition only, Mongolia – true to tradition – looked west rather than south. In 1991 Mongolia embraced democracy and a minimalist *laissez-faire* market economy, in strong contrast to its big neighbour in the south, the People's Republic of China.

Mongolia has embraced full financial liberalization and capital account convertibility. Starting in May 1997, a zero tariff regime was implemented, except on alcohol. The country has more than fulfilled the requirements foreseen in the Multilateral Agreement on Investment (MAI). In short, Mongolia has followed the rules for success as spelled out by the Washington institutions: Mongolia has been a 'model pupil'. Why then did the 1990s bring the Mongolian economy to the brink of collapse, see real wages plummet and make 'real' jobs a rarity, while simultaneously destroying the fragile ecological balance of the sub-Arctic country, risking permanent desertification?

These problems are not of a transitory nature. In my opinion the coercive advice of the Washington institutions has unleashed classical Malthusian mechanisms leading the country into vicious circles of poverty and environmental degradation. I shall attempt to show that although nineteenth-century classical economics understood the mechanisms that today make Mongolia increasingly poorer, the economists of the Washington institutions have failed to apply the basic insights of their founding fathers, the classical economists. The Washington institutions have ignored centuries of theory and evidence testifying to the different behaviour of economic activities under international specialization: an international specialization in diminishing-return activities, without a national increasing-return sector, has never failed to be a formula for economic and social disaster.

The only strong institution in Mongolia for most of the twentieth century was the state. Other institutional pillars – such as family or clan, and religion – were consciously deconstructed under the Soviet-influenced regime. The communist regime achieved impressive scores on human development indicators, especially on social indicators such as health, education, maternal and infant mortality, and higher education. This achievement was all the more remarkable because it took place in a nation with a relatively low level of GDP and with a widely scattered rural population (see Malhotra 1998 for a discussion).

The year 1990 brought the collapse of the COMECON trading system and opened up Mongolia for trading in dollars. Mongolia's manufacturing industry, geared to adding value to the country's raw materials, immediately felt the impact of the loss of foreign markets. It is unclear to what extent the overvalued currencies of the former COMECON countries contributed to the collapse of their manufacturing industry. Exchanging the currencies of the COMECON nations at their official exchange rate rather than at their value on the black market seemed like a gesture of generosity to the East Germans who had their marks converted 1:1 to West German marks. To the extent that this policy was followed, it brought disaster to the local manufacturing industry in the former communist countries.

Table 6.2 shows the precipitous fall in important sectors of Mongolian manufacturing industry. Table 6.3 shows an index of industrial production in all industrial branches where output is measured in quantities. (Due to problems with previous inflation, a few sectors where output is only measured in value were not included.) As can be observed, in the majority of industrial sectors (29 out of 52), output has been reduced by more than 90 per cent since 1989. No manufacturing industry other than alcohol has declined less than 50 per cent. In 15 manufacturing industries production has either ceased completely or been reduced to less than 1 per cent of its 1989 level. The only industries showing an increase in production are mining, alcohol production (the only industry still enjoying some protection) and the collection of bird down. As we shall see, the growth of the latter category – down collection – corresponds to a general 'primitivization' of the economy back to traditional animal herding. Whereas animal herding combined with a growing manufacturing sector produced increasing standards of living under the communist regime, the virtual disappearance of manufacturing has caused a precipitous economic decline, even in the herding sector.

In real (as opposed to monetary) terms, the economic shock that hit Mongolia and the other COMECON countries was initially twofold. First, the fairly elaborate internal division of labour within the Council collapsed with the opening of borders and the dollarization of trade. This hit the export sector of all the previously centrally planned nations. Second, the industries producing for the domestic market were hit by a combination of overvalued currencies, relative inefficiency, lack of knowledge of their own costs and of marketing skills, and faltering demand from people who had lost their jobs in the export sector. In 1991 the IMF planned to increase the imports of consumer goods (International Monetary Fund 1991, p. 30).

Herein lies the enormous difference between the transitions of the 1990s and the reconstruction of a war-torn Europe after the Second World War: in the late 1940s, economists and policy-makers still internalized the seventeenth- to nineteenth-century common sense that a nation with even an inefficient manufacturing sector will be infinitely better off than a nation with no manufacturing sector at all. No one would have dreamed of demanding free trade between Europe and the United States in May 1945. It was obvious that the manufacturing sector of Europe had to be rebuilt first. This was the essence of the European Reconstruction Programme (Marshall Plan). The Washington institutions subjected Mongolia to a Marshall Plan in reverse: a fairly conscious and premeditated destruction of Mongolia's manufacturing sector, which laid the country open to the grim Malthusian mechanisms of increasing poverty.

The solution for the increasing number of Mongolians who had lost their livelihoods in the manufacturing sector was to return to the way of life of their forefathers as herdsmen. The number of herdsmen tripled during the 1990s (Table 6.8), adding 8 million grazing animals to the fragile steppe. While the number of herdsmen tripled, the number of animals increased only 33 per cent, however. The traditional agricultural sector could only absorb the labour shed by manufacturing and by a shrinking public sector at the cost of greatly reducing the number of animals per herder. With no alternative employment, labour productivity thus becomes the first victim as the diminishing-return activity – in this case, raising animals – pushed towards the limits of ecological sustainability. Avoiding this problem of running resource-based industries into diminishing returns was at the core of the Australian argument for building a manufacturing sector (see Reinert 1980 and 1996a for discussion). Today the economic policy of escaping the traps of diminishing returns – which was crucial for the build-ing of European civilization for centuries – has seemingly not even been considered by the Washington institutions. The overhanging dangers of diminishing returns in a globalized economy are totally ignored in today's discussion (Reinert 1996a). Also gone without a trace is the common sense that rebuilt European manufacturing after the Second World War before opening those countries up for 'free trade'.

During the 1990s many Mongolians were driven back into subsistence agriculture. The average size of the herds decreased from 182 to 94 animals between 1989 and 1998. Today 80 per cent of herdsmen possess fewer than 200 head of livestock, and 67 per cent have fewer than 100 head of live-stock. 'In other words, [the] majority of herdsmen just survive without being involved in productive activities' (Batkhishig 2000, p. 45). We observe the kind of 'primitivization' of the economy that is typical when a whole community is pushed against the 'flexible wall' of diminishing returns. The same phenomenon can be observed with the depletion of fish stocks in Asian fisheries: so few fish are left that modern fishing boats can no longer be profitably used. At the same time, wages collapse so the only way for fishermen to survive is to go back to their traditional ways: subsistence fishing (Endresen 1994, Reinert 1996a). In the mines of Bolivia the same phenomenon appears when jobless miners with picks and spades manually rework the refuse from old mining activities in search of minerals.

For communities specialized in diminishing-return activities without the presence of an industrial sector, globalization will, almost as a natural law, bomb their productive sectors 'back to the Stone Age'. Without allowing for free labour migration, this is the inevitable effect of specializing in an economic activity subject to diminishing returns, be it herding, agriculture, mining or fishing. Neoclassical economics and the Washington institutions fail to distinguish between activities that, under specialization, behave like those of Microsoft and those that have one factor of production – such as land – limited by an act of God, as do the Mongolian herdsmen. The almost religious application of this simplified model is presently the source of much human suffering. The big paradox is that the politicians who are proudly featured on US paper currency – George Washington, Alexander Hamilton, Benjamin Franklin and Abraham Lincoln – all understood the need for a nation to engage in non-diminishing-return activities, and indeed they championed the nurturing and protection of increasing-return activities in the United States. The Washington institutions are not only undermining the economies of many poor nations, but by refusing to allow the Third World to follow the strategy followed by the United States they are also breaking faith with the economic ideals that built the United States.

During the mid-1990s, Mongolia experienced several mild winters. These mild winters helped to accommodate the more than 8 million additional animals on the steppe. When a winter struck which was normal or slightly colder than normal, in 1999–2000, a disaster of biblical proportions befell Mongolia: between 2 and 3 million animals starved to death. Typical of the present mainstream Zeitgeist – never questioning the Washington institutional wisdom but possessed by fear of climatic change – the Western press without exception reported the mass starvation in Mongolia as yet another sign of changing global weather. No one even hinted at the important piece of information that the number of dead animals corresponded to the increased number of animals over the previous two to three years.

In the winter of 1999–2000, Mongolia had reached what John Stuart Mill calls 'the flexible wall of diminishing returns'. If diminishing returns are reached for example in fisheries, there are always a few more fish which can be caught, but at rapidly increasing costs. Diminishing returns constitute 'a highly elastic and extensible band, which is hardly ever so violently stretched that it could not possibly be stretched any more, yet the pressure of which is felt long before the final limit is reached, and felt more severely the nearer that limit is approached' (Mill 1848, p. 177). Mongolia was grazing animals at the outer limits of this elastic band, and a climatic change that was within the normal range wiped out between 2 and 3 million animals.

Crucial in Malthusian mechanisms of underdevelopment is the fact that all of nature's bounties – land, fishing areas, mines – are available in different 'qualities'. Malthus assumes that the best land is cultivated first, and as a nation specializes in a resource-based activity, poorer land, mines or fishing areas will automatically lead the nation via diminishing returns into greater and greater poverty: 'the productive powers of labour as applied to the cultivation of land must gradually diminish and as a given quantity of labour would yield a smaller and smaller return, there would be less and less produce to be divided' (Malthus 1836, pp. 273–4). This is clearly an important mechanism at work in Mongolia, as 8 million animals were added to the fragile ecosystem during the 1990s. Having forgotten both global economic history and the history of their own profession, today's economists fail to connect the age-old paradox of the economic poverty of resource-rich nations to diminishing returns. Today's explanation of this phenomenon, centred on 'Dutch disease' (Sachs and Warner 1995), totally misses the core mechanisms at work in poor nations.

These were only the first rounds of deterioration that followed Mongolia's path into Malthusian diminishing returns. The further rounds of vicious circles in Mongolia are deeply tragic, but very interesting from a theoretical point of view. We find that traditional theoretical arguments about industrialization, both from Europe and the United States, proved correct as Mongolia's development process was put into reverse. As quoted earlier, David Hume – when discussing the economic policy of Henry VII, starting in 1485 – states that 'promoting husbandry . . . is never more effectually encouraged than by the increase of manufactures' (Hume 1768, vol. 3, p. 65). In Mongolia in the 1990s we could observe that the reverse is also true: as Mongolian manufacturing died out, Mongolian agriculture deteriorated. Not only did husbandry move into diminishing returns, but the productivity of the agricultural sector also deteriorated dramatically. We observe a 'primitivization' of the whole economy.

In Mongolia we also find that one historically important argument for protection of the manufacturing sector is still true: during the latter half of the nineteenth century many economists claimed that industry was of crucial importance to national wealth because if a nation specialized only in agriculture, it could not afford to import fertilizer. This was part of an important debate about the qualitative differences of agriculture and manufacturing as agents of economic development (see Esslen 1905 for a detailed discussion). Now when we find that Mongolian agriculture deteriorates for exactly the same reasons pointed out 150 years ago, it is time to unearth the same arguments, based on facts solidly observed over centuries. With the manufacturing sector gone, the Mongolian agricultural sector could no longer afford to purchase fertilizer and agricultural machinery. A very common observation in nineteenth-century Europe and the United States, along the same lines, was that the only farmers who achieved a reasonable degree of wealth were those working near increasing-return activities (see for example Leslie 1888). Again in Mongolia we see these synergies reversed.

Agricultural yield per acre in Mongolia fell by more than 50 per cent during the 1990s (Table 6.6). For cereal crops, the decline was 50 per cent, for oats 75 per cent. Yield per acre for the important animal fodder crops fell by an incredible 71 per cent, no doubt aggravating the situation for the 8 million pasturing animals added due to the collapse of the manufacturing sector.

The next turn of the screw of Malthusian/Myrdalian poverty mechanisms involves five parallel and simultaneous downward movements. In most cases these factors interact: Each one reinforces the others in a downward spiral:

1. The breakdown of the capacity to import (in Celso Furtado's terminology): as the manufacturing sector was treated to an extreme shock, almost overnight exports collapsed. Also Mongolian imports fell rapidly during the 1990s, by more than 50 per cent in current dollars (from $963 million in 1989 to $472 million in 1998). Exports fell even more, though, by 56 per cent (from $722 million in 1989 to $317 million in 1998, current dollars). The exports left are largely from the diminishing-return sectors, mining and raw mohair and cashmere. The permanent trade deficit now amounts to 50 per cent of the value of exports.

2. Collapse of agricultural productivity: combined with the lack of foreign exchange, increasing poverty of herders and farmers follows inevitably, as more and more marginal land is used (Malthus 1836). The combined effects of these two factors on agricultural productivity in Mongolia were enormous; both total harvest and yield collapsed (Tables 6.5 and 6.6). Addressing Mongolian agriculture in general, one of the participants in the March 2000 seminar in Ulaanbaatar writes: 'Activities like fertilization and applications of herbicides were terminated due to lack of funds, fuel and petroleum. [The] majority of equipment and machinery became obsolete. 90 percent of equipment and machinery currently utilized in crop producing business were purchased before 1990' (Batkhishig 2000, p. 46).

3. Institutional collapse: institutions that previously handled agricultural

extension and animal vaccination programmes disappear as government activities are reduced, further eroding animal health and agricultural productivity. The same type of institutional collapse hits human health, particularly support to women and young children (Malhotra 1998).

4. Sharp deterioration in the terms of trade (World Bank 2000b, p. 3): Mongolia has experienced a sharp reduction in its balance of payments because of both a decline in international copper prices and the fact that, compared to before, only a very small percentage of wool and cashmere is being processed locally.

5. A collapse in real wages: estimates indicate that overall real purchasing power of the average Mongolian has been halved since 1991 (Malhotra 1998, p. 40). A wage freeze went into effect in 1996, despite 56 per cent inflation that year and 17.5 per cent inflation in 1997. This phenomenon is well known also in Latin America since the 1980s; wage freezes are kept while inflation continues. The effect of this, unfortunately, is difficult to measure, as many poor countries do not break down their GDP data into the shares of income to wages and to other factors. In the 1980s and 1990s, increasing profits of the FIRE sector (Finance, Insurance, Real Estate) often compensated for the collapse of real wages in the national data, and therefore the phenomenon of real wage decline is not picked up in GDP figures. When Peru stopped publishing these data in 1990, wages and earnings of the self-employed had fallen continuously for ten years, in the end amounting to less than 25 per cent of GDP. (The normal industrial country average is between 60 and 70 per cent.)

These factors interact and reinforce each other. As manufacturing continues to shed jobs, more and more people have to take up traditional means of livelihood. However, the productive land is not able to carry the increased number of animals and therefore marginal land is put into use. As marginal land enters into production and overgrazing increases, the animals grow more slowly and become sickly. As manufacturing exports collapse, foreign currency ceases to be available for purchase of fertilizer and agricultural machinery. As wages collapse, demand for local industrial products is severely reduced. As even more people leave their jobs in the manufacturing sector to engage in subsistence agriculture, tax income is also reduced. As tax income is reduced, the government has to cut extension services to the agricultural sector, which again reduces the productivity of the agricultural sector. And so on.

At the core of these lock-in effects are diminishing returns. There is no indication that these vicious circles will not continue indefinitely. In the

2000 seminar there was no indication that the local representatives of the Washington institutions in Mongolia understood them.

It can be argued that diminishing returns is the only factually based assumption in the whole structure of neoclassical economics. Yet, when dealing with the Third World, this fact of life is ignored by the Washington institutions. The only way out of the vicious circles – as it has been for the last 500 years of world history – is for Mongolia to engage in increasing-return activities again. This will however be impossible without some targeted support for this sector, such as, for instance, the reintroduction of a ban or a tax on the export of raw materials. Such a tax on the export of raw wool was the policy measure which moved England out of poverty, starting more than 500 years ago. In 1995, the Asian Development Bank held up $17 million of a $30 million loan to Mongolia until Mongolia had dropped its export ban (Pomfret 2000). More than 50 textile mills closed, and now the Chinese process virtually all Mongolian wool. At the same time, the European Community uncontested follows the same kind of policy that Mongolia is not allowed to follow: many raw materials – such as fresh salmon – are allowed to be imported duty-free into the European Community, whereas industrialized products from the same raw material – for example, smoked salmon – are subject to high tariffs. Through the Washington institutions, the industrialized nations prohibit the Third World from following the types of economic policies that the industrialized nations themselves follow all the time.

Whereas the Washington institutions blindly apply neoclassical economics, the economic policy actually carried out by the wealthy countries themselves is continuously mitigated by common sense. As regards US economic policy, Paul Krugman complains, 'It is not just that economists have lost control of the discourse; the kinds of ideas that are offered in a standard economics textbook do not enter into that discourse at all' (Krugman quoted in Reder 1999, p. 6). Krugman is right: standard textbook economics generally is applied only in the Third World, through the Washington institutions. Here is also where it does the greatest possible harm. In an industrialized country, which already has its comparative advantage in increasing-return activities, the failure to distinguish increasing- from diminishing-return activities is relatively harmless in the short run. To a country like Mongolia the same failure is fatal.

The targeted support of increasing-return activities has been a mandatory passage point for all economies that have raised themselves out of poverty. Now this road is closed to the Third World through the conditions imposed by the IMF: 'XXVI. IMF to continue including policies on trade liberalization, elimination of state-directed lending on non-commercial terms to favoured industries, enterprises or institutions, and provision of non-discriminatory insolvency regimes, in its conditionality.'

The rich countries have, in effect, pulled up the ladder: the Washington institutions consistently refuse to allow poor countries to employ the same development policies that the rich nations used when they moved out of poverty.

The Washington institutions appear to see themselves as managers of neoclassical black box economies, inside which all economic activities are qualitatively alike. In the theory and policy of the Washington institutions there is no difference between the economic activities taking place in Silicon Valley and raising camels in the Gobi Desert. Today's global economy is based on a theory which 'proves' that a monoculture nation of animal herders in a sub-Arctic climate will achieve the same standard of living as the employees in Silicon Valley. I can only repeat with John Stuart Mill:

> It often happens that the universal belief of one age of mankind . . . becomes to a subsequent age so palpable an absurdity, that the only difficulty then is to imagine how such a thing can ever have appeared credible . . . It looks like one of the crude fancies of childhood, instantly corrected by any grown person. (Mill 1848, p. 3)

I propose that the economic management of the Third World countries since the early 1990s is just such a palpable absurdity. While the industrialized world experiences a new wealth explosion based on the increasing returns from a new 'productivity explosion', the majority of the world's population is struggling in national economies in which all the major activities butt up against diminishing returns (see Reinert 1980). The universal belief of the economics profession that lies behind the policies of the Washington institutions – a theoretical tradition in which the observation of historical facts is absent – is that the market under all circumstances will create economic harmony.

Had it been ethically acceptable to use human beings as guinea pigs, staging an experiment like Mongolia in the 1990s would have been highly interesting. We would have been able to test a theory and observe that centuries of economic theories based on observations of the real world were correct: the removal of increasing-return activities from Mongolia would unleash vicious circles of poverty, institutional collapse and environmental degradation. It is almost too cruel to be true that this experiment was actually carried out under the supervision and coercive advice of the Washington institutions, in the belief that free trade in this situation would cause increased welfare and 'factor price equalization'.

By treating all economic activities as being qualitatively alike, the economics profession fails to recognize the age-old mechanisms which cause the nations of the world to cluster in two convergence groups. One wealthy group is engaged in Schumpeterian increasing-return activities clustering at the top in increasing wealth. This group is mainly engaged in activities where all factors of production are expandable at costs that do not increase at the margin. The other convergence group of nations, the poor group, consists of nations that are principally engaged in activities subject to Malthusian diminishing returns, where one factor of production is limited by an act of God. The underlying mechanisms of increasing and diminishing returns will – if the process is left to the market alone – automatically produce this effect.

The notoriously inefficient communist planned economies proved the same point: their inefficient manufacturing sector provided a much higher national standard of living than what capitalism with a decimated manufacturing sector does today in the same nations. The salient feature of the 1980s and 1990s has been the loss of middle-income countries in the Second and Third Worlds. The main explanation of this loss of the middle class lies in the development of economic theory. Starting in the late fifteenth century, economic development in Europe became associated with increasing-return activities. It was recognized that not only were people working with machinery able to pay more taxes than the farmers and artisans, but also that the farmers and artisans working in manufacturing communities were richer than other farmers and artisans. Although challenged by Adam Smith and David Ricardo, the increasing–diminishing returns dichotomy was a cornerstone of economic policy all through the nineteenth century. In the 1950s it was still part of the common sense behind the reconstruction of Europe.

6.   A PARALLEL REALITY: THE WASHINGTON INSTITUTIONS OBSERVED

As mentioned in the introduction to this chapter, in March 2000 I was invited to Mongolia to present the paper 'The role of the state in economic growth' (Reinert 1999) at the conference 'Mongolian Development Strategy: Capacity Building'. The conference took place in the combined Parliament building and presidential palace in Ulaanbaatar. Most of the papers for this conference are reproduced in the book *Renovation of Mongolia on the Eve of the XXI Century and Future Development Patterns*, which was published both in Mongolian (in the Cyrillic alphabet) and in English (Batbayar 2000). The conference was organized by the Mongolian Development Research Center, a non-governmental organization established in 1998, financed by the Nippon Foundation, a private entity.

Very distinguished Mongolian authors presented papers. Professor D. Byambasuren, the former Prime Minister of Mongolia, presented 'National factors affecting development strategy of Mongolia' (Byambasuren 2000), and Professor P. Ochirbat, the former President of Mongolia, presented a paper on the role of the mining sector in Mongolian development (Ochirbat 2000).

Japanese authors at the conference contributed creatively to the evaluation of the Mongolian situation. A very positive characteristic of the Japanese experts working in Mongolia was their long experience in practical matters, for example in banking. One paper raised the issue of the damaging effect of the high interest rates, 35 per cent in real terms at the time (Fujimoto 2000a). Another paper addressed agricultural development (Kuribayashi 2000), and one compared the development in the republic of Mongolia with that of the Inner Mongolia Autonomous Region of China (Shinichi 2000).

Inner Mongolia (that is, China) now processes virtually all of Mongolia's cashmere and mohair. As opposed to the Soviet Union, which used to buy Mongolian manufactured goods, the Chinese purchase only raw materials: not canned meat but live animals on the hoof, and so on. In Inner Mongolia agriculture has intensified at the expense of herding. When flying from Ulaanbaatar to Beijing, one can clearly verify this from the air. The Chinese, however, seem aware of the problem of desertification. Grass areas in Inner Mongolia are strictly managed, and Inner Mongolia's cattle management and breeding practices are modern. Inner Mongolian farmers appear to have settled permanently and have managed to increase the number of cattle per capita to almost twice that of Mongolia (Shinichi 2000, p. 4).

Towards the end of the conference, the Washington institutions – in this case also including the United States Agency for International Development (USAID) – were scheduled to present their views on the future development of Mongolia. Having spent some time perusing the extensive statistical data available on Mongolia, I was keen to hear the analyses of the 'professionals'. I was disappointed.

First, none of the expatriate experts working in Mongolia bothered to show up in person to address this conference, held for members of Mongolia's Parliament and the highest-ranking national experts and policy-makers. Instead, the Washington institutions sent their bright, well-paid Mongolian assistants to present in English.

Second, the basic message of the World Bank and IMF representatives was a declaration of victory because inflation had been stopped. There was no mention that real wages had declined by half or that agricultural productivity had declined by more than half, no mention of the collapse of the manufacturing sector and of the balance of payments, nor of the 2 to 3 million animals that at the time were dying from starvation almost outside the windows of the conference room. The Washington institutions simply presented three scenarios for the future development of Mongolia: Mongolia would grow by either 3 per cent per year, 5 per cent per year or 7 per cent per year. Graphs were presented and discussed with no mention at all of how the present downward spirals could be stopped to allow for growth. Not only had the Washington institutions lost history, but this presentation bore very little relationship with Mongolian reality; it could have been (and probably is) presented in any country whatsoever. In addition, the World Bank presented a generic document in which the problems of the financial sector in Mongolia were built in (World Bank 2000a).

References to the problems in the real economy were few, but in his paper the USAID representative derided the Mongolians for their lack of entrepreneurship. On the other hand, a local politician complained that Mongolia was becoming a nation of cafés. Entrepreneurship was surfacing in the only sector where an overvalued currency was not sucking in imports, the traditional service sector. One cannot expect an entrepreneurial spirit to arise overnight, especially not with a 35 per cent real interest rate. It took Europe centuries to build up a spirit of entrepreneurship. One Prussian king complained that he had to grab his subjects by their nostrils and lead them to profits.

The USAID representative also derided the Mongolians for 'spending today all that they have today and not worrying about tomorrow' (Bikales 2000, p. 6). This would seem fairly normal for families who have seen their real income cut in half over a few years, in a country where more than a third of families live on less than $17 per month. Too many comments on Mongolia sound like Marie Antoinette's dictum, 'If they have no bread, let them eat cake.' The USAID paper – read by a Mongolian employee – points to the need for 'fostering a dynamic private sector, which will be the engine of growth' (Bikales 2000, p. 2). USAID does not mention the virtual impossibility of creating such a sector when the real interest rate is kept at 35 per cent, conditions under which not even General Motors would be able to make money. These complaints from a US official – whose government is the main architect and supporter of IMF policy – combined arrogance and lack of perception. Reading the US economic literature (for example Carey 1869, 1876) from the time England was attempting to keep the United States from manufacturing – when the United States was trying to avoid the trap of diminishing returns and commodity competition – would have been enlightening for the USAID mission.

In the important cashmere industry, 'Chinese processors can freely borrow money at 5 per cent p.a. or less, while [their] Mongolian counterparts can borrow a limited amount at 40 per cent p.a.' (Fujimoto 2000a, p. 2). This obvious block to any development is not discussed at all in either

the papers or the oral presentations of the Washington institutions including USAID.

Like the IMF, the USAID presentation initially holds up the image of
the mythical 'paths of annual growth rates of at least 5 per cent, and pref-
erably 7–8 per cent' (Bikales 2000, p. 1). It becomes clear that the assumption underlying the presentations of the extended Washington institutions
is that 'the market' will automatically grant these growth paths to all
nations that follow their rules of openness, regardless of what they produce.
We are back to the spectacle of an economics profession attempting to steer
a vehicle by manipulating monetary phenomena, without having any interest whatsoever in its propulsion system. The undeniable historical fact is
that no nation has ever reached a sustained growth path without a period
of nurturing and protecting increasing-return activities.

The USAID paper also scorns the Mongolians for regretting the loss of
manufacturing (incorrectly claiming that no other transition economy discusses this matter). The rhetoric is clear and straightforward, like a somewhat perverted Protestant ethic: the 'painful adjustments' imposed on
Mongolia inevitably will lead to growth. The papers insist that this must all
take place 'based on integration in the world economy', with no understanding whatsoever that historically no nation has ever come near the
growth rates they hold up for the Mongolians without the presence of a
manufacturing sector. The United States itself is the prime example of this.

Witnessing the presentations from the Washington institutions, I found
myself feeling increasingly estranged. These people hardly addressed the
realities of Mongolia at all, and when they did, it was with the unrealistic,
careless cynicism of 'let them eat cake'. It felt like being in a theatre watch-
ing Kafka's *Prozess* being performed. Like Joseph K. – Kafka's 'hero' and
victim – the Mongolians are overwhelmed by the decisions of institutions
that appear to be basing their decisions on a non-existent reality. The
growth paths that every country will achieve – 3, 5 or 7 per cent per year –
if they just 'open up' and globalize are not real; they are illusory and completely out of reach for a country engaged only in diminishing-return activities. In the case of Mongolia, Kafka's impersonal 'Courts' are the
Washington institutions which impose the laws of a 'reality' based on neoclassical economic theory. In this parallel 'reality' there is no reason why the
Mongolians should not be able to create a new Silicon Valley based on goat
herding. In the non-existent reality of neoclassical economics goat herding
and software engineering are qualitatively alike and equally good as carriers for economic development. In the harsh reality of Ulaanbaatar –
where poverty was increasing visibly and the newspapers were filled with
images of dying animals and their suffering owners – the whole scene
seemed surreal.

In the same slightly surrealistic vein, Jeffrey Sachs suggested in *The Economist* that Mongolia should specialize in software, not considering that most people here do not even have electricity or telephones. The idea is a good one if we work in a neoclassical framework devoid of context and assume 'perfect information' between Mongolian herdsmen and Silicon Valley engineers. The real context is that only 4 per cent of the mainly rural population have access to electricity, and that the 1.8 million inhabitants outside the capital have only 37000 telephones between them, not to mention a lack of money for computers and education.

The imposition of impersonal outsiders and their concealed rules have effects that are just as destructive to the Mongolians as they were to Kafka's Joseph K. In *Der Prozess* there is no correlation between what the authorities (in Mongolia's case, the Washington institutions) describe, and reality. In the end Joseph K. is destroyed through laws that he was never meant to understand (Kafka 1935/1994).

7. MONGOLIA: THE MARSHALL PLAN IN REVERSE AND THE CASE FOR REPARATIONS

Modern legal traditions in the United States admirably protect its citizens from the perils of professional malpractice and corporate irresponsibility. A jury award of $2.9 million in damages for the third-degree burns suffered by an elderly woman who spilled a cup of scalding hot coffee from McDonald's in her lap may seem exaggerated (and, indeed, it was later knocked down to $640000 by the judge), but to an outsider the US legal system as it applies to medical malpractice appears more logical. In this section I shall ask the following question, which is only partly rhetorical: what would happen if we applied the legal standards imposed on the medical profession to economists?

As we have seen, the perils suffered by a society producing only in diminishing-return industries has been documented in Genesis and in European economic policy since the late fifteenth century. It was a key feature in US economic theory and policy starting with Alexander Hamilton and Benjamin Franklin, throughout the nineteenth century, when Abraham Lincoln was a dominant politician supporting this view, and through most of the twentieth century. The core of the Economic Recovery Program (Marshall Plan) was to rebuild Europe's manufacturing industries to their pre-Second World War levels and beyond. The perils of subjecting a nation to a Morgenthau-type plan were acknowledged. The goal was to re-establish Europe in increasing-return activities in order to create enough wealth to withstand communist advances. The Marshall Plan – named after the

US Secretary of State George Marshall – was also in line with Alfred Marshall's suggestion of subsidizing increasing-return activities and taxing diminishing-return activities (Marshall 1890, p. 452). In 1953 George Marshall was given the Nobel Peace Prize for this work. From this perspective, the conditions imposed on Mongolia truly represent a Marshall Plan in reverse, both in the sense of the Economic Recovery Program and in the sense of Alfred Marshall's economics.

Mongolia was given assistance by the Washington institutions only on condition that the country not attempt to follow the principles of the Economic Recovery Program (Marshall Plan). A typical progress report for the Marshall Plan, published by the Economic Cooperation Administration in 1949, focused on the reconstruction of the increasing-return sector. The output of every industrial sector was recorded every month and carefully compared with previous months and with the basis year of 1936, the last 'normal' year (Economic Cooperation Administration 1949, pp. 28–9). The progress report for the Washington institutions in Mongolia, in contrast, appears to have focused narrowly on financial stability and lack of inflation. An exclusive focus on financial issues – virtually destroying the real economy by imposing a real interest rate of 35 per cent as of March 2000 – represents a total break with longstanding economic theories, with the traditional practice of good economic policy and with good judgement based on common sense.

One US college textbook in international trade theory seriously suggests that nations producing under increasing returns should pay compensation to nations specializing in diminishing-return activities:

> Thus the country which eventually specializes completely in the production of X (that is, the commodity whose production function is characterized by increasing returns to scale) might agree to make an income transfer (annually) to the other country, which agrees to specialize completely in Y (that is, the commodity whose production function is characterized by constant returns to scale). (Chacholiades 1978, p. 199; see also Reinert 1980)

I would argue that the perils of forcing a nation to specialize exclusively in diminishing-return activities, especially in a fragile ecosystem such as Mongolia's, are extremely well documented both in economic theory and in economic history. 'The Tragedy of the Commons' is a well-known phenomenon, and the concept of diminishing returns continues to be one of the first introduced in introductory economics at the universities where IMF and World Bank economists are educated. How could the economists of the Washington institutions fail to see this peril? How is it possible, as James Galbraith (2000) observes, that the economists who created this economic and environmental disaster are still the only economists who are listened to?

Economic policy in the core nations is never applied dogmatically. As Lionel Robbins – later Lord Lionel – shows in his book on economic policy, the English classical economists did not follow a *laissez fair* dogma in actual policy. These economists were sufficiently close to real life that economic policy was always filled with *ad hoc* interventions based on 'common sense' (Robbins 1952). This is even more true in the United States today, where, as we have seen, theoreticians such as Paul Krugman complain that textbook trade theory is virtually neglected as a basis for US economic policy. As the twentieth century advanced, neoclassical theory became more and more rigid and the economic practice of First World countries diverged more and more from textbook ideals. Only the Third World, and after 1990 also the Second World, became the testing grounds for the unmitigated application of 'pure theory', which had never before been tested to this extent. Joseph Stiglitz, the former chief economist of the World Bank, compared the IMF's handling of the Asian crisis of the late 1990s to the Holocaust (North 2000). The comparison could easily be extended to Mongolia.

However, even in 'pure' economic theory, diminishing returns is a core concept. After the Second World War, the United States, whose short-term business interest would have dictated free trade with Europe from May 1945, granted Europe a 15- to 20-year grace period before free trade was imposed. The European nations were for a long time permitted to look at foreign exchange as a scarce commodity, subject to rationing. In Norway the import of clothing was totally prohibited for 11 years after the Second World War in order to prepare the industry for free trade, and the import of cars for non-commercial use was freed only in 1960. European industrial tradition was much sturdier than Mongolia's, yet Mongolia was given no such grace period. Not allowing Mongolia a period of adjustment such as Western Europe received after the Second World War amounts to gross negligence and ignorance both of economic theory and of recent history.

The Mongolians are a hardy race. The huge loss of jobs in both the manufacturing sector and the government sector has left people with little choice but to go back to their old ways. The number of herdsmen – the traditional Mongolian occupation – has more than trebled since 1990. The number of animals has increased by more than one-third, by 8 million head, during the same period. But the land cannot feed the population of people who previously worked in the manufacturing and government sectors. More and more herdsmen with smaller and smaller flocks compete for a deteriorating and environmentally extremely fragile habitat. The annual population growth rate has fallen from 1.8 per cent in 1991 to 1.4 per cent in 1997, as people can no longer afford children. Support for children has gradually been withdrawn, increasing this problem (Malhotra

1998, p. 3). The support of the West will again be 'development assistance' which merely attempts to alleviate symptoms of problems that have been caused by the West in the first place.

In order to qualify for financial assistance, Mongolia was forced to give up its manufacturing sector. I have closely observed the same phenomenon in Ecuador, where assistance from the Washington institutions was given only on the condition that all assistance to increasing-return activities be terminated. In practice, no equivalent to the US government assistance to small business, subsidies to small businesses in particular sectors, assistance to high-tech industries, and the like are allowed in the Third World. On the federal level, the United States gets away with many subsidies of high-tech increasing-return activities since they come under the guise of defence, but there is little doubt that if IMF conditions were imposed on the level of US states, many if not all of the 50 states would be disqualified from receiving IMF and World Bank assistance. While the World Bank follows the recommendations of the University of Chicago economists, Mayor Daley of Chicago uses city and state money to finance and subsidize an incubator that is targeted at increasing-return high-tech activities. If the Unites States had been a poor country, this policy would have disqualified it from receiving any assistance from the Washington institutions. It is, in my view, crucial that we understand how the industrialized countries, as part of their day-to-day economic policy, continually break the rules that they themselves force upon the Second and Third Worlds.

I would argue that there are clear parallels between the Mongolian case as it has been handled by the Washington institutions and the US court cases that the tobacco industry lost: it can be demonstrated that the institutions in question acted with the knowledge that the product they were promoting – in this case, imposing a shock therapy and restrictions which forced the closing down of increasing-return activities in Mongolia – would seriously damage the health and well-being of their customers, the Mongolian people.

A Mongolian class action lawsuit against the IMF and the World Bank in a US court could focus on five aspects:

1. The Washington institutions have showed gross negligence by not flagging the risk of forcing Mongolia into exclusive specialization in diminishing-return activities. The detrimental effects of specializing exclusively in diminishing-return activities, such as Mongolia was forced into, are well documented in economic theory and economic history, and are taught even at the elementary level of economics in all Western universities.
2. A condition, like that imposed by the IMF, refusing Mongolia the right

to any kind of support in favour of increasing-return activities does not grant Mongolia the same rights as those enjoyed and practiced by all US states, cities and municipalities, and is consequently discriminatory.

3. The negligence shown by the Washington institutions is considerably exacerbated because no action has been taken even now, at this very advanced stage of the problem, when the diagnosis is clearly visible to anyone showing a minimum of interest in Mongolian economic data. The arrogance shown by the Washington institutions towards Mongolian civil society and institutions, such as the Mongolian Development Research Center, indicates a complete lack of interest in the productive side of the economy as long as short-term financial goals are met. The incentive structure in the Washington institutions, which judge economic success exclusively on financial issues, has led to the collapse of all increasing-return activities and to a real interest rate of 35 per cent in Mongolia. This incentive structure is applied contrary to economic theory and to all traditions of macroeconomic management in the developed world.

4. Fundamentally this is also an issue of the human rights of the Mongolians, individually and as a nation. As one of the Japanese experts in Mongolia argues, 'As there are human rights for individuals living in a country, so should all countries have a right to live and prosper' (Fujimoto 2000b, p. 2). In view of the accumulated experience of mankind, Mongolia is the victim of an 'experiment against reality'. As the late Archbishop Helder Camara of Brazil said, these people have been made poor in the name of economics (quoted in Reinert 1980). Arbitrary abstract principles of standard economics are, in practice, given precedence over human welfare.

5. The textbook solution to assist Mongolia's failing industry, to help it become more competitive on the world market and to cure the permanent balance of payment deficit, would be to devalue the local currency. Today the IMF is preventing this from happening, partly by keeping the real interest rate at 35 per cent. So Mongolia gets the worst of all worlds: a 'free market' when the market destroys its productive capacity, but no free market when the forces of the market would help it regain competitiveness. In a way that Thorstein Veblen would have recognized, we observe 'financial capitalism' destroying 'industrial capitalism', a development that in the long term will prove destructive to the financial side of the economy as well.

Reparations to the Mongolian people could focus on the huge share of GDP which has permanently disappeared, on the permanent loss of 50 per cent of the Mongolian people's purchasing power, on the permanent loss of manufacturing capacity and the permanent trade deficit amounting now to 50 per cent of the value of exports (that is on the simultaneous breakdown of the country's capacity to import and its ability to produce manufactured goods itself), and on the permanent damage to the environment through increased desertification in the fragile Mongolian ecosystem.

8.   TOWARDS THE GLOBAL VERSION OF 1848 AND A POSSIBLE WAY OUT

Nineteenth-century industrialization brought with it huge social ills. Books and articles addressing the 'social question' abounded in all languages well into the twentieth century. The social problems peaked in 1848, when most European nations experienced revolutions, England and Russia being the notable exceptions. Manchesterian liberalism and communism were opposite poles in the econo-political discussions, but very different forces cured the social ills. Both in the United States and in Germany dedicated politicians and economists consciously constructed institutions to create welfare states. The German Verein für Sozialpolitik created the operative institutions of the welfare state which were later copied throughout Europe (Verein für Sozialpolitik 1872–1932). The theoretical foundations for the economic theory undergirding the welfare state can also be found in the first 100 years of Schmollers Jahrbuch (1871–1972) and in the writings of the pre-war US institutional school of economics. On the political side, Otto von Bismarck saw that the socialists were right about the huge social problem, and the alliance between the enlightened and idealistic economists in the Verein für Sozialpolitik and Bismarck over time managed to resolve most of Europe's social ills.

More than half of the world's nations were poorer in the late 1990s than in 1990. A new technological wave is creating the 'social question' all over again. This time, however, the social question is not within each industrialized state; it is between industrialized states and the poor nations in the Second and Third Worlds. We are moving towards a new crisis in income distribution, a new 1848, but this time on a global scale. It is my firm conviction that only theories and attitudes similar to those that created the national welfare states will be able to move the world towards a global welfare state. Manchesterian liberalism had no chance of solving the social ills of nineteenth-century Europe. The present version of Manchesterianism – we could call it Washingtonianism – is based on the very same principles as Manchesterianism, and its chances of solving the world's poverty are nil.

What can bring the world out of this deadlock? Economists like those who formed the Verein für Sozialpolitik in 1872 – people who disliked communism as much as they disliked liberalism – cured the ills of Manchesterianism, the equivalent of the system today promoted by the Washington institutions. An individual whistle-blower, like Herbert Hoover in the case of Germany, no doubt helped save thousands of lives and prevented much human suffering (Baade 1955). I have mentioned that Joseph Stiglitz, the former chief economist of the World Bank, compared the intervention of the IMF in Asia to the Holocaust (North 2000). Stiglitz plays the role of the insider whistle-blower, as in Henrik Ibsen's (1882) *An Enemy of the People*. As in Ibsen's play, the very community he is in effect helping chastises Stiglitz, who makes the public aware that something is terribly wrong. This kind of whistle-blowing is unusual in the economics profession, because the appointment systems and career paths are structured in such a way that any person getting into a senior position in the system – and thus achieving credibility as a whistle-blower – will, almost by definition, have thoroughly absorbed the core assumptions of the ruling canon, in which the market is defined as a mechanism creating automatic harmony.

The fact that more than half of the world's nations were poorer in the late 1990s than in 1990 attracts as little press coverage as the German concentration camps did in the 1930s. Yet there are people who know. The report *Transition 1999* (United Nations Development Programme 1999) asserts that the transition to capitalism has 'literally been lethal for a great many people'. Compared to population projections based on demographic profiles and life expectancy recorded before 1990, 9.7 million men today are 'missing' in the transition economies. The 'transition' of Eastern Europe – in most cases from inefficient production of increasing-return products to diminishing-return economies – has been accompanied by great loss of life. As in the 1930s, those who want to know, know, but the matter is not publicly discussed.

The statistical records of the 1990s show beyond any doubt that the market fundamentalism – the quasi-religious thesis that preaches that markets are harmony-making machines – has caused great damage. A reaction is slowly mounting. Joseph Stiglitz's whistle-blowing and the refusal of the editor of the World Bank's development report to yield to the pressures from the US government to change the report are two examples of a mounting reaction. So are the protests in Seattle and Davos, and the establishment of ATTAC (the Association for the Taxation of Financial Transactions for the Aid of Citizens). These events, however, tend to be protests which do not lead to a better understanding of the problems at hand. In my opinion a large obstacle to better understanding of practical policy solutions is that the alterative and factually based economic theory – the Other Canon theory that built the United States – has virtually disappeared. A better policy can only be produced if we have a theory of what causes development to be so uneven.

Because the economics profession today fails to distinguish categories of economic activities, it fails to understand that whereas 'openness' of an economy is a necessary and indispensable policy ingredient for a nation with a strong presence of increasing-return activities, in a backward country the same 'openness' may initiate a maelstrom of Malthusian vortices as the weak increasing-return activities wither away, bringing the economy towards the flexible wall of diminishing returns.

In 1867 the US economist Henry Carey pointed out that Ricardian economics, from which today's standard economic theory descends, has a lot in common with medical quackery: quacks live in a world without categories of diseases and remedies, and they therefore have only one medicine which they claim will cure all illnesses (Carey 1869). It was standard in the nineteenth century in Canada and the United States to argue that backward nations needed a different economic policy from that of advanced nations.

The turnaround in economic theory that is suggested by The Other Canon group is not new. The market fundamentalism that swiped the policy of the countries in the Organization for Economic Cooperation and Development (OECD) towards the rest of the world during the 1990s bears strong similarities to the Ricardian euphoria that built across Europe from the 1820s, peaking in 1846. The backlash of 1848 followed in the form of widespread revolutions. Just as in the 1840s, today's problems in economic theory originate with the abstract system of David Ricardo. In the year 1900, looking back at the human suffering caused the last time the Ricardian system had been allowed to overrule common sense, the eminent Cambridge economics professor H.S. Foxwell wrote:

> Ricardo, and still more those who popularised him, may stand as an example at all times of the extreme danger which may arise from the unscientific use of hypothesis in social speculations, from the failure to appreciate the limited applications to actual affairs of a highly artificial and arbitrary analysis. His ingenious, though perhaps over-elaborated reasoning became positively mischievous and misleading when it was unhesitatingly applied to determine grave practical issues without the smallest sense of the thoroughly abstract and unreal character of the assumptions on which it was founded. (Foxwell 1899, p. xli)

This same criticism could be levelled at neoclassical economics for its devastating effects on welfare in the Second and Third Worlds. It is this kind of theoretical 'mischief' that has caused the loss of welfare in so many countries in the 1990s. The industrialized world has, for the last 50 years, attempted to cure the symptoms rather than the causes of underdevelopment in the Third

World. The Third World was 'put on the dole', like the unemployed of the European welfare states.

As it is now, non-governmental organizations move into newly impoverished countries such as Mongolia, attempting to ease economic pain. Also the World Bank tries to alleviate the symptoms of poverty rather than to spur development. We are experiencing the rise of palliative economics, a science that eases pain without even attempting to understand or address the root causes of that pain. Thus many parts of the Third World are slowly turning into gigantic hospices where the Florence Nightingales of the first world – both on the spot and through donations – do an admirable job of alleviating the pain of those dying prematurely. Our alternative is to develop the economic latecomers in the twenty-first century using the same methods as were used with the countries lagging behind England in the nineteenth century: letting the economic periphery become core by spreading increasing-return activities to them. This, however, requires understanding and distinguishing between the true causes and the mere symptoms of the phenomenon we call economic development.

The Washington conditionalities effectively make it impossible for any underdeveloped nation today to take the step into economic development. The policy of targeting increasing-return activities – whether identified under that label or not – has been a mandatory passage point for all nations without exception. The Washington institutions fail to see that a policy like the one forced on Mongolia amounts to an attempt to defy the laws of economic gravity as they have been observed since biblical times. No nation beyond the size of a city-state has ever reached economic development without targeting and cultivating 'good' economic activities (Reinert 2000a). Today's conditionality effectively outlaws the strategies that made it possible for Venice, England, the United States, continental Europe, Japan and Korea in sequence to catapult out of poverty on the virtuous circles created by increasing-return mechanisms. These mechanisms are, at any point in time, found in some activities rather than others. This makes for the activity-specific nature of economic development. Since institutions co-evolve with these economic activities, economic institutions are also activity-specific.

In order to acknowledge this crucial fact, standard economics has to go back to the roots of its own equilibrium theory, to Carl Menger. The tendency towards equilibrium must be seen as Menger and Marshall saw it: as a very rough map of the economic forces that would be at work if nothing happened, if no innovations and no economic progress were to take place. Menger saw this map as so inaccurate that no quantification should be attempted. After the economy had stopped changing, Menger envisioned a system with vacillation for decades before settling. Unfortunately the economics profession chose to work with Léon Walras's version of equilibrium theory, the theory of split-second equilibrium. The adoption of this thesis caused the economics profession to lose three important dimensions: time, space and the unevenness of economic growth.

Research in the 1990s showed that the world is converging into two groups of nations: a clustering of extremely wealthy nations and a cluster of increasing size in which the majority of nations are getting poorer. Standard economics is utterly helpless to explain this phenomenon. The Other Canon approach suggests that the forces creating the increasing gulf between the two groups of countries are two economic vortices. Nations specialized in Schumpeterian goods are catapulted towards ever-increasing welfare through a sequence of periodic productivity explosions, interspersed by quieter intervening periods of incremental innovation (Schumpeter 1942). On the other hand, nations specialized in Malthusian goods are – as in the Mongolian case – through the natural forces of the market driven into a downward spiral of increasing poverty and increasing environmental degradation. In this setting, Malthus was right: the natural wage level will be at the brink of starvation.

From the mid-eighteenth-century writings of economists such as James Steuart (1767), the rulers of Europe – the 'enlightened despots' in Wilhelm Roscher's term – understood the fundamental symbiosis between manufacturing and agriculture, between increasing-return activities and diminishing-return activities. This created the understanding that a nation with even an inefficient and undeveloped manufacturing sector would be much better off than a nation without any manufacturing sector at all. Targeting and cultivating incipient manufacturing allowed the creation of 'middle-income' countries. The sudden dismantling of any targeting and cultivating of increasing-return activities in Second and Third World countries through the shock therapy of the 1980s and 1990s in many cases effectively made their position as middle-income nations impossible.

Where do we go from here? The Washington Consensus has been through a slow learning process since the fall of the Berlin Wall. The first theory was 'get the prices right' and development would appear as out of a magician's hat. A first modification to this belief in spontaneous order saw to it that the dictum 'get the property rights right' was added. A third modification in the late 1990s was 'get the institutions right'. This position fails to grasp the activity-specific nature of economic institutions, what Richard Nelson calls the co-evolution of activities and institutions. It is virtually impossible to create among a hunting and gathering people an institution that has taken centuries to evolve in an industrial setting. On the other hand, the traditional institution distributing wealth in a family clan of a non-market society becomes 'corruption' in the eyes of the West.

Attempting to understand human institutions outside the logic provided by their respective productive systems is a key methodological flaw in today's development economics. Such understanding calls for an understanding also of non-market societies.

The next step – after 'get the institutions right' – will, in my view, have to be 'get the economic activities right'. In today's divided world we face two possible strategic options: we can either globalize the labour market and let the poor come to where the economic activities are that are able to create prosperity, or alternatively we can follow the nineteenth-century path and spread increasing-return activities that have a potential for technological change to the countries where the poor live. In my view these are the only two real options. The third option, instant globalization combined with palliative economics, is neither ethical nor feasible.

In order to spread wealth-creating economic activities to the poor, the theoretical foundations of the Washington Consensus will have to be replaced with the principles of the Other Canon. A succinct recommendation of Other Canon economic policy can be found in Marshall's *Principles of Economics* (Marshall 1890, p. 452): tax economic activities subject to diminishing returns and give bounties to activities subject to increasing returns. As the taxable base in the Third World is not very healthy, the support to build increasing-return activities will have to come from the First World. I suggest that this 'New Deal' in development ought to be financed by extending normal US product liability and medical malpractice reparations to the nations which collectively – through the economic malpractice of the Washington institutions – were led into the precipitous fall in living standards that hit a large number of the world's nations in the 1980s and 1990s.

APPENDIX 1:   ANTONIO SERRA: A NOTE ON THE HISTORY OF ECONOMIC THEORY AS IT RELATES TO UNEVEN ECONOMIC GROWTH

The first economist who explained uneven development – why the natural working of a market economy would make some nations rich and some poor – was the Neapolitan Antonio Serra, in 1613. Serra's work was republished in 1803, and the year before that a volume of eulogies was published in his honour (Salfi 1802).

Serra wrote at a time when 'public misery and crime spread [in Naples] . . . more and more people gave themselves over to public and ecclesiastic idleness . . . and assassinations increased' (Salfi 1802, p. 21). In his book, Serra explains how the poverty of Naples and the wealth of Venice originated in the fact that the economic activities in which the two states special-ized behaved according to different laws: as Venice specialized in manufac-turing, its unit costs fell, unleashing a virtuous circle of increasing sales, increasing production and increasing welfare. The volume-based low costs in Venice provided formidable barriers to entry for its competitors. As Naples specialized in harvesting the products of nature, the opposite phe-nomenon could be observed: unit costs increased and Naples was thrown into a vicious circle of falling income and poverty. European economic policy had followed Serra's principles starting in the late 1400s. They were expressed in the sixteenth- and seventeenth-century theories of 'good' and 'bad' trade (see King 1721, Pfeiffer 1764–78, Reinert 1998). However, Serra was the first to present a scientific explanation of how the mechanisms of wealth and poverty evolved around vortices moving economies up or down.

The rediscovery of Serra in 1802–1803 was timely. The industrial revolu-tion had again produced a few pockets of wealth and masses of poverty, and in 1798 Thomas Malthus had published his highly pessimistic view on the possibilities for mass welfare. Serra's idea of increasing returns deliv-ered the opposite message, and the nineteenth-century economists who laid the theoretical foundations for mass economic welfare all based their the-ories on Serra's dichotomy: wealth could be created and spread only by spreading to all nations economic activities which obeyed the laws of increasing returns. Friedrich List and Wilhelm Roscher – the economists who put increasing returns back into economic theory – both repeatedly quote Antonio Serra. Based on his ideas it was possible slowly to solve the scourge of nineteenth-century Europe, the 'social question'. There is a massive amount of literature on this economic theory (for example Verein für Sozialpolitik 1872–1932, Schmollers Jahrbuch for the same period, and the writings of the US institutional school).

In terms of understanding the causes of uneven economic development, the latter part of the twentieth century was a Dark Age. In economic policy Serra's principle of distributing and rebuilding increasing-return activities was a core principle behind the Economic Recovery Program (Marshall Plan), but in economic theory this insight was lost. Just as Fordist mass pro-duction started to dominate the industrialized world – where Serra's prin-ciple of increasing returns could be observed on a scale never before seen or imagined – the dichotomy of increasing versus diminishing returns was lost in economic theory. Because the concept of increasing returns was not compatible with the arbitrary choice of making 'equilibrium' into the only economic tendency, the historically observable fact that increasing and diminishing returns produce opposite results (wealth and poverty, respec-tively) was thrown out of economic theory (see Reinert 1980, 1996a, 1998 for more detailed discussions). This opened the way for the belief that globalization would produce 'factor-price equalization', that all nations would be equally wealthy under a regime of global free trade. In fact, according to late twentieth-century theory, the poor would benefit the most, since they lagged the most behind. In this chapter, using Mongolia as an example I have attempted to describe why the opposite results were produced as the few increasing-return activities in Mongolia were closed down by sudden world competition.

With the coming of 'new trade theory' in the early 1980s (Krugman 1980), increasing returns was again put on the map. Frank Graham's 1923 article (see Appendix 3) was the basis for this revival, but although Graham, a president of the American Economic Association, showed – as Serra did – that increasing and diminishing returns would produce opposite effects, by the 1980s the idea of equilibrium was so deeply entrenched that only half of Serra's and Graham's argument was resurrected. The diminishing-return side of the argument was essentially left out. By resurrecting only half of the practice and theory that had dominated economic policy in Europe for centuries and in the United States since 1820, understanding of the mechanisms that create poverty on the one hand and wealth on the other were lost. The half of the theory that was forgotten was the half concerning the mechanisms that keep poor nations poor, and neoclassical economics continued to view the world market as a machine creating automatic harmony. In 'International trade and the economic mechanisms of underdevelopment' (Reinert 1980) both increasing and diminishing returns were resurrected, based on Serra's theoretical insights.

As already pointed out, the increasingly globalized economy produces the opposite effects of what standard economic theory predicts. Instead of a convergence of world income (towards factor price equalization), we find that the nations of the world tend to cluster in two convergence groups, one rich and one poor. In many Latin American countries, 'real' jobs are becoming a rarity and poverty is on the rise. Poverty and disease have increased sharply in sub-Saharan Africa. Most of the former communist nations are considerably poorer than they were under the inefficient centrally planned economy. I argue that a key factor in this economic deterioration in the majority of the world's nations is the failure by the Washington institutions to recognize what most nineteenth-century economists believed: a nation with even an inefficient increasing-returns sector will be infinitely wealthier than a nation with no increasing-returns sector at all. Just as the spread of increasing-return activities to all European nations starting in the sixteenth century created even development, the loss of former 'middle-income' nations originates in the wholesale closing of increasing-return activities in Latin America and in the former centrally planned economies.

The purpose of this chapter has been to use the precipitous economic decline of the Republic of Mongolia during the 1990s as an illustration of the economic mechanisms by which the conditions imposed by the Washington institutions create vortices of increased poverty. Increasing and diminishing returns are at the core of the mechanisms that make globalization a blessing – indeed a necessity for further welfare creation – for some nations, but a curse for many others. A continuation of the present policies against the Second and Third Worlds can only reinforce the present division of the world into two convergence groups steadily moving apart in wealth and income.

Twentieth-century economic theory came to conceive of economics as a *Harmonielehre* (Robbins 1952): the world economy was assumed to be a machine producing automatic harmony. This is a natural result of the basic model. A model in which all inputs are alike throughout the process will never produce anything but an equality of outcome. During the first half of the twentieth century the common sense of the past prevailed over this model in practical policy. During the second half, mainstream economics had generally lost both the collective memory of the past and the habit of checking theory against reality. 'Pure theory' had been mistaken for 'science', and being relevant gradually came to be considered 'unscientific'. While common sense and practical men continued to dominate the policy making of the industrialized North, through the Washington institutions the South was fed an unprecedented diet of neoclassical economics in its pure form, unmitigated by the common sense of the past. The simplifying assumptions of standard economics ostensibly are there to clarify the conclusion. The Mongolian case shows that the assumption that all economic activities are qualitatively alike as carriers of economic development is wrong and has caused much harm. Only by leaving the highly abstract standard theory behind, by reintroducing 'The Other Canon' of economics that produced massive wealth in the nineteenth century, will it be possible to lift the majority of the world population out of acute poverty.

Joseph Schumpeter on Antonio Serra's 1613 Treatise

This man must, I think, be credited with having been the first to compose a scientific treatise, though an unsystematic one, on Economic Principles and Policy. Its chief merit does not consist in his having explained the outflow of gold and silver from the Neapolitan Kingdom by the state of the balance of payments, but in the fact that he did not stop there but went on to explain the latter by a general analysis of the conditions that determine the state of an economic organism. Essentially, the treatise is about the factors on which depend the abundance not of money but of *commodities* – natural resources, quality of the people, the development of industry and trade, the efficiency of government – the implication being that if the economic process as a whole functions properly, the monetary element will take care of itself and not require any specific therapy. (Schumpeter 1954, p. 195)

Before this, a general law of increasing returns in manufacturing industry, also in the form of a law of decreasing unit cost, had been stated explicitly and in full awareness of its importance by Antonio Serra,[3] much as it was to be stated in the nineteenth-century textbook. The restriction of increasing returns to manufacturing should be particularly noticed. Serra did not indeed assert that agrarian production was subject to decreasing returns. But the idea that *industrial and agrarian production as such follow different 'laws'* was as clearly expressed by him as if he had. Thus he foreshadowed an important feature of nineteenth-century analysis that was not completely abandoned even by A. Marshall. (Schumpeter 1954, p. 195, emphasis added)

APPENDIX 2:   STATISTICS FOR MONGOLIA, 1989–98

Table 6.2   Output of selected industrial commodities, 1989–98

	1989	1990	1995	1996	1997	1998
Sawn wood (thousand metres)	553.1	509.0	61.2	70.2	36.5	35.5
Leather jackets (thousands of pieces)	212.8	264.5	18.9	6.5	1.0	0.6
Skin coats (thousands of pieces)	180.2	138.1	16.8	14.9	2.6	0.5
Canned meat (tons)	1682.3	1108.5	431.7	339.2	650.8	322.0
Salt (tons)	4818.8	3811.9	497.3	429.3	240.4	201.6
Publications (millions of pages)	376.6	312.8	50.9	36.5	38.7	79.1
Porcelain (thousands of pieces)	3747.3	3138.3	688.5	150.6	49.3	24.2
Carpet (thousand m²)	2128.1	1971.2	595.7	667.0	643.6	587.7
Felt boots (thousands of pairs)	592.3	588.5	79.0	57.6	48.0	47.9
Suits (thousands of pairs)	182.6	201.8	1.2	1.0	1.2	1.6
Sheepskin (thousand m²)	1151.1	1510.5	193.5	22.4	5.2	–
Leather boots (thousands of pairs)	4140.0	4222.5	245.5	86.6	41.7	33.1

Source: National Statistical Office of Mongolia (1999).

Table 6.3 Index of industrial production (1989 = 100)

Year	1989	1990	1995	1996	1997	1998
Electricity (million KW/h)	100	94	73	73	75	75
Thermo-energy (thousand Gk)	100	107	100	94	95	96
Coal (thousand tons)	100	89	61	64	61	63
Fluorspar (thousand tons)	100	79	91	98	98	106
Copper concentrate	100	101	98	100	101	102
Molybdenum concentrates (thousand tons)	100	125	116	139	126	126
Bricks (million pieces)	100	88	12	15	9	10
Cement (thousand tons)	100	86	21	21	22	21
Lime (thousand tons)	100	108	54	57	60	58
Steel and concrete blocks (thousand m³)	100	101	8	10	8	7
Matches (million boxes)	100	76	58	36	6	3
Mineral cotton (thousand m³)	100	90	13	11	8	6
Khurmen block (thousands of pieces)	100	111	<1	<1	4	14
Spun thread (tons)	100	77	12	6	5	2
Combed down (tons)	100	96	168	207	173	201
Camel wool blankets (thousand metres)	100	100	21	34	26	24
Scoured wool (thousand m²)	100	96	12	8	8	5
Carpets (thousand m²)	100	93	28	31	30	28
Knitted goods (thousands of pieces)	100	103	13	7	8	9
Felt (thousand m²)	100	115	12	15	12	9
Felt boots (thousands of pairs)	100	99	13	10	8	16
Wool cloth (thousand running metres)	100	56	4	2	8	8
Overcoats (thousands of pieces)	100	121	<1	<1	<1	<1
Suits (thousands of pieces)	100	111	<1	<1	2	<1
Hides, large (thousand tons)	100	100	0	10	<1	<1
Sheepskin (thousand m²)	100	131	17	2	<1	–
Chevreau (thousand m²)	100	101	9	7	1	–

Table 6.3 (continued)

Year	1989	1990	1995	1996	1997	1998
Leather boots (thousands of pairs)	100	102	6	2	1	–
Leather coats (thousands of pieces)	100	86	31	11	<1	<1
Leather jackets (thousands of pieces)	100	124	9	3	<1	<1
Skin coats (thousands of pieces)	100	77	9	8	1	<1
Meat and meat products (thousand tons)	100	94	18	14	12	11
Canned meat (tons)	100	66	26	20	39	19
Sausages (tons)	100	95	11	12	14	11
Spirits (thousand litres)	100	101	62	60	78	82
Alcohol (thousand litres)	100	131	75	73	90	102
Flour (thousand tons)	100	95	80	46	32	33
Small intestine (thousand rolls)	100	97	10	6	5	14
Salt mining (tons)	100	51	6	6	11	<1
Salt (tons)	100	79	10	9	5	4
Bakery goods (thousand tons)	100	95	55	45	29	29
Confectioneries (thousand tons)	100	91	24	25	27	23
Milk, dairy products (million litres)	100	96	3	3	3	4
Mixed fodder (thousand tons)	100	56	22	9	7	7
Washing soap (thousand tons)	100	79	9	9	9	6
Toilet soap (thousand tons)	100	100	30	30	10	0
Publications (million signatures)	100	83	14	10	10	21
Porcelain (thousands of pieces)	100	84	18	4	1	<1
Installed metal constructions (thousand m³)	100	101	8	10	8	7
Doors and windows (thousand m²)	100	95	2	<1	<1	<1
Railway sleepers (thousand m³)	100	67	47	43	47	47
Sawn wood (thousand m³)	100	92	11	13	7	6
Ceramic tiles (thousand m³)	100	78	11	6	–	–

Source: Calculated from National Statistical Office of Mongolia (1999).

Table 6.4   Index of industrial production, new products (1995 = 100)

	1995	1996	1997	1998
Candles (thousands of pieces)	100	5	<1	7
Steel (thousand tons)	100	123	146	104
Metal foundries (thousand tons)	100	52	86	102
Injection syringes (million pieces)	100	214	306	151
Injection needles (thousands of pieces)	100	79	–	105

Source: Calculated from National Statistical Office of Mongolia (1999).

Table 6.5   Index of total harvest (1985 = 100)

	1985	1990	1991	1992	1993	1994	1995	1996	1997	1998
Total crop	100	81	67	56	54	37	29	25	27	21
Wheat	100	87	78	66	65	47	37	31	34	28
Potatoes	100	116	86	69	53	48	46	41	48	58
Vegetables	100	100	56	39	54	54	66	56	83	110
Fodder	100	88	35	23	19	5	3	3	2	2

Source: Batkhishig (2000), p. 46.

Table 6.6   Index of agricultural yields (1989 = 100)

	1989	1990	1995	1996	1997	1998
Cereals, total	100	88	58	53	61	50
Wheat	100	86	57	51	58	49
Barley	100	93	71	70	67	50
Oats	100	101	6	10	5	25
Potatoes	100	87	68	54	66	65
Fodder crops	100	111	43	49	56	29

Source: Calculated from National Statistical Office of Mongolia (1999).

The strategy of failure

Table 6.7   Index of number of livestock (1989 = 100)

	Total	Camels	Horses	Cattle	Sheep	Goats
1989	100	100	100	100	100	100
1990	105	96	103	106	106	103
1991	103	85	103	105	103	106
1992	104	74	100	105	103	113
1993	102	66	100	101	97	123
1994	109	66	110	117	97	146
1995	116	66	120	123	96	172
1996	119	64	126	129	95	184
1997	127	64	132	134	99	207
1998	133	64	139	138	103	223

Source: Calculated from Batkhishig (2000), p. 45.

Table 6.8   Number of herdsmen and herdsmen's households

	Herdsmen	Index	Households	Index
1989	135 420	100	68 963	100
1990	147 508	109	74 710	108
1995	390 539	288	169 308	245
1996	395 355	292	170 084	247
1997	410 078	303	183 636	266
1998	414 433	306	187 147	271

Source: Calculated from National Statistical Office of Mongolia (1999).

APPENDIX 3: FRANK GRAHAM'S THEORY OF UNEVEN DEVELOPMENT: INCREASING AND DIMINISHING RETURNS IN INTERNATIONAL TRADE: A NUMERICAL EXAMPLE

Stage 1: World income and its distribution before trade

Product	Country A			Country B		
	Man-days	Output per man-day	Total	Man-days	Output per man-day	Total
Wheat	200	4	800	200	4	800
Watches	200	4	800	200	3	600

World production: 1600 wheat + 1400 watches. In wheat equivalents: 3200
Country A's income in wheat equivalents: 1714 wheat
Country B's income in wheat equivalents: 1486 wheat
Price: 4 wheat = 3.5 watches

Stage 2: World income and its distribution after each country specializes according to its comparative advantage

Product	Country A			Country B		
	Man-days	Output per man-day	Total	Man-days	Output per man-day	Total
Wheat	100	4.5	450	300	3.5	1050
Watches	300	4.5	1350	100	2	200

World production with trade: 1500 wheat + 1550 watches. In wheat equivalents: 3271
Country A's income in wheat equivalents: 1993 wheat
Country B's income in wheat equivalents: 1278 wheat

APPENDIX 4: THE MONGOLIAN VICIOUS CIRCLES CONDENSED

1991: Free trade shock and collapse of COMECON trading area > fall in exports leads to galloping deindustrialization and loss of most activities subject to increasing returns (manufacturing) > lower demand and lower tax receipts lead to massive loss of other urban jobs, in both the services and the government sector > declining demand for people with higher education > wages collapse > lower wages reduce demand for manufactured goods even further > an overvalued currency favours imports over locally manufactured goods, increasing the crisis > return to the pastoral economy in the countryside > fast growth in diminishing-return activities, 8 million pasturing animals added by urban unemployed attempting to earn a new living > fragile ecosystem cannot support the increase in livestock (more than 2 million animals, roughly the increase in number of animals over the previous two years, starve to death during the winter of 1999–2000) > environmental degradation, perhaps permanent desertification > exports collapse even further (exports down by 56 per cent in current dollars since 1989) > breakdown of the capacity to import (trade deficit in 1998 equal to 49 per cent of exports) > terms of trade deteriorate as exports are now raw materials > very limited foreign exchange available to agricultural sector for industrial inputs such as fertilizer > institutional collapse in agricultural sector (animal vaccines programmes, agricultural extension) > complete collapse in agricultural productivity due to lack of fertilizers and the institutional collapse (yield per acre of important fodder crops down by 71 per cent since 1989; the least affected crop is potatoes with 'only' a 35 per cent drop in productivity; all other crops decline by at least 50 per cent) > fears of inflation and of bank failures cause IMF to keep both interest rates (real interest rate is 35 per cent) and currency exchange rate high, blocking the natural mechanisms which should have made Mongolian labour and products cheap on the world market, thus blocking the market mechanisms which would have given Mongolia a chance to become more competitive in world markets. There appears to be no factor in sight to invert these causal mechanisms. See Figures 6.1 and 6.2.

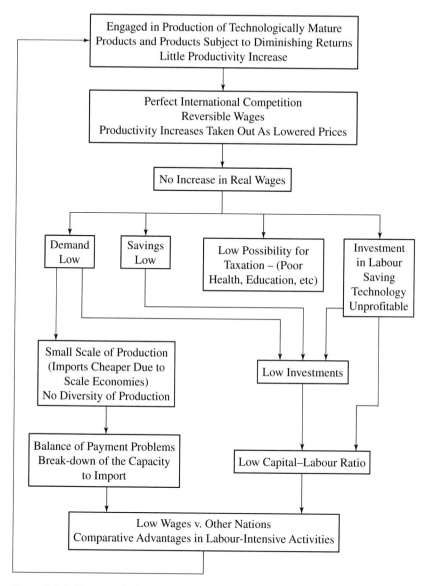

Note: It is futile to attack the system at any one point (for example increasing investment) when wages are still low and demand is absent. An instance of this is poor capital utilization and excess capacity in Latin American LDCs.

Source: Reinert (1980), p. 41.

Figure 6.1   The vicious circle of Morgenthau Plans

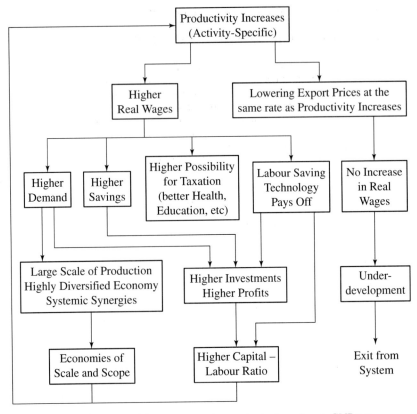

Note: In a closed system, with constant employment rate, the only way GNP per capita can grow is through the 'virtuous circle'. However, the system can be cut-off at any one point, for example if higher demand goes to foreign goods alone, the circle will break.

Source: Reinert (1980), p. 39.

Figure 6.2   The virtuous systemic effects of a Marshall Plan

NOTES

1. The author gratefully recognizes the partial financing of this project from the Royal Norwegian Ministry of Foreign Affairs. The opinions expressed in this essay are, however, his own, and do not necessarily reflect the views of the Ministry.
2. 1998 figures are from National Statistical Office of Mongolia 1999, unless otherwise noted.
3. Serra 1613, part 1, chapter 3: 'nell'artefici vi può essere moltiplicazione . . . e con minor proporzione di spesa.' (In manufacturing industry, output may be increased at less than a proportional increase in expense.)

REFERENCES

Abramowitz, Moses (1956), 'Resource and output trends in the United States since 1870', *American Economic Review, Papers and Proceedings*, May.

Abramowitz, Moses (1993), 'The search for the sources of growth: Areas of ignorance, old and new', *Journal of Economic History*, **53** (2), 217–43.

Arthur, W. Brian (1994), *Increasing Returns and Path Dependency in the Economy*, Ann Arbor, MI: University of Michigan Press.

Baade, Fritz (1955), 'Gruß und Dank an Herbert Hoover', *Weltwirtschaftliches Archiv*, **74** (1), 1–6.

Balabkins, Nicholas (1964), *Germany under Direct Control: Economic Aspects of Industrial Disarmament, 1945–1948*, New Brunswick, NJ: Rutgers University Press.

Batbayar, Tsendenambyn (ed.) (2000), *Renovation of Mongolia on the Eve of the XXI Century and Future Development Patterns*, Ulaanbaatar, Mongolia: Mongolian Development Research Center.

Batkhishig, B. (2000), 'Mongolian economic reform: guidelines, results and future trends', in Tsendenambyn Batbayar (ed.), *Renovation of Mongolia on the Eve of the XXI Century and Future Development Patterns*, Ulaanbaatar, Mongolia: Mongolian Development Research Center.

Bikales, William (2000), document presented by the United States Agency for International Development, Mongolia, at the International Conference on Capacity Building for Mongolian Development Strategy, Ulaanbaatar, Mongolia, March 23–24.

Byambasuren, D. (2000), 'National factors affecting development strategy of Mongolia', in Tsendenambyn Batbayar (ed.), *Renovation of Mongolia on the Eve of the XXI Century and Future Development Patterns*, Ulaanbaatar, Mongolia: Mongolian Development Research Center.

Carey, Henry C. (1869), *How Protection, Increase of Public and Private Revenues and National Independence March Hand in Hand Together: Review of the Report of the Hon. D.A. Wells, Special Commissioner of the Revenue*, Philadelphia, PA: Collins.

Carey, Henry C. (1876), *Commerce, Christianity and Civilization versus British Free Trade: Letters in Reply to the London Times*, Philadelphia, PA: Collins.

Chacholiades, Miltiades (1978), *International Trade Theory and Policy*, New York: McGraw-Hill.

Economic Cooperation Administration (1949), *Westdeutschland im Europäischen Wiederaufbauprogramm: Eine Wirtschaftsübersicht*, Frankfurt: Economic Cooperation Administration.

Endresen, Sylvi (1994*)*, *Modernization Reversed? Technological Change in Four Asian Fishing Villages*, PhD diss., University of Oslo, Department of Human Geography.

Esslen, Joseph (1905), *Das Gesetz des abnehmenden Bodenertrages seit Justus von Liebig: Eine dogmengeschichtliche Untersuchung*, Munich: Schweitzer.

Foxwell, H.S. (1899), foreword to Anton Menger, *The Right of the Whole Produce of Labour*, London: Macmillan.

Fujimoto, Atsushi (2000a), 'Inapplicability of the theory of positive real interest rates to highly inflationary economics', mimeograph distributed at the International Conference on Capacity Building for Mongolian Development Strategy, Ulaanbaatar, Mongolia, March 23–24.

Fujimoto, Atsushi (2000b), 'What Mongolia should do now for her mid-term and long-term economic development', mimeograph distributed at the International Conference on Capacity Building for Mongolian Development Strategy, Ulaanbaatar, Mongolia, March 23–24.

Galbraith, James (2000), 'How the economists got it wrong', *American Prospect*, http://www.prospect.org/print/V11/7/galbraith-j.html

Graham, Frank (1923), 'Some aspects of protection further considered', *Quarterly Journal of Economics*, **37**, 199–227.

Hume, David (1768), *The History of England*, 6 vols, London: T. Cadell.

Ibsen, Henrik (1882), *En Folkefiende*, Copenhagen: Gyldendal.

International Monetary Fund (1991), *The Mongolian People's Republic: Toward a Market Economy*, Washington, DC: International Monetary Fund.

International Monetary Fund (2000), *Mongolia: Statistical Annex*, IMF country staff report no. 00/26, Washington, DC: International Monetary Fund.

Kafka, Franz (1935/1994), *Der Prozess*, Frankfurt: Fischer.

King, Charles (1721), *The British Merchant, or Commerce Preserved*.

Krugman, Paul (1980), *Rethinking International Trade*, Cambridge, MA: MIT Press.

Krugman, Paul (ed.) (1988), *Strategic Trade Policy and the New International Economics*, Cambridge, MA: MIT Press.

Krugman, Paul (1996), *Development, Geography and Economic Theory*, Cambridge, MA: MIT Press.

Kuribayashi, Sumio (2000), 'Agricultural development in Mongolia and the role of official development assistance', mimeograph distributed at the International Conference on Capacity Building for Mongolian Development Strategy, Ulaanbaatar, Mongolia, March 23–24.

Leslie, T.E.C. (1888) 'The movements of agricultural wages in Europe', in *Essays in Political Economy*, Dublin: Hodges, Figgis & Co.

List, Friedrich (1841), *Das Nationale System der Politischen Ökonomie*, Stuttgart and Tübingen: Cotta.

Malhotra, Kamal (1998), *Mongolia. Rapid Economic Assessment: A Child-Focused Perspective*, Bangkok: Global South.

Malthus, Thomas (1820/1986), *Principles of Political Economy, Considered with a View to Their Practical Application*, Fairfield, NJ: Kelley.

Marshall, Alfred (1890), *Principles of Economics*, London: Macmillan.

Mill, John Stuart (1848), *Principles of Political Economy*, London: J.W. Parker.

Morgenthau, Henry, Jr (1945), *Germany Is Our Problem: A Plan for Germany*, New York: Harper.

Myrdal, Gunnar (1956), *Development and Under-Development: A Note on the Mechanisms of National and International Inequalities*, Cairo: National Bank of Egypt.

National Statistical Office of Mongolia (1999), *Mongolian Statistical Yearbook 1998*, Ulaanbaatar: National Statistical Office of Mongolia.

North, James (2000), 'Sound the alarm: Economist James Stiglitz rips Washington's "market Bolsheviks"', *Barron's*, 17 April.

Ochirbat, P. (2000), 'Development strategy of Mongolia: Minerals factors', in Tsendenambyn Batbayar (ed.), *Renovation of Mongolia on the Eve of the XXI Century and Future Development Patterns*, Ulaanbaatar, Mongolia: Mongolian Development Research Center.

Pfeiffer, Johan Friedrich von (1764–78), *Lehrbegriff sämmtlicher Ökonomischer und*

Cameralwissenschaften, 5 vols, Stuttgart: Johann Christoph Erhard, 1764–65 (part 1: vols 1 and 2) and Mannheim: Schwan, 1777–78 (parts 2 to 4).

Pomfret, John (2000), 'Mongolia beset by cashmere crisis; herders, mills struggle in new economy', *Washington Post*, 17 July.

Quesnay, François (1750), *Traité des Effets et de l'Usage de la Saignée*, Paris: d'Houry.

Reder, Melvin W. (1999), *Economics: The Culture of a Controversial Science*, Chicago, IL: University of Chicago Press.

Reinert, Erik S. (1980), 'International trade and the economic mechanisms of underdevelopment', PhD diss., Cornell University; Ann Arbor, MI: University Microfilms.

Reinert, Erik S. (1994), 'Catching-up from way behind: A third world perspective on first world history', in Jan Fagerberg, Bart Verspagen and Nick van Tunzelmann (eds), *The Dynamics of Technology, Trade and Growth*, Aldershot, UK and Brookfield, US: Edward Elgar.

Reinert, Erik S. (1996a), 'Diminishing returns and economic sustainability: the dilemma of resource-based economies under a free trade regime', in Stein Hansen, Jan Hesselberg and Helge Hveem (eds), *International Trade Regulation, National Development Strategies and the Environment: Towards Sustainable Development?* Oslo: Centre for Development and the Environment, University of Oslo.

Reinert, Erik S. (1996b), 'The role of technology in the creation of rich and poor nations: Underdevelopment in a Schumpeterian system', in Derek H. Aldcroft and Ross Catterall (eds), *Rich Nations – Poor Nations: The Long-Run Perspective*, Cheltenham, UK and Brookfield, US: Edward Elgar.

Reinert, Erik S. (1998), 'Raw materials in the history of economic policy; Or, Why List (the protectionist) and Cobden (the free trader) both agreed on free trade in corn', in G. Parry (ed.), *Freedom and Trade, 1846–1996*, London: Routledge.

Reinert, Erik S. (1999), 'The role of the state in economic growth', *Journal of Economic Studies*, **26** (4/5). A shorter version of this paper is published in Pier Angelo Toninelli (ed.) (2000), *The Rise and Fall of State-Owned Enterprise in the Western World*, New York: Cambridge University Press.

Reinert, Erik S. (2000a), 'Compensation mechanisms and targeted economic growth: Lessons from the history of economic policy', in Marco Vivarelli and Mario Pianta (eds), *The Employment Impact of Innovation*, London: Routledge.

Reinert, Erik S. (2000b), 'Full circle: Economics from scholasticism through innovation and back into mathematical scholasticism. Reflections around a 1769 price essay: "Why is it that economics so far has gained so few advantages from physics and mathematics?"', *Journal of Economic Studies*, **27** (4/5), 364–76.

Robbins, Lionel (1952), *The Theory of Economic Policy in English Classical Political Economy*, London: Macmillan.

Roscher, Wilhelm (1874), *Geschichte der National-Ökonomik in Deutschland*, Munich: Oldenbourg.

Roscher, Wilhelm (1882), *Principles of Political Economy*, Chicago, IL: Callaghan.

Sachs, Jeff and Andrew Warner (1995), *Natural Resource Abundance and Economic Growth*, National Bureau of Economic Research working paper 5398, Cambridge, MA: National Bureau of Economic Research.

Salfi, Franco (1802), *Elogio di Antonio Serra: Primo Scrittore di Economia Civile*, Milan: Nobile e Tosi.

Schmoller, Gustav/Schmollers Jahrbuch (1871–1972), *Jahrbuch für Gesetzgebung, Verwaltung und Rechtspflege des Deutschen Reichs* [varying titles], Leipzig: Duncker & Humblot.

Schumpeter, Joseph A. (1942), *Capitalism, Socialism and Democracy*, New York: Harper.

Schumpeter, Joseph A. (1954), *History of Economic Analysis*, New York: Oxford University Press.

Serra, Antonio (1613), *Breve trattato delle cause che possono far abbondare li regni d'oro e argento dove non sono miniere*, Naples: Lazzaro Scoriggio.

Shinichi, Kubota (2000), 'Inner Mongolian Autonomous Region: the shape of traditional production and the pressing transformation', mimeograph distributed at the International Conference on Capacity Building for Mongolian Development Strategy, Ulaanbaatar, Mongolia, March 23–24.

Steuart, James (1767), *An Inquiry into the Principles of Political Economy: Being an Essay on the Science of Domestic Policy in Free Nations*, 2 vols. London: Millar & Cadell.

United Nations Development Programme (1999), *Transition 1999: Human Development for Central and Eastern Europe and the CIS*, New York: United Nations Development Programme.

Verein für Sozialpolitik (1872–1932), *Schriften*, 188 vols.

Viner, Jacob (1937), *Studies in the Theory of International Trade*, New York: Harper.

World Bank (2000a), 'Economic and social development of Mongolia: contribution of the World Bank', mimeograph distributed at the International Conference on Capacity Building for Mongolian Development Strategy, Ulaanbaatar, Mongolia, March 23–24.

World Bank (2000b), *The World Bank and Mongolia*, country brief, Washington, DC: World Bank.

PART IV

Technical change and the dynamics of
income inequality

7. Technological revolutions, paradigm shifts and socio-institutional change

Carlota Perez

The last decades of the twentieth century were a time of uncertainty and extremely uneven development. People in many countries and in most walks of life felt uncertain about the future for themselves and their workplaces, about the prospects for their own countries and for the world as a whole. Inside each country and between countries there were strong centrifugal trends generating unprecedented growth and wealth at one end of the socio-economic spectrum and increasing poverty, deterioration and degradation at the other. Among those old enough to remember, there was widespread recognition that the erratic, uneven and unstable climate of the 1980s and 1990s was profoundly different from the 'golden age' of growth of the 1950s and 1960s. This recognition is probably at the root of the revival of interest in long waves.

This chapter puts forth an interpretation of the long-wave phenomenon which offers to provide criteria for guiding social creativity in times such as the present. In it, I define this period as one of transition between two distinct technological styles – or techno-economic paradigms – and of construction of a new mode of growth. Such construction would imply a process of deep, though gradual, change in ideas, behaviours, organizations and institutions, strongly related to the nature of the wave of technical change involved.

Indeed, contrary to what is usually assumed, I suggest that long waves are not merely an economic phenomenon, though they certainly have economic manifestations. Long waves affect the whole system, the entire structure of society worldwide. This explains why economists have such a difficult time proving or disproving the existence of long waves, although historical memory and the people of each period clearly distinguish the 'good times' from the 'bad times'. In fact I will argue that the instability of the present period has a techno-economic origin and a socio-institutional solution.

According to my interpretation, the long-term fluctuations that we call long waves are the result of successive couplings and decouplings of two

217

spheres of the system: the techno-economic on the one hand and the socio-institutional on the other. When a good coupling is achieved between those two spheres, there is a long period of two or three decades of stable growth, perceived as a time of prosperity. When a decoupling occurs, it results in an equally long period of irregular growth, recession or depression, perceived as a bad time. But why should this mismatch come about and what is the nature of the recoupling?

The causes for this behaviour of the system lie in important differences between the techno-economic and the socio-institutional spheres in terms of rhythms and modes of change. I suggest that there are mechanisms inherent in the way technologies diffuse which result in technological revolutions or changes of paradigm every 50 or 60 years, leading to long-term patterns of continuity and discontinuity in the techno-economic sphere which require matching transformations at the socio-institutional level. Yet inertial forces make the socio-institutional framework more resistant to change and rather slow to adapt to new conditions, except under critical pressure. Thus a mismatch occurs with each technological revolution and it takes decades to re-establish the coherence of the total system. But once a good match is achieved a period of prosperity ensues, leading to full deployment of the new wealth-creating potential.

If this is an acceptable explanation of the occurrence of long waves, the question remains as to what guides the adequacy of change in the institutional sphere. I suggest that each technological revolution, as it spreads, generates a set of best practice principles which serves as a conscious or unconscious paradigm for steering institutional change and for designing the social tools with which to master the new techno-economic potential.

Let us develop the argument beginning with the question of the great continuities and discontinuities in technology. For this we must examine the manner in which technologies evolve. This will be the content of the first section. In the second section we will see how and why technological revolutions gradually transform the whole productive system. In the third section I will discuss why the matching changes in the socio-institutional framework take time to occur. Finally, in the fourth section I will show how an understanding of the nature and characteristics of the emerging technologies can help in designing appropriate responses at the institutional level.

1. UNDERSTANDING TECHNOLOGY AND ITS MODE OF EVOLUTION

Everyone would agree that in order to assess the impact of technical change on society in general or on any particular aspect of human activity, it is necessary to have some basis for forecasting. If new technologies fall upon us like hailstorms or surprise us like earthquakes, there is little we can do as a society to master them or guide them for the common good. I will argue that in spite of the undeniable diversity of technologies, the unpredictable nature of inventions and the uncertain and risky nature of commercial innovations, there is a recognizable logic behind the main trends in technical change.

Let us begin by emphasizing that we shall view technical change not as an engineering phenomenon but as a complex social process involving technical, economic, social and institutional factors in a web of interactions. Single inventions as such do not change the world; widespread diffusion of waves of innovation does.

1.1   Inventions, Innovations and Diffusion

To develop the analysis we need a set of appropriate concepts for classification. The most basic are the Schumpeterian distinctions among invention, innovation and diffusion (Schumpeter 1939).

The invention of a new product or process occurs within what could be called the technoscientific sphere and it can remain there forever. By contrast, an innovation is an economic fact. The first commercial introduction of an innovation transfers it into the techno-economic sphere as an isolated event, the future of which will be decided in the market. In case of failure it can disappear for a long time or forever. In case of success it can either remain an isolated fact or become economically significant, depending upon its degree of appropriability – its impact on competitors or on other areas of economic activity. Yet the fact with the most far-reaching social consequences is the process of massive adoption. Vast diffusion is what really transforms what was once an invention into a socio-economic phenomenon.

So inventions can occur at any time, with different degrees of importance and at varying rhythms. Not all inventions become innovations and not all innovations diffuse widely. In fact, the world of the technically feasible is always much greater than that of the economically profitable, which, in turn, is much greater than that of the socially acceptable.

Thus our focus must be on innovation diffusion. Let us then establish a manner of classifying innovations which will help us understand the economic and social conditions for diffusion and will give us some insight into how meaningful trends in technical change can be discerned.

1.2   Incremental and Radical Innovations

Incremental innovations are successive improvements upon existing products and processes. From an economic point of view, this type of change lies behind the general rate of growth of productivity, visible in the aggregate. The frequent increases in technical efficiency, productivity and precision in processes, the regular changes in products to achieve better quality, reduce costs or widen their range of uses, are characteristic features of the evolutionary dynamics of every particular technology. The logic guiding this evolution, called 'natural trajectory' by Nelson and Winter (1977) and 'technological paradigm' by Dosi (1982), is analysable and makes the course of incremental change relatively predictable. Given a technological base and the fundamental economic principles, it is possible to forecast with a reasonable degree of certainty that microprocessors, for example, will become smaller, more powerful, faster in operation and so on. Once catalytic refining was introduced, it was natural – knowing the profile of demand for oil derivatives – to expect that technological evolution would lead to successive improvements geared to increasing the yield of gasoline to the detriment of the heavier products with lower demand and lower prices. After the discovery of Chilton's Law, according to which doubling plant capacity increases investment cost by only two-thirds, it was easy to predict a trend towards obtaining scale economies in a whole range of process industries. So the great majority of innovations occur in a continuous flow of incremental changes along expected directions.

A radical innovation, by contrast, is the introduction of a truly new product or process. As both Freeman (1984) and Mensch (1975) observe, because of the self-contained nature of the trajectories of incremental change it is practically impossible for a radical innovation to result from efforts to improve an existing technology. Nylon could not result from successive improvements to rayon plants, nor could nuclear energy be developed through a series of innovations in fossil fuel electric plants. A radical innovation is by definition a departure, capable of initiating a new technological course. Although radical innovations are more willingly adopted when the previous established trajectory approaches exhaustion, they can be introduced at any point, cutting short the life cycle of the products or processes for which they substitute. Some radical innovations give birth to whole new industries. Television, for instance, introduced not only a manufacturing industry but also programming and broadcasting services, which in turn widened the scope of the advertising industry. In this sense important radical innovations are at the core of the forces behind growth and structural change in the economy.

1.3   Birth, Development and Stagnation of a Technology

The combination of these two concepts allows us to visualize the evolution of a technology from introduction to maturity (see Figure 7.1). Every radically new product, when it is first introduced, is relatively primitive. In the initial period there is much experimentation with the product and its production process, in the market and among the initial users. Gradually it consolidates a position in the market and the main trends of its trajectory are identified. This ushers in a period of successive incremental improvements in quality, efficiency, cost-effectiveness and other variables, a process which eventually confronts limits. At that point, the technology reaches maturity. It has lost its dynamism and its profitability. Depending on the type of product, this cycle can last months, years or decades; it can involve a single firm, dozens of firms or thousands. As the technology approaches maturity there is often a shake-out, leaving only a few producers. There is also a high likelihood that, at maturity, the product will be replaced by another or the technology will be sold to weaker producers with lower factor costs (as happened in the migration of mature industries to the Third World in the late 1960s and 1970s).

Thus forecasting in relation to single technologies is on relatively firm ground and is, in fact, quite common in the daily practice of engineers, managers and investors. For each individual product or process, incremental change is not random and its destiny, unless another radical innovation appears, is to reach maturity and exhaustion. There are, then, moments of discontinuity and periods of continuity in the evolution of each individual technology.

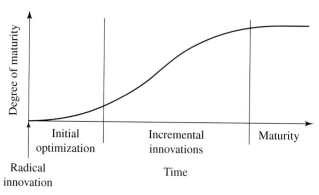

Sources: Nelson and Winter 1977, Dosi 1982.

Figure 7.1 Evolution of a technology (a technological trajectory)

This process on its own does not lead to long waves. Individual innovations – radical and incremental – are constantly happening in products and processes, in different industries and different places. Some are minor, some are major; some have long lives, others short ones. Indeed, if technologies developed isolated from each other the rise of the life cycle of some technologies would counter the maturity and decline of others. But technologies grow in systems.

1.4   New Technology Systems as Paths for Radical Innovations

Freeman, Clark and Soete (1982, Chapter 4) have defined new technology systems as constellations of innovations, technically and economically interrelated and affecting several branches of production. Rosenberg (1975) has described the way in which some innovations induce the appearance of others. Breakthroughs that increase the speed of operation of machine tools, for instance, induce innovative efforts in cutting alloys capable of withstanding greater temperatures and speeds. In general, incremental trajectories in a product, process or branch of industry tend to encounter bottlenecks which become incentives for innovations – even radical ones – in other industries. Nelson and Winter (1982) identify generic technologies whose natural trajectory of evolution encompasses that of a whole set of interconnected radical innovations. In petrochemical technology, for instance, one can identify several distinct but related systems: synthetic fibres, which transform the textile and garment industries; plastics, whose multiple impact, in the form of structural materials, generates whole new lines of equipment for extrusion, moulding and cutting, and whose versatility transforms the packaging industry and opens a vast universe of innovations in disposable products; and so on.

From the vantage point of a new technology system, then, there is a logic which joins successive interrelated radical innovations in a common natural trajectory. Once this logic is established for the system it is possible to forecast a growing succession of new products and processes, each of which, taken individually, appears to be a radical innovation, but when located within the system can be considered an incremental change. The series of durable consumer goods, made of metal or plastic with an electric motor, which begins with the vacuum cleaner and washing machine, goes through food processors and freezers, to later approach exhaustion with the electric can opener and the electric carving knife, is a banal example of this type of logic in the area of products. The succession of plastic materials with the most diverse characteristics, based on the same principles of organic chemistry, is an example in the field of intermediate products with enormous impact in generating innovations in the user industries. The 'green revolution' – the introduction of growing families of oil-driven agricultural machinery, together with multiple petrochemical innovations in fertilizers, herbicides and pesticides – is an example of the coherent evolution in the logic of a productive system.

The widespread impact of a new technology system stems from the 'wide adaptability' of the contributing innovations and from their multiple character (Keirstead 1948). The innovations are not merely technological. Each technological system brings together technical innovations in inputs, products and processes with organizational and managerial innovations. Further, they can induce important social, institutional and even political changes. The technological constellation of the 'green revolution' led to single-crop farming in great expanses of land and induced changes in the organization of production and distribution as well as in the structure of ownership. The automobile, the assembly line, the networks of parts suppliers, distributors and service stations, suburban living and commercial centres are only some of the elements of the technical, economic and social constellation gradually built around the internal combustion engine.

Yet technological systems, like individual technologies, eventually exhaust their potential for further growth and improvement. For a long time a new technology system provides multiple and growing opportunities for innovation and investment in complementary products, services or supplies. But the time comes when the system loses technological and market dynamism, reaches maturity, threatens the growth and profits of most of the firms involved and therefore stimulates a search for radical new products that will serve as the core of other new technological systems.

So at the level of technological systems we encounter the same phenomena of continuity and discontinuity in evolution. Again at first sight there is no reason to expect long waves to occur because of limits in the life cycle of technological systems. As with individual innovations, one could imagine a constant process of counterbalancing of the growth and decline of different systems in different parts of the economy. This would be the case if systems developed in isolation, but technological systems grow in interconnection with each other and with the surrounding economic, cultural and institutional environment.

1.5 Self-reinforced Processes of Growth and Exhaustion

The consequences of the exhaustion of a system are not overcome as simply as those of the obsolescence of individual products. When a system reaches maturity and loses dynamism, not only the producing firms are obliged to face change, but also all the social and institutional arrangements that had been set up around the system. The process of substitution is not one of eradication but of a slow and painful change in the proportions of the new against the old, but the end result is a radical change in the structures involved. Such was the case when cargo railways and ships were gradually replaced by trucks and aeroplanes, when natural materials were replaced by synthetics, when the reign of radio was replaced by that of TV and when vinyl records were replaced by CDs. Everyone from suppliers to consumers had to adapt in one way or another and these changes usually implied a reshuffling of the relative positions of all players (often including the elimination of some and the emergence of new ones), together with changes in the rules of the game. So once we visualize individual technologies within technological systems we can begin to understand the complex set of interactions that take place as technologies diffuse and the difficulties that discontinuities in technical change can create for the parts of society involved.

The deployment of each technological system involves several interconnected processes of change and adaptation:

1. The development of surrounding services (required infrastructure, specialized suppliers, distributors, maintenance services and so on).
2. The 'cultural' adaptation to the logic of the interconnected technologies involved (among engineers, managers, sales and service people, consumers and so on).
3. The setting up of the institutional facilitators (rules and regulations, specialized training and education and so on).

This adaptation of the economic, cultural and institutional environment to the requirements of technological systems is not passive. The environment in turn shapes the development of the systems in very important ways, including cases of significant resistance to diffusion, such as the resistance to nuclear energy. For our purposes, though, there is one particular phenomenon with far-reaching consequences: the social environment becomes a powerful selection mechanism for the inclusion or exclusion of particular innovations, making it easier and easier to invest in products and services belonging to the system and much less comfortable to invest in unrelated innovations

The adaptations that occur around a particular system generate conditions that strongly favour innovations that are compatible with – or can be fitted into – the systems already in place. What they provide, in fact, is a free and ready-made advantage for other similar products. After all homes have electricity, you can bring to market as many electric products for the home as you can invent. After grocers and homes have freezers, you can innovate all you want in frozen foods. After textile machinery handles synthetics, you can introduce further and further varieties of new fibres. Brian Arthur (1988) has shown how these 'lock-in' phenomena occur even at the level of individual products selecting among competing technologies. The triumph of VHS and the gradual exclusion of BETA technology in video cassettes, even though many experts held that BETA was superior, is an example of how certain market conditions favouring early diffusion of a particular product or technology can result in a permanent bias.

So the development of a system produces externalities facilitating radical innovations which follow well-trodden general trajectories or which are capable of creating related trajectories. This is because, among other things, these externalities reduce the expenses of introducing an innovation and convincing users, which are often the highest costs and the most difficult to recover in the market.

The consequences of this phenomenon are twofold. First, many potential innovations are either excluded or submitted to the existing logic, leaving out some of their most radical uses. When transistors first appeared, for instance, they became a means of making radios and other electrical appliances small enough to be portable. The early integrated chips in the 1960s were used mainly for hearing aids and a couple of minor military applications. The idea of putting them into computers existed, but the economic and market conditions for the success of this much farther-reaching application had not yet appeared. In fact, existing systems induce a sort of blindness which affects even the most forward-looking engineers and entrepreneurs. In the early days of electricity Werner Siemens thought that wiring every home was a utopia, and when IBM brought out the first commercial computers T.J. Watson Sr, IBM's CEO, thought that the world market would be saturated with a few such machines.

The other consequence of these increasingly powerful externalities is that the greater the development of a system, the shorter the life cycle of each radical innovation within it. The life cycles of the radical innovations that appear in the later stages of the development of a system are usually much shorter than those of the earlier ones. This is partly because the major innovations are generally those which give birth to the system while the later ones tend to be complementary. But it is also because once the supplies have been standardized, the habits established and the users conditioned, it takes very little time to make the whole series of incremental innovations and to reach market saturation and 'vegetative' growth. It took decades for every home to have an electric or gas cooker, a refrigerator and a washing machine, but it took only a few years to reach the great majority of possible consumers of electric can openers and electric carving knives.

So the mesh of mutual adaptation between technological systems and the economic, cultural and institutional environment tends to make the whole structure self-reinforcing, both in its development and in its exhaustion, in its inclusion and in its exclusion mechanisms. The problem arises when the firms that operate within mature systems face a serious threat to growth, profits and even survival.

1.6   Technological Revolutions as Rejuvenation of All Systems

In the early 1970s it was widely agreed (and feared) that the automobile industry had reached maturity. Its markets had lost dynamism and grew extremely slowly, if at all, inventories piled up, productivity stagnated and profits were threatened. Many experts declared that automobiles had become 'commodities' and that the future lay in complete standardization by moving towards the 'world car': engines would be produced in one country, gear boxes in another, bodies in the next, and so on, in order to increase productivity through maximizing economies of scale. This was the way imagined by the mentality of the time to confront the maturity of that technological system.

Few could foresee what actually happened. Japanese industry developed a different way of organizing production and markets, which at first threatened to overtake much of the world automobile industry but instead led to a thorough revamping of all firms and their forms of insertion, competition and interrelation. In the end, through a synergistic combination of the new managerial style and the introduction of information technology into production processes, products, administration and markets, the industry was completely renewed and set on a different and very dynamic trajectory of incremental innovation (Altshuler et al. 1982, Womack et al. 1990).

So maturity does not inevitably end in the marginalization of a system, nor is it necessary that a radical innovation in the core product itself should come to the rescue and replace the previous mature product. Both can and sometimes do occur. What is more likely to take place, especially at those times – such as the 1970s – when many interrelated systems tend to come to maturity more or less simultaneously, is that a general solution appears in the form of a technological revolution. What happens then is the diffusion of a new set of generic technologies, capable of rejuvenating and transforming practically all existing industries, together with the creation of a group of new dynamic industries at the core of radically new technological systems. These are the technological revolutions described by Schumpeter (1939) as 'gales of creative destruction'. They have occurred about every 50 or 60 years and they lie at the root of the so-called long waves in economic growth.

Schumpeter and many others after him have emphasized the powerfully dynamic nature of each of those great waves of new technologies as well as their capacity to profoundly modify the world around them (see for example Landes 1969, Nye 1990). Society has recognized their overarching influence by referring to the periods when these great technological changes have diffused as the Industrial Revolution, the Railway Era, the Age of Electricity and the Age of the Automobile. The industries at the core of these revolutions do indeed become the propellers of growth for a considerable length of time. They also lead to the proliferation of whole new industries and services complementary to the production and use of the new products, as was discussed above for technological systems of major importance.

Yet I suggest that they do much more than that. Technological revolutions change the 'commonsense' criteria for engineering and business behaviour across the board. In fact, in my view, each technological revolution merits that name, not only for the importance of the new industries it ushers in and the new technical possibilities it opens but also – and perhaps mainly – because it radically modifies the 'best practice frontier' for all sectors of the economy.

Each of these revolutions is in fact a constellation of technological systems with a common dynamic and including a set of generic technologies of widespread applicability. Its diffusion across the length and breadth of the productive sphere tends to encompass almost the whole of the economy and ends up transforming the ways of producing, the ways of living and the economic geography of the whole world.

Such all-pervasive revolutions generate, therefore, massive and fundamental changes in the behaviour of economic agents. What type of mechanism would be capable of serving as guiding force for a shift of this sort?

2. TECHNO-ECONOMIC PARADIGMS AS COMMONSENSE MODELS TRANSFORMING THE PRODUCTIVE SPHERE

2.1 A Cheap Input as Vehicle of Diffusion

Due to the exclusion mechanisms we have been discussing, the appearance of revolutionary new technologies will not automatically guarantee adoption from branch to branch and on a world scale. Diffusion in the early phase demands a simple vehicle of propagation, accessible to millions of individual decision agents and coherent with their decision-making criteria. That vehicle is long-term cost effectiveness. Although many of the products of each technological revolution can be inaccessibly expensive at first (as were computers, for instance), at the core of each of these great waves of innovation there is a key input which is very cheap, offers to remain cheap and, in conjunction with a constellation of generic innovations, radically transforms – in its favour – the relative cost structure confronting entrepreneurs, managers and engineers (Perez 1983).

Behind the spread of railways and the steam engine in the mid-nineteenth century there was an abundance of cheap coal. Behind the spread of electricity, heavy chemistry and heavy civil engineering at the turn of the twentieth century we find the Bessemer and Siemens Martin processes that made steel as cheap as iron. Behind the spread of asphalt roads and automobiles, electricity in every home and plastics and synthetics for every purpose, we find cheap petroleum and technologies that made energy and petrochemical products less and less expensive. Behind the present information and telecommunications revolution we find ever cheaper and more powerful electronic chips (Freeman and Perez 1988).

In each case the key input – or 'key factor' as I have called it (Perez 1985) – represents the new generic technologies in economic terms and steers engineering and investment decisions towards their intensive use.

2.2   Diffusion is Self-reinforced

So I suggest that there are two main reasons why a set of truly new technologies is able to spread in a world still dominated by the old: (1) the exclusion mechanisms have been weakened by the signs of exhaustion of the prevailing technologies, and (2) there are obvious changes in the relative cost structure which are seen to be permanent and act in favour of the new technologies. Therefore investment capital in search of better profits sees a good direction in which to plunge.

The process of switching over becomes self-reinforcing through several feedback loops. The greater the diffusion of its applications, the greater the demand for the 'key factor', which leads to economies of scale and lower costs, which in turn widens the range of applications. The more the new technology spreads, the more profitable it is to set up as a supplier to it or as a distributor, which further facilitates propagation. The more investment tends to incorporate the new technologies and equipment, the more the product mix of equipment producers moves to respond to this new dynamic demand and the more difficult it becomes to find the old type of equipment in the market. (This occurs even in consumer products: imagine the difficulties experienced by someone in the 1990s insisting on buying or finding maintenance services for a traditional manual – or even electric – typewriter.) The more consumers learn about using the products associated with the new technologies, the easier it is for them to accept the next product or the next generation of the same product. The more the process of innovation leads to extraordinary profits and growth in new industries and firms, the more likely are the waves of imitation, and so on and so forth.

2.3 A New Paradigm as a Quantum Jump in Potential Productivity for All

Yet the process overflows beyond the propagation of the key factor and the growth of the industries related to it. Each technological revolution also generates a wave of organizational innovation which, in synergy with the new generic technologies of widespread applicability, offers a quantum jump in productivity for all industries, however old and established (Perez 1986).

The principles of mass production, which applied the continuous flow of the chemical industry to the assembly of identical fabricated products, were first fully developed for the automobile but then diffused across all sectors. Ford's dictum in the 1920s, 'You can have any colour as long as it is black', could have been applied to mass charter tourism in the 1960s and 1970s. Du Pont's organizational innovation in its corporate structure, the 'm-form' with its many layers, functional departments and divisions, was originally created just for Du Pont, but it became the model for effectiveness and efficiency in all industries until very recently. Today the adaptability of the Japanese managerial network has been found to be one of the most appropriate forms of organization to take advantage of the flexibility of information technology. So it is diffusing through more and more sectors and being adopted and creatively adapted to different conditions locally and globally.

So each technological revolution brings a set of new industries, with a low-cost input at the core, and a set of generic all-pervasive technologies and organizational principles capable of renewing all the other productive activities.

2.4 A Techno-economic Paradigm as an Overarching Logic for the Technological Systems of a Period

This set of interrelated technical and organizational innovations gradually comes together as a best practice model – or a 'techno-economic paradigm' (Perez 1985) – capable of guiding the diffusion of each specific technological revolution. As it spreads, this new paradigm gradually takes root in collective consciousness, replacing the old ideas and becoming the new 'common sense' of engineers, managers and investors for the most efficient and 'modern' productive practice across the board.

Although for the direct actors this is often largely an unconscious process in response to changing circumstances, the underlying logic of change can be observed and analysed and its common general principles can be identified. Doing so – and helping change to occur – has become the business of thousands of consultants in this transition.

What this means is that each technological revolution establishes an overarching paradigm as the techno-economic common sense for a long period of five or six decades. This general logic guides not only the course of incremental innovations during each period but also the search for radical innovations and the evolution of successive and mutually reinforcing new technological systems. It also guides the upgrading and modernization of existing industries to bring them into harmony and synergy with the dynamic new industries.

2.5   Difficult Assimilation: The Shaping of a Paradigm Takes Decades

The process I have been describing does not flow easily; it can take decades. The construction and propagation of a paradigm is protracted and difficult, due to the many obstacles encountered in the economic actors themselves and in their environment.

At first there are the pioneers and the early adopters, who can go a long way in impressive growth of production and profits. But they soon encounter the limits to their full development within the environment of the old paradigm.

One of the areas of strong resistance to diffusion is found in the leadership of established firms. It is difficult to believe that the 'normal' way of doing things has become old style and ineffective. In Table 7.1 I suggest what it means to change managerial common sense, aspect by aspect, element by element (Perez 1989). Those who have vast experience in applying the old principles find themselves forced to learn a new way of thinking and behaving in order to get optimum results. Yet this internal resistance tends to be overcome by the threat to profits and growth from the exhaustion of the old technologies and practices, together with the increasing examples of success with the new paradigm and sometimes by the direct pressure in the market from competitors who have adopted it.

Another set of obstacles comes from the lack of adequate externalities. Each paradigm develops in strong feedback interaction with a particular infrastructural network. The deployment of information technology propels and is propelled by vast telecommunications systems, which must be reliable, low-cost, powerful and of high capacity and great flexibility. Without that, diffusion is stalled. That same sort of interaction characterized the deployment of automobiles and truck transport, which both facilitated and was spurred by the establishment of the networks of roads and fuel distribution services. A similar feedback loop takes place in relation to specific types of related suppliers and distributors, rules and regulations, trained personnel at various levels, and so on.

In other words, those elements which, when in place, are destined to

Table 7.1   The new versus the traditional paradigm: a radical and difficult shift in managerial common sense

	Conventional common sense	New efficiency principles and practices
Command and control	Centralized command	Central goal-setting and coordination
	Vertical control	Local autonomy/horizontal self-control
	Cascade of supervisory levels	Self-assessing/self-improving units
	'Management knows best'	Participatory decision-making
Structure	Stable pyramid, growing in height and complexity as it expands	Flat, flexible network of very agile units
		Remains flat as it expands
Parts and links	Clear vertical links	Interactive, cooperative links between functions, along each product line
	Separate, specialized functional departments	
Style and operation	Optimized smooth-running organizations	Continuous learning and improvement
	Standard routines and procedures	Flexible system/adaptable procedures
	'There is one best way'	'A better way can always be found'
	Definition of individual tasks	Definition of group tasks
	Single-function specialization	Multiskilled personnel/ad hoc teams
	Single top-down line of command	Widespread delegation of decision making
	Single bottom-up information flow	Multiple horizontal and vertical flows
Personnel and training	Labour as variable cost	Labour as human capital
	Market provides trained personnel	Much in-house training and retraining
	People to fit the fixed posts	Variable posts/adaptable people
	Discipline as main quality	Initiative/collaboration/motivation
Equipment and investment	Dedicated equipment	Adaptable/programmable/flexible equipment
	One optimum plant size for each product	Many efficient sizes/optimum relative
	Each plant anticipates demand	Organic growth closely following

Table 7.1   (continued)

	Conventional common sense	New efficiency principles and practices
	growth	demand
	Strive for economies of scale for mass production	Choice or combination of economies of scale, scope or specialization
Production programming	Keep production rhythm; use inventory to accommodate variation in demand	Adapt rhythm to variation in demand
		Minimize response time ('Just-in-Time')
	Produce for stock; shed labour in slack	Use slack for maintenance and training
Productivity measurement	A specific measure for each department (purchasing, production, marketing and so on)	Total productivity measured along the whole chain for each product line
	Percent tolerance on quality and rejects	Strive for zero defects and zero rejects
Suppliers, clients and competitors	Separation from the outside world	Strong interaction with outside world
	Foster price competition among suppliers Make standard products for mass customers	Collaborative links with suppliers, with customers and, in some cases, with competitors (basic R&D, for instance)
	Arm's-length oligopoly with competitors	
	The firm as a closed system	The firm as an open system

generate a virtuous circle of self-reinforced diffusion are at first, by their absence, its main obstacles. This is because each technological revolution must make its way in a world fully adapted to the requirements of the previous techno-economic paradigm.

So as all these changes take place in the economy, many – even most – of the adaptations and readaptations that the social, cultural and institutional environment had effected suddenly become obsolete and counterproductive. However, this is not visible at first.

3.   STRUCTURAL CHANGE IN THE ECONOMY AND SOCIO-INSTITUTIONAL INERTIA

The process of gradual abandonment of a declining productive model and of growing adoption of the new is not readily perceived as such. Existing institutions take a long time to grasp the pervasiveness of the transformations taking place in more and more points of the economic system. Traditions, established routines and past successes with the usual practices make it difficult to capture the meaning and the threat of these successive changes as a source of institutional mismatches and problems. The new technologies are very visible indeed – as were mass production, plastics and the automobile in the 1920s and 1930s and as information technologies have been in recent times – but their consequences take a long time to reach public awareness. Even those who realize the importance of the technological and economic changes do not often connect them with a need for adaptations in their own sphere of influence or changes in their own behaviour.

3.1   Institutional Inertia: The Upswing Delayed

Even when the need for change is understood, social institutions and the general framework of socioeconomic regulation (Aglietta 1976) have a natural inertia, partly as the result of past successes and partly due to vested interests. It is only when the diffusion of the new paradigm has reached a certain critical mass, imposing its new modernizing logic upon the rest of the productive system, that both the painful consequences of the process of 'creative destruction' and the obstacles to a full – and beneficial – deployment of the new potential become fully visible.

Indeed the social consequences of each transition are vast and profound, as is the human suffering. The consequences include widespread unemployment (Freeman and Soete 1994); the obsolescence of qualifications at all levels; the destruction of the livelihood of many; the geographic dislocation of people and activities; and the rapid growth of wealth at one end and poverty at the other end of the socio-economic spectrum, within each country and between regions and countries (Tylecote 1992) (see Figure 7.2). It is then that the social pressure for change is clearly felt, that the erstwhile effective recipes applied by governments and other institutions are revealed as powerless and that the need for a deep institutional renewal becomes more and more self-evident. But the necessary transformation is not easy nor can it happen quickly. There ensues an increasingly severe mismatch between a socio-institutional framework geared to supporting the deployment of the old paradigm and the new requirements of a techno-economic sphere brimming with change. Further, the persistent application

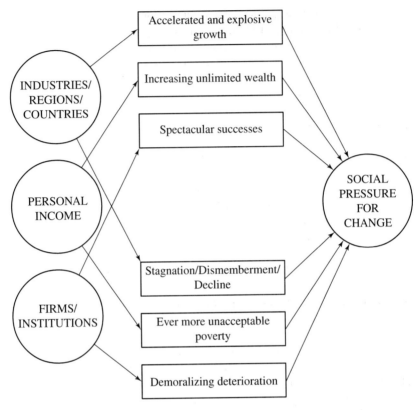

Sources: Perez after Tylecote 1992.

*Figure 7.2   The transition period: sociopolitical impact of centrifugal
                trends*

of the now obsolete practices can actually aggravate the situation and contribute to a collapse (as in the crash of 1929 and the ensuing crisis of the
1930s).

So during paradigm transitions there are very intense transformations in
technology and the economy and a high level of inertia and confusion in
the socio-institutional sphere. This difference in rhythms of change leads to
a decoupling of the two spheres. The ensuing turbulence and tensions are
characteristic of the downswing decades of Kondratiev long waves. The
upswing decades begin as structural coherence is re-established by means
of vast socio-institutional innovations in response to the requirements of
the new paradigm and geared to facilitating the full transformation in the
productive sphere.

Thus long-wave transitions are processes of 'creative destruction' not only in the economy, as shown by Schumpeter, but also in the socio-institutional sphere. The problem is that in such periods institutions face a chaotic and unaccustomed situation which requires much deeper changes than the great majority of their leaders and members have ever experienced. The difficulty is increased by the fact that there are no proven recipes and change has to take place by trial-and-error experimentation under the pressure of the very high social costs of the techno-economic transformation.

3.2   The Example of the Previous Socio-institutional Framework

Last time around, to overcome the Great Depression of the 1930s and to rebuild the economy after World War II, it was necessary to surmount the prevailing notions about the superiority of free-market mechanisms and accept the establishment of massive and systematic state intervention in the economy, generally following Keynesian principles. There is a very impressive list of institutional innovations which diffused widely in order to foster and regulate the growth of markets for mass production. At the national level it goes from the direct manipulation of demand mechanisms through fiscal, monetary and public spending policies to the official recognition of labour unions, collective bargaining and the establishment of a social security net, passing through the drastic reduction of the work week and year. Some of these innovations were made in the post-war period; some had existed before in some countries, for a short or long time. The important fact is that they were adopted almost everywhere, with all the variety resulting from vast differences in social, cultural, historical, political and other factors.

On the international level these national arrangements were complemented by the economic, political and military hegemony of the United States in the West (holding the Cold War balance with the Soviet system), Bretton Woods, the United Nations with all its specialized agencies, the GATT, the Marshall Plan, the IMF, the World Bank, gradual decolonization and other institutions and measures geared to facilitating the international movement of trade and investment as well as to maintaining political stability.

Today almost every one of these innovations, relatively effective and widely accepted until the 1970s, is under question. Some have already been partly or radically modified in one way or another. Indeed a successful transition will depend on the establishment of new rules of the game, regulatory mechanisms and institutions adapted to the new conditions. The process of institutional change has been under way nationally, locally and internationally with different visions and outlooks. Among the more coherent proposals are some that make an explicit connection with the nature of the present wave of technical change (Soete 1991).

3.3   Long Waves as Coupling and Decoupling of the System

In summary, I propose that long waves are related to the internal coherence of the system. They result from the fact that the techno-economic sphere experiences vast processes of widespread transformation and renewal – or changes of paradigm – about every half century, which in order to deploy their full growth potential require equally vast changes in the socio-institutional framework. Yet the changes in the economy take place at a much faster pace than in social institutions. The resulting mismatch, which historically has lasted two or three decades, brings about the 'bad times' (or the downswing of the long wave). When structural coherence is regained, through a succession of socio-institutional changes which achieve a good match, then there are two or three decades which are experienced as the 'good times' (or as the upswing of the long wave). The process then unfolds as shown in Figure 7.3.

4.   TECHNO-ORGANIZATIONAL PARADIGMS AS GUIDELINES FOR CHANGE IN THE SOCIO-INSTITUTIONAL SPHERE

The question remains as to what guides adequate institutional change. Not just any change will do, however positive. The techno-economic paradigm is the best source of guidelines for social and institutional design. This implies that the viable changes have a recognizable direction, but I am not making a case for mere technological determinism.

4.1   The Wide Space of the Possible

What a paradigm determines is the vast range of the possible, and that space is very wide indeed. In the previous paradigm we can recognize at least four major modes of growth: Keynesian democracy, fascism, socialism and, in the Third World, what we could call 'state developmentalism'. There can be no doubt at all that these are profoundly different socio-institutional systems. Moreover the variety of versions of each 'model' was enormous. And yet at a certain level of abstraction they all share certain common features, which stem from the fact that the same mass production paradigm is the logic guiding wealth-creating activities in the production sphere. Among these shared characteristics one could mention:

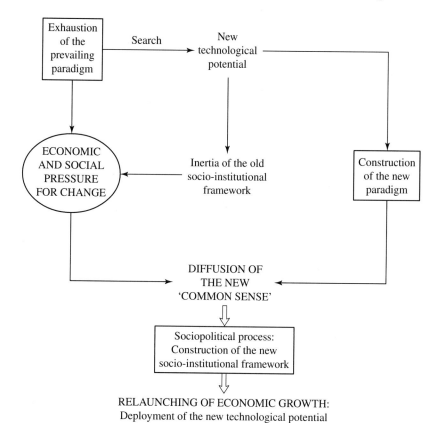

Figure 7.3   The process of creative destruction in long-wave transitions

1. An important role for a central government actively engaged in the economy, whether very directly or more indirectly.
2. The erection of the state as the main agent of redistribution of wealth, which is seen as the prevalent form of social justice.
3. A drive towards the 'homogeneity' of consumption styles within the nation-state, with an effort to reduce internal differences of nationality, language and so on.
4. Central representation of the provinces, generally by some form of direct elections.
5. 'Mass' character of political parties and other associations.
6. Government by one or very few main political parties (rarely more than two, even in countries with very democratic systems).
7. A separation of political leadership from 'technical' management (with measures for a degree of continuity of the latter).

The interesting phenomenon is that these similarities among systems otherwise so divergent have only become clearly visible with the diffusion of the new principles of decentralization and the increasing strength of the ideas which question the previously accepted role of the state. Furthermore, one can now also see a parallel between the typical forms of organization of the traditional big corporations and that of hospitals, universities, ministries and governments in general. As firms have begun to change to more open globalized networks, other structures have begun to question the effectiveness of their own forms of organization.

I am suggesting, then, that as the new wealth-creating potential unfolds in the economy, its logic propagates throughout society, modifying the commonsense criteria that guide all sorts of organizations and eventually resulting in maximum social synergy. Thus, understanding the nature of the paradigm can provide the most appropriate tools for becoming a fully conscious and effective actor in the process of institutional modernization.

4.2   The Notion of a Paradigm Can Be Understood on Three Levels

In practice each techno-economic paradigm is constructed and diffuses on three interrelated levels:

1. As a set of real new technological systems which grow and diffuse in the productive sphere (in the present case these would be the microelectronics, software and computer-related industries, plus modern telecommunications and all the services connected with them).
2. As a new 'best practice' model adapted to the new technologies and capable of taking best advantage of them. This model diffuses across all industries and productive activities, modernizing them and establishing the emerging managerial common sense for investment and innovation (at present this would be the flexible organizational model – in its 'Japanese' and other versions – fused with the consistent application of information technology).
3. As a more general set of 'commonsense' principles for organizational and institutional design (this would involve general principles such as decentralization, networking, interaction between the organization and its users or beneficiaries, continuous improvement, participation, consensus-building and so on). These principles can be said to conform to a techno-organizational paradigm.

These levels can be seen as a series of overlapping waves in time. The first to diffuse widely is the set of new technologies. Then, as it becomes clear that these cannot yield their promised fruits without organizational change, the new managerial model develops further and further and increasingly propagates. Finally, the third level develops as the paradigm overflows outside the economic sphere. When productive organizations discover the advantages of the new paradigm, so do many of their leaders, participants and observers. That is how the paradigm, in the form of general guidelines or principles, is gradually constructed in the minds of more and more people and starts becoming the new common sense for effectiveness more or less everywhere.

Obviously the variety of forms of adoption and application is immense. Technology enters a world where other very powerful influences, such as history, culture and politics, shape the manner in which it is taken up (or partly rejected) in each particular country or region, productive sector or territory, nation or social group. The power of these shaping forces is naturally greater the further one goes from the hard technology core towards the realm of ideas. In other words, the variety of forms of adoption increases as one goes from the first to the third level in the propagation of a paradigm.

Since it is in the third level that the new paradigm provides the criteria for viability and the guidelines for designing effective institutions and social action, it should be clear why the diversity of applications and forms of adoption was so great in relation to the previous mass production paradigm.

It is also at this third level that the old paradigm remains alive beyond its usefulness and becomes an obstacle to the new. For this reason, at each transition the traditional left–right divide is made more complex by the appearance in each group of another divide, which is between the old and the modern ideas, those looking backwards and those looking forward (see Figure 7.4).

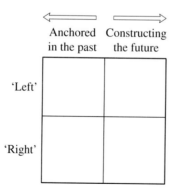

Figure 7.4 Political positions in the transition

4.3   General Principles: Many Forms of Application

So what the paradigm provides is not the goals but the forms and the technical and organizational tools with which to pursue them. Therefore the space for institutional creativity is very wide. Within it, the various social forces play out their confrontations, experiments, agreements and compromises. The result is the framework – or frameworks – which will ultimately mould, orient, select and regulate the actual paths the new potential will follow.

This means that each crisis, each period of technological transition, is a point of indeterminacy in history. A quantum jump in potential productivity opens the way for a great increase in the generation of wealth. But the specific sociopolitical framework that will handle – or squander – this new potential has to be designed and established. This, in turn, is what determines the mix of commodities that will compose that greater wealth and the way they will be produced and their benefits distributed. Historically, each transition has modified both the conditions of the various social groups within each country and the relative position of countries in the generation and distribution of world production.

However, the task is so ambitious that it is difficult to envisage. If someone in the 1920s or 1930s had held that in less than three decades practically all colonial empires could be dismantled and that in North America and Europe there could be full employment and most industrial workers could own cars and houses full of electrical appliances, he or she would have been met with general disbelief.

4.4   The Politics of Transition

The question of social and institutional change is political. Ideologies and vested interests have great power in determining the particular outcomes from the wide space of the viable at each transition. The level of political consensus, conflict or confusion strongly influences the speed and the ease or difficulty with which the new mode of growth is established.

Yet whatever the political position, it certainly makes a difference how one understands the present period. Insisting on the dichotomy between state and market, as the alternative automatic solutions, can only prolong the agony and retard the establishment of an appropriate socio-institutional framework. It is likely to be much more fruitful to see the present as a transition between two distinct modes of growth.

This means accepting the past with its ideas and its institutions, its successes and its failures, its promises and its achievements, as the way the societies of the time found to take advantage of the potential of a specific techno-economic paradigm, now exhausted. It also means facing the future with a commitment to the construction of a framework capable of making the best social use of the new wealth-creating potential. This implies a readiness to pursue a deep understanding of the characteristics and requirements of the new paradigm and a willingness to assimilate change and promote creativity at all levels and in all spheres.

Historically these transition processes have been long and difficult, with a very high cost in human suffering. It is to be hoped that a better understanding of the nature of the transformation could help to alleviate the social cost and to quicken the success of institutional experimentation.

REFERENCES

Aglietta, M. (1976), *Regulation et crises du capitalisme*, Paris: Calmann-Levy.

Altshuler, A., M. Anderson, D. Jones, D. Roos and J. Womack (1982), *The Future of the Automobile*, London: Unwin Paperbacks.

Arthur, W.B. (1988), 'Competing technologies: an overview', in G. Dosi, C. Freeman, R. Nelson, G. Silverberg and L. Soete (eds), *Technical Change and Economic Theory*, London: Pinter, pp. 590–607.

Dosi, G. (1982), 'Technological paradigms and technological trajectories', *Research Policy*, **11** (3), 147–62.

Freeman, C. (1984), 'Prometheus unbound', *Futures*, **16** (5), 494–507.

Freeman, C., C. Clark and L. Soete (1982), *Unemployment and Technical Innovation: A Study of Long Waves in Economic Development*, London: Pinter.

Freeman, C. and C. Perez (1988), 'Structural crises of adjustment, business cycles and investment behaviour', in G. Dosi, C. Freeman, R. Nelson, G. Silverberg and L. Soete (eds), *Technical Change and Economic Theory*, London: Pinter, pp. 38–66.

Freeman, C. and L. Soete (1994), *Work for All or Mass Unemployment: Computerised Technical Change in the Twenty-first Century*, London: Pinter.

Keirstead, B.S. (1948), *The Theory of Economic Change*, Toronto: Macmillan.

Landes, D.S. (1969), *The Unbound Prometheus: Technological Change and Industrial Development in Western Europe from 1750 to the Present*, Cambridge: Cambridge University Press.

Mensch, G. (1975), *Das technologische Patt*, Frankfurt: Umschau.

Nelson, R. and S. Winter (1977), 'In search of a useful theory of innovation', *Research Policy*, **6** (1), 36–76.

Nelson, R. and S. Winter (1982), *An Evolutionary Theory of Economic Change*, Cambridge, MA: Harvard University Press.

Nye, D.E. (1990), *Electrifying America*, Cambridge, MA: MIT Press.

Perez, C. (1983), 'Structural change and assimilation of new technologies in the economic and social systems', *Futures*, **15** (5), 357–75.

Perez, C. (1985), 'Microelectronics, long waves and world structural change: new perspectives for developing countries', *World Development*, **13** (3), 441–63.

Perez, C. (1986), 'Las nuevas tecnologias: Una vision de conjunto', in C. Ominami (ed.), *La tercera revolucion industrial: Aspectos internacionales del actual viraje tecnologico*, Buenos Aires: RIAL, Grupo Editor Latinoamericano, pp. 43–90.

Perez, C. (1989), 'Technical change, competitive restructuring and institutional reform in developing countries', SPR Publications, discussion paper no. 4, World Bank, Washington, DC. Published in Spanish in *El Trimestre Economico*, **233** Mexico, January–March 1992, pp. 23–64.

Rosenberg, N. (1975), *Perspectives on Technology*, Cambridge: Cambridge University Press.

Schumpeter, J. (1939), *Business Cycles*, New York: McGraw-Hill.

Soete, L. (1991), *Technology in a Changing World*, Paris: Technology/Economy Programme, Organisation for Economic Cooperation and Development.

Tylecote, A. (1992), *The Long Wave in the World Economy*, London: Routledge.

Womack, J., D. Jones and D. Roos (1990), *The Machine That Changed the World*, New York: Ranson Associates.

8.   Income inequality in changing techno-economic paradigms

Chris Freeman

This chapter discusses the relationships among technical change, economic growth and income distribution. The first section of the chapter concentrates on technical change and unemployment; it is fairly clear that the prevalence of mass unemployment will tend to aggravate inequalities in income distribution. The second section of the chapter discusses the effects of technical change on the earnings of those who are employed. Both in relation to unemployment and in relation to the earnings of those who are employed, the chapter argues that waves of technical change have profound long-term effects on income distribution.

Formal growth theory and growth models (Romer 1986, Grossman and Helpman 1990) have at last begun to recognize that the combination of technical change and increasing returns to scale, which Antonio Serra first explored (Reinert 1996, 1999), are at the heart of the process of economic growth. However, most formal models still ignore the cyclical aspects of growth. This chapter therefore first of all argues that the study of long cycles is essential to an understanding of the relationship between technical change, economic growth and income distribution.

1.   UNEMPLOYMENT AND TECHNOLOGY

At the simplest level, it is obvious that the standard of living for all of us depends on the achievements of science and technology. Since Adam Smith's *Wealth of Nations* and Alfred Marshall's comments on *Knowledge as the Chief Engine of Production*, the role of technical change in economic growth has been universally accepted by all schools of economists. The so-called New Growth Theory gives to research, development and education a more central role than earlier growth models, but no economist of repute had ever denied their importance.

However, it is one thing to pay lip service to the importance of science and technology in economic and social change but quite another thing to study this interdependent relationship in depth, that is, to study the actual process of technical change in firms, in industries, in nations and in the world economy. In the first half of this century almost the only economist to attempt this was Joseph Schumpeter, and for this reason research on the economics and sociology of technical change is usually described as neo-Schumpeterian. Its relevance to the problems of income distribution and social cohesion is not immediately obvious, and I shall argue that to understand this relationship requires the exploration of cycles of investment and the associated problems of employment, skills, unemployment and profitability.

Schumpeter suggested in his magnum opus on *Business Cycles* (1939) that waves of new investment were generated by the diffusion of new technologies. Following the Russian economist Nikolai Kondratiev, he argued that successive industrial revolutions led to long cycles of about 50 years' duration (see Table 8.1). In Schumpeter's theory, the ability and initiative of entrepreneurs, drawing upon the discoveries and ideas of scientists and inventors, create entirely new opportunities for investment, growth and employment. The exceptional profits made from these innovations are then the decisive signal to swarms of imitators, generating bandwagon and multiplier effects throughout the system. Schumpeter studied the extraordinarily rapid growth of the cotton and iron industries in the first industrial revolution, of steam power and railways in the second and of electrification in the third.

In a passage which is seldom referred to, John Maynard Keynes (1930) fully acknowledged the significance of these influences on investment behaviour:

> In the case of fixed capital it is easy to understand why fluctuations should occur in the rate of investment. Entrepreneurs are induced to embark on the production of fixed capital or deterred from doing so by their expectations of the profits to be made. Apart from the many minor reasons why these should fluctuate in a changing world, Professor Schumpeter's explanation of the major movements may be unreservedly accepted.

The big investment booms of the 1850s and 1860s, of the *belle époque* before the First World War or of the golden age of the 1950s and 1960s were followed by fairly prolonged periods of recession, depression and high unemployment. In Schumpeter's scheme, these recessions were the combined result of the erosion of profits and the slow-down of growth in the previous wave of technology and the disruptive effects of the emergence of new technologies and a new infrastructure to unleash the next wave. His theory is still controversial; opposition has come both from more orthodox mainstream economists, including Keynesians who have been preoccupied with the

Table 8.1 Long Waves

Kondratiev Wave	Cycle	Recession trough	Key Factor(s)	Carrier Branches	Infrastructures
1st	1780s–1840s	1820s 1830s	Cotton yarn Iron	**Cotton textiles** Ship building	Ports Canals Water power Roads Ships, barges
2nd	1840s–90s	1880s 1890s	Coal Coal gas	**Steam engines** Railways Mechanization Gas Machine tools	Iron–rail networks Telegraphy Steam ships Gas light and heat
3rd	1890s–1940s	1920s 1930s	Steel	Electrification Electrical and heavy engineering Non-ferrous metals	Electric power Steel ships Global steel rail networks Telephones
4th	1940s–90s	1980s 1990s	Oil Natural gas	**Automobiles** Consumer durables Refineries Automation	Motor highways Airlines Tankers Roll-on, roll-off
5th	1990s–?	?	Microelectronics	**Computers** Video, telephone equipment Software, info services	'Information highways' E-mail Air freight

shorter business cycles, and from orthodox Marxists, who drove Kondratiev to an early death in the 1930s. Orthodox economic theory has tended to accept purely econometric attempts to refute Schumpeter's long-wave theory, but recently a Portuguese economist (Louçã 1997) has provided a powerful critique of econometrics and reinforcement for neo-Schumpeterian theories of the long wave.

If the test of a theory in the social sciences, as in the natural sciences, is its predictive power, then the ideas of Kondratiev and Schumpeter come out of this test in the twentieth century extremely well. At a time when more orthodox Marxists were predicting the collapse of capitalism and the final crisis in the 1930s, Kondratiev pointed to the possibility of a new capitalist growth boom. When the biggest ever boom materialized in the 1950s and 1960s, long-wave theorists such as Mandel pointed to the probability of a new deep recession. This was at a time when many economists and government advisors, such as those at the Organization for Economic Cooperation and Development (OECD), assumed that the problem of mass unemployment would never return. Even in the 1970s they continued to believe this despite the mounting evidence of structural unemployment (see, for example, OECD 1977 [McCracken Report]). In the 1930s, however, many economists had believed the opposite: that unemployment would remain permanently at a high level. Even William H. Beveridge and Keynes in the early 1940s were pessimistic about the possibilities of achieving a 3 per cent level of unemployment and thought 8 per cent a more realistic target. The definition of 'full employment' as 3 per cent or less came relatively late in the deliberations of Beveridge and his colleagues. Mainstream economics thus showed a persistent inability to understand or cope with the problems of structural change and unemployment related to new technologies. Yet the prevalence of mass unemployment for quite long periods has been one of the major causes of inequality in income distribution and related social problems.

In what was to become the accepted definition of 'full employment', it was often assumed that about 1 per cent would be 'frictional' unemployment – the simple gaps in the movement of people between jobs, which would occur in any changing economy; a further 1 per cent would be 'regional' unemployment caused by delays in the movement of people between regions; and 1 per cent would be 'structural' unemployment – longer-lasting unemployment associated with changes in technology, skills and industrial organization (Beveridge 1946).

In fact, unemployment in the 1950s and 1960s, as in the 1850s and 1860s, fell well below 3 per cent throughout almost the whole of Europe (Table 8.2). In the 1980s and 1990s it was well below 3 per cent in the East Asian 'Tigers', but almost everywhere else, and especially in Europe, it reached

Table 8.2   Unemployment in the 1990s (% of workforce)

	1959–67 average	1982–92 average	1992	1995
USA	5.3	7.1	7.4	5.6
Canada	4.9	9.6	11.3	9.5
Germany[a]	1.2	7.4	7.7	9.5
France	0.7	9.5	10.4	11.6
Italy	6.2	10.9	11.6	12.1
UK	1.8	9.7	10.0	8.2
Spain	2.3	19.0	18.4	22.9
Japan	1.5	2.5	2.2	3.1
Belgium	2.4	11.3	7.3	9.9
Denmark	1.4	9.1	9.2	7.1
Finland	1.7	4.8	13.1	17.3
Ireland	4.6	15.5	16.7	12.4
Netherlands	0.9	9.8	5.6	7.3
Norway	2.1	3.2	5.9	5.7
Sweden	1.3	2.3	5.3	9.2
S. Korea	n.a.	2.5	2.4	2.3
Singapore	n.a.	2.9	2.7	2.6

Note: [a] 1959–92 = German Federal Republic

Source: European Commission (1996).

levels described by M. Paye, the Secretary-General of the OECD, as 'disturbing, perhaps alarming' (OECD 1993). The relatively low levels of unemployment in the 'Tigers' were clearly related to their high overall growth rate, averaging 7 per cent or more over long periods in the 1970s, 1980s and 1990s, but also to the high rate of structural change, as shown in the output and exports of their information and communications technologies (ICT) industries (Table 8.3). Europe suffered from the reverse problem of low rates of growth, relatively poor performance of the ICT industries and other high-tech industries and an inadequate level of aggregate investment. Since 1997 the Asian countries have suffered from the problems of overcapacity and the instability of investment, collapsing from the very high levels of the boom period. The bubble economy in Japan and its collapse in the 1990s added to the instability of the entire region and of the world economy.

The social consequences of these failures in economic policy and in structural adjustment are very severe indeed. The continuing high levels of

Table 8.3   Percentage share of office machinery and telecom equipment in total merchandise exports (ranked by value of 1989 exports)

	1980	1989
1. Japan	14	28
2. USA	8	13
3. FRG	5	5
4. UK	5	9
5. Singapore	14	34
6. South Korea	10	22
7. Taiwan	14	25
8. Hong Kong	12	16
9. France	4	7
10. Netherlands	5	7
11. Canada	2.5	4

Source: GATT

unemployment have undermined social services in many European countries because the payment of unemployment benefits and many other benefits indirectly associated with unemployment leads to budget deficits of a scale and duration which are hard to sustain and led to the deflationary Maastricht criteria for the European Monetary Union. The early social reformers, such as Beveridge, were absolutely right to assume that the welfare state depended on full employment. In her earliest social research in Liverpool, Eleanor Rathbone had demonstrated the close relationship between casual part-time employment, unemployment, poverty and malnutrition (Stocks 1949).

Persistent mass unemployment presents society with great dangers. It is an unmitigated social disaster as well as a loss of output, and the OECD was right to urge that the restoration of full employment in Europe should be a high priority for both economic and social reasons. The IMF medicine for Asian countries poses the danger of undermining their achievements in the development of new industries, services and employment by drastically curtailing their rate of investment. In many Asian countries social services have never been fully developed, placing a greater strain on social cohesion when the recession began.

The future growth of employment in both Europe and Asia must depend, as indicated in the US estimates (Table 8.4), on three main categories:

Table 8.4   US occupational employment forecasts, 1990–2005 (total percentage growth of fastest-growing occupations)

Occupation	Projected growth
Systems analysts	79
Computer programmers	56
Information clerks	47
Home health aides	92
Child care providers	49
Nurses	44
Nursing aides	43
Cooks	42
Gardeners	40
Food counter workers	34
Food preparers	32
School teachers	34
Educational assistants	34

Source: US Bureau of Labor Statistics

1. Occupations related to the computerization of all industries and services: software engineering, design and programming and new tele-communications-based networking services.
2. Personal and public service occupations in health care, care for the elderly, child care, improvement of the urban and rural environment, and leisure activities.
3. Education, training and related professional occupations. These are closely related to the first category because the education and training system will make massive use of multimedia.

All three of these areas offer enormous scope for future growth of employment, but the third category is of exceptional importance because the entire economy will increasingly depend on the efficiency and scope of education, training and retraining. The US figures probably underestimate the potential growth of educational products and services and the associated growth of employment in publishing, multimedia and other 'cultural' industries closely related to the first category.

Whether for nursery schools or primary or secondary education, it is essential for education policy to play an active role in developing new ICT products in cooperation with industry. Developing new modules for new courses in every discipline and combination of disciplines and keeping them up to date are enormous educational undertakings. They will require the active participation of the teaching profession at all levels. A regular part of in-service teacher training and post-experience training should be participation in design and development teams for new course CD-ROMs and other materials in cooperation with publishers, video companies, information services and other related industries.

Far from leading to unemployment amongst teachers, the widespread use of ICT will enhance their importance although changing their role to that of guides and counsellors rather than instructors. Home learning will complement rather than replace schools for many social, economic and cultural reasons. Children learn from each other, and direct interaction with other children and teachers is essential if they are to develop the social skills and communication skills which are so important in our economic, social and political life. Scale economies and indivisibilities are just as important for equipment and materials in education as in other sectors of the economy (Freeman and Soete 1994). There is already a tendency for society to divide into 'information-rich' and 'information-poor' households, and any move towards 'de-schooling' would exacerbate these divisions. Schools provide the best opportunity for children from deprived households to obtain education and skills.

2.   TECHNICAL CHANGE AND EARNINGS DISPERSION

So far this discussion has focused on long waves of technical change and their effects on employment. It points to the conclusion that to cope with structural change and to return to high levels of employment, it is essential to restore high levels of investment and to overcome the mismatch of skills and qualifications which is an inevitable feature of technical change.

However, as the case of 'information-rich' and 'information-poor' households suggests, social inequality is not only a question of employment and unemployment. Each new wave of technical change brings with it many social benefits in the forms of new, more skilled occupations and professions and higher standards of living for many people based on the growth of new industries and services. But each wave also brings high social costs in the forms of erosion of old skills and occupations and the decline of some older industries, services and industrial areas. The main trends in the change from mass production to ICT are illustrated in Figures 8.1 and 8.2. They show the general decline in manual (blue-collar) occupations and the rise in service (white-collar) occupations in the 1980s. This uneven distribution of social costs and benefits occurs also on an international scale, with some

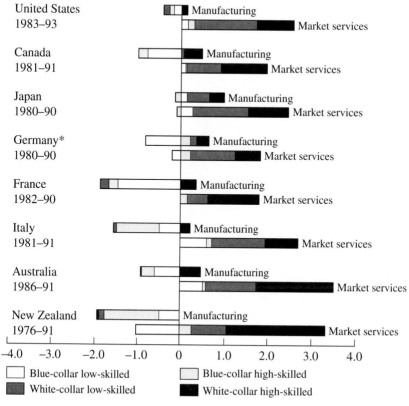

Notes:
See text for definitions.
* The white-collar high-skilled group in Germany excludes some occupations and is thus underestimated.

Source: OECD Secretariat calculations from national data; STI/EAS Division.

Figure 8.1 Employment growth breakdown by skill level in manufacturing and services

nations taking full advantage of the new technologies and others unable to do so. Reinert (1996) has demonstrated the 'collusive' effects in the distribution of the benefits of technical change associated with increasing returns to scale at the national level.

The effects of this uneven distribution of social costs and benefits are clearly visible in the statistics on income distribution for the 1980s and 1990s (Table 8.5). Twelve out of 17 OECD countries showed an increased dispersion of earnings in the 1980s, four showed no change and only one

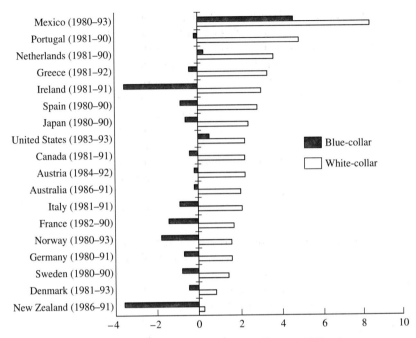

Source: OECD Secretariat calculations from International Labour Office data.

Figure 8.2   Employment growth for blue- and white-collar workers over the 1980s (average annual growth rate)

(Germany) showed a decrease. In the 1970s the reverse was true. In that decade only one country (the United States) showed an increase in inequality while most others showed a decrease in dispersion. These statistics are for income before tax. Taking into account that fiscal changes in the UK and many other countries were regressive in this period, the increase of inequality in incomes was substantial for those who were employed. These trends were aggravated in most countries in the 1990s, above all in Eastern Europe and China.

Similar changes took place in previous waves of technical change: the earnings of engine drivers and fitters in the nineteenth century, of electricians in the 1890s, of assembly line workers in the 1940s and 1950s and of software engineers and programmers in the 1980s were all well above the average earnings of their times. It is obvious that in any well-functioning market system, the shortage of workers in rapidly expanding industries will have these effects. The Japanese electronic employers in the 1980s agreed not to poach each other's workers and tried thus to avoid the wage-push

Table 8.5 *General pattern of changes in the dispersion of earnings in the 1970s and 1980s (hourly earnings or earnings of full-time workers)*

	1970s	1980s	Comments on extent and type of changes in dispersion
Australia	−	+	Increase in the dispersion from 1979 onwards
Austria	−	+	Increase from 1980 to 1989
Belgium		+	Slight increase due to gains at top over 1983–88
Canada	0	+	Increase mainly due to gains at top
Denmark		0	Slight gains at top and bottom
Finland	−	0	Slight gains at top and bottom
France	−	−/+	Decrease in dispersion ended in 1983
Germany	0	−	Decrease mainly due to gains at bottom
Italy	−	0	Gains at top and bottom
Japan		+	Increase due to gains at top
Netherlands	0	−/+	Slight decrease to 1984, then slight increase
Norway		0	Gains at top and bottom
Portugal		+	Increase between 1985 and 1990
Spain	− −/0	+	Sharp decrease in mid-1970s, rise in 1980s
Sweden	0	0/+	Increase after 1986, except for low-paid women
United Kingdom	−	+ +	Increase from 1979 onwards
United States	+	+ +	Increase for men only in 1970s; strong gains at top in 1980s

Notes:
+ Increase in dispersion; + + Strong increase; − Decrease; − − Strong decrease; 0 No clear change (perhaps changes at top and bottom working in opposite directions); +/− Increase followed by decrease (etc.); Blank No information available

Source: OECD (1993).

effects of the extremely rapid growth of that industry. This was a fairly typical response to this problem, even though it has rarely been effective outside Japan. Consequently, periods of rapid structural change and high unemployment have generally been associated with increased inequality of incomes.

The combined effect of prolonged periods of high unemployment together with this increased dispersion of earnings and increasingly regressive taxation has been to create or to enlarge an 'underclass' in the United States, Britain, Russia, France, Spain and many other countries. A huge underclass already existed in Mexico, Brazil and most other countries of Latin America and Africa, and this is growing even faster. A rise in social tensions, crime and ethnic hostility is evident almost everywhere and clearly associated with the loss of social cohesion and increasing insecurity of employment. One of the early responses to the East Asian crisis was seen in the attempts to expel immigrant workers and hostility to 'foreigners'.

In the past when alarm bells rang, whether in the 1830s, the 1880s or the 1930s, ultimately they led to programmes of social reform, educational reform, employment policies and fiscal changes designed to mitigate the worst effects of these problems of structural change and to share the burdens more equally.

In his highly original and thorough analysis of long waves in the world economy, Andrew Tylecote (1992) studied two aspects of inequality which he designated as inequality in the North and in the South respectively. He suggested that in the North the dispersion of incomes which widened in the downswing of each long wave was superimposed on a long-term secular trend towards greater equality in income distribution. No such tendency was yet apparent in the South, with the exception of a few countries in East Asia. Moreover the inequality gap between average per capita incomes in most of the underdeveloped countries of the South and countries in the North has widened enormously in the last century. Tylecote argues that deep inequality is actually harmful for long-term growth, whether in the South or the North, and a similar point is made in the World Bank report (1993) on the 'East Asian miracle' and by Persson and Tabellini (1994). It is a tragic effect of the present crisis that the more equal income distribution which the World Bank reported in East Asia is now being undermined.

In his classic paper on 'Economic growth and income inequality', Simon Kuznets (1955, p. 20) argued that

> one might assume a long swing in the inequality characterizing the secular income structure: widening in the early phases of economic growth . . . becoming stabilized for a while; and then narrowing in the later phases . . . The long swing in income inequality is also probably closely associated with the swing in capital formation proportions – in so far as wider inequality makes for higher, and narrower inequality for lower, country-wide savings proportions.

An American economist, Brian Berry, following in the tradition of Kuznets, suggested that income dispersion increased in four different periods of American history since 1776 (Berry et al. 1994). Whereas Kuznets suggested that wide dispersion of incomes was characteristic of the early stages of industrialization and economic growth, diminishing with maturity, Berry proposed that alternating periods of wider and lesser dispersion correspond to long (Kondratiev) cycles of economic development. Like Tylecote, Berry maintained that 'it is in the immediate post stagflation decade that inequality surges' (p. 10). These surges of inequality in the 1820s, 1870s, 1920s, 1980s and 1990s were associated with the downturn of the long wave, with major structural changes, with demand for new skills (Williamson and Lindert 1980) and with exceptionally high profits in new industries.

Initially, strongly pro-business governments tend to aggravate the growing inequality, believing that a dose of strong medicine is needed to set the economy right, but ultimately, according to Berry's analysis, this leads to a political revulsion against the hardships which these policies incur (Jackson and the Homestead Act in the 1830s, antitrust legislation and other reforms in the 1890s, and the New Deal in the 1930s and 1940s). Williamson and Lindert (1980, p. 33) concluded from their study of inequality in America, 'In contrast with the previous periods of wealth leveling, the twentieth-century leveling has not been reversed.'

As Berry points out, this conclusion was too hasty. The United States and the United Kingdom have led the way in the reversal of that trend in the 1980s and 1990s. In the UK, the share of the lowest quintile (20 per cent) of household disposable incomes fell from 10 per cent of the total in 1979 to 6 per cent in 1992, while the share of the top quintile rose from 35 to 43 per cent over the same period (Table 5.19 in Central Statistical Office 1995). To reverse these trends anywhere will not be easy. John Kenneth Galbraith (1992) has pointed to the political coalition favouring inequality, and the opposition to fiscal changes favouring greater equality is every-where formidable. New ways of thinking and policy making are urgently needed.

We can only speculate about two policy changes which have been proposed by a group which reported in 1997 to the Directorate of Social Affairs within the European Union (European Commission 1996, 1997). This group proposed first that the EU and all its member countries should examine the potential of a new tax, the so-called bit tax, to redress the gulf between the 'information-rich' and the 'information-poor'. Fiscal policy must always change with the changing structure of the economy and polit-ical realities. Principles of public finance dictate that any tax should justify three basic criteria:

1. enlargement of the revenue base;
2. economy in collection; and
3. social equity.

At first sight, the bit tax would seem to satisfy all these requirements and offer the possibility of significant redistribution, both nationally and inter-nationally. It has been attacked as a 'Luddite tax', but the rate of growth of ICT transactions is so rapid and the lock-in effects are so strong that a low rate of levy would have only marginal effects and might indeed improve efficiency in the information technology industries. However there are important technical problems which must be resolved before any tax could be introduced. It would probably have to be a transmission tax and could not simply be levied on numbers of bits (Soete and Kamp 1997).

The group's second proposal relates to the measurement of inflation and the argument has also been advanced by a recent report to the Senate Finance Committee. The indexing of price inflation depends on the selection of a 'basket' of commodities and services and measuring the changes in the prices of this selection. The chairman of the EU group, Luc Soete, has argued that this selection is out of date as it understates some of the information services which are now commonplace (Soete and Kamp 1997). The prices of ICT goods and services have generally been falling since the late 1980s, in contrast to the general inflationary trends. Yet the inflation index still reflects to some extent the old structure of the economy. The very use of the word 'basket' reflects the old goods-based structure of the economy when these indices were first introduced. They have of course been revised since then, but the report to the Senate Finance Committee maintained that US inflation has been overestimated by between 1 and 2 per cent. Luc Soete has calculated that inflation in the EU has been overestimated to a greater extent.

This has major implications for macroeconomic policy and social policy, as the overestimation of inflation has led to unnecessarily restrictive policies and higher rates of interest in Germany, France and other European countries. This has slowed down growth and raised unemployment. The understanding of structural change and technical change is thus fundamentally linked to the great social problems which confront us. This is even more true of James Tobin's proposal to tax speculative transactions on the foreign exchange markets, which were a major source of the instability in the East Asian markets in 1997 to 1998. All of these examples seem to indicate the type of new thinking and policy-making which will be needed to overcome the recessionary trends in the world economy which now confront us.

REFERENCES

Berry, B.J.L., E.J. Harpham and J. Elliott (1994), 'Long swings in American inequality: the Kuznets conjecture revisited', University of Texas at Dallas, mimeograph.
Beveridge, W.H. (1946), *Full Employment in a Free Society*, London: Allen & Unwin.
Central Statistical Office (1995), *Social Trends*, London: HMSO.
European Commission (1996), *Building the European Information Society for Us All: First Reflections of the High-Level Group of Experts*, Interim Report, January, Brussels: EC, DGV.

European Commission (1997), *Building the European Information Society for Us All*, Final Policy Report, April, Brussels: EC, DGV.

Freeman, C. and L. Soete (1994), *Work for All or Mass Unemployment*, London: Pinter.

Galbraith, J.K. (1992), *The Culture of Contentment*, London: Sinclair Stevenson.

Grossman, G. and E. Helpman (1990), 'Comparative advantage and long-run growth', *American Economic Review*, **80**, 796–815.

Keynes, J.M. (1930), *A Treatise on Money*, London: Macmillan.

Kuznets, S. (1955), 'Economic growth and income inequality', *American Economic Review*, **45**, 1–28.

Louça, F. (1997), *Turbulence in Economics: An Evolutionary Appraisal of Cycles and Complexity in Historical Processes*, Cheltenham, UK, and Lyme, CT: Edward Elgar.

OECD (1977) [McCracken Report], *Towards Full Employment and Price Stability*, Paris: OECD.

OECD (1993, 1994), *Employment Outlook*, Paris: OECD.

Persson, T. and G. Tabellini (1994), 'Is inequality harmful to growth?' *American Economic Review*, **84** (3), 600–621.

Reinert, E. (1996), 'The role of technology in the creation of rich and poor nations: Underdevelopment in a Schumpeterian system', in D.H. Aldcroft and R. Catterall (eds), *Rich Nations – Poor Nations: The Long Run Perspective*, Aldershot: Edward Elgar, pp. 161–88.

Reinert, E. (1999), 'The role of the state in economic growth', *Journal of Economic Studies*, **26** (4/5), 268–326.

Romer, P. (1986), 'Increasing returns and long-run growth', *Journal of Political Economy*, **94** (5), 1002–37.

Schumpeter, J.A. (1939), *Business Cycles*, 2 vols, New York: McGraw-Hill.

Soete, L. and K. Kamp (1997), 'The "BIT tax": The case for further research', University of Maastricht, Maastricht Economic Research Institute for Technology, mimeo.

Stocks, M. (1949), *Eleanor Rathbone: A Biography*, London: Gollancz.

Tylecote, A. (1992), *The Long Wave in the World Economy*, London: Routledge.

Williamson, J. and P.H. Lindert (1980), *American Inequality: A Micro-economic History*, New York: Academic Press.

World Bank (1993), *The East Asian Miracle*, Washington, DC: World Bank.

9. Information technology in the learning economy: challenges for developing countries

Dieter Ernst and Bengt-Åke Lundvall

The engine of growth should be technological change, with international trade serving as a lubricating oil and not as fuel.

(Lewis 1978, p. 74)

Both the pace and the acceleration of innovation are startling; nay terrifying ... No one can predict the ... range of skills which will need to be amassed to create and take advantage of the next revolution but one. (And thinking about the next but one is what everyone is doing. The game is already over for the next.)

(Anderson 1997)

Research in industrialized countries has shown that the ability to learn determines the economic success not only of firms and industries but also of whole regions (industrial districts) and countries (OECD 1996a, 1996b, 1996c). This has given rise to the concept of the learning economy, which is based on the following propositions (Lundvall and Johnson 1994; Lundvall 1994, 1996): learning is an interactive, socially embedded process; its efficiency depends on the institutional setup, the national innovation system. The content of the knowledge generated through learning is critical: tacit knowledge is essential for adjusting to change (flexibility) and for implementing change (innovation).

This chapter inquires how the concept of the learning economy can be applied to the requirements of developing countries (DCs). Its main purpose is to develop an analytical framework for understanding how learning and capability formation can foster industrial upgrading, with special emphasis on the spread of information technology (IT). Under what conditions can DCs use this set of generic technologies to improve their learning capabilities? As a growing amount of knowledge becomes accessible through worldwide information networks, the establishment of national IT capabilities should help to accelerate knowledge creation and diffusion. But the IT revolution also poses new challenges: it increases the inequality of access to knowledge while accelerating the pace of economic and technical change. To cope with these new opportunities and challenges it is imperative that DCs broaden their capability base. This chapter emphasizes the need to improve learning capabilities in all parts of the economy. We argue that IT should not be regarded as a potential substitute for human skills and tacit knowledge. Instead, its main role should be to support the formation and use of tacit knowledge. We proceed in four steps.

First, we describe the challenges DCs face today in their attempts to cope with globalization and to upgrade their industrial sectors. We show that trade has lost its predominant role as the engine of growth; instead DCs are eager to participate in the international production networks (IPNs) of transnational corporations. This requires upgrading DCs' sources of competitiveness: a shift is necessary to an alternative development paradigm, with learning and capability formation as the core elements of development strategy.

Second, we explain why tacit knowledge is essential for adjustment to rapid change in markets and technology as well as for innovation. We show that as globalization of competition, shorter product cycles and rapid technical change have combined to increase uncertainty, tacit knowledge has increased in importance.

Third, we discuss how the diffusion of IT affects the access to tacit knowledge for local agents in DCs. We show that a massive transfer of tacit knowledge into information systems in principle provides DCs with better access to new recipes (process technology as well as products) developed in rich countries. At the same time, IT speeds up the rate of economic change and increases uncertainty, with the result that DCs must permanently restructure and upgrade.

Finally, we ask which institutional features of a national production system are best suited to improving the diffusion of tacit knowledge. We compare two stylized models of the learning economy, the Japanese versus the American model,[1] focusing on the role of tacit knowledge. The Japanese model explicitly promotes and exploits tacit knowledge whereas the American model seeks to reduce the importance of tacit knowledge and to transform it into information – that is, into explicit, well-structured and codified knowledge. The American model emphasizes market selection, competition, income inequality and strict control by financial markets as ways of promoting learning whereas the Japanese model emphasizes co-operation, social cohesion and long-term social relationships.

We show that each of these models has peculiar strengths and weaknesses. Their usefulness to any particular DC depends on its stage of development. Neither model gives a complete answer. DCs need to develop their own hybrid forms of institutions which combine the advantages of both models in a way which is appropriate to their idiosyncratic needs and capabilities.

1.   THE CHALLENGE FOR DEVELOPING COUNTRIES

DCs have gone through a long history of unequal integration into the world economy. As W.A. Lewis observed in 1980: 'For the past hundred years the rate of growth of output in the developing world has depended on the rate of growth of output in the developed world. When the developed grow fast, the developing grow fast, and when the developed slow down, the developing slow down' (Lewis 1980, p. 555).

This linkage continues to hold.[2] Yet the forms of this integration have changed considerably, and this has had important implications for development strategies. These changes result from the combined impact of globalization and the spread of a set of generic technologies, especially IT, with a large potential for productivity enhancement. The result is that learning and knowledge creation, more than ever before, determine the success or failure of development strategies.

1.1   Globalization

International trade was the main engine of growth for DCs until the mid-1970s, the period covered by W.A. Lewis's 1980 article. Lewis's main concern was that stagflation in industrialized countries would slow down North–South trade with the result that it could no longer act as an engine of growth. He suggested strengthening South–South trade through a variety of selective regional trading blocs among DCs.

This well-intentioned scenario did not materialize. Attempts to promote South–South trade almost invariably ended in failure. World trade remains highly concentrated on industrialized countries and the concentration is rising: the North's share of world trade rose from 81 per cent in 1970 to 84 per cent in 1989.[3] North–South trade has fallen as a proportion of the total and the share of South–South trade remains insignificant.

World trade growth slowed during the 1980s and 1990s relative to output growth: the ratio fell from 1.65 in 1965–80 to 1.34 in 1980–90 (World Bank 1992, Tables 2 and 14). Trade continues to grow considerably faster than gross domestic product does, however. This implies that an increasing share of production goes to foreign markets. This raises the importance of foreign markets relative to domestic markets. The result is that a country's relative income, its welfare, becomes more dependent on the ability of its firms to compete against imports in the domestic market and against other producers in foreign markets. This is as true for DCs as for industrialized countries.

Since the mid-1970s Japan and later a handful of so-called newly industrializing economies (NIEs), primarily in Asia, have emerged as important new competitors in a variety of industrial manufacturing sectors. Over time their focus has shifted from low-end, labour-intensive products (such as textiles and household appliances) to capital- and knowledge-intensive products (such as cars and computer-related products). Furthermore, since the mid-1980s international investment has grown considerably faster than international trade (UNCTAD 1996). By the 1990s sales by the foreign affiliates of transnational corporations (TNCs) far outpaced exports as the principal vehicle to deliver goods and services to foreign markets. Increasingly the focus of international market share expansion has shifted from exports to international production, with the result that a growing number of national economies have become mutually interconnected through cross-border flows of goods, services and factors of production.

This has destabilized established patterns of competition: formerly stable national oligopolies have been considerably eroded.[4] Competition today cuts across national and sectoral boundaries – hence the term 'global competition'.[5] Firms are now forced to compete simultaneously in all major growth markets. Cost leadership has to be combined with product differentiation. This has led to a rapid expansion of international production: new production sites have been added with breathtaking speed at lower-cost locations outside the industrial heartlands of Europe, North America and Japan.

Yet quantitative expansion is only part of the story. Of equal importance are qualitative changes: a shift from partial to systemic forms of globalization. In order to cope with the increasingly demanding requirements of global competition, companies are forced to integrate their erstwhile stand-alone operations in individual host countries into increasingly complex IPNs.[6] Companies break down the value chain into discrete functions and locate them wherever they can be carried out most effectively and where they are needed to facilitate the penetration of important growth markets. Reduction of transaction costs is one important motivation. Of equal importance, however, are access to clusters of specialized capabilities and contested growth markets and the need to speed up response time to technological change and to changing market requirements.

1.2 The Neoliberal Concept of Globalization

Pressure to liberalize capital and financial markets has further accelerated the pace of globalization. Yet relatively little of the literature dealing with DCs has addressed the impact of globalization.[7] The dominant view is that globalization will act as a powerful equalizer, over time leading to greater uniformity of development potentials.[8] Among nations, liberalization reduces distortions in international trade; as more and more nations liberalize, national policies converge. Convergence is also expected among firms. Faced with similar constraints, firms are expected to converge in their organization and strategies, irrespective of their national origin (Vernon 1971, 1977; Graham and Krugman 1992). Boyer summarizes the underlying logic: 'Everywhere firms facing the same optimizing problems find the same solution in terms of technology, markets and products, for there is one best way of organizing production – a single optimum among a possible multiplicity of local optima.'[9]

This dominant view also argues that globalization will accelerate the decline of the nation state as the relevant unit of policy-making and that anything which smacks of industrial policy is unlikely to improve local competitiveness. Governments, in this view, should concentrate on the pervasive deregulation and liberalization of national economies. The more willing a government is to embrace sweeping liberalization, the more this country can use international trade and investment as engines of growth.

1.3   The Critical Importance of Local Capabilities

We disagree with this neoliberal concept of globalization. Nothing is predetermined about the impact of globalization.[10] It can increase geographical inequality if left to the invisible hand of the market and to the quite visible hand of TNCs because TNCs have become much more selective and demanding in their choice of locations. Low labour costs are taken for granted, and alternative locations are judged by the quality of certain specialized capabilities which the TNC needs in order to complement its own core competencies. Countries which cannot provide such capabilities are left out of the circuit of international production. Thus, vast areas of the international economy – involving a majority of the world's population – have experienced a dramatic decline in their development potential.

Those countries which can provide such capabilities and, as a result, can attract higher value-added investments may benefit, however. Leading multinationals construct IPNs in order to gain quick access to lower-cost external capabilities which are complementary to their own competencies. In order to mobilize and harness these external capabilities, multinationals are forced to broaden their capability transfer to individual nodes of their IPN.[11] This opens up new entry possibilities for small, specialized suppliers in DCs. Although in some cases (screwdriver contract assembly, for example) such entry may be short-lived, it is not necessarily. Outsourcing requirements have become more demanding and have moved up to include a variety of high-end support services such as engineering, product design, and research and development. This creates new gaps and interstices which can be addressed by small, specialized suppliers. Over time they may be able to upgrade their position from simple contract manufacturers to providers of integrated service packages, and hence increase the benefits which they can reap from network participation.

Successful late industrialization in Korea and Taiwan are cases in point.[12] Take the development of Korea's electronics industry, which arguably has been the most impressive example of such successful late industrialization: An industry which barely existed 25 years ago has been able to transform itself into a credible international competitor in a very short time.[13]

Rather than letting foreign firms establish local subsidiaries and decide on the speed and scope of technology diffusion, Korean firms focused on learning and knowledge accumulation through a variety of links with foreign equipment and component suppliers, technology licensing partners, OEM clients and minority joint venture partners. By licensing proven foreign product designs and by importing most of the production equipment and the crucial components, Korean electronics producers were able to focus most of their attention on three areas:[14]

1. The mastery of production capabilities, initially for assembly but increasingly also for related support services and for large mass production lines for standard products.
2. Some related minor change capabilities, ranging from reverse engineering techniques to analytical design and some system engineering capabilities which are required for process re-engineering and product customization.
3. Some investment capabilities, especially the capacity to carry out at short notice and at low cost investments to expand capacity and/or modernize plants and to establish new production lines.

In order to succeed, Korean electronics firms had to develop the knowledge and skills necessary to monitor, unpackage, absorb and upgrade foreign technology. Equally important was a capacity to mobilize the substantial funds for paying technology licensing fees and for importing 'best practice' production equipment and leading-edge components.[15] Most Korean electronics producers arguably would have hesitated to pursue such high-cost, high-risk strategies had they not been induced to do so by a variety of selective policy interventions by the Korean state. Getting relative prices 'wrong' has been important (Amsden 1989). By providing critical externalities such as information, training, maintenance and other support services and finance, the Korean government has fostered the growth of firms large enough to hurdle high entry barriers.

Because of these particular historically conditioned circumstances Korea's electronics firms were able to reverse the sequence of technological capability formation (Dahlman et al. 1987). Rather than proceeding from innovation to investment to production, they could take a shortcut and focus on the ability to operate production facilities according to competitive cost and quality standards. Production capabilities thus were used as the foundation for developing capabilities in investment and adaptive engineering, and product and market development and process innovation were postponed to a later stage of development. Through judicious reverse engineering and other forms of copying and imitating foreign technology and by integrating into the increasingly complex IPNs of American, Japanese and some European electronics companies, Korean electronics firms were able to avoid the huge cost burdens and risks involved in R&D and in developing international distribution and marketing channels.

1.4 The Role of the State

The Korean approach to capability formation reflects the fact that markets are notoriously weak in generating such capabilities. They are subject to externalities: investments in capabilities are typically characterized by a gap between private and social rates of return (Arrow 1962). National policy interventions must compensate for these market failures. In addition to the subsidies and tax incentives suggested by Arrow, these interventions require a variety of organizational and institutional innovations. There is now a much greater need for national and regional policies to develop local capabilities which can attract high value-added investment.

But there is also now more space for national policy and politics to vary and to make a difference. A growing body of research on economic policy making in advanced industrial countries has demonstrated that choice is possible in terms of institutions and policy instruments and that this applies to macroeconomic as well as industrial and technology policies.[16] The same is true for DCs. The real question, then, is no longer whether national policies can make a difference but rather what kind of policies and institutions are most conducive to improving local competitiveness.

Few people understand the time dimension involved. Policy requirements keep changing over time for two reasons: increasing complexity and greater exposure to the international economy. As a DC moves from simple and labour-intensive to more complex products, much more sophisticated policies are required because entry barriers tend to rise with increasing complexity. This implies that local enterprises need to have access to more demanding externalities which would enable them to overcome their disadvantages in terms of size and weak proprietary assets.

Externality requirements vary, depending on the market segment and the stage of development of a particular industry. Obviously they are less demanding for textiles than for semiconductors. And within the same product group (semiconductors, for example) such requirements become much more complex once the focus shifts from low-end discrete devices for consumer applications to higher-end design-intensive devices.

Greater exposure to the international economy is a second reason why industrial development policies need to develop over time. Increasing complexity of the domestic industry necessitates more international linkages. Such linkages are necessary to facilitate local capability formation. They encompass not only critical imports of key components and capital equipment and inward FDI; such linkages also involve participation in IPNs as well as in a variety of specialized and informal 'international peer group' networks which are essential carriers of knowledge creation.

The dynamics of change thus is of crucial importance for industrial development policies. Peter Evans's model of four archetypal roles which the state has played in industrial transformation can help in this context (Evans 1995).

Among 'developmental states' such as Korea, Brazil and India, and in the information sector in particular, Evans argues, one can distinguish four archetypal roles the state has played, sometimes separately and sometimes in combination. These are (1) the custodian role, in which the state regulates the market, generally privileging the policing function over promotional policies; (2) the 'demiurge' role, in which the state acts as entrepreneur, not just to provide public goods but out of an assumption that private capital is not adequate to fund the whole gamut of production; (3) the midwife role, in which instead of substituting for the private sector the state tries to shape it out of a belief that the capacity of the private sector is malleable; and (4) the husbandry role, in which the state takes a long-term view, recognizing that even if it successfully induces private groups to tackle promising sectors in its role of midwife, that may not be sufficient. As global changes challenge these firms, the state must continue to cajole and assist private groups to meet these challenges by signalling opportunities, reducing risks, engaging in R&D and so on.

According to Evans (1995, p. 14), 'sectoral outcomes depend on how roles are combined'. Brazil and India 'made less use of midwifery, got bogged down in restrictive rule making and invested heavily in direct production of IT goods by state-owned enterprises. Their efforts to play custodian and demiurge were politically costly and absorbed scarce state capacity, leaving them in a poor position to embark on a program of husbandry which would help sustain the local industries they had helped create.' Not so Korea, which built up firms through midwifery and then through husbandry helped them to meet competitive challenges in IT.[17]

In addition to cross-country comparisons, this classification can guide our understanding of how industrial development policies have changed over time in a given country. The case of Taiwan illustrates how the state has moved from the custodian which regulates the market to the 'demiurge' which takes on productive activities itself rather than leaving them to private capital (Ernst 2000c). Once the limits to these two functions of the state were reached during the 1960s, the Taiwanese state then moved on to midwifery and husbandry, actively introducing a variety of institutional and policy innovations which allowed small enterprises to grow and to become more efficient while providing an environment conducive to learning and innovation.

1.5   A Focus on Learning and Capability Formation

As a result of globalization, DCs today face new challenges: in order to sustain access to markets and technology, they need to continuously upgrade the sources of their competitiveness. This has given rise to debates on the role firm strategies and government policies can play in the transition from traditional forms of competitiveness, based on cheap labour, natural resource endowments and currency devaluation, to more sustainable forms of competitiveness, based on a wide diffusion of technological capabilities and organizational competence. One important example is the current debate between accumulation theorists,[18] for whom growth is largely a result of 'a rapid movement along prevailing production functions' (Krugman 1994), and innovation theorists who argue, following Schumpeter, that development requires learning and innovation.[19]

Our research does not support the assumption that development can be reduced to efficiency gains due to capital accumulation – that is, investment (Lundvall 1992; Ernst 1994b, 2000c). In siding with Nelson and Pack (1995), we argue that investment needs to be complemented by learning and the formation of capabilities in order to achieve sustainable development. That economic growth requires innovation is as true for DCs as it is for OECD countries. Recent econometric analysis, for example, shows that 'the main factors influencing differences in international competitiveness and growth across countries are technological competitiveness and the ability to compete on delivery . . . Cost-competitiveness does also affect competitiveness and growth to some extent, but less so than many seem to believe' (Fagerberg 1988, 370–71).

To put it bluntly, there is no way to reduce poverty other than to place learning and knowledge creation at the centre of development strategy. Foreign aid and windfall profits from oil and other natural resources can produce sustained development only if these resources are channelled into the formation of local capabilities. The question is what specific learning requirements DCs face today.

We distinguish two components of technological knowledge. The first component covers all codifiable items such as engineering blueprints and designs and the underlying generic scientific knowledge plus management manuals and handbooks describing system features, performance require-ments, materials specifications and quality assurance criteria and the organizational methods and routines which are used to implement them. As Nelson has shown, this component also includes individual practition-ers' knowledge of the way such scientific, engineering and organizational principles are applied and of how things work in practice (Nelson 1990).

The second component of technological knowledge is tacit and firm-specific. It is embodied in the organizational routines and collective exper-tise or skills of specific production, procurement, R&D and marketing teams. This is the part of technology which differentiates firms and which cannot be exchanged among them, as it is derived from and tied to the localized and collective learning experience of a given company through its own development of technological capabilities.[20] Whereas the first element of technology may be traded between firms, the second element is the essence of firm-specific competitive advantage. It is non-tradable and relies on learning, either within a firm or within an IPN.[21]

Technological learning in DCs faces two challenges: acquiring the codified knowledge element of technology and developing tacit, firm-spe-cific knowledge. Access to codified knowledge may at times be constrained by patenting, aggressive IPR strategies and the proliferation of 'high-tech neomercantilism'.[22] This first challenge results from some basic failures of international technology markets. Although not even the tightest technol-ogy appropriability regime can prevent technology leakages, such restric-tions can substantially delay the actual entry of such knowledge into the public domain. Codified knowledge remains subject to the constraints of entry deterrence strategies pursued by both firms and governments (Ernst and O'Connor 1992, Chapters 1 and 2). Technology leaders, for instance, can substantially increase the cost of external technology sourcing by charging high licensing fees.[23]

This first challenge is of particular relevance to countries like Korea and Taiwan, which today confront the 'successful catching-up trap' (Ernst and O'Connor 1989). As these countries move closer to the technological fron-tier, they face a number of new constraints with regard to access to tech-nology and markets. Access to codified knowledge becomes more difficult and costly, especially if it involves new product designs and core compo-nents. Although such access to technology constraints is real and often quite serious, it would be misleading to focus our attention exclusively on it. Both Korea and Taiwan have reached a critical level in the development of their domestic capabilities. One way or another they will always be able to circumvent such access to technology constraints.[24]

This brings us to the second challenge for DCs, which is far more important than the first. In addition, it applies to all kinds of DCs. Even if all firms can gain access to a common pool of codified knowledge, they must undertake a costly and invariably time-consuming learning process in which they develop the tacit capabilities required to use, adapt and further develop the imported technology.

2.   THE CRITICAL IMPORTANCE OF TACIT KNOWLEDGE

The creation of tacit knowledge is the decisive prerequisite for successful development. A weak tacit knowledge base, in our view, constitutes a major barrier which delays or in some cases even obstructs international technology diffusion to DCs. This implies, of course, a broad definition of knowledge and learning. Wealth-creating knowledge includes practical skills established through learning by doing as well as competencies acquired through formal education and training, and it includes management skills learnt in practice as well as new insights produced by R&D efforts.

It is important to emphasize that learning takes place in all parts of the economy, including in so-called low-tech and traditional sectors. Indeed, learning in traditional and low-tech sectors may be more important for economic development than learning in a small number of insulated high-tech firms. The learning potential (technological opportunities) may differ between sectors and technologies but in most broadly defined sectors there will be niches where the potential for learning is high.

Finally, all kinds of labourers have skills and learning capacity, including those misleadingly called 'unskilled workers'. We make this point in order to avoid having the learning economy hypothesis lead to a neglect of the developmental potential of those parts of the economy which rely less on formally acquired knowledge.

In short, tacit knowledge is at least as important as formal, codified, structured and explicit knowledge.[25] Both types of knowledge hang together; they are symbiotic. Even though codified knowledge can be exchanged, to make it operational a firm needs to develop supporting tacit knowledge. This is in line with Edith Penrose's observation that 'a firm's rate of growth is limited by the growth of knowledge within it' (Penrose 1959, pp. xvi, xvii). Nonaka and Takeuchi (1995) have convincingly demonstrated that a firm's learning efficiency critically depends on an institutional set-up which facilitates a spiral-type interaction between tacit and codified knowledge.

One difficulty with such a broad definition of knowledge is that it is not easy to illustrate empirically the validity of the basic hypothesis. Almost all indicators of knowledge-intensity and learning activities refer to formal education and R&D efforts, and generally they support the hypothesis of the learning economy. It can be shown that modern economic growth is biased in the direction of more intensive use of human capital, that sectors intensive in their use of trained labour and in their investments in R&D are the ones expanding their employment most rapidly and, finally, that there is a strong tendency towards a polarization in labour markets in favour of skilled labour (Foray and Lundvall 1996). But these indicators, even if pointing in the right direction, give a biased picture of the learning economy. They do not reflect the importance of tacit knowledge and the results of learning taking place within regular economic activities of marketing, production and development.

2.1   What Is Tacit Knowledge?

The distinction between tacit and non-tacit knowledge is not always clear; it might be helpful to illustrate the distinction with some examples. The first would be the classical one of the skilled worker or artisan who uses tools and materials to form a final product. It could be a baker who mixes flour with milk and eggs to produce pancakes. If the quality of ingredients and the process equipment were completely standardized and the environment completely stable, this tacit knowledge could easily be reduced to a formula (2 eggs + 1 cup of flour + 1 litre of milk = 5 pancakes) which non-experts could use with success and which could be easily transferred. But if the ingredients vary in quality and the environment is unstable the proportions and the work process need to be adapted to get good results. This example illustrates that the degree of complexity and the rate of change in quality and environment may determine how far tacit knowledge might be transformed into non-tacit knowledge.

A second example of tacit knowledge involves the management of firms. Should firm A take over firm B or should it leave things as they are? To make such a decision involves the processing of an enormous amount of information and attempts to analyse a multitude of relationships between ill-defined variables. 'Guesstimates' and hunches about future developments are crucial to the outcome. Evaluating the human resources in the other firm is a complex social act. In this case there is no simple arithmetic to refer to (depending on future developments, $1 + 1$ may equal -2, $+2$ or even $+10$). It is obvious that the competence needed in this case is not easily transferred through formal education or information systems. It should also be observed that the decision is unique rather than one in a series of very similarly structured problems. Attempts to design formal decision models to cope with this kind of problem will not be meaningful; the knowledge remains tacit and local. Of course it is possible to learn the skills of artisans and business leaders, but this learning will typically take place in a kind of apprenticeship in which the apprentice or the young business administrator learns by operating in close cooperation with more experienced colleagues.

In short, tacitness has its roots in complexity and in variations in quality. It prevails in situations where there is a need to use several different human senses simultaneously, where skilful physical behaviour is involved and where understanding social relationships is crucial. Globalization and the spread of IT have reinforced these reasons for tacitness, as they have dramatically accelerated the pace of change in economic life. If we were in a steady state (circular flow), a gradual movement from tacit toward non-tacit knowledge might take place. But because the long-term economic success of agents increasingly reflects their ability to adapt to change (flexibility) and their ability to impose change (innovation), tacit knowledge will remain crucial for economic success.

3.   THE IMPACT OF INFORMATION TECHNOLOGY

3.1   Codification of Knowledge

There is a strong normative bias in Western civilization in favour of explicit and well-structured knowledge and there are permanent efforts to automate human skills. One historical example is Taylorism's effort to transfer the knowledge of skilled workers to machinery. Present efforts to develop general business information systems and expert systems move in the same direction.

So far automating human skills has proved to be economically successful only in relation to relatively simple, repetitive tasks performed in a reasonably stable environment. Highly automated process industries may be extremely cost-efficient, but when their products are superseded by more attractive substitutes, these industries leave behind them rust-belt problems that are difficult to solve.

Let us take a closer look at how IT affects different elements of knowledge. It is claimed that the increased use of IT enhances both the incentives and the possibilities for codifying knowledge (David and Foray 1995). We suggest that the connection between the IT revolution and the learning economy is more complicated.

While some skills will be transformed into a codified form, demand will grow for complementary tacit knowledge. The very growth in the amount of information which is made accessible to economic agents increases the demand for skills in selecting and using information intelligently. For this reason experience-based learning might become even more important than before. The major impact of the IT revolution on the process of learning might, however, be that it speeds up the process of change in the economy. The codification, standardization and normalization of certain parts of the knowledge stock increases the rate with which some stages in the innovation process are progressing, and the diffusion of this kind of knowledge might also be accelerated. In order to see why skills and the formation of skills will remain a core element behind economic performance, we need to take into consideration the relationship between learning and change.

3.2 Learning and Change

Learning and change are closely related and the causality works both ways. On the one hand, learning is an important and necessary input in the innovation process. On the other hand, change imposes learning on all agents affected by the change. In this context it is important to note that a significant and growing proportion of the labour force is designated to promote change; for the rest of the labour force, change is imposed from above.

In a market economy there is a strong incentive to create and exploit novelty. Producing the same thing in the same way is not very rewarding in the long run. Finding new and more efficient methods of production and introducing new and more attractive products to the market are necessary for survival in most competitive markets. Learning in connection with production and in an interaction with users is fundamental to success in process and product innovation (Lundvall 1985). Learning involves finding and defining the problems to be solved – developing an agenda for problem solving – as well as forming the know-how necessary for problem-solving. Being able to learn from earlier experiences and to use the experiences from earlier rounds of problem solving is also important.

Learning creates change and promotes innovation. But it is equally true that the change instituted by innovating actors imposes further change on the other agents. When a competitor introduces a more efficient process or a more attractive product, the pressure for change increases. Consumers, when confronted with new products, have to change their behaviour as well. And change involves learning. In this sense learning is a self-reinforcing process.

3.3   Acceleration of Learning and Change?

We hypothesize that the rate of change and learning in the economy has accelerated since the 1980s. There is little doubt that over a longer time span this has been the case: change has accelerated enormously since the beginning of the industrial revolution, and people have been forced to learn to do things differently in order to survive.

But what about the shorter term? It is not easy to find reliable and valid indicators in this field. The number of scientific articles is growing exponentially, but this might have more to do with the institutional context than with an increase in the rate of learning. Patent statistics and other indicators of technical progress may also indicate an acceleration, but again the institutional setting may be more important than the actual rate of learning in explaining such patterns. The rate of growth of the economy is actually slower than in the 1950s and the 1960s, and changes in the sectoral composition of production and employment do not give any clear indication of structural change. Although changes in the structure of employment seem to have slowed down in the 1980s, the output of sectors during the same period seems to have accelerated slightly (OECD 1994a, 1994b).

Given the difficulty of obtaining reliable and valid data, let us turn to anecdotal evidence of three trends. First, in 1993 the theme of the annual conference of European R&D managers – EIRMA – was 'Accelerating Innovation', and among the experts present there was little doubt that there had been an acceleration since the 1980s at least in some crucial respects. The key to success in innovation, they agreed, was speed – moving as rapidly as possible from the original idea to the introduction of the innovation in the market. The major theme at the conference was how to attain this goal. When these strategic agents of change accelerate their activities they impose the need for more rapid learning on the other agents in the economy.[26]

A second tendency which involves a broader set of actors than the R&D-intensive firms is the movement towards flexible specialization, in which producers compete through rapid response to volatile markets. This movement has been widely recognized by scholars and consultants, and many firms have drastically changed their organization in order to meet this challenge. Again rapid change demands the ability to learn and to respond to new needs and markets.

A third phenomenon has to do with the introduction of competition into sectors which have previously been protected from it. Competition may come from the opening of national markets for services to imports or from deregulation and privatization of activities. In this process the rate of change will accelerate even more rapidly than it will in sectors which have been used to competition. The rate of learning will accelerate throughout the organization; new learning will include the development of completely new management concepts as well as new organizational forms.

There are thus several indications of an acceleration of change and learning. Easier access to codified knowledge may be one factor reinforcing these tendencies since some elements in the process of innovation now will take place with less delay than before. The truth might be more complex than we want it to be, however; while change has accelerated in some dimensions and segments of the economy, it might have slowed down in others. Let us now look at one of the few, but very original, attempts to measure the rate and costs of change.

Anne P. Carter (1994, 1996) introduced a new perspective on economic change. Her analysis, which covers only manufacturing, demonstrates that there is a strong correlation between the proportion of non-production workers and the rate of change in a sector. Sectors with high proportions of non-production workers grow more rapidly, their rate of productivity grows more rapidly and they include among them the most science-based activities. On this basis, Carter argues that the majority of non-production workers are engaged in either promoting or adapting to change. R&D personnel are most visible in promoting change, but many other professions do this as well. Why would one need so many engineers, accountants, sales personnel and managers if there was no or very little change?

3.4 An Alternative Perspective: IT as a Flexible Tool Supporting Interactive Learning

The most fundamental problems of IT have to do with difficulties in absorbing, allowing for and promoting change. In a stable environment characterized by a high degree of standardization in inputs and outputs, it would be possible and economically attractive to build information systems which substituted for at least some of the functions which had previously been performed by skilled labour and human intelligence. But when materials, processes, products, markets and regulations all change, efforts to mechanize often prove counterproductive – they become barriers to flexible adaptation. It is also difficult to pursue innovative activities in an organizational environment in which human skills are automated.[27]

In short, the main impact of IT is not to reduce the importance of tacit knowledge but rather to speed up specific phases of the innovation process. Such a speed-up might increase the demand for tacit skills. When the rate of change accelerates it confronts all economic agents with a need to analyse and react to a complex and rapidly changing flow of knowledge. We know that the exclusive use of strictly analytical models does not work in such situations. We conclude that tacit knowledge – in the forms of gut reactions, creativity and pragmatic intuition – is needed both to adapt to change and to impose change. We further conclude that attempts to impose overly ambitious analytical models hamper rather than stimulate decision-making in such a context.

IT may be regarded from a different perspective, in which the emphasis is upon its potential to reinforce human interaction and interactive learning. Here the focus is not upon its ability to substitute for tacit knowledge but rather on its ability to support and mobilize tacit knowledge. E-mail systems connecting agents sharing common local codes and frameworks of understanding can have this effect, and broad access to data and information among employees can further the development of common perspectives and objectives for the firm. Multimedia exchange may be helpful in transferring elements of tacit knowledge, for instance, by using combinations of voice and pictures interactively.

Let us assume an 'information economy' where all practical knowledge has been successfully transformed into simple recipes which can be accessed and applied by everyone. In such an economy – which corresponds to the assumptions of complete mobility of technical knowledge made in neoclassical trade theory – there would be no transnational corporations, and regional disparities in wealth would reflect only differences in the accumulation of tangible capital.

Introducing tacit knowledge, including shared tacit knowledge rooted inside firms or in local knowledge-intensive networks of firms, changes the workings of global competition completely. In such a world it becomes profitable for firms to exploit their specific knowledge assets all over the world and it becomes clear why the access to such knowledge for local agents in less developed regions is limited. This implies also that any kind of systematic changes in the borderlines between tacit knowledge and information are of fundamental importance for the prospects of DCs.

An optimistic scenario would be one in which a massive transfer of tacit knowledge into information systems gives DCs access to new recipes (process technologies as well as new products) developed in the rich countries at a lower cost and much more rapidly than before. This would imply an acceleration of the catching-up process and prospects of narrowing global inequalities.

The experience of East Asian firms with learning from IPNs, described in the first part of this essay, provides reason for cautious optimism. The crux of such arrangements is an increased exposure to modern methods of organizing not only production but the complex interaction between different stages of the value chain. This indicates that participation in IPNs can help, over time, to accelerate the formation of a variety of technological and organizational capabilities, provided that (1) a certain minimum threshold of such capabilities already exists, (2) DC firms pursue active strategies of learning and technology acquisition, and (3) the government and other intermediary institutions in the DC play a very active role as suppliers of necessary externalities.

The main remaining institutional problem in such a world would be to establish appropriately balanced intellectual property right (IPR) regimes which on the one hand stimulate the creation of new technology and on the other hand do not restrict the diffusion of new knowledge to late industrializing countries.

Two alternative scenarios which are less optimistic and more realistic must be considered. One is that access to the new recipes is limited by ability to master the language and codes connected to IT and that access can be gained only by countries and firms having a well-trained labour force with an ability to master symbolic languages. But there are much more mundane and fundamental constraints. In a great number of DCs, especially in the so-called least-developed countries, many firms are not logging on to the Internet. Either they lack computers or Internet access nodes and providers, or the cost of telecommunications is prohibitive (Ernst 1997a). Research is needed to uncover the content and structure of network linkages which firms in the Third World are maintaining, and how these network linkages affect the firms' access to tacit knowledge.[28]

These constraints prevent many DCs from catching up economically with the industrialized countries. It will not be easy to overcome these constraints. Most of these countries have experienced a drastic decline in inflows of foreign capital, both concessionary and commercial. Access to capital has further deteriorated as a result of the crisis of the global finance markets caused by the bursting of the 'bubble economies' of East Asia. Most of the incoming capital is used for the purchase of equipment, leaving very little for crucial investments in human capital. Without such investments, DCs are doomed to perpetual exclusion from the marvels of the learning economy.

But this is only part of the story and much more is required in order to reap the benefits of IT. In essence, DCs need to create institutions to provide both the incentives and the externalities necessary for domestic learning, which we define as learning within the domestic economy by both national and foreign actors. Learning efficiency is critically dependent on the existence of such institutions. They are shaped by the interaction of policies, firm strategies (including those pursued by interfirm networks) and markets. Such institutions need time to develop, and there is no single optimum solution. Each individual country has to find the idiosyncratic mix of policies, market structure and firm organization which best fits its own strengths and weaknesses. Nor is there any guarantee of success: institutions can also experience malignant growth or they can get stuck with obsolete features which once were useful but now have become barriers to a further upgrading of local capabilities. In short, the dynamics of institutional change matter, but nothing is predetermined about the impact of these processes on capability formation (Ernst 2000a).

Probably the greatest challenge for DCs, however, results from the fact that IT accelerates creative destruction. Let us consider a third scenario which follows from our earlier discussion. This scenario takes as its starting point that IT, in the context of globalization, speeds up the rate of economic change and that, as a result, the need for rapid learning of tacit as well as codified knowledge has dramatically increased. This requires not only increasing investment in human and fixed capital but also constant and frequently drastic changes in existing strategies and organizational patterns. Both constraints are real and difficult to overcome.

Developments in Korea show that even if sufficient investment resources are available, the rigid and hierarchical structure of firm and industry organization and of regulatory institutions can act as a major barrier to such change.[29] Accumulating tacit knowledge, required for a quick response to changing markets and technologies, has turned out to be a bit easier in the very different organizational and institutional context of Taiwan (Ernst 2000c). This has important implications for DCs in terms of what institutional set-up is most conducive to learning and capability formation.

4.   WHAT KIND OF LEARNING ECONOMY IS APPROPRIATE FOR DEVELOPING COUNTRIES?

4.1   The New Challenge Recapitulated

We have seen that the spread of IT has changed the role of information: IT enhances the divisibility and storage of information, its processing, transportation and communication, and consequently its accessibility and tradability. In principle, this has improved access to codified knowledge. Yet, in order to benefit from this improved access, DCs need to strengthen their tacit knowledge base.

This has far-reaching implications for the process of knowledge creation: Its effectiveness critically depends on linkages and interactions among participants in this process. Knowledge generation within a society 'is strongly influenced by the network of relations among its firms . . . with externalities, communication and interdependence playing crucial roles' (Antonelli 1997, p. 2).

The same is true for international networks (Ernst 1997b). For DCs, such international linkages are of critical importance in overcoming the vicious circle of underdevelopment (Ernst 2000a). Many of these countries are stuck with a truncated sectoral specialization, dominated by low-end, homogeneous products (commodities) with limited productivity-enhancing potential.[30] The limited size of the domestic market constrains the degree of specialization and places tight restrictions on its ability to function as a buffer against heavy fluctuations in international demand. Insufficient domestic market size also constrains the development of sophisticated 'lead users' which could stimulate innovation.[31] It also limits the scope for technological spillovers.[32] Finally, the limited size of the national knowledge and capital base restricts the choice of industries in which such nations might successfully specialize.

At least in principle, the spread of IT could help to break this vicious circle. By allowing for increasing specialization in the production of knowledge, it could improve the chances for DCs to participate in and to benefit from IPNs. Knowledge generation now shifts from vertically integrated hierarchies to networks: 'The vertical integration structure of knowledge, characteristic since the Second World War, is being progressively replaced by the institutional creation of an information exchange market, based on real-time, on-line interaction between customers and producers' (Antonelli 1997, p. 3). In other words, the spread of IT facilitates and promotes the formation of separate and specialized knowledge markets.

4.2 Two Competing Models of the Learning Economy: The Japanese versus the American Model

Under what conditions can DCs benefit from these developments? And, more specifically, what types of institutional arrangements are most conducive to enhancing the formation of learning capabilities? In what follows, we compare two stylized models of the learning economy, the Japanese versus the American model.[33] The models differ in their approach to tacit knowledge.[34] The Japanese model is explicit in its promotion and exploitation of tacit knowledge whereas the American model is driven by a permanent urge to reduce the importance of tacit knowledge and to transform it into information – that is, into explicit, well-structured and codified knowledge. The American model emphasizes market selection, competition, income inequality and strict control by financial markets as ways of promoting learning, whereas the Japanese model emphasizes cooperation, social cohesion and long-term social relationships. Furthermore, the two models differ in terms of firm organization (including the organization of interfirm networks) and in their approaches to international linkages through trade and investment.

4.3   Knowledge Creation in Japanese Firms

Nonaka and Takeuchi (1995) give a series of examples of how large and well-managed Japanese TNCs organize the process of product innovation in ways which explicitly take into account the important role of tacit knowledge. Japanese managers do not give their innovation teams detailed instructions. Instead they promote the search for innovative solutions by formulating metaphors and analogies. These are based on management's intuition and they leave ample room for creativity and the formation of new intermediate concepts. An intermediate layer of project team leaders makes these open concepts interact with the tacit knowledge of skilled workers and engineers. They formulate somewhat more concrete slogans and gradually the new product is conceptualized.

All through the process face-to-face interaction and hands-on experimentation are given high priority. IT is used to give all participants easier access to banks of information to support knowledge creation, but these efforts are always combined with direct human interaction. They are not regarded as substitutes for it.

Nonaka and Takeuchi argue that the organizational model best suited to the creation of new knowledge is a 'hypertext organization' in which there is one regular divisional structure which is overlayered with ad hoc horizontal teams directly aiming at creating new products and new knowledge. Members of these teams should be taken completely out of their regular functions and divisions.[35] The analysis is limited to management strategies in connection with product development in big knowledge-based firms. It is however possible to extend the basic perspective in order to understand other characteristics of the Japanese innovation systems such as the long-term close interfirm relationships, the labour market and the lifetime employment contracts, the patient capital market with a long-term perspective, and so on.[36]

In short, the Japanese model of the learning economy places mid-level team leaders at the centre of innovation. Top management gives direction to innovation in the form of metaphors and analogies. They establish frameworks promoting direct social interaction (face to face) and hands-on experimentation in order to mobilize and develop tacit knowledge at all levels of the firm. Monetary incentives are secondary and income differences are suppressed. Job circulation is stimulated in order to avoid narrow specialist perspectives. Markets are characterized by long-term relationships between sellers and buyers, and they transmit qualitative as well as quantitative information. Direct interaction with customers is a key element when marketing new products.[37] The creation of trust and communication channels is crucial to the success of developing and introducing new products.

4.4 Key Elements of the American Model

Central to the American model is an attempt to transform tacit knowledge into explicit knowledge through the automation of human skills. This is in line with a strong normative bias in Western civilization in favour of explicit and well-structured knowledge and the high priority given to formal natural science as the ideal for all other sciences. Engineering and especially disciplines with weak science bases have much lower status. In practical life there are permanent efforts to structure and formalize or automate tacit knowledge. Economists tend to share and reinforce this bias because economic models have even greater difficulty analysing tacit knowledge than analysing information.[38]

Typical of the American model is a hierarchical understanding of competence – competence is concentrated at the top. Operators on the shop floor have very limited roles in learning and knowledge creation. This goes hand in hand with an approach to labour management which emphasizes top management as the authority selecting competent teams and designing material incentives to stimulate the top teams in the firm. If anything, this model assumes that compensation is biased against the most competent participants. This model does not accept the idea that social cohesion could promote learning and innovation.

In product markets, American firms favour low entry barriers and fierce competition, which are perceived as creating the best environment for experimentation and for eliminating inefficient non-innovative firms. Interfirm cooperation as a solution is still considered second best to the free play of market forces. The most important function of the financial market is to intervene and enforce a shift in top management when it fails to produce the return on investment required by the market. Capital markets combining takeover threats, junk bond markets and venture capital are presented as the ideal. Little is said about the problem of short-termism in Anglo-Saxon financial markets.

Finally, one of the basic credos of the American model is that the government should not intervene in the market mechanism because government is by definition incompetent when it comes to recognizing and correcting its own mistakes – a key competence of successful firms. There is no reference to historical cases where active governments have stimulated economic development by indicating broad trajectories for industrial development.

In short, the American model is characterized by a clear hierarchy, and the main responsibility for promoting innovation rests at the top. This responsibility is performed by hiring, firing and promoting competent people and by designing incentive systems. Monetary incentives predominate: inequality in competencies should be reflected in inequalities in earnings. Specialized expertise is crucial to problem solving.

Finally, competition dominates interfirm relationships. Industrial markets as well as markets for consumption goods are regarded as characterized by arm's-length and anonymous relationships between sellers and buyers. Markets serve as media for information exchange when the tacitness of knowledge constrains the scope for organizational learning.

4.5   Hybrid Models and Economic Development: Implications for Developing Countries

We have seen that both models of the learning economy have peculiar strengths and weaknesses. For any particular DC, their usefulness depends on its stage of development. The American model promotes short-term static allocation efficiency but neglects two equally important types of efficiency problems: distributive and learning efficiency. For DCs, this may have negative consequences for long-term capability formation.[39] The Japanese model, in turn, is conducive to rapid capability formation, which can facilitate economic catching up. This, however, comes at a cost in static allocation efficiency and reduced speed to market.

For the majority of DCs, the main concern is to create the necessary institutions to provide incentives for and externalities necessary for domestic learning. For these countries, the US model has less to offer than the Japanese model: its disregard of the importance of tacit knowledge leads to a misconception of the role of IT in the learning economy. For those countries, however, which have reached a certain degree of development and need to upgrade their existing institutions, neither of the stylized models gives the full answer. These countries need to develop hybrid institutions which combine the advantages of both models in a way which is appropriate to their idiosyncratic needs and capabilities.

Such pragmatic new combinations may become more realistic in a world in which the two models converge. On the one hand, the reason American firms have regained their competitiveness is that they have started to use organizational solutions which are much closer to the Japanese model than the American ideology would indicate. On the other hand, the ongoing debate about industrial restructuring in Japan emphasizes the limitations of the old catching-up strategy and the need to borrow institutional elements from the US model in order to promote individual entrepreneurship and short-term flexibility.[40]

NOTES

1. For related papers which compare the Korean and the Taiwanese models see Ernst 1994b, 1998a, 2000b.
2. Note, however, that this linkage did not hold during the two twentieth-century world wars, which led to breakdowns of the international economy. During these two wars countries such as Brazil, Argentina, colonial India and Egypt experienced bouts of growth based on import substitution. Classic sources include Hirschman 1968 and Furtado 1970. For a review of these debates see Ernst 1973.
3. 'North' refers to developed market economies, virtually identical with OECD member countries. UNCTAD 1991, Table 3.4, in Appendix 1.
4. See the growing literature on 'contestable markets', which shows that high concentration can go hand in hand with high contestability or openness to entry (Baumol et al. 1982). For a review of this literature see UNCTAD 1997, part 2, 'Foreign direct investment, market structure and competition policy'. For a case study of how globalization affects competition in the electronics industry see Ernst 1998b.
5. The following is based on Ernst 1997b, Chapter 1.
6. The concept of an IPN is an attempt to capture the spread of broader and more systemic forms of international production which cover all stages of the value chain and which may or may not involve equity ownership. This concept allows us to analyse the globalization strategies of a particular firm with regard to four questions: (1) Where does a firm locate which stages of the value chain? (2) To what degree does a firm rely on outsourcing? What is the importance of interfirm production networks relative to the firm's internal production network? (3) To what degree is the control over these transactions centralized or decentralized? (4) How do the different elements of these networks hang together? The IPN concept has been developed in studies prepared for the OECD (Ernst 1994a), the Sloan Foundation (Ernst 1997b) and the Brookings Institution (Ernst 2000b).
7. For a detailed analysis of the impact of globalization on industrialization in DCs see Ernst and O'Connor 1989, 1992. For an analysis of how Korea and Taiwan have tried to cope with the globalization challenge see Ernst 1994b, 1998a, 2000c.
8. For a typical example of this neoliberal globalization doctrine see Ohmae 1991.
9. Boyer 1996, pp. 47 and 40. We agree with Boyer's conclusion: 'This syllogism that equates globalization with convergence is logically flawed, and its premise may not correspond to the current state of the world economy' (p. 50).
10. The following is based on Ernst 2000a.
11. Consider a stylized IPN: it combines a lead firm, its subsidiaries, affiliates and joint ventures, its suppliers and subcontractors, its distribution channels and VARs (value-added resellers), as well as its R&D alliances and a variety of cooperative agreements (such as standards consortia). The lead company derives its strength from its control over critical resources and capabilities and from its capacity to coordinate transactions between the different network nodes. One such source of strength, for instance, is the intellectual property and knowledge associated with setting, maintaining and continuously upgrading a de facto market standard. This requires perpetual improvements in product features, functionality, performance, cost and quality. It is such 'complementary assets' which the lead firm increasingly outsources. For empirical evidence see Ernst 1997b.
12. On Korea see Amsden 1989 and Ernst 1994b. On Taiwan see Wade 1990 and Ernst 2000c.
13. The following is based on Ernst 1998a.
14. For the underlying conceptual framework of capability formation see Ernst et al. 1998. See also the excellent analysis in Bell and Pavitt 1993.
15. Already in the 1970s most Korean electronics firms had to pay roughly 3 per cent of their gross sales for technology licensing fees, a share which since then has increased to more than 12 per cent (Lee Jin-Joo 1992, pp. 132, 139).
16. For macroeconomic policies see Frieden 1991 and Frankel et al. 1992. For industrial and

technology policies see the contributions by Boyer and also by Wade in Berger and Dore 1996.

17. Although Peter Evans's classification is a highly innovative theoretical approach, it is hard to agree with his choice of Korea as the positive role model in the computer industry. Taiwan is much better qualified to play this role (Ernst 2000c). This is not to belittle Korea's tremendous achievements in consumer electronics and standard precision components such as DRAMs. For a detailed analysis see Ernst 1994b, 1998a.

18. Young 1993, Kim and Lau 1994, Krugman 1994.

19. Freeman 1982, 1991; Lundvall 1988, 1992, 1996; Bell and Pavitt 1993; Nelson 1993; Nelson and Pack 1995; Maskell 1996a, 1996b.

20. The nature of these technological capabilities has been analysed in Ernst et al. 1998.

21. For analyses of IPNs and their impact on technology diffusion see Ernst 1994a, 1997b.

22. Today's arsenal of policy instruments available for such 'high-tech neomercantilism' is impressive and includes subsidies for investment or research, restrictions on access to the domestic market by similar goods from foreign producers, restrictions on direct investment in the domestic market by foreign firms, and procurement policies which favour the domestic producer of a high-technology good. For evidence see Ernst and O'Connor 1989, p. 26 *passim*; Tyson 1992.

23. For evidence see note 15.

24. For evidence see Ernst 1994b, 2000c.

25. The concept of tacit knowledge was originally developed by Michael Polanyi (1966, 1978).

26. EIRMA 1993. In this context, it is relevant to quote from the introductory remarks of the EIRMA president, Dr E. Spitz: 'In a time of intensive global competition, speeding up the innovation process is one of the most important ingredients which enable the company to bring to the market the right product for the right price at the right time . . . We know that it is not only the R&D process which is important; we have to put emphasis on the integration of technology in the complete business environment, production, marketing, regulations and many other activities essential to commercial success. These are the areas where the innovation process is being retarded. This subject is a very deep seated one which sometimes leads to important, fundamental rethinking and radical redesign of the whole business process. In this respect, especially during the difficult period in which we live today, where pressure is much higher, our organisations may, in fact, need to be changed' (EIRMA 1993, p. 7).

27. The difficulties with automating tacit knowledge do not rule out new attempts to formalize and structure tacit knowledge; it is reasonable to assume that the growing importance of IT will further stimulate such attempts. Already one can see a number of new applications which change the character of knowledge creation at certain stages of the innovation process. Computer-aided development and testing of drugs and aircraft and computer-aided design in many other areas illustrate successful transfers of problem-solving skills from humans to computers (Foray and Lundvall 1996, pp. 14–15).

28. On some of these issues see UNCST (forthcoming), Chapters 3 and 5.

29. For evidence see Ernst 1994b, 1998a.

30. The classical source remains Fajnzylber 1989.

31. Von Hippel defines 'lead users of a novel or enhanced product, process, or service' as those which 'face needs that will be general in the market place, but . . . [who] face them months or years before the bulk of that marketplace encounters them' and who will 'benefit significantly by obtaining a solution to those needs' (Von Hippel 1988, p. 107).

32. Innovation theorists (Lundvall 1992, Nelson 1993) as well as new growth theorists (Grossman and Helpman 1991, 1993) assume that technological spillovers are primarily domestically generated. If this is so, then large countries will benefit more from an investment in R&D than smaller countries, where some of the spillovers of R&D are likely to benefit their trading partners (Zander and Kogut 1995).

33. Both models are ideal types which do not exist in real life. There are, of course, substantial variations among both American and Japanese firms. There are also instances of selective convergence between the models. On both issues see Ernst 1997b, 1997c.

Nevertheless, the two models capture essential differences in the process of knowledge creation which reflect the very distinct patterns of economic development and institutions in the two countries. See also note 1.

34. There are, of course, equally important criteria for comparing different paradigms of the learning economy. For instance, American and Japanese firms differ substantially in how they approach the development and application of IT. For a discussion of some of these issues see Ernst 1997b, 2000b.

35. The analysis is much more complex than indicated by this summary. For instance, Nonaka and Takeuchi develop a model of knowledge creation which assumes the process to be a spiral movement from tacit to explicit and then back to tacit knowledge. The conversion between these forms plays a crucial role in the theory. This point is worth critical attention. In some of Nonaka and Takeuchi's examples it is not clear whether what is illustrated is an interaction between the different forms of knowledge or a conversion of one into the other.

36. For an attempt to cover these broader aspects of knowledge creation in Japanese firms see Fruin 1997.

37. The case of Nissan developing its Primera model for the European market is an extremely interesting illustration of how Japanese firms try to absorb local tacit knowledge from their potential markets (Nonaka and Takeuchi 1995, pp. 200ff).

38. Eliasson (1996) shows that the fascination with automation in the form of generic business information systems again and again has proved out of proportion with reality. An enormous number of articles has been written on the fully automated factory, but the real counterpart has been of negligible importance. The same has been true for office automation. This bias has been costly for many firms. The case studies of Hatchuel and Weil (1995) show that so far automating human skills has been economically successful only for simple, repetitive tasks performed in a reasonably stable environment. Their work on expert systems shows that even when the tasks are reasonably simple, the mode of operation of the expert system developed will differ radically from the operation of the expert.

39. This is in line with research on the 'specialization dilemma'. Andersen (1996, p. 105) shows that specialization may involve substantial trade-offs. Pushing static allocation efficiency gains to the limit could undermine a firm's and a country's capacity for knowledge creation.

40. For an analysis of these issues see Ernst 1997b, 2000b.

REFERENCES

Amsden, A. (1989), *Asia's Next Giant: South Korea and Late Industrialization*, New York: Oxford University Press.

Andersen, E.S. (1996), 'The evolution of economic complexity: A division-of-coordination-of labor approach', in E. Helmstaedter and M. Perlman (eds), *Behavioral Norms, Technological Progress, and Economic Dynamics: Studies in Schumpeterian Economics*, Ann Arbor, MI: University of Michigan Press.

Anderson, R. (1997), 'R&D knowledge creation as a bazaar economy', paper presented at OECD–IEE workshop on 'Competition and Innovation in the Information Society', 19 March, Paris.

Antonelli, C. (1997), 'Localized technological change, new information technology and the knowledge-based economy: the European evidence', Laboratorio di Economia dell'Innovazione, Università di Torino.

Arrow, K.J. (1962), 'The economic implications of learning by doing', *Review of Economic Studies*, June, **29** (3), 155–73.

Baumol, W.J., J.C. Panzer and R.D. Willig (1982), *Contestable Markets and the Theory of Industrial Structure*, New York: Harcourt Brace Jovanovich.

Bell, Martin and Keith Pavitt (1993), 'Technological accumulation and industrial growth: contrasts between developed and developing countries', *Industrial and Corporate Change*, **2** (2), 157–211.

Berger, S. and R. Dore (eds) (1996), *National Diversity and Global Capitalism*, Ithaca, NY: Cornell University Press.

Boyer, R. (1996), 'The convergence hypothesis revisited: Globalization but still the century of nations?', in S. Berger and R. Dore (eds), *National Diversity and Global Capitalism*, Ithaca, NY: Cornell University Press.

Carter, A.P. (1994), 'Production workers, meta-investment and the pace of change', paper prepared for the meeting of the J.A. Schumpeter Society, Munster, August.

Carter, A.P. (1996), 'Measuring the performance of a knowledge-based economy', in OECD, *Growth and Employment in the Knowledge-Based Economy*, Paris: OECD.

Dahlman, C., B. Ross-Larson and L. Westphal (1987), 'Managing technological development: lessons from the newly industrialising countries', *World Development*, **15** (6), 759–75.

David, P. and D. Foray (1995), 'Accessing and expanding the science and technology knowledge-base', *STI Review*, OECD.

EIRMA (1993), *Speeding Up Innovation*, conference papers for the EIRMA Helsinki conference, May.

Eliasson, G. (1996), *Firm Objectives, Controls and Organization*, Amsterdam: Kluwer.

Ernst, D. (1973), 'Wirtschaftliche Entwicklung durch Importsubstitutierende Industrialisierung: Das Beispiel Lateinamerikas', *Das Argument*, **15** (4–6), 3–82.

Ernst, D. (1994a), 'Network transactions, market structure and technological diffusion: Implications for South–South cooperation', in L. Mytelka (ed.), *South–South Cooperation in a Global Perspective*, Paris: Development Centre Documents, OECD, pp. 89–129.

Ernst, D. (1994b), *What Are the Limits to the Korean Model? The Korean Electronics Industry under Pressure*, Berkeley Roundtable on the International Economy (BRIE), University of California, Berkeley.

Ernst, D. (1997a), *Developing a Competitive Information Service Sector in Jamaica: What Changes Are Required in Jamaica's National System of Innovation*, report prepared for the Division on Investment, Technology and Enterprise Development, UNCTAD, Geneva.

Ernst, D. (1997b), *From Partial to Systemic Globalization: International Production Networks in the Electronics Industry*, report prepared for the Sloan Foundation project on the Globalization in the Data Storage Industry, Graduate School of International Relations and Pacific Studies, University of California, San Diego, published as *The Data Storage Industry Globalization Project Report 97-02*, Graduate School of International Relations and Pacific Studies, University of California, San Diego.

Ernst, D. (1997c), 'Partners in the China circle? The Asian production networks of Japanese electronics firms', in Barry Naughton (ed.), *The China Circle*, Washington, DC: Brookings Institution Press, pp. 210–53.

Ernst, D. (1998a), 'Catching-up, crisis and industrial upgrading: Evolutionary aspects of technological learning in Korea's electronic industry', *Asia Pacific Journal of Management*, **15** (2), 247–83.

Ernst, D. (1998b), 'High-tech competition puzzles: how globalization affects firm behaviour and market structure in the electronics industry', *Revue d'Economie Industrielle*, **85**, 1–28.

Ernst, D. (2000a), 'Globalization and the changing geography of innovation systems: A policy perspective on global production networks', *Journal of the Economics of Innovation and New Technologies*, special issue on 'Integrating policy perspectives in research on technology and economic growth', ed. Anthony Bartzokas and Morris Tenbal.

Ernst, D. (2000b), 'Globalization, convergence and diversity: The Asian production networks of Japanese electronics firms', in M. Borrus, D. Ernst and S. Haggard (eds), *Rivalry or Riches: International Production Networks in Asia*, Ithaca, NY: Cornell University Press, pp. 112–48.

Ernst, D. (2000c), 'Inter-organizational knowledge outsourcing: what permits small Taiwanese firms to compete in the computer industry?', *Asia-Pacific Journal of Management*, special issue on 'Knowledge creation management in Asia', August.

Ernst, D., L. Mytelka and T. Ganiatsos (1998), 'Export performance and technological capabilities: A conceptual framework', in D. Ernst, T. Ganiatsos and L. Mytelka (eds), *Technological Capabilities and Export Success: Lessons from East Asia*, London: Routledge, pp. 5–45.

Ernst, Dieter and David O'Connor (1989), *Technology and Global Competition: The Challenge for Newly Industrialising Economies*, Paris: OECD Development Centre Studies.

Ernst, Dieter and David O'Connor (1992), *Competing in the Electronics Industry: The Experience of Newly Industrialising Economies*, Paris: OECD Development Centre Studies.

Evans, P. (1995), *Embedded Autonomy: States and Industrial Transformation*, Princeton, NJ: Princeton University Press.

Fagerberg, J. (1988), 'International competitiveness', *Economic Journal*, **98** (June), 355–74.

Fajnzylber, F. (1989), 'Technical change and economic development: Issues for a research agenda', paper presented at World Bank seminar on 'Technology and Long-term Economic Growth Prospects', Washington, DC, November.

Foray, D. and B.-Å. Lundvall (1996), 'The knowledge-based economy: From the economics of knowledge to the learning economy', in OECD, *Employment and Growth in the Knowledge-Based Economy*, Paris: OECD Documents.

Frankel, J., S. Phillips and M. Chinn (1992), 'Financial and currency integration in the European monetary system: the statistical record', Working Paper 1.3, Center for German and European Studies, University of California, Berkeley.

Freeman, C. (1982), *Economics of Industrial Innovation*, London: Pinter.

Freeman, C. (1991), 'The nature of innovation and the evolution of the production system', in OECD, *Technology and Productivity: The Challenges for Economic Policy*, Paris: OECD.

Frieden, J.A. (1991), 'Invested interests: the politics of national economic policies in a world of global finance', *International Organization*, **45** (4), 425–51.

Fruin, Marc (1997), *Knowledge Works: Managing Intellectual Capital at Toshiba*, New York: Oxford University Press.

Furtado, C. (1970), *Economic Development in Latin America*, New York: Cambridge University Press.

Graham, E. and P. Krugman (1992), *Foreign Direct Investment in the United States*, Washington, DC: Institute for International Economics.

Grossman, G.M. and E. Helpman (1991), *Innovation and Growth in the Global Economy*, Cambridge, MA: MIT Press.

Grossman, G.M. and E. Helpman (1993), 'Endogenous innovation in the theory of growth', National Bureau of Economic Research (NBER) working paper no. 4527, Cambridge, MA.

Hatchuel, A. and B. Weil (1995), *Experts in Organisations*, Berlin: Walter de Gruyter.

Hirschman, A.O. (1968), 'The political economy of import-substituting industrialization in Latin America', *Quarterly Journal of Economics*, **82** (1), 2–32.

Kim, J.I. and L.J. Lau (1994), 'The sources of economic growth in the East Asian newly industrialized countries', *Journal of Japanese and International Economics*, 235–71.

Krugman, P. (1994), 'The myth of Asia's miracle', *Foreign Affairs*, December, pp. 62–77.

Lee Jin-Joo (1992), 'The status and issue of management dynamism and four case studies in the Republic of Korea', in Asian Productivity Organization (APO), *Management Dynamism: A Study of Selected Companies in Asia*, Tokyo: APO.

Lewis, W.A. (1978), *The Evolution of the International Economic Order*, Princeton, NJ: Princeton University Press.

Lewis, W.A. (1980), 'The slowing of the engine of growth', *American Economic Review*, **70** (4), 555–64.

Lundvall, Bengt-Åke (1985), *Product Innovation and User-Producer Interaction*, Aalborg: Aalborg University Press.

Lundvall, Bengt-Åke (1988) , 'Innovation as an interactive process: From user–producer interaction to the national system of innovation', in G. Dosi et al. (eds), *Technical Change and Economic Theory*, London: Pinter.

Lundvall, Bengt-Åke (ed.) (1992), *National Systems of Innovation: Towards a Theory of Innovation and Interactive Learning*, London: Pinter.

Lundvall, Bengt-Åke (1994), 'The learning economy: challenges to economic theory and policy', paper presented at EAEPE Conference, 27–29 October, Copenhagen.

Lundvall, Bengt-Åke (1996), 'The social dimension of the learning economy', DRUID working paper no. 1, Department of Business Studies, Aalborg University.

Lundvall, B.-Å. and B. Johnson (1994), 'The learning economy', *Journal of Industry Studies*, **1** (2), 23–42.

Maskell, P. (1996a), 'Learning in the village economy of Denmark: The role of institutions and policy in sustaining competitiveness', DRUID working paper no. 96-6, Department of Industrial Economics and Strategy, Copenhagen Business School.

Maskell, P. (1996b), 'The process and consequences of ubiquification', paper prepared for the DRUID workshop, January 1997, Department of Industrial Economics and Strategy, Copenhagen Business School.

Nelson, R. (1990), 'US technological leadership: where did it come from and where did it go?', *Research Policy*, April, 97–116.

Nelson, R. (ed.) (1993), *National Innovation Systems*, London: Oxford University Press.

Nelson, R. and H. Pack (1995), 'The Asian growth miracle and modern growth theory', manuscript, School of International and Public Affairs, Columbia University.

Nonaka, I. and H. Takeuchi (1995), *The Knowledge-Creating Company*, Oxford: Oxford University Press.

OECD (1994a), *The OECD Jobs Study: Evidence and Explanation*, Paris: OECD.

OECD (1994b), *The OECD Jobs Study: Facts, Analysis, Strategies*, Paris: OECD.

OECD (1996a), *Growth and Employment in the Knowledge-Based Economy*, Paris: OECD.

OECD (1996b), *Science, Technology and Industry Outlook 1996*, Paris: OECD.

OECD (1996c), *Transitions to Learning Economies and Societies*, Paris: OECD.

Ohmae, K. (1991), *The Borderless World: Power and Strategy in the Interlinked Economy*, New York: Harper & Row.

Penrose, Edith (1959), *The Theory of the Growth of the Firm*, 3rd edn (1995), Oxford: Oxford University Press.

Polanyi, M. (1966), *The Tacit Dimension*, London: Routledge & Kegan Paul.

Polanyi, M. (1978 [1958]), *Personal Knowledge*, London: Routledge & Kegan Paul.

Tyson, L.D. (1992), *Who's Bashing Whom? Trade Conflict in High-Technology Industries*, Washington, DC: Institute for International Economics.

UNCST (forthcoming), *Building Knowledge Societies for the Twenty-first Century: Effective National ICT Strategy Design*, New York: United Nations.

UNCTAD (1991), *Handbook of International Trade and Development Statistics 1990*, New York: United Nations.

UNCTAD (1996), *World Investment Report 1996*, New York: United Nations.

UNCTAD (1997), *World Investment Report 1997*, New York: United Nations.

Vernon, R. (1971), *Sovereignty at Bay: The Multinational Spread of US Enterprises*, New York: Basic Books.

Vernon, R. (1977), *Storm over the Multinationals: The Real Issues*, Cambridge, MA: Harvard University Press.

Von Hippel, E. (1988), *The Sources of Innovation*, New York: Oxford University Press.

Wade, R. (1990), *Governing the Market: Economic Theory and the Role of Government in East Asian Industrialization*, Princeton, NJ: Princeton University Press.

World Bank (1992), *World Development Report 1992*, Washington, DC: World Bank.

Young, Alwyn (1993), 'The tyranny of numbers: Confronting the statistical realities of the East Asian growth enterprise', Sloan School, MIT, July.

Zander, U. and B. Kogut (1995), 'Knowledge and the speed of the transfer and imitation of organizational capabilities: an empirical test', *Organizational Science*, **6** (1), 76–92.

10.   Diversity: implications for income distribution

David B. Audretsch

As recently as the early 1990s scholars and industry observers predicted, if not the death of Silicon Valley, then its slowdown.[1] For example, in a much-cited article in the *Harvard Business Review* Charles Ferguson (1988, p. 61) argued:

> Fragmentation, instability, and entrepreneurialism are not signs of well-being. In fact, they are symptoms of the larger structural problems that afflict US industry. In semiconductors, a combination of personnel mobility, ineffective intellectual property protection and tax subsidies for the formation of new companies contribute to a fragmented 'chronically entrepreneurial' industry. US semiconductor companies are unable to sustain the large, long-term investments required for continued US competitiveness . . . Personnel turnover in the American merchant semiconductor industry has risen to 20 percent compared with less than 5 percent in IBM and Japanese corporations . . . Fragmentation discouraged badly needed coordinated action – to develop better process technology and also to demand better government support.

A decade later, not only is Silicon Valley thriving but, as *The Economist* pointed out, average pay in Silicon Valley rose between 1995 and 1996 by 5 per cent in real terms, to $43,510, compared to a mere 1 per cent increase to $28,040 for the rest of the country.[2] Despite high production costs, environmental destruction and overall congestion, reports of Silicon Valley's demise were premature.

The purpose of this chapter is to suggest that differences in the distribution of income across regions are likely to grow. As a result of globalization, those regions whose economies are based on routinized economic activity will experience a downward pressure on incomes because the cost of diffusing routinized economic activity across space to lower-cost locations is relatively low. By contrast, those regions whose economies are based on search economic activity will experience growth in incomes because it is costly to diffuse search economic activity across space.

The extent to which firms and individuals are homogeneous or heterogeneous shapes the relative efficiency of routinized and search activities.

Homogeneity is conducive to routinized activity but impedes search activity. Diversity promotes search activity but raises the cost of routinized activity. An implication is that as the comparative advantage of the developed nations of Western Europe and North America shifts away from routinized activities and towards search activities, those organizations able to harness diversity will tend to emerge as the most successful. The income gap will continue to grow between those economic agents and regions engaged in search activity and those engaged in routinized activity.

1.   WHY DOES DIVERSITY MATTER?

1.1   New Economic Knowledge

The starting point for most theories of innovation is the firm. In such theories the firm is exogenous and its performance in generating technological change is endogenous. For example, in the most prevalent model found in the literature of technological change, the model of the knowledge-production function formalized by Zvi Griliches (1979), firms exist exogenously and then engage in the pursuit of new economic knowledge as an input into the process of generating innovative activity.

The most decisive input in the knowledge-production function is new economic knowledge. And as Cohen and Klepper (1991, 1992a, 1992b) conclude, the greatest source generating new economic knowledge is generally considered to be R&D. Certainly a large body of empirical work has found a strong and positive relationship between knowledge inputs such as R&D on the one hand and innovative outputs on the other hand.

The knowledge-production function has been found to hold most strongly at broader levels of aggregation. The most innovative countries are those with the greatest investments in R&D. Little innovative output is associated with less developed countries, which are characterized by a paucity of production of new economic knowledge. Similarly, the most innovative industries tend to be characterized by considerable investments in R&D and new economic knowledge. Industries such as computers, pharmaceuticals and instruments are high not only in R&D inputs which generate new economic knowledge, but also in innovative outputs (Audretsch 1995). By contrast, industries with little R&D, such as wood products, textiles and paper, tend to produce only a negligible amount of innovative output. Thus, the knowledge-production model linking knowledge-generating inputs to outputs holds at the more aggregated levels of economic activity.

Where the relationship becomes less compelling is at the desegregated microeconomic level of the enterprise, establishment or even line of business. For example, although Audretsch (1995) found that the simple correlation between R&D inputs and innovative output was 0.84 for four-digit standard industrial classification (SIC) manufacturing industries in the United States, it was only about half (0.40) among the largest US corporations.

The model of the knowledge-production function becomes even less compelling in view of the recent wave of studies revealing that small enterprises serve as the engine of innovative activity in certain industries. These results are startling because, as Scherer (1991) observes, the bulk of industrial R&D is undertaken in the largest corporations; small enterprises account for only a minor share of R&D inputs. Thus the knowledge-production function seemingly implies, as the Schumpeterian hypothesis predicts, that innovative activity favours those organizations with access to knowledge-producing inputs – large incumbent organizations (Schumpeter 1911, 1942). The more recent evidence identifying the strong innovative activity of small firms raises the question: where do new and small firms get innovation-producing inputs, that is, knowledge?

One answer, proposed by Audretsch (1995), is that although the model of the knowledge-production function may be valid, the implicitly assumed unit of observation – the firm – may be less valid. The reason why the knowledge-production function holds more closely for more aggregated degrees of observation may be that investment in R&D and other sources of new knowledge spills over for economic exploitation by third-party firms.

1.2   The Appropriability Problem Revisited

A large literature has emerged focusing on what has become known as the appropriability problem. The underlying issue revolves around how firms which invest in the creation of new economic knowledge can best appropriate the economic returns from that knowledge (Arrow 1962). Audretsch (1995) proposes shifting the unit of observation away from exogenously assumed firms to individuals – agents with endowments of new economic knowledge. As J. de V. Graf (1957) observed:

> When we try to construct a transformation function for society as a whole from those facing the individual firms comprising it, a fundamental difficulty confronts us. There is, from a welfare point of view, nothing special about the firms actually existing in an economy at a given moment of time. The firm is in no sense a 'natural unit'. Only the individual members of the economy can lay claim to that distinction. All are potential entrepreneurs. It seems, therefore, that the natural thing to do is to build up from the transformation function of men,

rather than the firms, constituting an economy. If we are interested in eventual empirical determination, this is extremely inconvenient. But it has conceptual advantages. The ultimate repositories of technological knowledge in any society are the men comprising it, and it is just this knowledge which is effectively summarised in the form of a transformation function. In itself a firm possesses no knowledge. That which is available to it belongs to the men associated with it. Its production function is really built up in exactly the same way, and from the same basic ingredients, as society's.

But when the lens is shifted away from focusing upon the firm as the relevant unit of observation to individuals, the relevant question becomes: how can economic agents with a given endowment of new knowledge best appropriate the returns from that knowledge?

The appropriability problem confronting the individual may converge with that confronting the firm. Economic agents can and do work for firms, and even if they do not, they can potentially be employed by an incumbent firm. In fact, in a model of perfect information with no agency costs, any positive economies of scale or scope will ensure that the appropriability problems of the firm and individual converge. If an agent has an idea for doing something different than is currently being done by the incumbent enterprises – in terms of a new product or process or organizational structure or management approach – the idea, which can be called an innovation, will be presented to the incumbent enterprise. Because of the assumption of perfect knowledge, both the firm and the agent would agree upon the expected value of the innovation. But to the degree that any economies of scale or scope exist, the expected value of implementing the innovation within the incumbent enterprise will exceed that of taking the innovation outside of the incumbent firm to start a new enterprise. Thus, the incumbent firm and the inventor of the idea would be expected to reach a bargain splitting the value added to the firm by the innovation. The payment to the inventor – in terms of either a higher wage or some other means of remuneration – would be bounded between the expected value of the innovation if it were implemented by the incumbent enterprise on the upper end, and by the return which the agent could expect to earn if she used it to launch a new enterprise on the lower end. Or as Frank Knight (1921, p. 273) observed,

> The labourer asks what he thinks the entrepreneur will be able to pay, and in any case will not accept less than he can get from some other entrepreneur, or by turning entrepreneur himself. In the same way the entrepreneur offers to any labourer what he thinks he must in order to secure his services, and in any case not more than he thinks the labourer will actually be worth to him, keeping in mind what he can get by turning labourer himself.

Thus, each economic agent would choose how to best appropriate the value of his endowment of economic knowledge by comparing the wage he would earn if he remains employed by an incumbent enterprise, w, to the expected net discounted present value of the profits accruing from starting a new firm, π. If these two values are relatively close, the probability that he would choose to appropriate the value of his knowledge through an external mechanism such as starting a new firm, $Pr(e)$, would be relatively low. On the other hand, as the gap between w and π becomes larger, the likelihood of an agent choosing to appropriate the value of her knowledge externally through starting a new enterprise becomes greater:

$$Pr(e) = f(\pi - w) \tag{1}$$

1.3 Asymmetric Knowledge, Transaction Costs and the Principal–Agent Relationship

As Knight (1921) and Arrow (1962) emphasized, new economic knowledge is anything but certain. In addition, substantial asymmetries exist across agents both between and within firms (Milgrom and Roberts 1987). The expected value of a new idea or a potential innovation is likely to be anything but unanimous between the inventor of that idea and the decision-maker or group of decision-makers of the firm confronted with the task of evaluating proposed changes or innovations. In fact, it is because information is not only imperfect but also asymmetric that Knight (1921, p. 268) argued that the primary task of the firm is to process information in order to reach a decision:

> With the introduction of uncertainty – the fact of ignorance and the necessity of acting upon opinion rather than knowledge – into this Eden-like situation [that is, a world of perfect information], its character is entirely changed . . . With uncertainty present doing things, the actual execution of activity, becomes in a real sense a secondary part of life; the primary problem or function is deciding what to do and how to do it.

Alchian (1950) pointed out that the existence of knowledge asymmetries would result in the inevitability of mistaken decisions in an uncertain world. Later, Alchian and Demsetz (1972) attributed the existence of asymmetric information across the employees in a firm as resulting in a problem of monitoring the contribution accruing from each employee and setting the rewards correspondingly. This led them to conclude, 'The problem of economic organization is the economical means of metering productivity and rewards' (Alchian and Demsetz 1972, p. 783).

Combined with the bureaucratic organization of incumbent firms to make a decision, the asymmetry of knowledge leads to a host of agency problems, spanning incentive structures, monitoring and transaction costs. It is the existence of such agency costs, combined with asymmetric information, which not only provides an incentive for agents with new ideas to appropriate the expected value of their knowledge externally by starting new firms, but also with a propensity which varies systematically from industry to industry.

Coase (1937) and Williamson (1975) argued that the size of an (incumbent) enterprise will be determined by answering the question, 'Will it pay to bring an extra exchange transaction under the organizing authority?' (Coase 1937, p. 30). In fact, 'other things being equal, a firm will tend to be larger the less likely the [firm] is to make mistakes and the smaller the increase in mistakes with an increase in the transactions organized' (Coase 1937, p. 24).

Holmstrom pointed out the existence of a bureaucratization dilemma, in which 'to say that increased size brings increased bureaucracy is a safe generalization. To note that bureaucracy is viewed as an organizational disease is equally accurate' (Holmstrom 1989, p. 320).

To minimize agency problems and the cost of monitoring, bureaucratic hierarchies develop objective rules. In addition, Kreps (1991) argues that such bureaucratic rules promote internal uniformity and that a uniform corporate culture in turn promotes the reputation of the firm. These bureaucratic rules, however, make it more difficult to evaluate the efforts and activities of agents involved in activities which do not conform to such bureaucratic rules. As Holmstrom (1989, p. 323) points out:

> Monitoring limitations suggest that the firm seeks out activities which are more easily and objectively evaluated. Assignments will be chosen in a fashion that is conducive to more effective control. Authority and command systems work better in environments which are more predictable and can be directed with less investment information. Routine tasks are the comparative advantage of a bureaucracy and its activities can be expected to reflect that.

Williamson (1975, p. 201) also emphasizes the inherent tension between hierarchical bureaucratic organizations and the ability of incumbent organizations to appropriate the value of new knowledge for innovative activity outside of the technological trajectories associated with the core competence of that organization:

> Were it that large firms could compensate internal entrepreneurial activity in ways approximating that of the market, the large firm need experience no disadvantage in entrepreneurial respects. Violating the congruency between hierarchical position and compensation appears to generate bureaucratic strains,

however, and is greatly complicated by the problem of accurately imputing causality.

This leads him to conclude:

> I am inclined to regard the early stage innovative disabilities of large size as serious and propose the following hypothesis: An efficient procedure by which to introduce new products is for the initial development and market testing to be performed by independent investors and small firms (perhaps new entrants) in an industry, the successful developments then to be acquired, possibly through licensing or merger, for subsequent marketing by a large multidivision enterprise . . . Put differently, a division of effort between the new product innovation process on the one hand, and the management of proven resources on the other may well be efficient. (Williamson 1975, pp. 205–6)

This model analysing the decision of how best to appropriate the value of new economic knowledge confronting an individual economic agent seems useful when considering the actual decision to launch a new firm taken by entrepreneurs. For example, Chester Carlsson started Xerox after his proposal to produce a (new) copy machine was rejected by Kodak. Kodak based its decision on the premise that the new copy machine would not earn very much money, and in any case Kodak was in a different line of business – photography. It is perhaps no small irony that this same entrepreneurial start-up, Xerox, decades later turned down a proposal from Steven Jobs to produce and market a personal computer because it did not think that a personal computer would sell, and in any case Xerox was in a different line of business – copy machines (Audretsch 1995). After 17 other companies, including IBM and Hewlett-Packard, rebuffed him for virtually identical reasons, Jobs resorted to starting his own company, Apple Computer.

Similarly, IBM turned down an offer from Bill Gates, 'the chance to buy ten percent of Microsoft for a song in 1986, a missed opportunity that would cost $3 billion today'.[3] IBM reached its decision on the grounds that 'neither Gates nor any of his band of thirty-some employees had anything approaching the credentials or personal characteristics required to work at IBM'.[4]

Divergences in beliefs with respect to the value of a new idea need not be restricted to what is formally known as a product or even a process innovation. That economic agents choose to start a new firm because of divergences in the expected value of an idea applies to the sphere of managerial style and organization as well. One of the most vivid examples involves Bob Noyce, who founded Intel. Noyce had been employed by Shockley Semiconductor, which is credited with being the pioneering semiconductor firm. In 1957 Noyce and seven other engineers quit Shockley Semiconductor en masse to form Fairchild Semiconductor, which is considered the start of what is today known as Silicon Valley. Although Fairchild Semiconductor had 'possibly the most potent management and technical team ever assembled' (Gilder 1989, p. 89):

> Noyce couldn't get Fairchild's eastern owners to accept the idea that stock options should be part of compensation for all employees, not just for management. He wanted to tie everyone, from janitors to bosses, into the overall success of the company . . . This management style still sets the standard for every computer, software, and semiconductor company in the Valley today . . . Every CEO still wants to think that the place is run the way Bob Noyce would have run it. (Cringley 1993, p. 39)

Noyce's vision of a firm excluded the dress codes, reserved parking places, closed offices and executive dining rooms, along with the other trappings of status which were standard in virtually every hierarchical and bureaucratic US corporation. But when he tried to impress this vision upon the owners of Fairchild Semiconductor, he was rebuffed. The formation of Intel in 1968 was the ultimate result of the divergence in beliefs about how to organize and manage the firm.

The key development at Intel was the microprocessor. When longtime IBM employee Ted Hoff approached IBM and later DEC with his new microprocessor in the late 1960s, 'IBM and DEC decided there was no market. They could not imagine why anyone would need or want a small computer; if people wanted to use computers, they could hook into time-sharing systems' (Palfreman and Swade 1991, p. 108).

2. THE GEOGRAPHY OF SOURCES AND INCENTIVES

2.1 The Selection Mechanism

At the heart of the evolutionary theory proposed by Richard Nelson and Sidney Winter (1982) is the selection mechanism in the economy across diverse alternatives. It is the existence of alternative and competing ways of doing things, ideas and proposed solutions – that is, diversity – which confronts economic agents and institutions with a choice. Most generally considered, diversity represents (1) the simultaneous existence of different possible actions, and (2) a differential in the valuation of potential actions by economic decision-makers. The selection mechanism in the economic process serves to select some of the proposed actions while rejecting others.

The selection mechanism occurs at many different levels. For example, an individual with several different ideas about what action to take must choose one to the exclusion of the others. That is, the most micro level of what Nelson and Winter (1982) term the 'selection environment' actually takes place within the context of the decision-making process by individual economic agents. A second locus of selection occurs within organization units of firms and a third across those organization units. Notice that all of these selection environments are inherently non-market in that they rely upon an internal mechanism for selecting across alternative actions. That is, given a set of diverse alternatives, first the individual economic agent and then the organization selects across those alternatives to eliminate some and choose others. An internal selection environment is based on subjective valuation in that the decision-making unit of observation – an individual or hierarchical bureaucracy – places an implicit value on one action.

The market provides another selection environment. As a result of the selection mechanism of the market, only a subset of the diverse alternatives tends to survive. A rich body of literature has shown that as the duration of any period increases, fewer of the original diverse alternatives tend to survive. At the same time, the conditional likelihood of surviving into the next time period increases as the number of time periods which have already been survived increases (Audretsch 1995).

For example, Audretsch (1995) shows both theoretically and empirically that the act of creating a new firm is the result of diversity with respect to the valuation of new ideas or potential innovations. My model suggests that (uncertain) knowledge asymmetries combined with high transaction costs result in individual economic agents deciding to start a new firm. Divergences in the expected value regarding new knowledge lead some economic agents to value any given idea (potential innovation) more than other agents, including those involved in the decision-making process of incumbent firms. When such divergences occur and an agent chooses to exercise what Albert O. Hirschman (1970) has termed exit – rather than voice or loyalty – and the agent departs from an incumbent organization to launch a new enterprise, then who is right, the departing agent or those agents in the organizational hierarchy who, by assigning the new idea a relatively low expected value, have effectively driven the agent with the potential innovation away? *Ex post* the answer may not be too difficult, but given the uncertainty inherent in new knowledge, the answer is anything but trivial a priori.

Thus, when a new firm is launched its prospects are shrouded in uncertainty. If the new firm is built around a new idea – that is, a potential innovation – it is uncertain whether there is sufficient demand for the new idea or whether some competitor will have the same or even a superior idea. An additional layer of uncertainty pervades a new enterprise: it is not known how competent the new firm really is in terms of management, organization and workforce. At least incumbent enterprises know something about their underlying competencies from past experience.

The initial condition of not just uncertainty but greater degree of uncertainty *vis-à-vis* incumbent enterprises in the industry is captured by Boyan Jovanovic (1982). Jovanovic presents a model in which the new entrants, which he refers to as entrepreneurs, face costs which not only are random but also differ across firms. A central feature of the model is that a new firm does not know what its cost function is (that is, its relative efficiency) but rather discovers this through the process of learning from its actual post-entry performance. In particular, Jovanovic (1982) assumed that entrepreneurs are unsure about their ability to manage a new firm start-up and therefore their prospects for success. Although entrepreneurs may launch a new firm based on a vague sense of expected post-entry performance, they only discover their true ability – in terms of managerial competence and of having based the firm on an idea which is viable in the market – once their business is established. Those entrepreneurs who discover that their ability exceeds their expectations expand the scale of their business, whereas those discovering that their post-entry performance is less than commensurate with their expectations will contract the scale of output and possibly exit the industry. Thus Jovanovic's (1982) model is a theory of noisy selection, in which efficient firms grow and survive and inefficient firms decline and fail.

The role of learning in the selection process has been the subject of considerable debate. On the one hand is the Lamarckian assumption that learning refers to adaptations made by the new enterprise. Those new firms which are the most flexible and adaptable will be the most successful in adjusting to whatever the demands of the market are. As Nelson and Winter (1982, p. 11) point out, 'Many kinds of organizations commit resources to learning; organizations seek to copy the forms of their most successful competitors.'

On the other hand is the interpretation that the role of learning is restricted to discovering if the new firm is viable in terms of the product as well as the production process. Under this interpretation the new enterprise is not necessarily able to adapt or adjust to market conditions, but receives information based on its market performance with respect to its fitness in terms of meeting demand most efficiently *vis-à-vis* rivals. The theory of organizational ecology proposed by Michael T. Hannan and John Freeman (1989, p. 132) most pointedly adheres to the notion that 'individual organizations are characterized by relative inertia in structure'. That is, firms learn not in the sense that they adjust their actions as reflected by their core identity and purpose, but in the sense that they adjust their perception. What is learned, then, is whether the firm has 'the right stuff', but not how to change that stuff.

Audretsch (1995) shows that the process of firm selection in markets apparently revolves around two driving selection mechanisms. The first is the gap between the size of the firm and the minimum efficient scale (MES) of output. The greater this gap is, the greater the growth rates of surviving firms tend to be but the smaller the likelihood of firm survival is. Since the variance of new firm start-up sizes is low relative to the variance in the MES levels of output, it is essentially the degree of scale economies which determines the extent of this gap and therefore the severity of this market selection mechanism.

The second selection mechanism in markets is the degree of uncertainty inherent in the nature of the product being sold and in how to produce it. In highly innovative industries this selection mechanism plays a more important role. In environments where innovation is relatively less important this selection mechanism plays less of a role.

2.2   Search versus Routine

As Knight (1921, p. 199) pointed out, uncertainty is the result of possessing only partial or bounded knowledge: 'The essence of the situation is action according to *opinion*, of greater or less foundation and value, neither entire ignorance nor complete and perfect information, but partial knowledge.' In fact, it is the fundamental condition of incomplete knowledge which leads Arrow (1983) to focus on the firm as an organization whose main distinction is processing information. As March and Simon (1993, p. 299) argue, 'Organizations process and channel information.' But as Arrow (1985, p. 303) emphasizes, 'The elements of a firm are *agents* among whom both decision making and knowledge are dispersed . . . Each agent observes a random variable, sometimes termed a signal . . . Each agent has a set of actions from which *choice is to be made. We may call the assignment of signals to agents the* information structure and the choice of decision rules the decision structure.'

How will economic agents and ultimately hierarchical organizations respond when confronted with incomplete knowledge? Knight's answer is 'differently' because agents differ in 'their capacity by perception and inference to form correct judgements as to the future course of events in the environment' (Knight 1921, p. 241). In addition, there are differences in 'men's capacities to judge means and discern and plan the steps and adjustments necessary to meet the anticipated future situation'. This is to say that different economic agents confronted with the same signal, in Arrow's

(1985) terms, or simply with incomplete information, in Knight's terms, will respond differently because they have different sets of experiences from which to evaluate that incomplete information.

Like Nelson and Winter (1982), March and Simon (1993, p. 309) emphasize the role of established routines in the functioning of organizations:

> The process of gaining individual expertise by coding experience into recognition/action pairs is paralleled by organizational processes for developing pairings between rules and situations . . . Organizations are collections of roles and identities, assemblages of rules by which appropriate behavior is paired with recognized situations . . . These are developed in an organization through collective experience and stored in the organizational memory as standard procedures . . . Organizations turn their own experience as well as the experience and knowledge of others into rules that are maintained and implemented despite turnover in personnel and without necessary comprehension of their bases. As a result, the processes for generating, changing, evoking, and forgetting rules become essential in analysing and understanding organizations.

As long as new information is consistent with the routines established in an organization, it will be processed by economic agents and a decision-making hierarchy in a manner which is familiar. New information under the routinized regime is familiar turf for organizations. A more fundamental problem arises, however, when the nature of that new information is such that it can no longer be processed by the familiar routines. Under these circumstances the organizational routines for searching out new relevant information and making (correct) decisions on the basis of that information break down. And it is under such information conditions that divergences tend to arise not only among economic agents in evaluating that information, but between agents and organizational hierarchies.

If each economic agent were identical, such divergences in beliefs would not arise. The greater the degree of homogeneity among agents, the greater the tendency will be for beliefs in evaluating uncertain information to converge. But individuals are not homogeneous. Rather, agents have varied personal characteristics and different experiences which shape the lens through which each agent evaluates where to get new information and how to assess it. That is, reasonable people confronted with the same information may evaluate it very differently, not just because they have different abilities but because each has had a different set of life experiences which affects the decision-making process. Perhaps this helps to explain why IBM, for all its collective knowledge, not to mention resources, was proven wrong about its early rejection of the minicomputer. Steve Jobs, a college dropout, was able to see something that the decision-making hierarchy at IBM did not. After all, Jobs emerged from the milieu of computer 'hackers' and 'freaks' in Northern California, which provided him with experience and knowledge unavailable to the IBM decision-makers, who generally lived in upper-middle-class East Coast residential areas such as White Plains, north of New York City.

Thus, to some extent the phenomenon of the establishment of a new firm represents not just imperfect information but a diverse population of economic agents. That is, diversity in the population of economic agents may ultimately lead to diversity in the types of firms populating the enterprise structure. And to some extent these diverse firms represent experiments based on differing visions about the product and how to produce it.

Diversity also is the source of the high degree of turbulence which is experienced in the United States and, increasingly, in other developed nations. That is, industrial markets are characterized by a high degree of churning. It took the two decades of the 1950s and 1960s for one-third of the Fortune 500 companies to be replaced by new additions. In the 1970s it took the entire decade to replace one-third of the Fortune 500. By contrast, in the 1980s it took just five years for one-third of the Fortune 500 to be replaced (Audretsch 1995).

3. THE SPATIAL INCOME DISTRIBUTION

3.1 Innovation

The emergence of a recent literature (re)discovering the importance of economic geography might seem paradoxical in a world increasingly dominated by e-mail, faxes and electronic communications superhighways. Why should geographic proximity matter when technology has advanced in a manner which has drastically reduced the cost of transmitting information across geographic space? The answer posited by Audretsch and Feldman (1996), Audretsch and Stephan (1996) and Feldman (1994a, 1994b) is based on a key distinction between information on the one hand and tacit knowledge on the other. Although the costs of transmitting information may be invariant to distance, the cost of transmitting knowledge and especially tacit knowledge rises with distance. Geographic location and proximity to the source matter in the transmission of tacit knowledge because face-to-face contact is the most effective and economical mode of transfer. Thus, Glaeser et al. (1992, p. 1127) characterize the Marshall–Arrow–Romer model as suggesting that 'intellectual breakthroughs must cross hallways more easily than oceans and continents'.

This model is consistent with anecdotal evidence. For example, a survey of nearly 1000 executives located in America's 60 largest metropolitan areas ranked Raleigh/Durham as the best city for knowledge workers and for innovative activity. *Fortune* magazine reports:

A lot of brainy types who made their way to Raleigh/Durham were drawn by three top research universities. . . . US businesses, especially those whose success depends on staying atop new technologies and processes, increasingly want to be where hot new ideas are percolating. A presence in brain-power centers like Raleigh/Durham pays off in new products and new ways of doing business . . . Dozens of small biotechnology and software operations are starting up each year and growing like kudzu in the fertile business climate.

Considerable evidence has been found suggesting that location and proximity clearly matter in exploiting knowledge spillovers. Not only have Jaffe et al. (1993) found that patent citations tend to occur more frequently within the state in which they were patented than outside of that state, but Audretsch and Feldman (1996) found that the propensity of innovative activity to cluster geographically tends to be greater in industries where new economic knowledge plays a more important role.

3.2   Diversity versus Specialization

Despite the general consensus which has now emerged in the literature that knowledge spillovers within a given location stimulate technological advance, there is little consensus as to exactly how this occurs. The contribution of the knowledge-production function approach was simply to shift the unit of observation away from firms to a geographic region. But does it make a difference how economic activity is organized within the black box of geographic space? Political scientists and sociologists have long argued that differences in the cultures of regions may contribute to differences in innovative performance across regions, even holding knowledge inputs such as R&D and human capital constant. For example, Saxenian (1990) argues that a culture of greater interdependence and exchange among individuals in the Silicon Valley region has contributed to a superior innovative performance than is found around Boston's Route 128, where firms and individuals tend to be more isolated and less interdependent.

In studying the networks in California's Silicon Valley, Saxenian (1990, pp. 96–7) emphasizes that it is the communication between individuals which facilitates the transmission of knowledge across agents, firms and even industries, and not just a high endowment of human capital and knowledge in the region:

It is not simply the concentration of skilled labor, suppliers and information that distinguish the region. A variety of regional institutions – including Stanford University, several trade associations and local business organizations, and a myriad of specialized consulting, market research, public relations and venture capital firms – provide technical, financial, and networking services which the region's enterprises often cannot afford individually. These networks defy sectoral barriers: individuals move easily from semiconductor to disk drive firms or from computer to network makers. They move from established firms to start-ups (or vice versa) and even to market research or consulting firms, and from consulting firms back into start-ups. And they continue to meet at trade shows, industry conferences, and the scores of seminars, talks and social activities organized by local business organizations and trade associations. In these forums, relationships are easily formed and maintained, technical and market information is exchanged, business contacts are established, and new enterprises are conceived . . . This decentralized and fluid environment also promotes the diffusion of intangible technological capabilities and understandings.[5]

Though economists tend to avoid attributing differences in economic performance to cultural differences, there has been a series of theoretical arguments suggesting that differences in the underlying structure between regions may account for differences in rates of growth and technological change. In fact, a heated debate has emerged in the literature about the manner in which the underlying economic structure within a geographic unit of observation might affect economic performance. One view, which Glaeser et al. (1992) attribute to the Marshall–Arrow–Romer eternality, suggests that an increased concentration of a particular industry within a specific geographic region facilitates knowledge spillovers across firms. This model formalizes the insight that the concentration of an industry within a city promotes knowledge spillovers between firms and therefore facilitates innovative activity. An important assumption of the model is that knowledge externalities with respect to firms exist, but only for firms within the same industry. Thus, the relevant unit of observation is extended from the firm to the region in the tradition of the Marshall–Arrow–Romer model and in subsequent empirical studies, but spillovers are limited to the relevant industry.

By contrast, restricting knowledge externalities to occur only within the industry may ignore an important source of new economic knowledge – interindustry knowledge spillovers. Jacobs (1969) argues that the most important source of knowledge spillovers are external to the industry in which the firm operates and that cities are the source of considerable innovation because the diversity of these knowledge sources is greatest in cities. According to Jacobs, it is the exchange of complementary knowledge across diverse firms and economic agents which yields a greater return on new economic knowledge. She develops a theory which emphasizes that the variety of industries within a geographic region promotes knowledge externalities and ultimately innovative activity and economic growth.

The extent of regional specialization versus regional diversity in promoting knowledge spillovers is not the only dimension over which there has been a theoretical debate. A second controversy involves the degree of competition prevalent in the region, or the extent of local monopoly. The

Marshall–Arrow–Romer model predicts that local monopoly is superior to local competition because it maximizes the ability of firms to appropriate the economic value accruing from their innovative activity. By contrast, Jacobs (1969) and Porter (1990) argue that competition is more conducive to knowledge externalities than is local monopoly.[6] It should be emphasized that by local competition Jacobs does not mean competition within product markets as has traditionally been envisioned within the industrial organization literature. Rather, Jacobs is referring to the competition for the new ideas embodied in economic agents. Not only does an increased number of firms provide greater competition for new ideas, but greater competition across firms also facilitates the entry of a new firm specializing in some particular and new product niche. This is because the necessary complementary inputs and services are likely to be available from small specialist niche firms but not necessarily from large, vertically integrated producers.

The first important test of the specialization versus diversity theories to date has focused not on gains or innovative activity but on employment growth. Glaeser et al. (1992) employ a data set on the growth of large industries in 170 cities between 1956 and 1987 in order to identify the relative importance of the degree of regional specialization, diversity and local competition in influencing industry growth rates. The authors find evidence which contradicts the Marshall–Arrow–Romer model but is consistent with Jacobs's theory. However, their study provided no direct evidence on whether diversity is more important than specialization in generating innovation.

Feldman and Audretsch (1999) identify the extent to which the organization of economic activity either is concentrated or, alternatively, consists of diverse but complementary economic activities, and how this composition influences innovative output. We ask the question: does the specific type of economic activity undertaken within any particular geographic concentration matter? To consider this question we link the innovative output of product categories within a specific city to the extent to which the economic activity of that city is concentrated in that industry or, conversely, diversified in complementary industries sharing a common science base.

To systematically identify the degree to which specific industries share a common underlying science and technology base, Feldman and Audretsch (1999) rely upon a deductive approach which links products estimated from their closeness in technological space. They use the responses of industrial R&D managers to a survey by Levin et al. (1987). To measure the significance of a scientific discipline to an industry, the survey asked: 'How relevant were the basic sciences to technical progress in this line of business over the past 10–15 years?' The survey uses a Likert scale of 1 to 7, from least important to most important, to assess the relevance of basic scientific research in biology, chemistry, computer science, physics, mathematics, medicine, geology, mechanical engineering and electrical engineering. Any academic discipline with a rating greater than 5 is assumed to be relevant to a product category. For example, basic scientific research in medicine, chemistry and chemical engineering is found to be relevant to product innovation in drugs (SIC 2834).

Feldman and Audretsch (1999) then use cluster analysis to identify six groups of industries which rely on similar rankings for the importance of different academic disciplines. These six groups reflect distinct underlying common scientific bases.

To test the hypothesis that the degree of specialization or, alternatively, diversity as well as the extent of local competition within a city shapes the innovative output of an industry, Feldman and Audretsch (1999) estimate a model where the dependent variable is the number of innovations attributed to a specific four-digit SIC industry in a particular city. To reflect the extent to which economic activity within a city is specialized, we include as an explanatory variable a measure of industry specialization which was used by Glaeser et al. (1992) and is defined as the 1982 share of total employment in the city accounted for by industry employment in the city, divided by the share of US employment accounted for by that particular industry. This variable reflects the degree to which a city is specialized in a particular industry relative to the degree of economic activity in that industry which would occur if employment in the industry were randomly distributed across the United States. A higher value of this measure indicates a greater degree of specialization of the industry in that particular city. Thus, a positive coefficient would indicate that increased specialization within a city is conducive to greater innovative output and would support the Marshall–Arrow–Romer thesis. A negative coefficient would indicate that greater specialization within a city impedes innovative output and would support Jacobs's theory that diversity of economic activity is more conducive to innovation than is specialization of economic activity.

To identify the impact of an increased presence of economic activity in complementary industries sharing a common science base on the innovative activity of a particular industry within a specific city, a measure of the presence of science-based related industries is included. This measure is constructed analogously to the index of industry specialization, and is defined as the share of total city employment accounted for by employment in the city in industries sharing the science base, divided by the share of total US employment accounted for by employment in that same science base. This variable measures the presence of complementary industries relative to what the presence would be if those related industries were distributed randomly across the United States. A positive coefficient of the presence of science-based related industries would indicate that a greater presence of complementary industries is conducive to greater innovative output and would lend support to the diversity thesis. By contrast, a negative coefficient would suggest that a greater presence of related industries sharing the same science base impedes innovation and would argue against Jacobs's diversity thesis.

The usual concept of product market competition in the industrial organization literature is typically measured in terms of the size-distribution of firms. By contrast, Jacobs's concept of localized competition emphasizes instead the extent of competition for the ideas embodied in individuals. The greater the degree of competition among firms, the greater will be the extent of specialization among those firms and the easier it will be for individuals to pursue and implement new ideas. Thus the metric relevant to reflect the degree of localized competition is not the size of the firms in the region relative to their number (because, after all, many if not most manufacturing product markets are national or at least interregional in nature) but rather the number of firms relative to the number of workers. In measuring the extent of localized competition we again adopt a measure used by Glaeser et al. (1992), which is defined as the number of firms per worker in the industry in the city relative to the number of firms per worker in the same industry in the United States. A higher value of this index of localized competition suggests that the industry has a greater number of firms per worker relative to its size in the particular city than it does elsewhere in the United States. Thus, if the index of localized competition exceeds 1, then the city is locally more competitive than other American cities.

In Feldman and Audretsch (1999) the regression model is estimated based on the 5946 city-industry observations for which data could be collected. The Poisson regression estimation method is used because the dependent variable is a limited dependent variable with a highly skewed distribution. By focusing on innovative activity for particular industries at specific locations, Feldman and Audretsch (1999) find compelling evidence that specialization of economic activity does not promote innovative output. Rather, the results indicate that diversity across complementary economic activities sharing a common science base is more conducive to innovation than is specialization.

CONCLUSIONS

An important impact of globalization has been to shift the comparative advantage of the leading developed nations in Western Europe and North

America away from routinized economic activity towards search activity. An important implication of globalization is that in a world where diffusion costs are relatively low and large wage differentials exist across geographic space, routine economic activity tends to be transferred out of the high-cost *Standort* (location) to lower-cost locations. The telecommunications revolution has rendered this just as true for information-based economic activity as for manufacturing activities.

Income differentials across geographic space can only be maintained by engaging in economic activity in which the cost of diffusing that activity across space is high. Whereas the cost of diffusing routine economic activity across geographic space is relatively low, the cost of diffusing search activity is high. Thus, the comparative advantage of high-wage locations is shifting to knowledge-based search activity and away from routine activity.

Homogeneity, in both the underlying population and the enterprise structure, is more conducive to routinized economic activity. Homogeneity across economic agents reduces the cost of transactions, resulting in efficiency gains for routinized economic activity.

By contrast, heterogeneity, in both the underlying population and the enterprise structure, is more conducive to knowledge-based innovative activity. Such diversity is the driving force behind knowledge spillovers. Thus, those geographic regions which comprise diverse economic agents engaged in knowledge-based economic activity, which does not costlessly diffuse across space, are likely to experience rapid increases in income, while those regions based on homogeneous economic agents engaged in routinized economic activity are likely to experience a relative decline in income.

NOTES

1. I would like to thank Professor Erik Reinert for his helpful suggestions along with those made by the other participants in the Oslo conference.
2. 'The valley of money's delight', *The Economist*, 29 March 1997, special section, p. 1.
3. 'System error', *The Economist*, 18 September 1993, p. 99.
4. Paul Carrol, 'Die offene Schlacht', *Die Zeit*, **39**, 24 September 1993, p. 18.
5. Saxenian (1990, pp. 97–8) claims that even the language and vocabulary used by technical specialists is specific to a region: 'A distinct language has evolved in the region and certain technical terms used by semiconductor production engineers in Silicon Valley would not even be understood by their counterparts in Boston's Route 128.'
6. Porter (1990) provides examples of Italian ceramics and gold jewellery industries in which numerous firms are located within a bounded geographic region and compete intensively in terms of product innovation rather than focusing on simple price competition.

REFERENCES

Alchian, Almerin (1950), 'Uncertainty, evolution, and economic theory', *Journal of Political Economy*, **58**, 211–21.

Alchian, Almerin and H. Demsetz (1972), 'Production, information costs, and economic organization', *American Economic Review*, **62**, 777–95.

Arrow, Kenneth J. (1962), 'Economic welfare and the allocation of resources for invention', in R.R. Nelson (ed.), *The Rate and Direction of Inventive Activity*, Princeton, NJ: Princeton University Press, pp. 609–26.

Arrow, Kenneth J. (1983), 'Innovation in large and small firms', in J. Ronen (ed.), *Entrepreneurship*, Lexington, MA: Lexington Books, pp. 15–28.

Arrow, Kenneth J. (1985), 'Informational structure of the firm', *American Economic Review*, **75** (2), 303–7.

Audretsch, David B. (1995), *Innovation and Industry Evolution*, Cambridge, MA: MIT Press.

Audretsch, David B. and Maryann P. Feldman (1996), 'R&D spillovers and the geography of innovation and production', *American Economic Review*, **86** (3), 630–40.

Audretsch, David B. and Paula E. Stephan (1996), 'Company–scientist locational links: the case of biotechnology', *American Economic Review*, **86** (3), 641–52.

Coase, R.H. (1937), 'The nature of the firm', *Economica*, **4** (4), 386–405.

Cohen, Wesley M. and Steven Klepper (1991), 'Firm size versus diversity in the achievement of technological advance', in Z. Acs and David B. Audretsch (eds), *Innovation and Technological Change: An International Comparison*, Ann Arbor, MI: University of Michigan Press, pp. 183–203.

Cohen, Wesley M. and Steven Klepper (1992a), 'The anatomy of industry R&D intensity distributions', *American Economic Review*, **82** (4), 773–99.

Cohen, Wesley M. and Steven Klepper (1992b), 'The tradeoff between firm size and diversity in the pursuit of technological progress', *Small Business Economics*, **4** (1), 1–14.

Cringley, Robert X. (1993), *Accidental Empires: How the Boys of Silicon Valley Make Their Millions, Battle Foreign Competition, and Still Can't Get a Date*, New York: Harper Business.

Feldman, Maryann P. (1994a), *The Geography of Innovation*, Boston, MA: Kluwer Academic Publishers.

Feldman, Maryann P. (1994b), 'Knowledge complementarity and innovation', *Small Business Economics*, **6** (5), 363–80.

Feldman, Maryann P. and David B. Audretsch (1999), 'Innovation in cities: science-based diversity, specialization and localized competition', *European Economic Review*, **43**, 409–29.

Ferguson, Charles H. (1988), 'From the people who brought you voodoo economics', *Harvard Business Review*, **87** (May/June), 55–62.

Gilder, George (1989), *Microcosm*, New York: Touchstone.

Glaeser, Edward L., Hedi D. Kallal, Jose A. Scheinkman and Andrei Shleifer (1992), 'Growth of cities', *Journal of Political Economy*, **100** (4), 1126–52.

Graf, J. de V. (1957), *Theoretical Welfare Economics*, Cambridge: Cambridge University Press.

Griliches, Zvi (1979), 'Issues in assessing the contribution of R&D to productivity growth', *Bell Journal of Economics*, **10** (1), 92–116.

Hannan, Michael T. and John Freeman (1989), *Organizational Ecology*, Cambridge, MA: Harvard University Press.

Hirschman, Albert O. (1970), *Exit, Voice, and Loyalty*, Cambridge, MA: Harvard University Press.

Holmstrom, Bengt (1989), 'Agency costs and innovation', *Journal of Economic Behavior and Organization*, **12**, 305–27.

Jacobs, Jane (1969), *The Economy of Cities*, New York: Random House.

Jaffe, Adam B., Manuel Trajtenberg and Rebecca Henderson (1993), 'Geographic localization of knowledge spillovers as evidenced by patent citations', *Quarterly Journal of Economics*, **63** (3), 577–98.

Jovanovic, Boyan (1982), 'Selection and the evolution of industry', *Econometrica*, **50** (2), 649–70.

Knight, Frank H. (1921), *Risk, Uncertainty and Profit*, New York: Houghton Mifflin.

Kreps, David (1991), 'Corporate culture and economic theory', in J. Alt and K. Shepsle (eds), *Positive Perspectives on Political Economy*, Cambridge: Cambridge University Press, pp. 119–33.

Levin, R.C, A.K. Klevorick, R.R. Nelson and S.G. Winter (1987), 'Appropriating the returns from industrial research and development', *Brookings Papers on Economic Activity*, 783–820.

March, James G. and Herbert A. Simon (1993), 'Organizations revisited', *Industrial and Corporate Change*, **2** (3), 299–316.

Milgrom, Paul and John Roberts (1987), 'Information asymmetries, strategic behavior, and industrial organization', *American Economic Review*, **77** (2), 184–93.

Nelson, Richard R. and Sidney G. Winter (1982), *An Evolutionary Theory of Economic Change*, Cambridge, MA: Harvard University Press.

Palfreman, Jon and Doron Swade (1991), *The Dream Machine: Exploring the Computer Age*, London: BBC Books.

Porter, Michael (1990), *The Competitive Advantage of Nations*, New York: Free Press.

Saxenian, Anna Lee (1990), 'Regional networks and the resurgence of Silicon Valley', *California Management Review*, **33** (1), 89–112.

Scherer, F.M. (1991), 'Changing perspectives on the firm size problem', in Z.J. Acs and D.B. Audretsch (eds), *Innovation and Technological Change: An International Comparison*, Ann Arbor, MI: University of Michigan Press, pp. 108–18.

Schumpeter, Joseph A. (1911), *Theorie der wirtschaftlichen Entwicklung: Eine Untersuchung über Unternehmergewinn, Kapital, Kredit, Zins und den Konjunkturzyklus*, Berlin: Duncker & Humblot.

Schumpeter, Joseph A. (1942), *Capitalism, Socialism and Democracy*, New York: Harper and Row.

Williamson, Oliver E. (1975), *Markets and Hierarchies: Antitrust Analysis and Implications*, New York: Free Press.

11. Convergence, divergence and the Kuznets curve

Ådne Cappelen

The study of economic growth has again become a major area of interest for both applied and theoretical economics. This chapter relates some of these developments to the empirical study of economic growth focusing on Europe. My main concern is with the distribution of income over time, not only between countries but also between regions within countries. I discuss the link between income levels and the distribution of income of individuals as depicted by the Kuznets curve (Kuznets 1955). The empirical convergence literature (see Abramovitz 1986, Baumol 1986) suggests that incomes of the richest countries in the world seem to converge, but this is not the case for the world as a whole. Barro (1991) and many subsequent studies based on an explicitly neoclassical growth model have shown that if one controls for differences in factor accumulation, countries seem to converge at the same rate but to different steady state levels of income. Thus conditional convergence is taking place. However, the distribution of income levels between regions in a steady state is not made explicit in most of these latter studies.

In this chapter I first illustrate the changes in the dispersion of income between most of those countries in Europe which today are members of the European Union. I use long historical time series of gross domestic product (GDP) per capita, relying on Maddison (1995) in order to show that there have been periods of convergence as well as divergence in incomes among these countries. Thus, care should be taken when interpreting estimated growth equations which use only a subset of observations excluding periods of divergence. This conclusion echoes the argument by De Long (1988) with regard to the subset of countries chosen for empirical growth studies that the exclusion of countries for which data series are not sufficiently long will bias the conclusion towards support for the convergence hypothesis.

The next section defines some measures of convergence and refers to theoretical arguments put forward to explain differences in the level and growth of regional incomes. Then I present some empirical evidence on mainly European national and regional convergence. These results are then compared with the distribution of personal income in relation to the level of income; these are related through the so-called Kuznets curve.

1.   THEORIES OF CONVERGENCE

The hypothesis of convergence of GDP per capita among countries or regions has been intensively tested in recent years. This hypothesis exists in three versions:

1.   Absolute convergence. Regions converge in the long run irrespective of their initial conditions. This is often called absolute beta-convergence; it implies that poor countries grow faster than rich countries and that the growth rate of real per capita GDP is negatively related to the initial level of real per capita GDP. If we have beta-convergence, the dispersion of regional GDP per capita will tend to decrease, in which case we have so-called sigma-convergence. However, one may have beta-convergence without observing sigma-convergence.
2.   Conditional convergence. Regions with similar structural characteristics converge, independent of initial conditions. This is the prediction of the traditional neoclassical growth model. If one controls for factors which characterize the steady state growth path of GDP per capita, one should still find that the growth rate is negatively related to initial income. However, one may not observe absolute convergence but still have conditional convergence.
3.   Club convergence. Regions with similar structural characteristics converge only if their initial conditions are similar as well. In this case neither absolute nor conditional convergence is observed.

As shown by Mankiw (1995) and many others, the neoclassical model of economic growth leads to a steady state growth rate which is independent of initial conditions and where the growth rate (per person) depends only on the rate of growth of technology. If technology is a public good, then in a steady state all countries should experience the same per capita growth. However, the steady state level of income per capita depends on several structural characteristics which are not normally assumed to be equal between regions. Conditioned on these characteristics, the neoclassical model predicts convergence. The hypothesis of conditional convergence is often supported by empirical evidence which shows that initial income is negatively related to growth even after controlling for other explanatory variables. However, many have stressed that this result is supportive not just of the neoclassical model but also of models based on technology diffusion (see Barro and Sala-i-Martin 1995). To discriminate between rival hypotheses one must either look for other empirical evidence or use other criteria such as how reasonable it is to assume that technology is a public good. However, the hypothesis of conditional convergence is rejected by many studies (see Bernard and Durlauf 1995 and studies cited therein).

Club convergence, on the other hand, implies that even if certain structural features of economies are similar, they may not converge because of initial factors. Or, stated differently, history matters. The possibility of club convergence is ruled out by assumption in the standard neoclassical model because agents are assumed to be homogeneous. If, however, agents are allowed to be heterogeneous, the dynamic system of the neoclassical growth model could lead to multiple steady state equilibria in spite of diminishing returns to capital. This possibility is usually discussed within a model with different factor endowments between individuals (a most reasonable hypothesis, in my view) so that we have different saving ratios out of wage income and capital income. The one-sector model with overlapping generations is one example of extensions of the neoclassical model that may produce multiple equilibria (see Galor 1996 for a discussion). Durlauf and Johnson (1995) present empirical evidence in favour of multiple steady states using cross-section data.

Allowing for heterogeneous agents is reasonable if one wants to discuss the effects of human capital for economic growth. This leads one to consider income distribution effects. Galor and Zeira (1993) examine private education decisions in a simple overlapping-generations model in which initial wealth differs between individuals. They find that countries with unequal wealth distribution accumulate less human capital and experience less growth than countries in which the middle class is relatively large. Garcia-Penalosa (1995) shows that in countries where education costs are relatively low compared to average wealth (which is typically the case in rich countries) an increase in inequality reduces growth because fewer people can afford higher education. Thus countries that are similar in their structural characteristics as well as initial per capita output but differ in their initial distribution of income may converge to different steady state equilibria. This hypothesis has been supported by a number of recent empirical studies such as Alesina and Rodrik (1994), Persson and Tabellini (1994) and a study based on data for Norwegian counties (Aaberge et al. 1996).

2.   GROWTH IN EUROPE: A LONG-RUN PERSPECTIVE

Based on national data on GDP per capita, there is substantial evidence showing that some convergence between countries took place in Europe during the twentieth century (see Verspagen 1995). However, there are few studies of how the very wide dispersion of per capita income between regions and countries in Europe came about in the first place. What factors caused per capita income to diverge between countries and regions in Europe until somewhere around 1850, before they started to converge?

In Landes (1969) the title of Chapter 4 is 'Closing the gap', and the opening sentence of that chapter reads: 'The period from 1850 to 1873 was Continental industry's coming-of-age.' This suggests that before 1850 there was divergence in incomes between European countries. The GDP per capita figures in Table 1-3 of Maddison (1995) indicate that there indeed was divergence in Europe between 1820 and 1850. The countries with per capita income significantly above the average in 1820 (the Netherlands, the UK and to some extent Belgium) increased their relative income further compared to many other countries (Finland, Germany, Italy, Ireland, Spain and Sweden) which fell behind. If we move even further backwards in history and rely on the figures in Maddison (1982), we see considerable convergence between France, the Netherlands and the UK from 1700 to 1820. Figure 11.1 shows the standard deviation of GDP per capita for all EU members except Greece and Portugal from 1820 to 1992. The increase in the dispersion in European incomes between 1820 and 1850 is striking.

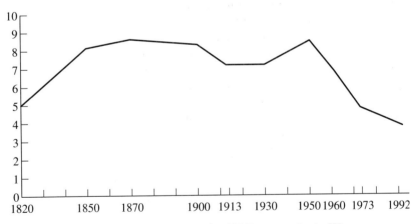

Figure 11.1   Coefficient of variation for GDP per capita in Western European (EU) countries, 1820–1992

In a number of recent studies Williamson and colleagues (Williamson 1995, Williamson 1996, O'Rourke and Williamson 1996, and O'Rourke 1996) have compared post-Second World War convergence with similar developments in the late nineteenth century. Using their evidence along with the figures from Maddison (1995), the following epochs of European economic growth can be distinguished:

1820–50: Divergence
1850–1913: Convergence
1913–45: Divergence
1945–90: Convergence

According to Williamson (1995) the periods of convergence were ones with overall fast growth and globalization, whereas the period between the world wars was characterized by low growth and de-globalization. Most important, globalization was the critical factor in contributing to convergence in the form of mass migration and trade. It is worth noticing that according to Williamson it was not capital deepening *per se* that caused convergence (as is the case in the traditional neoclassical model) but rather factor mobility. This view is not supported by Barro and Sala-i-Martin (1995, p. 413) in their concluding section on convergence: 'The evidence here is not definitive, but suggests that migration plays only a minor role in the convergence story.'

The globalization that took place in the second half of the nineteenth century manifested itself in many ways. First, international trade increased. This was due both to policies (Europe moved towards free trade following the Cobden–Chevalier treaty in 1860) and to technological change as railways and steamships lowered transportation costs. However, again according to the figures in Maddison (1995), the growth rate in world exports was higher during 1820–70 (4.2 per cent annually) than during 1870–1913 (3.4 per cent). Thus it is not obvious that the period of divergence (1820–50) was one of low growth in exports.

Second, there was a lot of factor mobility. Emigration from Europe to countries in the New World was particularly important in Ireland, Britain, Scandinavia and Italy. International labour mobility produced large shocks to the labour force in many countries and contributed significantly to the convergence in many of the countries that were involved, according to O'Rourke (1996) and O'Rourke and Williamson (1996), whereas the lack of emigration from the Iberian peninsula caused this region to diverge. There were also large capital flows within Europe and between Europe and other regions. For a country like Norway, large inflows of capital from Europe (Britain in particular) financed the take-off of the Norwegian resource-based industrial sector.

Moving on to the period between the two world wars, the volume of world exports did not recover from its previous peak in 1913 and was actually lower in 1929 (when trade peaked between the wars) than in 1913. This happened in spite of continued large reductions in transport costs; it coincided with the reimposition of trade barriers. Thus divergence and low export growth went together during the interwar period. This is also the case after the Second World War, when world trade increased dramatically by historical standards (7.0 per cent annual growth on average between 1950 and 1973) and there was convergence of incomes between most European countries. During this post-war period tariffs were reduced and transportation costs were reduced further.

Does the view that globalization promotes growth and convergence fit recent evidence? First, the process of convergence in incomes seems to have come to a standstill; indeed, some divergence has occurred. This is not as apparent between European countries as it is on a global level. As we shall see below, even at the regional level in Europe convergence has stopped and there are signs of greater inequality in personal income distribution. Although I think it is fairly uncontroversial to state that capital markets were substantially liberalized during the 1980s both globally and within the Organization for Economic Cooperation and Development (OECD) area, labour markets have gradually become less open. However, within the EU restrictions on both labour and capital mobility have been largely eliminated. It has become more difficult for non-Europeans to enter Europe. Markets for services have gradually been liberalized, but many commodity markets may have become slightly less open during the 1970s and 1980s because of an increase in non-trade barriers. In Europe the establishment of the internal market has significantly reduced non-tariff barriers, but it may not have lasted long enough yet for the effects on GDP to be visible.

All in all, my view is that convergence in GDP per capita among the present members of the EU seems to have slowed down after 1973 and may even have stopped. This conclusion is also supported by looking at regional data for Europe. It is perhaps in this light that the reduction of regional inequality is formulated as an explicit goal of EU policy in the 1987 Single European Act. One argument in line with Krugman and Venables (1995) is that market integration may initially involve divergence, followed by convergence later, due to the interactions of economies of scale, transportation costs and their effect on industry location and relative wages.

Looking beyond the European experience, the long-term global picture is one of divergence in GDP per capita (Maddison 1995). This is due to several well-known factors. Nearly all African and Latin American countries grew slowly during the twentieth century. In Asia the growth experience is very different, with some countries hardly growing at all (Burma,

Bangladesh, India and Pakistan) while others have been growing very fast by any standard (Taiwan, South Korea and Japan). The lack of convergence in incomes is, however, underestimated by looking only at those countries for which we have more or less reliable GDP figures. We know that many countries which today are extremely poor and can barely feed their populations (Mozambique and Ethiopia, to name just two obvious examples) cannot possibly have grown at all during the last century. Going a bit further, one may 'guesstimate' a minimum sustainable level of GDP per capita that a country can have and use this as an indicator of the maximum growth rate any country might have had during the past century. Based on the figures in Maddison (1995), a level of US$300 (in 1990 international dollars) can serve as an approximation of this minimum level. Using this figure as a level of GDP per capita for those countries where no figures are available for 1820, the United States had four times this level in that year as opposed to eight times in 1850, 14 times in 1900, 32 times in 1950 and 72 times that level in 1992 (which in fact is the observed ratio between Ethiopia and the United States that year). Narrowing the analysis of convergence to the present 'advanced' countries is obviously not a sensible way to limit one's sample, a point made forcefully by De Long (1988).

It is by now generally accepted that absolute convergence in GDP per capita has not taken place at a global level. Indeed, it is worth pointing out that even among countries within Europe, there are fairly long periods of time during which divergence in GDP per capita has occurred. Thus even for countries which are quite homogenous and where one could expect the assumption of similar structural characteristics to be reasonable as defined by the traditional neoclassical growth model, divergence may very well be observed.

3. THE REGIONAL DISTRIBUTION OF INCOME IN EUROPE

There is a number of empirical studies of economic growth and convergence among regions in Europe. This section summarizes some of the more recent studies rather than providing yet another study. I will present information to answer the following questions:

1. How much variation in GDP per capita is there among regions in Europe and how can this distribution be characterized?
2. Is the dispersion in GDP per capita in Europe declining, or do we observe convergence?
3. If we observe convergence, is it a steady process?

4.   How does the European process of regional convergence compare with other international evidence?

In answering the first question, I shall rely on figures for GDP per capita for nomenclature of territorial units for statistics (NUTS) II regions and in purchasing power standards (PPS) based on Eurostat (1994). For 1980 these figures show that a number of regions had only 40 per cent of EU12 average income while a number of regions had income 40 per cent higher than the average (even after excluding rich regions such as Groningen due to gas, and Hamburg and Brussels due to the difference between residents and workers). The ratio between the poorest and the richest region was roughly 1:4. In 1991 the inclusion of the new German Länder increased the dispersion further, but even after excluding this group of regions the dispersion was more or less the same as in 1980 if not wider. I shall return to measures of dispersion below.

What is perhaps more interesting than this max–min distance is the form of the density distribution of GDP per capita. As is apparent in Figures 11.2 and 11.3, the cross-regional distributions of GDP per capita are far from being normal. Two conclusions can be drawn from this feature of the data. First, the distribution is not well characterized using only mean and standard deviation as is the case with the normal distribution. One of the popular measures of convergence, the so-called sigma-convergence, which is based on the standard deviation, does not have an intuitive interpretation in this case, as opposed to when distributions are normal. Second, the shape of the distribution lends some support to the hypothesis of convergence clubs. This hypothesis states that regions may converge to different income levels (Quah 1996b). My results on density distribution differ somewhat from those of Quah (1996a) because he excludes Greece and Portugal from his sample. The regions of these two countries are essential for establishing the lower end of the distributions in Figures 11.2 and 11.3.

An alternative way of interpreting the data in Figures 11.2 and 11.3 would be to say that many European regions seem to converge to their own steady states, each of which is different from that of other regions. This would be the case if we have conditional convergence. Given certain regional characteristics with regard to the saving ratio, population growth, depreciation rate and the like, the kind of distribution we see in these figures is what we will observe in a steady state. Obviously this will tell us nothing about whether the poor are catching up with the rich (Quah 1996b).

One might object to the relevance of studying the distributions in Figures 11.2 and 11.3 by saying that these are mere snapshots of the regional income distribution in a single year. Idiosyncratic shocks to income could cancel out if aggregated over several years. From a policy perspective large economic

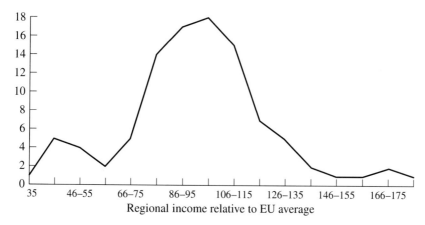

Figure 11.2   Regional GDP per capita 1991 (PPS) in EU12, excluding new German Länder and French Dept. D'Outre-mer (frequencies in %)

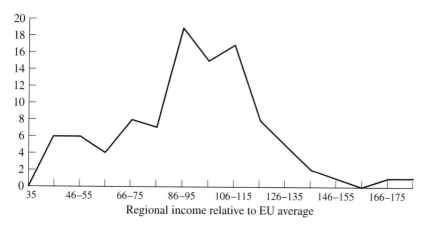

Figure 11.3   Regional GDP per capita 1980 (PPS) in EU12 (frequencies in %)

differences between regions in any one year may not be a problem if they are only temporary. One could even say that if there is much income mobility between regions, large differences could indicate that the European economies are dynamic. Friedman (1962) has expressed this view in more general terms. If this were the case, differences in average income over several years should be much smaller. However, looking at Figure 11.4, which shows the distribution of average relative income for the same regions in both 1980

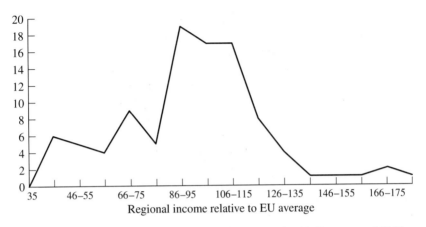

Figure 11.4 Regional GDP per capita (PPS) in EU12 (average of 1980 and 1991, frequencies in %)

and 1991, one can clearly see that this is not the case in our sample of 145 identical regions in the EU. The average distribution is not more concentrated around the mean than the 1980 distribution; it is actually very similar. Thus those regions that were poor in 1980 were also poor in 1991, suggesting that there was very little income mobility between regions in Europe during the 1980s.

Let us now turn to questions 2 and 3 on the process of convergence among European regions. An interesting way to describe the regional dynamics in Europe from 1980 to 1991 is to study whether or not low-(high-) income regions are moving towards (away from) the average EU income. Table 11.1 takes the initial (1980) relative level of income as the starting point and shows how many countries converged towards or diverged from the mean by 1991.

Of the total number of regions (five regions had stable relative income and are not included in the table) just as many converged as diverged. Slightly more than half of all movements are small in the sense that the relative change in income is equal to or less than 5 per cent of the initial relative income.

Table 11.1 Number of EU regions converging or diverging, 1980–91

Relative income in 1980	Converging	Diverging	Sum
Below average	35	50	85
Above average	35	20	55
Sum	70	70	140

The conclusion from this exercise is that nothing much happened to the distribution of relative incomes in EU12 during 1980 to 1991. At least there is no evidence of systematic convergence. This conclusion is in line with Fagerberg and Verspagen (1996), who conclude with reference to the recent development that 'the postwar trend towards convergence in levels of productivity and income levels across Europe may have come to an end'. Also there are still substantial differences in regional per capita GDP in EU12.

Neven and Gouyette (1995) use a somewhat shorter window (1980–89) and find that there is a tendency for convergence even during the 1980s as a whole but that the degree of convergence varies over time and between southern and northern regions of Europe, with less convergence in the South. They also find when estimating beta-convergence that the process of convergence tended to slow down in the later part of the 1980s when one controls for differences in industrial structure. Defining convergence as a Markov process, they conclude that poor and rich regions tend to be quite stable over time and that the mobility is low at the lower end of the income spectrum, indicating that the poorest regions in Europe are likely to stay poor. This is in line with the results of Table 11.1 even if that table is a much cruder way of describing the transitions that took place during the 1980s.

Canova and Marcet (1995) also provide support for these conclusions, using both regional data for 1980–92 and country data for a longer period. Their study is mainly concerned with estimating the rate of convergence. They use time series for GDP growth for each geographical unit (region or country) as opposed to using average growth rates for longer periods. This enables them to estimate steady state growth for each unit separately, and they find that regions do converge to their own (unconditional) steady state. They conclude that the 1980s was a decade in which heterogeneities across countries became more marked and that poor regions cannot expect to become as well off as rich regions unless some structural changes occur. They also found that in spite of some tendency towards convergence, the steady state levels of per capita income would show large inequalities.

Barro and Sala-i-Martin (1995, section 11.4) discuss convergence across European regions since 1950. Their data show clear signs of convergence for the period as a whole but also signs of convergence coming gradually to an end by 1980, in line with the data presented above. They also present data for the dispersion of regional GDP per capita within the largest European countries, which also show convergence but again with a tendency for convergence to come to a halt in the 1980s.

For some of the Nordic countries there exist regional income data based on income statistics for tax purposes. These data are not directly comparable to GDP figures, but they still measure most of GDP from the income side. An interesting aspect of these data is that they are available for smaller geographical regions than NUTS II and also contain data for individual households or taxpayers. We can thus study the individual income distribution within the region, between regions and within the country. Persson (1995) studies 24 Swedish counties for the period 1906–90 using real per capita income net of government transfers. According to his figures the regional dispersion (measured by the standard deviation of log real per capita income) was fairly constant between the two world wars, started to decrease in the late 1930s and decreased a lot until 1950. There was a further decrease in the 1960s but no decrease at all in the 1980s. A very similar story applies to Denmark according to Dilling-Hansen et al. (1994). They use income statistics for 12 Danish counties for the period 1935–90. It is quite remarkable how similar the results are to those of the Swedish study, with a substantial convergence in income from the mid-1930s to 1950, followed by a decade of stability, and then some further reduction in regional dispersion during the 1960s and 1970s and finally stability from 1980 to 1990.

These results for European countries resemble those for US states and Japanese prefectures. Barro and Sala-i-Martin (1995) present data for US states and Japanese prefectures showing the same pattern as in Europe: little convergence (if any) between the First and Second World Wars, rapid convergence from 1940 to 1950 (and also to 1960 in the United States) and no convergence in the 1980s (there is even divergence in the United States). Thus as an answer to the fourth question raised above, regional dynamics in Europe show many common features with regional development in the United States and Japan. The regional data even seem to have some of the same features as the national data discussed earlier.

The obvious question that arises from these empirical studies is: What are the economic factors that produce similar regional results within different countries? First, it seems that these factors cannot mainly be country-specific because they apply to many (perhaps most) OECD countries. Barro and Sala-i-Martin (1995, p. 393) suggest (perhaps as a joke) that 'The rise in dispersion was reversed at the end of the 1980s (apparently as soon as Mr. Reagan was no longer President), and dispersion fell through 1992.' Taken seriously, however, this could suggest that there were certain policies ('Reaganomics') adopted by many countries that produced increased regional dispersion. Thus the results are country-specific but related to similar policies in most OECD countries. The second conclusion is that convergence is not a stable process. In fact, it seems to be much more erratic than what follows from a typical capital deepening process, which is the driving force in the neoclassical growth model.

4. ECONOMIC GROWTH AND INCOME DISTRIBUTION: THE KUZNETS CURVE

Kuznets (1955) introduced the famous inverted U-shaped relationship between inequality and income, which states that the distribution of income first becomes more unequal as income increases before inequality decreases with income. This relationship received much attention in the development debate in the 1970s and was adopted by the World Bank in order to predict trends in inequality. If we use the concepts introduced by modern growth theory as presented earlier, individual incomes within a country should first diverge and then converge as the country becomes richer if the Kuznets curve is valid. Looking at data for 60 countries, Ahluwalia (1976) shows that this cross-section of countries seems to support the Kuznets curve. However, this finding has been criticized by Anand and Kanbur (1993), who find that the inverse U curve is not inverse at all – that is, the exact opposite of the Kuznets curve.

How does the Kuznets curve fit with the phases of absolute divergence and convergence presented earlier? To answer this, one really needs time series on income distribution for many countries and over long periods of time. Such data are not readily available, but they exist for some countries. A summary of some of these data are given by Lindert and Williamson (1985). Their conclusion is that it is only the falling part of curve which seems robust, whereas increasing inequality at early stages of economic development or from low levels of income is not supported by data. An alternative has been to use figures on wage differentials between different groups of skilled and unskilled labour. In Brenner et al. (1991) a number of papers on various country experiences are collected; by and large they seem to support the divergence story of the period 1820–50 followed by a long period of convergence. Data for 1854–1913 in Williamson (1996) also supports the general trend of lower wage dispersion during this period, but with large ups and downs within this time span. The divergence period between the two world wars in terms of per capita GDP is not borne out in data on income and wage inequalities.

Data on income inequality and wage dispersion for the period 1950–80 generally show decreasing inequalities in most OECD countries. However, since 1980 (the exact year varies between countries) inequality seems to be increasing. This is so both for incomes in general and for wages. Thus the long-run trend towards less inequality seems to have been broken. For a recent summary of these developments see Gottschalk and Smeedling (1997). This change may coincide with at least a tendency for the process of convergence to have halted. It is, of course, much too early to conclude that a diverging phase has started, but the data on dispersions of income on many levels of aggregation at least show that convergence is not taking place. Looking back at history, we should not be surprised by this. The attempts to explain the relationship between economic development and the distribution of income clearly indicate that no close correlation should be expected.

Several factors have been suggested in order to explain the Kuznets curve. The movement of the labour force from agriculture and rural areas to the more modern urban and industrial sectors implies an increase in income for those who move but, at the same time, a more unequal distribution of total income. As more and more people move to urban areas the low-paid rural jobs become relatively less important and inequality then decreases. The relevance of this explanation put forward by Kuznets (1955) depends on the levels and changes in the intersectoral income differential and intersectoral inequality differential and on the proportion of the labour force that moves between sectors. Underlying a process of 'modernization' are changes in the demand and supply of various skills. The recent development towards higher dispersion of earnings in many OECD countries is partly explained by a relatively strong demand for skilled labour (the so-called capital–skill complementarity) and a more sluggish supply response, while trade and globalization more generally reduce demand for unskilled workers in these countries. This change in relative demand may also be thought of as the consequence of a change in the division of labour on a world scale without much migration of unskilled labour. The literature on the new economics of geography, which follows in the footsteps of modern trade theory, discusses this phenomenon extensively but is beyond the limits of this chapter.

5.   CONCLUSIONS, OR WHY ARE WE INTERESTED IN REGIONAL GROWTH?

The convergence controversy can be analysed from two perspectives. Some see it as part of an empirical project concerned with testing economic theory. Does the neoclassical model of economic growth fit the facts or should it be rejected in favour of, say, endogenous growth theory or theories of technology diffusion? This is partly the line of reasoning taken by Barro and Sala-i-Martin (1995) and Mankiw (1995). The other way of approaching the debate is from the perspective of economic policy. If equality in some form is important for politicians, it is of course important for them to know whether a market economy will bring about convergence between regions of the country – or of the world, for that matter. Politicians are probably also interested in knowing what policies will promote convergence in incomes.

On the other hand, the analysis of convergence has so far been only marginally preoccupied with the distribution of individual incomes. Based on most empirical growth studies, human capital is regarded as a very important factor in explaining economic growth (and conditional convergence). If policies are geared towards promoting education, however, and wages for skilled labour for some reason increase relative to the wages of the unskilled, a process of growth and convergence between countries may well be characterized by increasing individual inequality. Indeed, rising individual inequality is generally what seems to be the case in OECD countries for the last decade or two. Thus policies to promote growth by increasing human capital, which may produce regional convergence, may at the same time lead to more inequality at the individual level. That may pose new dilemmas for policy-makers. Thus, an integration of the analysis of the regional and individual distribution of income is warranted.

NOTE

Financial support from the European Union's Targeted Socio-Economic Research Program is gratefully acknowledged. The first version of this chapter was presented at a TSER seminar in Rome, May 1996.

REFERENCES

Aaberge, R., Å. Cappelen and K. Gerdrup (1996), 'Regional growth and income inequality in Norway', mimeograph, Statistics Norway.

Abramovitz, M. (1986), 'Catching up, forging ahead and falling behind', *Journal of Economic History*, **46**, 385–406.

Ahluwalia, M.S. (1976), 'Inequality, poverty and development', *Journal of Development Economics*, **3**, 307–42.

Alesina, P. and D. Rodrik (1994), 'Distributive politics and economic growth', *Quarterly Journal of Economics*, **109**, 465–90.

Anand, S. and S.M.R. Kanbur (1993), 'Inequality and development: A critique', *Journal of Development Economics*, **41**, 19–43.

Barro, R.J. (1991), 'Economic growth in a cross section of countries', *Quarterly Journal of Economics*, **106**, 407–33.

Barro, R.J. and X. Sala-i-Martin (1995), *Economic Growth*, New York: McGraw-Hill.

Baumol, W.J. (1986), 'Productivity growth, convergence and welfare: what the long-run data show', *American Economic Review*, **76**, 1072–85.

Bernard, A.B. and S.N. Durlauf (1995), 'Convergence in international output', *Journal of Applied Econometrics*, **10**, 97–108.

Brenner, Y.S., H. Kaelbe and M. Thomas (1991), *Income Distribution in Historical Perspective*, Cambridge: Cambridge University Press.

Canova, F. and A. Marcet (1995), 'The poor stay poor: Non-convergence across countries and regions', CEPR discussion paper no. 1265.

De Long, B. (1988), 'Productivity growth, convergence and welfare: Comment', *American Economic Review*, **78**, 1138–54.

Dilling-Hansen, M., K.R. Petersen and V. Smith (1994), 'Growth and convergence in Danish regional incomes', *Scandinavian Economic History Review*, **42**, 54–76.

Durlauf, S.N. and P.A. Johnson (1995), 'Multiple regimes and cross-country growth behavior', *Journal of Econometrics*, **10**, 365–84.

Eurostat (1994), *Rapid Reports*, Regions (Luxembourg).

Fagerberg, J. and B. Verspagen (1996), 'Heading for divergence? Regional growth in Europe reconsidered', *Journal of Common Market Studies*, **34**, 431–48.

Friedman, M. (1962), *Capitalism and Freedom*, Chicago, IL: University of Chicago Press.

Galor, O. (1996), 'Convergence? Inferences from theoretical models', *Economic Journal*, **106**, 1056–69.

Galor, O. and J. Zeira (1993), 'Income distribution and macroeconomics: the human capital connection', *Review of Economic Studies*, **60**, 35–52.

Garcia-Penalosa, C. (1995), 'The paradox of education or the good side of inequality', *Oxford Economic Papers*, **47**, 265–85.

Gottschalk P. and T.M. Smeeding (1997), 'Cross-national comparison of earnings and income inequality', *Journal of Economic Literature*, **35**, 633–87.

Krugman, P.R. and A. Venables (1995), 'Globalization and the inequality of nations', NBER working paper no. 5098, Cambridge, MA.

Kuznets, S. (1955), 'Economic growth and income inequality', *American Economic Review*, **45**, 1–28.

Landes, D.S. (1969), *The Unbound Prometheus*, London: Cambridge University Press.

Lindert, P.H. and J.G. Williamson (1985), *Growth, Equality and History*, discussion paper no. 1052, Harvard Institute for Economic Research, Harvard University, Cambridge, MA.

Maddison, A. (1982), *Phases of Capitalist Development*, Oxford: Oxford University Press.

Maddison, A. (1995), 'Monitoring the world economy, 1820–1992', Paris, OECD.

Mankiw, N.G. (1995), 'The growth of nations', *Brookings Papers on Economic Activity*, **1**, 275–326 (with discussion).

Neven, D.J. and C. Gouyette (1995), 'Regional convergence in the European community', *Journal of Common Market Studies*, **33**, 47–65.

O'Rourke, K.H. (1996), 'Trade, migration and convergence: An historical perspective', CEPR discussion paper no. 1319.

O'Rourke, K.H. and J.G. Williamson (1996), 'Around the European periphery, 1870–1913: Globalization, schooling and growth', CEPR discussion paper no. 1343.

Persson, J. (1995), 'Convergence in per capita income and migration across the Swedish counties, 1906–1990', seminar paper no. 601, Institute for International Economic Studies, Stockholm University.

Persson, T. and G. Tabellini (1994), 'Is inequality harmful for economic growth?' *American Economic Review*, **84**, 600–621.

Quah, D.T. (1996a), 'Regional convergence clusters across Europe', *European Economic Review*, **40**, 951–8.

Quah, D.T. (1996b), 'Twin peaks: Growth and convergence in models of distribution dynamics', CEPR discussion paper no. 1355.

Verspagen, B. (1995), 'Convergence in the global economy: a broad historical viewpoint', *Structural Change and Economic Dynamics*, **6**, 143–65.

Williamson, J.G. (1995), 'Globalization, convergence and history', NBER working paper no. 5259.

Williamson, J.G. (1996), 'Globalization and inequality then and now: the late nineteenth and late twentieth centuries compared', NBER working paper no. 5491.

Index